MW01687620

THE NEW GUARD

LITERARY REVIEW

P.O. BOX 866
WELLS, ME 04090
www.newguardreview.com

Writers for writers' sake.

Cover painting: *I'll Be Here All Week* 40"x 40", oil on canvas
© 2011 Matt Welch

Cover art photo by Jay York, 2013

For book orders please visit www.newguardreview.com

Printed by Walch Printing, 40 Walch Drive, Portland, ME 04103

ISBN: 978-0-615-95702-9

Volume III Second Printing

For our fellow writers and readers

Table of Contents

Table of Contents

Table of Contents

Editor's Note

You hold a big book in your hands, a book brimming with new voices. The voices lift and sing. Why not follow one of these voices as one might a beloved writer or luminary, why not search for last written word, why not revel in that new vision. Why not find a writer within these pages to follow, in the name of possibility. In the name of greater human achievement. We have now lost Chinua Achebe, Seamus Heaney, Lou Reed and Nelson Mandela; each died in 2013, each leaving us with their own singular, unfathomable absence. Of course, none could fill those shoes. Still, there is new work to find, always new work. It's up to all of us writers and readers to seek one another out, support one another and read one another's writing. All writers strive to give their best gift to the world. I feel writing is as a kind of prayer, a humble holding-forth, a way to meditate and give and commune and learn and love.

My own DNA is in this book, my care and hope. I'm proud to be a part of such an undertaking, from tip to tip, proud. Each writer included in this volume struggled to bring words to the page. Here we are, page after page of challenges met. I'm waving this book in the air. I'm holding it up, the writing of my fellows. Can you hear me cheering, wherever you are? Read! I am a circus hawker, a hype man, step right up. Read, read. Have a good sit-down, look it all over, see how consciousness abuts consciousness, bask away. And find that voice—one voice, at least, to match your own.

Shanna McNair
Wells, ME 2013

Stephen Dunn

Something Had to be Done

For B.

I've tried to believe the ancient Greeks
were wrong: you *can* count yourself happy
before the final verdict is in.

Let's bring in the Chorus for a song.

The kings and queens knew what they excreted
would make it down to us; it was the nature,
the gravity of things. So in the low places

happiness was a triumph
of engineering and ingenuity,
the very things the Chorus recommended

practicing-until practicing became an art.
We'd hear their mellifluous tones
amid the ambiguities of dawn,

the slate gray middle ground of dusk.
Who were they, really? The community?
A group of wise friends?

They seemed to understand
that you were beautiful,
and that beauty leaves us no choice.

We heard what we wanted to hear,
as the Greeks at Delphi did.
Something was telling us

something needed to be done.

The moon was full of itself.
I was doomed to feel its pull.
I had nightmares. I had mere dreams

full of cravings and scatological talk.
I worried about overly tidy men
who didn't know until too late

that it was their mothers they wanted.
The Greeks had it down all right.
I was sure, my sweet, I wasn't one of them.

The Chorus began to sing: *the fewer*
the words the more they are felt.
It was 2013, and words were

sprawling all over the place. If they named
what had to be done, they named
too much. No longer were there hints

hidden in the spaces at the end
of a line or a wish. My smartest friend
said if I wanted illumination

I'd have to learn to love the shadows
it creates. He said maybe
it isn't enough to love just one person.

You are beautiful, he said,
but so was Helen, and how different
the world would be if men like Paris

loved hundreds instead of one.
Troublemaker, troublemaker,
the Chorus sang, wanting as ever

for things to be better than they are.
Here in Garrett County we've all
been getting fat. It saves us from the perils
of attractiveness. When the rains come

we don't try to call out to Poseidon.
Most here believe in one God, and ask Him
to bless only us. I love you, my love.

I feel happy today, though I know today
is just a speck in time. Is that our song
the Chorus is singing? Or is it the wind

in the hemlocks, preceding a storm?

Barbara Hurd

A Pre-Mortem Promise

—after Stephen Dunn's *A Postmortem Guide*

I will not praise you
for your exceptional serenity.
Haven't I seen you
turn a peaceful sleep
into a nightmare of revenge
and loose balls from the schoolyards
of your youth?
Serenity? There's nothing sincere
to be said about that.
Your midnight bad guys are all kinds—
lifeguards, point guards, wrong referees—
and you're the dumb chicken of your past,
unbearably vengeful
within the safety of a dream.

I've witnessed them all.

And you bet I'll resist the temptation
of speaking of you as an angel.
The inadequately loved are the ones
who'd want all that feather-froth
and flighty desire. Being with you
means I'm not among them.

Know that I've admired in you
not just the fraught straining to be good
but the lapses, too, if they're followed
by the kind of remorse that reminds me

you're also a man who knows
that all art, including that of love,
depends on the power of revision.
Still, for accuracy's sake I might say
you've occasionally disappointed,
that your fruit cocktail from Del Monte's
makes a lousy flambé.

And since I know your stories,
understand I also know
they're more than mere rote
or entertainment.

I'll remind those who call, perhaps weeping
after news of your death,
that you, in fact, live on,
transformed into poems
that have nothing to do
with pomp or idle circumstance.
They are what you've made
of that skinny, big-eared kid
making moves on the courts of Queens,
evidence you learned long ago
to turn a restless heart
into a brilliant one.
Yes, I'll tell them
you had second chances,
that you knew joy
and were burned by books early on,
that you came through
properly scathed.

And I'll add that at the end of the day,
what you—scotch in hand
and a vest over your chest—
needed most was them.

But before all that weeping and wail,
I turn to you here in the high spirits
of this seventh-decade now
and, in all sincerity, say that
you're the one who's spoiled us all,
made our lives more radiant
by the richness of who you are.

I say that by example and word
you've shown us
a better way to be alive.

With love,
Barbara

Sharon Olds

The Signature

J is for the judge we drew,
A woman who looked sensual and witty, whom I felt we could
C ount on. She praised us for restraining our tendency to
Q uibble. She looked calm and wise, up there,
U nder the oak eagles and arrows.
E very time my almost ex and his
L awyer proposed some new or revised
I dea of a fair divvy, my lawyer said
N ot to worry, this is the top
E xcelsior justice, smart and fair.

S he signed the final settlement papers—
I find, today—ten days ago; for the
L ast ten days I have not in the slightest
B een married. In ink or ballpoint she formed
E ach letter of her name—not in pencil—slow or
R apid she wrote it. When she started, we were still
M arried,
A nd when she stopped her cursive, we were
N ot, and it had been done by her hand, with
N o dishonor—or dishonor subsumed in her honor.

Erin Belieu

Love Letter: Final Vistation

I come back to you
in the interregnum of wisteria,
            in the epoch of the armadillo's
fetching leprosy: storm season, mold season, season of
Savannah's ghosts rotting for
            the sozzled gawkers. Parked in
the public fountains, your banshees rattle
their Marley chains, carry signs that read
Will Work For Any
                        Human Sympathy.
            But there's none leftover:
we blew, we consumed, we squandered, we lavished,
we bounced that check high as a Super Ball and snickered
as it leapt away.
                        O, we were numb, dumb and increasingly
wasted; were pigs in the Piggly Wiggly, did ravage
and damage. We told the infected stories, mumbled them
drunk at the lip of the Devils' Pool. What is a kiss
but the mouth's potential for wreckage?
            I come back to you:
yes, wept for, wracked, and now unfamiliar. The cauldron's
cold in the shed and I can't put a hand to my planchette,
no matter where I look.
                                    Peace, peace, I free and
undream you. The priestess of nothing,
I am pleased to be plain.

Madeleine Blais

To Miami

I did not set out to fall in love in Miami, or to have it exert the kind of magnetic field over my life that it has. I am a New Englander by birth and disposition. I like understatement, the color taupe, and brief dignified greetings. I did not grow up speaking the languages of Miami, speaking garish, speaking pink, speaking effusiveness and showy displays of affection.

My first sighting of Florida was on a perfect September sun-washed day in 1976, made a little less perfect due to rumors of a hurricane. I-95, as it heads south from Ft. Lauderdale into Miami, struck me as a deranged strip of highway, with as many as seven lanes on either side and with a daunting mix of drivers. Multi-tasking tourists, pointing out sights, slathering on sunscreen, consulting maps, and careening across lanes to get to the exit they almost sped by. Ramshackle pick-up trucks with sun-wrinkled sinewy men packed into the beds along with lawn mowers and rakes and machetes. Semis filled with beef and bedding and citrus. Senior citizens driving under the speed limit. Aging guys in pricey convertibles driving over it. College students with music pulsing driving way over it. The occasional mom in a station wagon. Tour buses, cops, motorcyclists.

Through a connection at the University of Miami, the guy I was with and I had a free place to stay in a drab brown sunless faculty apartment for the first month while the professor who normally occupied it was away on sabbatical, so we slid off of 95 onto US One and sought an address across from the university, east of the highway, struck as we traveled by how different everything looked: the colors of the buildings, how they were made out of concrete, not wood, and how even the messages on the billboards were unusual, with their ads for exterminating companies with a big fake roach climbing all over the top and for Bacardi rum and for gleaming cars from The Collection. We overshot our mark and found ourselves turning onto Sunset Drive, passing a store where a lady named Connie Banko made custom bathing suits.

Custom bathing suits: Janzten wasn't good enough?

Connie Banko's store provided the first sign of the kind of indulgence fostered by the tropics, the steamy undulating lip-smacking surrender to luxury.

Up north, trees shed leaves.

In Florida, people shed inhibitions.

The few shoppers out in the heat moved in slow motion, carrying umbrellas to block the sun. Nearby a bakery emitted the sleepy smell of fresh bread.

Once I was away from the locomotion and the chaos of Interstate 95, my take on Miami changed and I saw it as sleepy and satisfied: a well-fed cat dozing on a pink stucco windowsill warmed by an average year round temperature of approximately eighty degrees.

Florida embodied the dream opposite of what I was used to in the North.

Florida was New England turned inside out.

On our first free day a few weeks later, we decided get to know the town better and to drive over to Miami Beach for a swim. We took the MacArthur Causeway: no traffic to speak of at that time of year, just the Goodyear Blimp off to the south and birds looping over the water in search of tasty prey. The MacArthur appears in certain sections to sit in the bay as if floating on an inner tube. To the north I saw what I considered the most posh enclaves imaginable: private islands named Palm, Star, and Hibiscus. The Beach itself radiated much less prosperity, the side streets filled with unimposing little shops, selling Judaica: Torah pointers and mezuzahs and menorahs. At least the days of "always a view, never a Jew" were long over on Miami Beach. Boutiques sold tired-looking beach cover-ups and shapeless dresses: *schmatas,* they were called, by the salesladies and customers alike, Yiddish for rags. A neutral term, accepting, not critical. Drugstores sold medical supplies geared toward shoring up human infrastructure, trusses and denture creams and nose guards.

Miami Beach was a ghost town in the early fall, and the old people who sat on the porches of the hotels were ghostly as well.

Yet here was water, blue and tangy, free for the taking.

We were the only ones in it for miles.

Slowly, I came around.

The subtropical air plumped my spirits and I could see first-hand the power of the landscape.

The poet Elizabeth Bishop called Florida "the state with the prettiest name," and she was right, not just about the name.

How can you be from New England and not thrill at the light?

The sun is a blast of bleach and hygiene: in Florida the dirt does not seem dirty.

I am not a place slut. I have standards, but coming from the dour northern reaches of the U.S. and having gone through eight years of Latin lockstep with the nuns, I never imagined a locale could be so playful, so dedicated to ease, so lacking in inhibition. It was the mirage I had been secretly dreaming of all those years when I shook slush off of my mittens and tried to care about Julius Caesar's insane number of battles.

In the hip part of Miami, (back then, we were talking Coconut Grove, pretty much exclusively) people congregated in the well-named Peacock Park and wore outlandish clothes, sheer, short, tight, with sequins.

Or they wore no clothes.

In either case the goal was obvious: to outshine the sun, to get noticed.

Unbidden but insistent, the theme song from *Midnight Cowboy*, "Everybody's Talkin'," came to mind, its kind-hearted friendly rhythms, at odds with the lonely fate of the movie's two protagonists, as they head to Miami where *the sun keeps shining through the pouring rain.*

The old people called Miami Beach, with a certain well-earned immigrant irony, their *schtel* by the sea, evoking images of past ghettos in Eastern Europe where loud talk and the promise of candlelight and challah on Fridays softened hardships.

The residents of South Beach appeared grateful to have the sun to warm them, especially when memories could not.

Pristine ocean, next to shabby hotels.

Miami Beach offered just the kind of jolting contradiction that journalists covet.

Why not? I thought.

This could work.

Judith Podell

LETTER TO THE IRS

April 15, 2013

Dear Internal Revenue Service,

This is a love letter. Bet you don't get many of those. [1] You and I met at a job fair in Washington DC, back when women with law degrees were novelty acts. Your experience with women was limited to secretaries, clerk typists, and the girls at the Lone Star. [2] I looked into your pale eyes and said, "Speak to me about ERISA." [3]

Aha! A live one, you thought.

When you asked about my long-range career goals I lied and said I wanted to be a GS-13.

I signed on to protect and defend the Constitution.

Mind if I call you Irving? You've been called worse. Some think hating you is the highest form of patriotism. I, on the other hand, think of you as the man I married in 1975 when I was fresh out of law school and saddled with debt.

There's a wistful quality about you, Irving. At parties you stand around the clam dip and hope beautiful women will flirt with you. You wear cheap suits that are too big in the shoulders and use Old Spice aftershave. You are tone-deaf, near-sighted, humor-impaired, and partially color-blind, which is maybe why your socks don't match.

Your eyes are the color of cocktail onions bottled in brine. You are officially apolitical, like death itself.

You thrive under fluorescent light, much like the philodendrons and spider plants I kept in my cubicle to remind me that green is the color of life as well as money. The work was exceptionally dry, highly technical, and at times dangerously boring. The Internal Revenue Code itself is a living creature, you told me once as you dumped a fresh pile of prototype 401(k) plans on my desk to review for compliance. 'Live cases' you called them.

You are partial to veterans, men who almost became priests, and big fish from small southern towns where everyone works for the mills. People for whom institutional loyalty is second nature. I was loyal to you in my fashion. "Taxes are the price we pay for a civilized society," [4] I'd respond when taunted.

You are furtive about your trysts with high priced call girls who so often steal your wallet, but not about those long lunches in the Lone Star.

You're so not my type. You know nothing about jazz nor do you subscribe to High Times for indoor gardening hints. You haven't spent your adult life studying t'ai chi so you could become a better surfer.

"What's foreplay?" you asked me once; and when I explained, you said it would take too long.

Oh Irving! You saved me from a life of shared apartments in rough neighborhoods, storefront clinics, second hand clothing and ramen noodles in exchange for the best years of my life, the prime time of my days (Monday through Friday with a half hour for lunch). Financial dependency laced with resentment? I'd call it old-fashioned married love, not unlike my grandmother's marriage, which lasted 50 years most of them unhappy. I was only going to stay till I finished my first novel, which would surely be a bestseller, like Fear of Flying. [5] Please don't laugh. We were all young once, except you.

Like many women I shaped myself to your needs, which were foreign to my nature, and consoled myself with fantasies of secret stardom. Attempts were made to ignite passion in hotels that did not have room service. I was Joan Didion[6] with a migraine in Detroit but we'll always have Fresno. That motel had a swimming pool and the nighttime sky stayed pink. We pretended I was Joni Mitchell and you were Crosby, Stills and Nash. I'm glad you talked me out of the tattoo. Some might call it Stockholm syndrome, but I say love the one you're with. [7]

Writing was my true love, but you came first.

Thirty years passed, not as a dream. More like a situation comedy in real time with no laugh track. Your gradual loss of self-esteem was painful to behold.

I watched you experiment with hair gel and try to squeeze your stout self into Euro-styled suits. You wanted to look more 'corporate'. Tried to pass yourself off as MasterCard or LL Bean. I protested when you changed our mission statement.

Instead of "taxpayer assistance" we would provide "customer service," and "customer satisfaction."

I drew the line at language abuse.

"Customers?" I said. "They're taxpayers, not customers. Real customers can take their business elsewhere. No one says 'I was going to sign up with IRS but AOL offered me free Internet porn.'"

You looked right through me with those cocktail onion eyes. It was as though I hadn't spoken.

I skipped out on my retirement party. Didn't even say goodbye.

Our divorce was final and I was bitter at first about The Wasted Years.

I should have been more gracious, especially in light of the pension.

Writers need patrons or grants or some means of earning a living while we are learning our craft, and even afterwards. You kept me on a short leash in terms of time but left me to write whatever I chose so long as it did not reveal sensitive taxpayer information.

You were my first and best teacher.

You taught me that proper punctuation has the force of law.

With love and gratitude,

Judith Podell, GS-13

---

[1] David Foster Wallace's unfinished novel The Pale King comes to mind.

[2] Topless bar in Washington DC across the street from the FBI building. Rumored to have been acquired by the FBI from a seizure.

[3] The Employee Retirement Income Security Act of 1974 (ERISA), a heartbreaking work of staggering complexity, intended to ensure that the private pension system would provide meaningful benefits to employees through a series of tax incentives. It was widely believed that this could be accomplished through a complex network of regulations containing loopholes big enough to drive a truck through.

[4] Oliver Wendell Holmes, Jr. quote that is carved above the entrance of IRS Headquarters at 1111 Constitution Avenue.

[5] Published in 1973. Arguably the Great Jewish American Feminist Comic novel. Certainly the first, and a hard act to follow.

[6] The anti-Erica Jong.

[7] Title of song by Stephen Sills. Don't think the original expression was his.

Van Newell

We'll Leave the Refrigerator Light on For You

In 1983 Pat Benatar sang that love is a battlefield, a scholarly observation no doubt, but I think love of food is another battlefield and I think it is a battle we enjoy losing. A school cafeteria switches to baked fries instead of regular fried fries and a libertarian cries foul at a Parent Teacher association meeting. Personally I do miss not chicken fried steak (which is a steak fried in chicken batter). Many people, especially here in the South, would rather go down with the food ship. You'll forgive us if we have a thing for lost causes.

Due to the numerous small towns dotted across the Southern states, many people that live here tend to think that the South as a rather small, sparsely-populated part of America. But it is nine hundred miles from Little Rock to Daytona Beach, and a thousand miles from New Orleans to Richmond and obviously the immense variety in climate and landscapes in between influences the local diet. Rice was plentiful in Charleston and made the city incredibly wealthy in the 1800s. Wealth still resides there. The city is a tenth the size of Atlanta but has a Louis Vuitton boutique.

And across the South wherever there is food, there is lust. I've heard many, many sermons over the thirty-four years I have been attending church. The subjects range from the antichrist to Zachariah, yet rare is the sermon where you will hear the admonishment of gluttony when it comes to food. With lust comes desire and I do not think it is too much of an exaggeration to say that cooking shows are a kind of crypto-pornography; they invite lust, without the effort of romance and courting (i.e. preparations). Instead we are quickly shown the mixing of materials, intercoursing if you will, in the beginnings of a dish, desert, etc. and then instantly shown the meal. If you will allow me to add a word to the lexicon, a "pornucopia" of food and its displays. Once your eyes have been inflamed by the sights, what can one do, except head to the grocery store to assemble one's own culinary debasement, the mind coarsened by unrealistic expectations of what one saw on the screen.

There are more chef celebrities than stars in the sky but one reason I believe for Paula Dean's meteoric rise is that she reminds people of themselves, or as a nice neighbor, friendly and plump, using butter as a staple rather than Vietnamese cabbage. People admire those with whom they identify; New Yorkers understandably gravitate towards No Reservations, college students at Ohio State love Man vs. Food. So too with Southern cooks and Southern food.

Here in the South, pride in one's ability to fulfill hungry guests and family members has led to numerous entrepreneurial enterprises. Atlanta man Truett Cathy decided to fry a chicken breast in peanut oil in 1946, eventually leading him to found Chic-fil-A, a billion dollar business rivaled only in cultish devotion by In & Out Burger or the television show, Glee. Waffle House, basically a Denny's *sans* the frills, is a southern staple and was the place where everyone in high school could buy cigarettes out of those machines with the pulleys. You could play a song off the jukebox and smoke there inside while you ate an undercooked $1.99 waffle the size of a pizza.

The people of the South are lovers of the flesh, but not in the Biblical sense, rather, in the Bible belt we love to consume flesh. To many of the old folks, gambling, alcohol, smoking, "living in sin," were, with varying degrees, frowned upon, so what were they allowed to do? Eat. I've never heard a sermon or read a church sign admonishing the faithful not to be gluttons. One of my history professors knew Martin Luther King Jr. and the only comment he made in class about Dr. King was "that man could eat."

In a place where agrarian work, planting, farming, and sharecropping were what most did, consumption of food was considered a necessary virtue. Thinking about how many calories one burns in an hour doing Pilates or playing their Kinect on their Xbox 360? Now multiply that hour by ten hours in the sun and you can see how people could eat sausage and eggs and butter and were still thin. I look at the pictures of my wife's great grandparents from the 1930s and 1940s. Her great grandfather was a sharecropper, thin, but not gaunt, and his skin darkened from being in the sun all day plowing a mule. He cut a rather thoughtful figure because he wore glasses and wore mostly white clothing. His favorite entree was "lights," which were the lungs of a pig. His wife's favorite parts were the neck bones, the ears, and the tail.

The meat was always salted, then hung up in a smokehouse, a small one room shack with a dirt floor in which a small fire was kept smoldering for a whole week. With twelve children all hungry from working in the fields and doing their chores as well, the offal was always eaten as well.

At the beginning of the past century the surplusing of weigh brought with it no stigma or sense of shame. Rather, a glorious girth evoked in our culture some sense of merriment: Santa Clause for instance. Or, if you wish, trace the girth back to Victorian England: Dickens' Mr. Pickwick. Or Oliver Hardy, of the 1930s comedic duo Laurel and Hardy, who grew up outside Augusta, Georgia, pleasantly plump and who no doubt won the admiring affections of America. Fat meant no shame because fat meant no trace of poverty. I have not seen the entire catalog, but I have never seen a fat person in a Dorothea Lange photograph. Sixty five years later, another plump son of Georgia, Wayne Knight, landed the role of Newman on Seinfeld, my favorite character on the show, in fact. Knight would be my choice for the role of Ignatius J. Reilly if *The Confederacy of Dunces* movie ever gets made. For my ninth grade English class we read *To Kill a Mockingbird.* Ditto for tenth grade. By eleventh grade I was sensing a pattern. If you remember the novel you may recall how the young boy Walter Cunningham asks for more syrup, a treat for a poor boy in Depression era Alabama. In the novel, the Cunningham men represented the southern emasculated everyman. Too proud to beg but too starving and stuck to do otherwise so that his children would not starve. Senator Richard Russell of Georgia helped push through the National School Lunch Act of 1946 to fed poor school children which helped subsidize farming in the South. Numerous young men who had volunteered for World War II had been rejected because they were too malnourished to undergo the rigors of basic training which in turn alarmed the armed forces. From a general's point of view, adolescent health was a matter of national defense.

Fast forward to today, the South, and America for that matter, will still defend her love of food. Just go to a buffet. Many of us growing up were told to finish our plates, that children were starving in vaguely oriental places. Our parents and grandparents who had grown up with little food then saw these oases of opulence where one could eat. We seem almost hardwired to be attracted to buffets if we do not have the money to eat at nicer establishments. Our minds rationalize it to us thusly, it is a great value. Buffets were exported west to Las Vegas, the price raised to twenty-five dollars and the menu broadened to include all the crab legs one could consume with a flute of vaguely constructed bitter grape water disingenuously christened as "champagne."

Ironically, the most popular chain restaurant here where I live in Birmingham, a city of over one million people, is the Cheesecake Factory, a place Southerns have come to love for the platter-sized portions (I recently ended my relationship with said factory due to their charging me two dollars and ninety five cents for a Coca-Cola). The thought being to your average customer, I might be paying fifteen dollars for this chicken and pasta but they give me three chicken breasts and a pound of buttered noodles.

Barbecue pork and chicken, though, are the staples of the inland South. For years, out-of-towners visiting the University of Alabama in Tuscaloosa would find their way to the worst-guarded secret: Dreamland; a restaurant that for decades served only two things, ribs and white bread. In recent years, they have committed heretical acts such as allowing the serving of sides of macaroni & cheese and turnip greens. But on the plus side of heresy, Dreamland is the only place I have ever heard of that will UPS their ribs to you. Anyone can say it with flowers, but I think it takes a man of high character, wisdom, and refinement to say it with ribs. Only now after ten years of marriage has my wife forgotten that our first Valentine's together that we spend was at Dreamland. We were seated at a table underneath a neon sign that read in soft baby blue font NO FARTING. I did not feel like waiting an hour and forty minutes for all the soup, salad, and breadsticks I might want from the Olive Garden. Others have been grafted into the barbecue body politic as well. Dimitri's is a locally-owned Greek barbecue establishment that combines various Europeans accents, feta, spices, etc. to plates of pork. None dare call it fusion.

Of course, having lived in the South off and on for much of my life there are roads not taken when it comes to authentic experiences. Some I had never heard of and I live here. Most people have had gumbo in one form or another, but I was informed recently that truly authentic Cajun gumbo requires Nutria meat in the stew. Nutria are classified as rodents, and when viewed on Wikipedia, appear to be beavers. Authenticity and poverty seem to go hand in hand. Why else would one consume a rodent unless they had to? (Indeed, the concept of "selling out," a term always used to condemn those who are loosing the bonds of being poor and blue collar.) A friend's coworker recently lamented the fact that women nowadays are "always having you to take them somewhere nice. Applebee's, Chili's, O'Charley's." Eating good in whatever neighbor may depend simply on economy of scale, a four dollar Hardee's/Carl's Jr. hamburger versus a nine dollar Red Robin hamburger versus a sixteen dollar Kobe beef hamburger at aforementioned factory.

A few years ago I donated most of my CDs to the local thrift store because I wanted another write-off on December 31st. The music had already been uploaded to my iPod but then five months later my Volvo station wagon blew a head gasket and soon after I procured a Chevrolet Cobalt with a salvage title (which' is a car that has been totaled in a wreck and then brought back to life through a junkyard or mechanic. These cars cost and are worth considerably less. Do not ever buy them. Ever.). There was no auxiliary input in the Cobalt for me to play my wife's iPod (which had been procured by redeeming all my Citibank rewards points for three years) and thus on my hour and ten minute commutes to work, I listened to the radio. There was a sports talk radio show called The Roundtable on WJOX 94.5 which I enjoyed listening to because they cared about making an entertaining show rather overanalyzing sports. The two co-hosts, Ian and Lance, were interviewing San Diego Chargers linebacker Takeo (pronounced tuh-KEY-oh) Spikes who is from Sandersville, Georgia. When the topic turned to food Spikes remarked about his family tradition of eating raccoons. Ian and Lance were taken aback, and a wager was made between the two of them that whoever lost the March Madness basketball bracket would have to consume Jambalaya a la raccoon entree. Ian lost but I believe the listeners of The Roundtable won. Two raccoons were caught and put down, then skinned and ridden of glands. A local sporting goods store decided to host the event and a large crowd gathered, ten deep, patiently waiting their own turn to sample the raccoon which was described vaguely as greasy. An anonymous source related to me that Ian "shit for the entire weekend." On a side note, I felt like that previously mentioned verb/noun when I discovered a football player I have never heard of has three hundred and ninety thousand followers on twitter and I still have eleven.

But there are nice, normal foods and nice, normal people here as well. The Ned Beattys of America can truly transverse our trails without fear. Look, the South has quickly changed as much as the rest of the country and it is only the outliers where time has slowed to a more conservative advancement of culture.

On the down side, the same phenomenon is occurring everywhere in America is occurring even more acutely here: Our bodies are paying the price for the good food we feed them. Almost everyone I see parking in handicapped spots and getting out of their cars are not older people with bad hips or in wheelchairs but rather obese people, some not even fifty, waddling along. Al Roker made it cool, and safe, to have lap band surgery. Of course, I will lump myself in with them with my being in my thirties and already on cholesterol medication, weighting twenty five pounds more than my father who is a good three inches taller than me.

And I don't know if we are really that conscious of it. Instead, it is rather one of those "Oh, I suppose I am" moments rather a consuming obsession. But since so many of us are, sigh, overweight or more, it does not only seem normal, but boringly pedestrian to the point none of us really notices until we come into contact with an extreme example. Self-obsession is a very, very rare thing here. The obsession rather turns to college football from August to January. From January to May, American Idol, Alabama having blessed the nation with Ruben Studdard, Taylor Hicks, and Bo Bice. America, you are welcome. From May to August family reunions that swell to hundreds of participants. Introspection is not particularly frowned upon, it is just not thought about really. Who has time for it what with going to work and coming home and making dinner and then taking the kids out for t-ball practice and finally tucking them into bed until you fall asleep in their bed and wake up at two in the morning? Self-reflection, I suppose, is for those who are eighty-five and older. America's new retirement age.

I am sure it is the same for many other agrarian-based rural and semi-rural areas be they Nebraska, Vermont or Oklahoma; showing off and flaunting wealth is seen as immodest, unbecoming, and gaudy. I've never asked their gross worth, but I have three friends that I safely assume to be millionaires. One in his thirties, one in his forties, one in his fifties. Respectively, they drive a Volvo, a Ford truck, and a Chevrolet Suburban. On the other side of the coin, when I was temping in a law firm in Calabasas, California a few years back, a coworker, still living with his parents, told me he was purchasing an Escalade. The insurance was going to be higher than the car payment. In Hollywood, Cameron Diaz wasn't even forty when she had plastic surgery. My wife's second cousin goes around her small town with just one breast, having survived cancer, and no one bats an eye. I like to think people take a certain amount of pride in not caring about their appearance or others. When I was a kid, I thought people with money bought clothes at JC Penny.

Alas, pride has been both our glory and downfall. Our food, we know to be delicious, and we know in the back of our minds, that, like smoking, it is bad for us. The South has been known to be attached to lost causes and moral victories. I recently read part one of Shelby Foote's narrative of the Civil War and I see how this culture of pride, both foolish and noble, not has been inherited. Our hearts are simply too full—large, and overflowing with passion, be it for good or for ill.

We may drive by nicely manicured nursing homes and we may visit a relative there and see that it's not *One Flew Over the Cuckoo's Nest* but we still shrug our shoulders and drink down bad bourbon and cheap beer then take another puff of flavor country and the next morning dig into hash browns and cheese grits and bacon and sausage gravy with biscuits knowing that it is preferable to die happy and slightly corpulent at sixty five. We are just trying to get to heaven quicker. Then again, we in the South have been in the wrong on occasion. On occasion. But as far as the food goes, our love handles and cankles are living alters to savored-and-devoured food. A Waffle House original composition is still available for customer's perusal. The title: Why would you want to eat anywhere else? Love and food are both battlefields and if you are going to surrender to one, you will probably surrender to the other as well. Just do not surrender at the same time because it did not work out well for Caligula or George Costanza.

Edie Clark

The Love of Many Strangers

I live alone in a house with thousands of letters stashed under the eaves. Beneath the fragrant boards of my roof, they hunch in old cardboard cartons (my grandmother's); in leather-bound suitcases (words exchanged between my parents during World War II); in baskets, the tender missives bundled with ribbons or string.

Some of these are my own letters, between my first boyfriend and I. He was a poet and a corporal in the Army. I was 16. He was 25. We exchanged poems, one for one, through the mail. I was spending the summer babysitting for a family near the Fort Devens army base and while I washed dishes or changed diapers, I kept one eye on the front window for the mailman to come, mid-day. Most days did bring me a poem, and his devotion. After a while, he was sent to Viet Nam and I never heard from him again, which brought a searing first heartbreak. Or my next, the 6'8" mechanic who worked at the garage near my college dorm. He was Jewish, told wonderful stories that often made me laugh or cry, as in the case of the story of his 4'9" grandmother who escaped the pogroms of Eastern Russia with only the family's samovar. And when we were out on drives along the backside of the New Jersey waterfront, from behind the wheel of his old Ford pick-up, he would sing Yiddish ballads in a curiously melancholy way. At night, he was studying for his MBA at Temple University. Once again I thought this was the man for me. My parents did not approve. There were other problems and eventually I escaped the city for rural New England, where I have lived ever since. That was when he wrote me, the most open expression of his desire ever: *"Have you had enough of your hippie life? Are you ready to come home?"*

And from the one who finally made me understand what love means, I have only three letters, written during the very first part of our courtship. After that, we were together almost all the time. Why write? Paul has now passed away of cancer (I would write to him now of my fidelity if I thought they could be delivered). But I treasure these three, which are subtly crafted, shy, not wanting to give much away, as was his way.

Large plastic storage bins, the lids duct-taped shut to prevent them from bursting open, hold the mother lode: pop open the lids and, like fish in the hold, envelopes of all colors and sizes are revealed, a wide variety of scripts, scrawls, and chicken-scratch directing them from all over the map to me. Most, if not all, of these are from people I have never met, people who have read what I have written over the years and who have then sat down and on note cards or lined paper or formal stationery, applied their ballpoints or their ink pens or sometimes even their No. 2 pencils to the paper to tell me that—they deeply appreciate my writing. (*"I love what you do!" "You are a treasure." "Your writing is like a kind of poetry. It makes me* feel.*"*) I have hardly ever thrown any of them away because they seem like such touching expressions of a feeling that, necessarily, cannot be shared or even returned.

I answer all these but only a few have turned into long-term correspondences. Nettie Armant, of New Orleans, was one who wrote to me for years. For reasons of her own, she connected with the essays I wrote but she also connected with New England, about which I write a lot and I have for more than thirty years. Nettie claimed she had read me since my first day. But *she had never been to New England.* It was hard to figure out the source of her enchantment. Nettie was a native of New Orleans, born and bred, and she wrote to me of her memories and of her passion for that old city (and for Mardi Gras—she often sent me beads and doubloons after the celebrations). That made sense. But her curious affection for a place she'd only ever imagined was, I suppose, her appreciation for me. From the very first letter she ever wrote to me as well as the last, she signed every one: *"I love you. Nettie."*

Of all the many communications in these bins, Nettie's are perhaps the most intense from someone I have never met. It's an odd feeling, to be loved in an imaginary way by these faceless people for whom I feel nothing except supreme gratitude. (I eventually became very fond of Nettie. I shed tears when I learned she had died. By then I knew her life story which unfolded for me, letter by letter, each one written in her child-like script, sometimes written on paper saved from another project, or on the backs of postcards of the New Orleans of the 1950s. From these scribbles, I knew how she and her husband had survived the Depression, living on canned beans. I learned of their spare but passionate marriage and the joy they found in small moments. She wrote of the sudden loss of her husband, for whom she grieved without end. How could I not love such a soul?)

But the letters between my parents during World War II bear the heaviest weight under the eaves. When they died, they left me this legacy of their star-crossed union, birthed (perhaps) by a world war. The complication, for the most part, was a man named Tom, who had a great passion for my mother and who asked her to marry him as he went off to war. She demurred; she wasn't sure. My father had had his sights set on my mother since their early days, his sister being my mother's best friend through school. And he too had asked for her hand. He was already in North Africa. After Tom left for the South Pacific, my mother wrote to him and accepted his marriage proposal, regretful she had not told him before he left. My mother's letter was returned to her, the pink envelope stamped DECEASED. As were a handful of others which drifted into her parents' home in New Jersey for weeks after the word of his death had reached her, all bearing the same heartless bureaucratic stamp. Perhaps more than anything, the idea that Tom had never received any of her letters stunned her the most. His to her during that time, written from the jungles of New Guinea, were full of doubt and despair:

> *One topic that comes up every day is the question about when will our mail come and what can be delaying it. Most of our waking thoughts are about home and it is hard to go day after day without news. It is increasingly difficult to write because we can't say anything about what we are doing and as we don't hear from home, there doesn't seem to be anything to say. I think it's sort of a joke for me to write for my letters have nothing in them worth reading. . . .I think of you constantly. Please write often. I long to hear from you. Don't ever forget me, darling. Always, Tom*

These were his last words to my mother, which took a month to arrive in her parents' mailbox. By then, he was dead, shot down and killed on his first mission.

When my parents died, these letters (more than a thousand) came to me, all of them, which spelled out the confusions of their emotions about this divisive war and the glacial pace of its communications. Men died quickly. Word of their deaths arrived much later. I read them all—the ones that were marked DECEASED had never even been opened. My mother, of course, knew what they said—why open them? And then I wrote a book about this story, a book that, like the unopened letters, for years remained unpublished, my own private heartache. Perhaps this manuscript is the longest love letter I have ever written—to my parents, with whom I did not always get along and for whom I had always had mixed emotions. Until their deaths. I was forty-five when they died (they passed away within two months of each other, my mother first, followed by my father who literally died of a broken heart) and I miss them terribly, maybe most of all for the stories they could have told me. These letters, these keys to their souls, are now a book which is called *What There Was Not To Tell*, because whenever I asked my father to tell me about the war, he always answered, with a shrug, "There's nothing much to tell."

It took me months to organize, read, transcribe and catalog these—and they were just the raw material for the book which was fifteen years in the making and all my previous years had not given me nearly as much insight into who they were. Certainly, they showed me what there was not to tell, made me live through a war, and provided a great deal of sorrow, in every way imaginable.

During my growing up years, my mother kept Tom's letters in a small shopping bag in a corner of her closet. They were full of doubt and despair as in his whole time spent in the jungles of New Guinea (a place he did not like at all), he never once received a single word from my mother, in spite of all she had written and sent to him.

> *It is difficult to write because I haven't heard from you in so long. The mail service is slow and a stack of our mail must be sitting some place. Every day I look eagerly to see if I have a letter from you for I love every word from you and every day that passes without word is a disappointment. My life is constantly colored with thoughts of you and hopes. I wonder how your days pass, what you are doing and what you are thinking about. You are the wonderful and beautiful part of my life and it's devilish to have a curtain of silence between us.*

This ill-fated correspondence haunted my mother for the rest of our lives. She never got over the idea that Tom had never known she returned his ardor. In his will, required of him by the War Department before he left for battle, he left everything to my mother, which amounted to a car and a moldy bag of clothing and rusted razors and blades, which arrived a year and a half after his death, shipped on the slow boat from the steamy heart of New Guinea. The car, a 1937 Ford convertible, remains in our family. Tom's parents became my third set of grandparents and we traveled often to see them, my father at the wheel of our station wagon for the long journey from New Jersey to Long Island. One, from my father to my mother, was written when he received the news of Tom's death—almost six months after the fact. Everything in that war came in slow motion, like an echo from a distant canyon. In it, he said:

> *I wouldn't want you to forget him or stop thinking about him. Not even for a short while. If I were killed and never returned — I wouldn't want you to forget me. I'd want you to think about me often. But I'd want you to think of all the fun and all the grand times we had together. Of our crazy days. Of the beautiful music we enjoyed together. And the drives we went on. I'd want you to feel pleased that you meant so much to me. I love you because you are gay and happy and I'd never want to be the cause of your misery.*
>
> *Tom was very lucky to have your feelings toward him change and to have you want to marry him. And he was most unfortunate never to have known about it or been able to enjoy what he had wanted for so long. . . . Whenever I get back and we are together again, I want to talk with you about Tom and I want you to talk and talk about him. And I'll never let you forget him, as if you could. But when I get back, I want to see the Dittie I used to know—and the Dittie that Tom knew. . . .*

And he meant it. Growing up, I couldn't understand how or why my father allowed Tom (who was supposedly his rival) to crowd our home but then I didn't understand war and the way a man can feel when he comes home completely unscathed after almost four years in the dirt and sand of Italy and North Africa while others never returned. That war, about which my father had so little to say, completely altered his life. My father was a good and patient man. He was, as well, a friend of Tom's and said of him, in one of his letters to my mother, *"Tom is a better man than I."*

As a result of reading their letters, my respect for my parents increased many times over. As well as my feelings about war—how the death of one soldier can affect so many others, as well as the next generation who never knew the one who died.

Finally, a much lighter weight in my attic, I found a letter written by my great-grandmother to my aunt, who many years later passed it to me. My great-grandmother, known in the family as Nana, wrote (in curly European script) to encourage my aunt as she passed through her apparently difficult adolescence. At the time Nana wrote, she was elderly, thinking back on the days when she was crossing the Atlantic on board a ship (called The City of Berlin) filled with others on their way to a new life in America. Nana left Queenstown, Ireland, in 1875. She was eighteen and had with her a small satchel of clothing and a batch of her favorite poems, copied out on single sheets of paper. On a windy but sunny day, she carried the treasured verse up on deck to sit and read them, to buck up her spirits. I can only imagine how difficult that crossing must have been for her, alone and so young. When she got to the deck, a gust of wind grabbed the poems from her hand and in an instant she watched them fly off into the void of the great wide sea. "And so, at this great age, I write to you that, when those poems escaped my hand, I felt that all was lost. I didn't feel I could go on. But, I did, and here I am. And so will you be as well." The letter was so much the better in that, when my aunt read Nana's message to her, she already knew that Nana had done well and had lived a full and colorful life in her new land. And by the time I read it, more than a generation later, I knew that as well.

Maybe all letters are love letters. I have defended the evolution of the letter to e-mail, saying that these communications are the same as letters, just delivered in a different way. "People will always write letters," I have said. "We eventually accepted typewriters, didn't we?" But I wonder if future generations will have the e-mails in the same way that I have these documents—now not just news but history, physically occupying space in my attic, in my drawers, on my desk, the infinitely varied handwriting as readily identifiable to me as a face or a hand—my father's perhaps the most beautiful handwriting I have ever seen, formal, sweeping, like calligraphy, and my grandmother's scrawl the most difficult to decipher (in college, I used to offer free doughnuts to anyone who could read me what she wrote and have them make sense). My mother always wrote on pink stationery, the paper stiff and very lightly imprinted with Swiss dots, spelling out her message in plump, cheerful lettering. She never used anything but blue ink, drawn into her pen from an inkwell. The envelopes were perfect squares and sat high in the stack of mail as I carried it back to my kitchen from my mailbox. I imagine that e-mails, though capable of being just as passionate, just as strong expressions of these emotions, will not be kept in the way that these treasures have been, through the generations, bundled and tied like precious documents. And I would never have had the wisdom of my great-grandmother, or the details of her story, if my aunt had not saved the letter and passed it to me.

Letters that I have kept from relationships of my past have provided an amazing perspective as I have moved along in life. What was I doing dating a twenty-five-year-old soldier when I was but sixteen? I always thought it was about the poems but reading them now I wonder if it was not more about his service in the military. And the messages from Nettie and her like? I don't think I could ever have kept on writing if not for their enthusiasm and their encouragement. After a while, I felt a responsibility to them, to keep writing.

Those men with whom I was so infatuated grew more distinct within the perspective of time, as did our youthful emotions. Were it not for this collection of words from generations of my ancestors, my great-grandmother would have remained a stranger to me. And I would never have known this New Orleans lady named Nettie, who was otherwise every bit a stranger: I never even saw her face. I might even say that my parents might never have emerged from their parental costumes. Knowing them all my life had not brought them alive or objectified them as these letters did. These interpreters of relationships, these channels to my past, somehow conveyed to me the love of many strangers. Reading them now may have come too late for the past but not, one hopes, for the future.

Ian Withrow

To Ray

Dear Ray,

He said they found you, he being Gordon Lachance, in the story that made the movie some twenty years back. He thought Ace had something to do with it, though he wasn't exactly sure. Neither that dime store hood nor anyone from his gang ever received any credit. Ace must have placed an anonymous call, Gordie figured. Safest measure for everyone involved.

He said they found you.

So why were you here?

I've always had a hard time getting you out of my head. Ever since I was young, when I first saw your tallow face plastered across the big screen of the Wilma Theater in downtown Missoula. The crusted gore across your forehead worked like a leech on the innocent folds of my brain, as did the congealed blood crusted like dried globs of raspberry currant on the underside of your nose. You wore a green shirt, I remember, and your hair was a dark reddish color accented with highlights of yellowed grass. Your eyes were smoky hoarfrost, the icy afterglow rippling to the rhythm of my adolescent heart. And the words, as if you were whispering in my ear: *Watch out for woodchuck intestines in the blueberry pie.*

When I was ten years old, I found you at a birthday party. Not mine. Ronnie Callahan's. I was only there because my mom told me it would be impolite not to show. I told her I didn't care about being polite. Told her, "He doesn't even like me, Mom. He says my butt looks like wolverines fighting in a sack when I run." But my mother, being my mother and inherently proud, said I didn't have a choice. "Just smile and laugh," she cheered as she dropped me off at the arcade where the party was being held. "Kill them with kindness, son."

And I wanted to; wanted nothing more than to smile them all into early graves. I just didn't have the courage. Thirty minutes into the party I found myself alone at a bench by the front registers. Listening to the electronic bop and whir of the arcade and watching a teenager rack up the high score on a Galaga machine while the rest of the partygoers huddled around The Simpsons game in the back. I was about to get up to buy some candy with my meager stack of arcade tickets—something that certainly would've earned plenty of teasing from Callahan and his cronies—when I noticed a single pale hand sticking out from beneath the pinball machines.

"Brower," I hissed, because I saw your familiar frosty eyes glimmering in the deep shadows. A thin black line of ants trundled across your hand. Then larger bugs—beetles, cockroaches, worms. The shadows shifted, and I knew you were opening your mouth. Knew you were about to whisper. Knew I was about to hear something I wasn't ready to understand. I screamed. Ran to the payphone and called my mom. I was home before the candles on Ryan Callahan's birthday cake began to smoke.

Gordie said everyone heard about your absence on the radio. That they all knew you were from Chamberlain and that you had gone out with one of your mother's pots to pick blueberries, never to return. He said the authorities took to the woods, game wardens and volunteers, and the question on everyone's mind that summer was the same.

What happened to Ray Brower?

Two weeks after my twentieth birthday I found you again. I was in college then, Princeton, housed in a dormitory infamous for its brick walls and waffle-stamped ceilings. Having suffered a broken ankle in a recent football game—an injury that would mark the beginning of the end of my well-intended yet poorly realized athletic career—I had crutched down to the basement in the middle of the night to use the bathroom. Moving carefully because it was always so perfectly black down there in those late New Jersey nights, I hobbled to the nearest urinal and began fumbling with the drawstring of my sweatpants.

It wasn't until I heard the slumping sound behind me, the squeal of shoe on wet linoleum, that I turned around and saw you there. Propped against the wall in a seated position. One leg tucked beneath your hips, the other out and to the side.

My casted ankle screamed with pain as I crashed down on the urine-soaked floor and closed my eyes against the nausea boiling in my guts.

"Jesus Christ!" I cried.

And you answered, *cherry PEZ!* Which probably equates to the same prayer for a boy who never tasted the hormonal fireworks of someone else's chapped lips. Flies swirled about your head like the fighter planes in the old *King Kong* classic and there was that smell about you. Rotting blueberries, overcooked beef stew.

By the time I opened my eyes you had disappeared.

I spent the next thirty minutes staring at a vacant wall while tears trickled down my cheeks and cold urine soaked into my sweatpants. Later, when I was safely beneath the covers of my dorm room bed, I was sure I'd heard the hollow whistle of a faraway train reverberating through the drainage pipes in the bathroom floor.

A dead body is supposed to bring closure. That's how it works in books and movies, anyway. Just a glimpse of the corpse drifting along the bottom of a murky lake, a passing glance at the pile of bones hidden in the walls of the abandoned mansion atop the hill north of town, and all ghosts disappear. A puff of blue smoke, accompanied by a mournful violin, and everyone is allowed a great sigh of relief. The haunting is over; the final loose end effectively woven into that high-arcing thread that keeps everything in order, every meaning in its proper place.

And that's how it went with you, Ray. Or at least that's what you did for Gordie, Vern, Teddie, and Chris. The moment those four boys cleared the brush from your face you became their rite of passage, their magic corridor where fear becomes experience and death, an intimate thing. You forged new perspectives in the hearts of young men, and as those final layers of innocence were ripped away like blood-engorged leeches from soft and sensitive skin, hardened scars emerged.

For those boys you were the end of an era, because you were once a boy in search of something. And you died.

Last night I found you at the foot of my bed. Don't deny it. I saw you standing there. The moon poured light through my bedroom window and your eyes were like gleaming balls of bone. Dark liquid dribbled from your nose and ears, and your jaw sagged. Revealing an upper row of teeth that seemed to hover above your black and lifeless tongue. As you know, I live by the train yard, now, and the midnight collisions of coupling boxcars rumbled like thunder through the walls of my house.

"Why are you here?" I tried to scream, and managed only a wet choking sound.

You remained motionless. Said nothing. You were no longer wearing the green shirt. Instead, it was a white under-tee with sweat stained armpits, and *What the fuck* is *Goofy?* written out in chicken scratch penmanship across the front.

"Why are you here?" I tried again. This time the words came.

You reached out and dropped a folded piece of paper on my comforter. It landed without a sound.

Then I blinked and you were gone.

Scrambling to the foot of my bed, I pawed the comforter for the mysterious paper. Unfolding it, I saw, by the light of the moon, what looked to be a crudely drawn treasure map.

Vern's Penny Jar, it said. *For Vern's eyes only. Sincerely.*

I spent the entire night staring at the ceiling. Of course, I wondered about the map and what it was supposed to mean. But I also wondered about you, Ray. About what were you *really* doing out on those train tracks, for instance, because it sure as hell wasn't to pick blueberries. "Boys don't go out to pick blueberries with pencil and paper," Gordie said. I say, rare is the boy who goes off alone to pick berries at all; I don't care how enjoyable the pie. If you ask me, it must have been a rite of passage that brought you there—something about young love, or your parents, or to prove some primal validation about your ability to survive on your own. That would make sense. I can buy into that.

But why were you here?

And yet even as I ask I think a part of me already knows.

There's a train coming. Not one of steam and steel, of wood and wheel, but fear and defeat and pain. It runs on a bed of burning time, and the boxcars in tow are marred with stenciled labels, big and bold: *FINANCIAL RUIN. MORAL INADEQUACY. DOUBT. FAILURE. FAILURE. FAILURE.* Yes, it's coming. Even now I feel the tracks trembling beneath my feet. And the trestle seems too far to cross in time.

Gordie said his hometown felt smaller when he returned from discovering your body. He said he's carved out a nice career as a writer, and that he gets headaches—stress-aches, he calls them—more often than not. He said he's the only one still around from that group of four. All the rest, he said, have died.

It's because they stopped searching for you, isn't it? It's because they forgot how to run. And, I suppose if there's a purpose to this letter, it's this: I wanted to thank you. Thank you for the unanswered questions, the vague nostalgic clues. Thank you for reminding me that I'm supposed to keep looking. Reminding me that it's not the discovery that matters so much, but the constant journey for more. The rite of passage. The magic corridor that molds and reforms and keeps you one step ahead of that oncoming train. Thank you for being the warning, Ray, and the memory, and everything in between.

I'll never forget you, because the trestle is long and my train is coming.

And I'd like to run.

I'm listening to my iPod as I write this. Ben E. King. I believe you know the song. And you know something? I won't be afraid. As long as you stand by me, Ray. You're a good friend, in so many ways.

Hugs and Kisses. Here's to another ten years.

—Ian

Kate Levin

ANGEL

—Excerpted from *Punk Prophet,* a novel-in-progress

It's 8 o'clock in the fucking morning, and I'm awake. I lie in bed and smoke. I live across from an elementary school, and I can hear all the laughing and cheer as they gather in the play yard and wait to be allowed up to classes. The general ruckus floats in through my window, and I look over at Bodhisattva—in bed with me. I'm jealous of his sleeping state.

As I look at his closed eyes, his dark eyelashes flush against his cheek, and the pillow smooshing his mouth into a crumple, it occurs to me that he's just a child too. I know I'm getting bitter. I smoke, and I know it's time to end this thing with Bodhisattva.

Not yet. No. I can't just give him up. I'd miss this too much; I'd miss our time together. His skin. Fuck, but it's wearing on me. I'm not gonna be able to stay in this much longer. I'm not gonna kick him out of my life—at this point I can't even kick him out of my bed. But right now I want to talk about that day; that day and the moment that I knew, that I knew it was over. When I woke up to the sound of the morning schoolyard, and I smoked, and I considered my future with Bodhisattva.

The children play, my curtains flap, Bodhi continues to sleep, and I continue to smoke.

It came to me a couple days ago. I was putting on makeup, and Bodhi walked into the room. His black jeans were riding low on his hips, the top unbuttoned. I was drawn to his skin, flashes of the water beading below his belly button, the trail of dark hair. He had just used my shower. He stood behind me, wrapping his arms around my shoulders and breasts and the damp of him soaked through my shirt, the damp of his cheek and hair up against my neck. And even as I felt myself wanting him, felt those zings of lust—It wasn't enough anymore.

But I won't change that easily. I'll chew on this feeling, let it cumulate—feel the emptiness when we talk, in our quiet moments in bed. Hear it whispering to me, when we share day to day intimacy—feel it poisoning everything.

But fuck this is a lousy feeling. It should be good. Maybe if I honored it, this moment could be ok—'cause I'd know it's time to move on, and how can you be sad when you know? But I'm ignoring that feeling. I'm clinging to what I want instead of what I know.

So, I put out my cigarette and lay back down, pulling the covers up. I roll over and wrap my arm around Bodhi, spooning up against his back. The sound of the children gets fainter, as it's now 8:30 and I know they're getting into lines in their little cement yard, being led into the school.

Something changes in the room, and I know that Bodhisattva is awake. We pretend to sleep in the morning light, and I listen to him breathe. Both of us are facing my open window, and the curtains move in the breeze, filtering the light a shade of blue.

Now would be the moment, if I were to tell him. I can feel it developing, bubbling up under his skin. Waiting to burst. I silently rehearse the words I want to say, that I can't say yet.

His heart beats under my fingers, and these chorus' ride through my brain, a letter to Bodhi…to us…

> Dear _______,
> Dear ~~Bodhi~~,
> Dear Love,
>
> I'm not so sure I know your face anymore, Love. Your hair has changed, your face has changed, your bodytouch keeps changing. You don't like to be held. As time passes I will think more of what didn't happen, what we missed, the times we didn't kiss, didn't talk, didn't touch.
>
> Love: some say you don't exist, like the Loch Ness Monster, like GOD. I think I see you every day. You're following me, Love. Don't think I won't see you around me. I will catch you quickly in the lights reflecting in the east river, subways riding in one clear strip of window light, in music, the perfect riff, the groove of James Brown, in still evenings when music syncs over stereo with window light and air, the

milky blacks and grays of photography with film grain, strong cups of coffee lined up in rows, Cuban, Costa Rican, tins of beans out on gourmet floors, scratch of nostalgia from record needles, commuter-worn paperbacks read on subways, singular thoughts of brilliance at 2am, cold nights with moon above and snow frozen to cement, the Buffalo roaming through poetry readings of NYC—.

Will that be enough—these momentary glimpses of you?

You leave me, Bodhi, you keep fading—your ghostly image smudged in my brain.

Love,
Angel

Leslie Z. Anderson

To Faith

October 5, 2013

Oh, Faith[1]—

This morning I put my June on the school bus—snot clinging to her pouty upper lip before dripping to the pavement—and again I thought of you. Month two of Kindergarten and Junie is despondent over forgetting the homework. *Ridiculous, homework for such a little one! Robbing childhood!* Of course I didn't say any of that as I tried to comfort her there in the street, while the other mothers and fathers looked on, while my two maniac dogs pulled their leashes and consequently my right arm nearly out of the socket while my left held the backpack of her older sister, stooped to tie those sneakers that don't even fit…You would have said the right words in June's little ear. You would have at least had a Kleenex in your pocket, for God's sake.

Jim is in Brussels. I'm in despair.

Not for lack of a warm body in my bed, mind you, but for the extra set of hands at bath time. The baby is six months now but still nursing around the clock, so I have all the middle-night tenderness I can handle, tugging at my breasts for the foreseeable future. How mean and how sad that makes me, in all the ways that you know. And that's why I love you, I suppose. That knowing.

I think of you so often; why not just come out with it? I return over and over again to the stories, seeking guidance, but inevitably get lost in the moment—your moments—and my own smothering admiration. You were no hinting Heloise. Faith in the afternoon, Faith in a tree; you were always there for your Richard and Tonto, their father, your father, your lovers, and all the politicians and armies who conspired to employ the boys of your life for national gain. Or was it national defense? You were those boys' defense, at any rate, and you had a lot to say about that too. I love the mother you were to all of them and are —by the great transitive properties of kitchen sink fiction—to me.

Three days ago I thought of you in the playground. I climbed to the top of the monkey bars and surveyed the territory. Like you I judged the other mothers and fathers, their children and their parenting, their pocketbooks and politics. You know what? Not much has changed, not really, in all this time, and my heart nearly burst with a yearning to hear you laugh at it all. At me. It is funny, isn't it? This *living* we are all so damn busy with.

I know I need to wean her. There's a job to hold down, real-world problems to speak out against; there's sex to be having. I wonder, would you be disappointed to see how we mothers, nearly four decades removed, have allowed thickets to grow over the paths your generation created? (But honestly, Faith. Stop nursing my baby? I say let her have the milk a few more months. It's the most good I may do in my lifetime and you know that too.)

Ah well. I hope you that you don't mind this outpouring. I just wanted you to know, is all. You're such a bright, burning light in this mother's heart.

With love,
Leslie

---

[1] Grace Paley, Enormous Changes at the Last Minute. 1974.

Mark Wagstaff

BURN LINES

MY MUM LET ME EAT WITH A SPOON till I was seven so I never learnt the niceties or much respect. Waiting for someone to open this door I could admire the roses, nod approval at the collaborative way all the windows down the street sparkle. Even notice those lads kicking ball got machine–fresh kit. I could form positive opinions of this neighbourhood that—with due care and time—might lead to enduring friendships, to possibilities years from now. But I was the kid ate dinner with a spoon, so I just price everything.

This woman who opens the door I'd call a declining market. That shirt must have been smart once, and her hair's a tended garden a couple of months after the gardener was let go. There's spider silk on the porch light; says a lot.

"Yes?"

Hear that, in her voice there? Doesn't like visitors. Visitors make demands. I feel sorry a bit but life's not charity is it? "This Frater Road, love? Couldn't see a sign at the top. Warren round here innit? Took ages to find you. I come about the room."

Now I'm not saying everyone who lets a room got the shiny knuckles of repo men in their gullet. Some are glad of the company, or saving for something special. A few honestly think it's wrong to leave a room empty. A few got other reasons. And round here with the stadiums and all that's going on any of your mates down the pub would tell you it's mad not to cash in.

She's Karen. I already knew. These girls getting dragged towards middle age, their hair and dreams getting faded, they're always Karen or Tina or Chrissy or Jane—names that lit them bright in good years now deserted, so just that wispy remembrance of girlhood—that name—remains. I get time to consider these things, in between keeping busy.

Someone said to Karen: with the stadiums and that you could make a bit letting out that damp room at the top. Be glad you did, they said, come Christmas. What's really sad is she's made an effort: the nets look rinsed, she's made the bed neat with the pillows on top of the duvet. There's scrappy, knock–off flowers in a vase. The flowers get me a bit. I'm not guessing this house is typically top–to–toe blooms—she's actually gone out, got them somewhere, come back, realised she's nothing to put them in, dug a vase out the hall cupboard or begged off a neighbour, washed it, cut and spread the flowers, chose to put them just so on the bedroom side. She's thought: whoever sees that will pay the asking price straight off. They won't quibble or take snide looks at the stains round the window, or notice the wallpaper's coming away and the carpet's bald as a park soccer pitch. They'll see flowers, and call this place home.

"Ah this is nice." I lie with ease. "Like the flowers."

Karen's tall—taller than me: she has trouble getting jeans with the length. She's lived here ten years though she wants to move one day; presumably the same one day that we'll all get everything done. Money's scarce—doesn't say so of course but I reckon there's nothing bought new in this house in a twelve month. She's got obligations: seventeen years old, called Kellie.

I lay on my latest bed, listening how evening settles. Telly from downstairs, music from Kellie's room off the landing; few cars but this is a quiet street, the way I've come to like it. I used to be one for a rave up, I've breached my share of the peace. But I come to appreciate much more the clicks and sighs of quiet nights when the whole world sounds foggy: the only discord the screams of cats or a burglar alarm far away.

Show my face in the morning but don't interfere. People are rightly protective of their routines. Karen seems to have some part time job—her fingernails are short and jagged. Kellie already twigged the college course she's on will take her nowhere and goes out, huddled up in resentment. I'm too busy really to feel sentimental but a bit concerned for my housemates. An air of gloom in domestic arrangements makes each day hard country.

Once they're out I search the place. It's a bit optimistic expecting jars of cash in the kitchen cupboards; I look anyway, despondent at white label cans, uniform and slapdash as rations. Sitting room is Karen's den: celeb magazines, some failed knitting, piles of snide letters from debt—mongers. Not left out of course. In a drawer with some holiday snaps—looks like Crete. Does her well, a bikini. Lottery tickets, scratch cards, scrappy bits of paper with premium rate numbers. Contests I bet. Bent contests. Last year's telly, scrag ends of booze; small but fair selection of physical music.

The troubled feeling I get from it all goes large in her bedroom. Women rightly have their pride: don't guess Karen's over the moon about those sheets. It's not where you'd bring someone back. She's put the good bedding in my room, left herself stuff that wouldn't scrub fresh on an all–day boil wash. Still a bit warm deep down in the dented mattress. One dent–dead centre. Her wardrobe's got some quite nice things, but aged from when they were bezzies. There's a story on these hangers: looks that were nearly hot five, six years ago; going out clothes, dancing clothes. Jeans gone up two sizes, labels gone downmarket. Dressing for expectations that have tightened. She doesn't waste cash on fancy lingerie.

Careful round Kellie's door: kids set traps. Every wall thick with posters, glossy offcuts of next big whatevers; her graffiti got smart, sick humour. Don't get involved in gear on the floor—she'll have instinct for anything moved. Cheap end electronics. No value whatever. One corner tidy—no celebs: pictures of girls—teams of girls—tracksuits zipped tight, hair smoothed back; holding up medals to catch the passing eye. And this explains it. Carbon fibre tube, rubber stoppers each end. Hard to resist giving it a twirl. Manage a double before I drop it. There's a knack, twirling these. Kellie's got medals. Good on her. Medals furnish a life.

Lay on my bed at ease to be living with poor people. They got nothing. That relaxes me. Almost lets me sleep. But I got duty, things to get done. So I'm touring the street and it's plain to me Karen's house lets the neighbourhood down. I don't mind, but understand how folks who shelled out on that triple glazing or the rather fine basement kitchen peeking up through railings might look at her place, might feel it impairs their investment. I appreciate effort people put in, getting their dream home together. Shocking always when dreams get spoiled.

Take a detour where the stadium waits, a few weeks short of its moment. Never comfortable where police got guns: they hold them like they got no plan what to do. Desultory action men, look as close to dropping the things as making some peace. Finished and tested, a while from now this place will sing with endeavour: cheers for the fast and strong; more will leave disappointed. I've no flag to wave. Moving here was a business decision.

Sledge turns up first: I'm satisfied he's upset at buying a drink. His sour face of an uglier, outsize Muppet draws me through knots of engineers on lunch from the Comms Centre. Slumped at his beer, posture so bad he can tip it straight in; among the techie chat, vintage shirts and experimental sideburns he's a leftover old dosser. Sledge really gets hands–on in a task.

"Where have you been?" He doesn't sit up: his voice sprawls round beneath my chin.

I answer the top of his head. Scraps of peanut shells fleck his hair. "Round the stadium."

"Lap of honour?"

"Good to check it. Before it's busy."

He makes a noise like your mum when you ask for a lend out her purse. "You done any work?"

So I tell him about my new neighbourhood: what I've seen of basement kitchens, knock–through lounges, big tellies cheering up darkened rooms, tablets left on desks. Tell him cars, cleanliness, cameras. Offer thoughts on where odds might be kind. Sledge keeps pouring beer in his mouth, grunting, shoulders flexing then falling back when they realise they got nowhere to go. He wants to make a start before, "This bloody circus." Too distracting he reckons, too busy. I give him some numbers, tell him nothing's guaranteed. Check pockets on the way out and go shopping.

I offer to cook the steak. Karen says keep it till Sunday surprised—not entirely pleased—I bring her so much stuff. She says there's no need—I pay rent. Dusting the lightest sugar across my voice I say it's no trouble: I've got to eat and we share the same house. She says she didn't mean to sound ungrateful. I say let us know what you want bringing in.

After I help her wash up I go out. Could never say spring's my favourite time of year. I understand in the day there's gonna be hustle; at night I like streets to myself. Go out dead of winter, snow to here: I don't mind. In spring everyone thinks they got rights on the night. Young guys leaning on cars bust out tunes, girls double–dutch on the corner shouting rhymes, working the moves that'll make them famous one day. Old boys sit huffing beer in postage stamp front gardens, their women stood beside open doors, arms folded, staring into some other time. Kids run around in PJs—their mums know it's time to go in but the air's so warm, the kids so happy; enough early nights in winter. For me quiet nights are more welcome; winter cold that sends everyone scurrying in crackles steely and swift in my bones. Nowhere quiet tonight. Houses open front to back —right through to their barbecue smoke. So full of cargo, rich and static, but clustered with people and flies. Go sit in the park, watch day disappear but the hollers of kids loading up in the playground kicks lumps from the twilight.

In my new street a car pulls up. I slow a bit, from curiosity and natural caution. Kellie gets out, in trackies with a sports bag. Says something—female voices answer. Waves once as the car moves off. Just catch sight of a tracksuit passenger side. Walk to the end and back: give her chance to get in. She's young still, don't guess best pleased mum took a lodger. They probably rowed about it. I don't have time or need to build trust but I'm soft so I stay out her way.

People don't run to schedule though. I'm quiet with keys so their voices don't stop till I shut the front door heavy. Chuck a friendly look in the sitting room: Karen in her armchair, white label beer in one hand, satellite remote in the other. Kellie stood between her and the screen, bit flushed with her tracksuit zipped, hair pulled and pinned and pummelled up into a twist. Her eyes immune to evening warmth lay a chill on me; don't want her to know I feel it so I drop some 'luvverly wevver' stuff that flies like lead. I'm quiet with stairs but Kellie is teenage suspicious. I go on up not hearing anything said.

Police park two doors down. I walk by, see through the jumbled curtains a man gesturing round his front room, making fuss as two officers bulked with kit give him minimum face time. He's still got a house, and furniture, but doesn't see things that way. He jabs round the room, hands flying, while these big nods stare, too equipped to do much else. I feel a bit sorry and that but life's not fair.

Most days I've got people to see. Their scratchy air of excitement works hell on my sunny nature. Rattner in his bolthole behind The Prince's Feathers spills plans for his game of a lifetime like I'm his best fan. He's got this map—no lie—this map of Stratford pinned on what's left of his corkboard. Points up rat runs, safe houses, friendly retailers like a general speccing out some sweaty war. A million happy people, he tells me. A million empty wallets. Two million phones, tablets, cameras—no end of them music players. Watches, rings—all manner of lost property. His skin glows sour yellow with the wonder of it all. The biggest pocket pick in history, right here in London Town. He's recruited all stripes of loafers and flakes—students, catalogue models, them East European gypsy girls with the nice hair—running goods for his army of razorblade dodgers. He wants Sledge's crew hard at it in the empty streets back home. Offers me various unspecified positions for unquantified rewards. I tell him it's all good. Since I was last in my class to tie laces I'm wary of ambition. Don't want to give him the brush—that would be suicide. So I lay him some chat how I'm here to help and leave when his phone starts ringing. Hit daylight bemused at Rattner's Olympic spirit. Treat myself to a prostitute on the way home but my heart's not in it.

Poor people get letters. The bourgeoisie are strictly digital; my world leans on rushed words and violence; it's the poor get snail mail. Now I'm not so blunt to ask Karen what that letter says—I'll find out anyway—so I go: "Fancy a brew?" in chirpy, lodgerly manner. Make one anyway when she don't answer, asking, with all the innocence: "Going the games?"

She has this way of taking a breath, half–turning so her ashy hair scrabbles and falls from her shoulder—such a perfectly unconscious move it's almost dancing. "No." She thinks a moment. "That why you here?" She's not asked before.

"Not really." Give her tea and sit across from her. "I'm not really that sporting."

"Don't think anyone cares." She glances at the letter.

"Be glad when it's over I 'spect. All the disruption. Parking. Police."

"There was a break–in. Coupla doors down." She folds the letter, puts it down but can't seem to let it go—her fingers test at it; specks of dirt freckle her nails.

"Not friends I hope?" Through steam off my tea, check what colour her eyes are. Yeah. Would be.

Karen's face got no habit of emotion. A sort of flicker runs through it: could be pity, disgust, toothache—anything. "Don't really know people round here."

"Keep themselves to themselves?"

Her nails scratch on the letter. "Not being funny and that but you got next week's rent? I got work and I need to go shopping…"

"Got the next two weeks."

Her neck takes a slight jolt. "No. Just next week. Don't want to get ahead."

There's a fight when Kellie comes in. She got a teen voice for a row. Karen's more subdued, but the gist is I hear Kellie say: "One thing, one thing in my life and you won't let me." There's a mumble, some clatter and Kellie sings out: "Don't you think I've had enough?" She catches light: "It's okay for you to have beer and go out." Air rises. "You go out. You went out last month. But I got one thing." A storm of fat trainers hitting thin carpet and from the battlefront halfway upstairs: "I ain't never surprised he left you." A slammed door—sudden, sharp music.

Give it ten, then another ten for comfort. Pad on down to the living room looking cheerful. "I'm popping out for some chips. Want anything?"

I'm not big on watching telly, 'specially when it's cranked loud to soundclash upstairs beats. Karen was a bit awkward about chicken and chips and wine. It was the wine. Just bargain bin from the firetrap corner shop but she kept saying she couldn't. I told her I couldn't drink it all, which made no sense but seemed to help. She said sorry for the glasses. Wrong glasses for wine. Too tall and that. Try saying it don't matter but she's not the type to think making do's okay.

We watch this weird shit people watch in the evening, and I'm pondering the cost of smart–end tellies against the value of what's on when Kellie comes flying downstairs in a jangle of arcade bling. Not seen her dressed out before. She's got this shiny black dress—twenty years back I'd have stood up but now I think it's too short. Her hair frizzed out, face done like she wants a fight and a mile of impressive leg tone. I'm speculating how quick she could make off with a sack of cameras when Karen jumps in.

"Where you going?"

"Out," says Kellie, reasonably.

Karen checks the time. "Got college."

"Holidays nearly."

"Your course…"

"I," says Kellie, loud as her muscles are hard, "am going out."

The slam leaves one of them domestic silences I'm not really that clever with. This has all become my business at a difficult time. I tip out more wine; Karen says softly, "Seventeen and knows it all."

I got sympathy for kids with all the unemployment and that. These games is a huge opportunity: dipping, scamming, daylight mugging. Prostitution. Huge opportunity. "Bet you were a girl at her age." I mean it nice and hope the wine will ride it to her a kind way.

She looks at me, eyes all reflections. "Her age I was married."

I look back at the screen. Some bloke cracking jokes that ain't funny. There's softness through his body. "Got burn lines, see? On the picture. Need a new telly."

Hardly know she's stood up she's so quiet. "Leave these things. I'll do it in the morning." Watch her out the door. Count slow steps upstairs.

Over the road gets a widescreen delivered, round the corner acquires new hardware. Rattner likes gadgets—says technology gives his outfit professional edge. I see places getting alarms, porch cameras fitted. A locksmith's busy next door, looking shifty how locksmiths do. He'll be in demand when everyone's out at the egg–and–spoon. A house, any house, big or small, is a box. Now there's no such thing as a box you can't open with pressure applied just the right way. People set cameras but most of these cameras are trash. I know: Sledge says about it in his precise, involved way of a drunk trainspotter. Cameras, dogs, infrareds. Private patrols in noddy uniforms. Your house is still a box.

Sledge gets busy, the neighbourhood gets more nervous. Start to recognise the bored, irritable young coppers who come out time after time days after the action. Guess they're dreaming of some bigger role for themselves when the hoop–la kicks off and there's crowds to control and, maybe, the chance of real damage. Not for them, though, in their bulky vests and under–spec cars. They'll be rolling the stripy tape and fetching biscuits. At Kellie's age I thought everything was people's own fault, except mine. Now I see we're all moving parts, gadgets with limited function. We maybe start off as widescreen hearts but with only so much life to go round we shrink to our own small picture. Maybe quick, like those lads with their life in the force planned out. Maybe after a bit of messy, wasteful resistance.

There's a sour rhythm at home. Don't like that. Karen says she ain't worried —got nothing to steal. But she's scared of losing the nothing she's got; I'm not free to reassure her. There's things she's not telling: hiding letters, being too careful. Bad air between her and Kellie, non–stop. In my busy life there's more than this but it concerns me. I like people to be happy, so far as possible.

Rattner comes down to recce the site. I don't want his car near my street — we drive round a bit while his lads crack jokes and he slags my neighbourhood.

"Take all this down," he says. "Have car parks."

Tell him there's plenty sweeties in the shopfront.

He grips on my leg. It hurts. "You're wasting yourself you know that? Doing what? Housebreakers' tipster? Moving every few weeks. Out all weathers. You're a tramp."

Tell him I pull sweet percentage but Rattner's guiding heresy is it ain't about the sheckles. "What we're doing here is pulling off something substantial. Oi." He raps on the driver's head. "There's a space over there. Am I driving? What we're doing…" he's a visionary thug "is laying foundations. Know what substantial means? Of substance. With substance. It's not just nicking some fancy phones and heaving 'em through Stansted. We're building businesses to service a market. And buying up nods to do the runaround for us."

We can't get up close on the site. Every time I come by the security gates push a bit more down the road. Rattner talks in widescreen: a movie man setting up shots he explains where the crowds will be, where his boys and girls go in, how they get out: words like 'footfall' 'throughput' 'traffic' buzz around the spring day—jam–weary wasps too fat to fly, too ripped to land. The conveyor for shifting merchandise runs through the operation—no one's caught with more than a couple of phones, that's the theory. A relay of hand to hand shipping, while people run and jump and swim oblivious to the big show.

I've no clue why Rattner thinks I'm his boy. Wasp words: 'logistics' 'strategy' buzz my way. Get a sense too that it's softer skills he's after. A lot of his dippers are young, bit foreign. He's not got time, he says, and I see myself as nursey, sorting everything from their lunch money to finding the right lawyer's nark. To breaking fingers when merchandise goes freelance. I take a sub from him—not that I feel especially ambitious. But it's not just him got investments.

He insists we launch a few drinks. Regret it when I'm late home and Karen's out. "Poncing cash," Kellie says, her back to me at the sink. I assume Kellie's dad was a stocky man with Afro hair and thin skin. She's a powerful shape: it invades everything she does. Unloading her bag in the washing machine her arms yank and flick away clothes: a clear yearning to throw something hard. She's got good balance, squatted like that. She ain't sexy.

"What's your sport?"

She ignores me.

"You go training?"

With impressive control she stands straight up, swivels on a heel tap. Not tall as Karen—every inch works hard for its keep. She blocks the window, nervy light edging round her. "What's your game?"

If I close my eyes—which I don't much—might recall any one of the thousand people who asked me that in robust situations. "Football," I tell her. She looks like she might mouth back but goes on filling the washing machine. I nip upstairs—try her door on the way but it's locked.

When Karen comes in her skin's a sad shade of cream. Eyes dusty, hair overdue. I'm tightening screws in the kitchen cupboards—keeps me downstairs since Kellie's gone up—watch Karen offload shopping, put her keys on the hook, hang her thin leather in the hall and stand, staring at nothing. She's no more than forty–odd but looks done.

Dosing my voice I ask does she want dinner bringing in. Say I might go down the Indian. Or Chinese. I like Chinese. Ask has she been Stratford, seen the shops and that. She takes a minute, like thawing out. Says I'm good but I can't keep getting takeaway. She'll cook dinner. She's got mince. I say I'll get the drink then; next thing she's in the sitting room and the TV on loud. Lifestyle show, hot makeovers for the games. She maybe doesn't hear the knock at the door.

Loud, determined. A knock that knows you're there. I already got my jacket. Can't stay in just coz someone's outside. Tall lad, taller than me. Casual and business–ready. He asks is Karen around. Her full name.

"Not right now."

He checks me, positive I'm on some list. "When's she back?"

"You can talk to me." Pull the door to behind.

"It's a private matter."

"I won't breathe a word."

"Look," he says, bit lairy, "I'm not authorised to talk with anyone different. It's private business between her and my client."

"How much?"

He keeps on with the middleweight noise.

"What is it? Credit card? Loan?"

"It's an agreement for credit." He checks me again. "You her bloke?"

"You send her letters?"

He takes a step. I meet him. "We are required, by law, to take all reasonable action to contact debtors. To discuss their situation."

"To give them shit."

"To seek repayment. Who are you?" His breath bears down on my face in the fading evening air. He's big, but it's all in the game.

Grab on his shoulder. Surprised, his head ducks down. "I asked you a question sonny. How much?" It's just a few hundred. Night out and a cab home. Peel Rattner's sub from my jacket lining. "This is full and final settlement."

"It's short."

"I'll have a receipt."

His voice bleaches. "I can't settle this much short. Use your head. We can discount but I need more than this."

Give him all I got but the note I keep for bargain bin red and crisps. Get a receipt in big, stupid writing. He gets his cockiness back before the end of the street.

When I get in from the shop Karen's out again—telly left on and her cuppa stone cold. I been in the habit of girls once or twice—how they act on that sense in their blood and moment by moment, doing just fine without all the sad scheming men need so they can fail. If I got any notion of people I wouldn't say Karen's life runs to any great plan.

A bit empty with wine and crisps and no one to share I hang about downstairs, then go up, churned with heavy dub from Kellie's room. Floor shakes. I'm used to it.

Give it half hour and go back down. She's still not home and night's gathering round the windows—see the neighbourhood's fearful faces twitch their curtains shut. Make some calls, deal some business. Distractions, and still she ain't back. Kellie's door flicks and shivers with the bassline. Take a couple of knocks, feeling stupid.

She cracks the door a bare fraction, stares like I'm the e–fit everyone's after.

"When's your mum back? I was gonna cook dinner."

"She ain't happy with you."

"Where's she gone?"

"Poncing cash. Fuck." She looks down sharpish: my foot jacking her door. "Fuck off."

It stings: she can throw some weight. She leans on the door. I push back. It cracks, sickly sounding.

Her voice goes wild. "Kill you. Swear. Got a knife."

"Don't show off."

Her room so heavy with bass can't hardly think. Tell her I used to skank on that when her mum still trusted the pill.

She puts the bed between us. "What you want?"

"Where's your mum?"

"Settled that bloke didn't you? It ain't none of your business."

"How's the athletics?"

"What?"

Her baton's on the bed among her medals. "You do contests?"

"National championships last three years. Solo multiple baton last year."

She picks up the baton, balances it a second, whirls it around her head in a dazzle of helicopter shears. "Baton's only part of it. It's whole body discipline."

"Have to be fit."

"It's not just this." She twirls. "Dexterity yeah—but you need strength and control." She stares, rock. "Discipline."

Her dad must have had a mean streak and mortal fear of failing. "You going to the games?"

"What you doing here? Who are you?"

"Are you? Going?"

She checks the team photos on the wall. "Twirling's not an Olympic sport."

"Maybe it should be."

"Maybe you should piss off where you come from."

Even if that was possible it ain't what I'd choose.

Karen blanks me when she comes in late, smelling of beer a bit. Lay on my bed, feel burn lines itch my body. Painkillers stopped working. I thought they'd stop working. In time I'll have better scars, an alibi how you should never assume a firework's dead till it's cold. But for now this scratchy pain nags day and night.

Down early this morning, catch Karen before she goes out. Her mood's no brighter but she's always an English summer. As I breeze in the kitchen I think: this is our first row. First time at each other's throats. We got a long race to run still but it's good to mark these occasions. I kick it off: saves time. "Missed you last night. I was gonna do dinner."

She smacks around from the cupboard doors that I tightened so much they swing slow like the hands of old clocks. "I was gonna cook dinner. I said I was gonna cook dinner."

"Wanted to give you surprise."

"Don't want your surprises." She turns her back, scrubbing up the kitchen side to look busy.

"Karen…"

"Had a good laugh did you? I scrape and ponce off this one and that one, and you settle up right out your pocket. Musta give you a good laugh."

My background, my training, is getting things done. How—almost never matters. So she goes off to work all pink and moody; Kellie I guess is off college or just not going; and I got nothing but business the whole day through. Scouting prospects, making plans—takes a good deal of my time. Even trekking up west to get new boots… I can't not leave the shop without paying. My life's a dare that became a habit.

All very festive in town. I'm not bothered much with their Sports Day. I'm not really so bothered with Rattner's bonanza, and when I'm round his office and he's banging on like a rep for some shady prize draw I find my thoughts wandering. We have this mad meeting in one of them chipboard hotels for the conference traffic. Notepads branded with the dumb thoughts of the workshy dead and them water bottles with rubber balls on top. He's talking logistics and percents while these suburban villains grin like cartoons and trouser the free sweeties. Rattner's one of them officers got a map and a plan and statistics and words—such words: all the cock on where the show's headed. But he got no… shall we say… feel what it's like when angry brothers with burned up eyes stick hardware in your spine and say it's your call to prayer. They don't register on the plan. They ain't got branded notepads.

Back home Old Bill's out again. Only a class neighbourhood gets so much helmet time. Fight down the urge to ask what's occurring, stride up to my front door the fully upright citizen. But not best pleased it's open. Not wide, just a small way, like someone's banged out and it didn't quite catch. Like accidental.

When you see it in movies, widescreen, a turned up room has the look of a beaten city after the bombs. But close to, in a place with not much to start, it's small derelictions that hurt. All the drawers whipped out the sideboard, chairs upended. Telly keeled over sideways—not surprised they left it, weighs a ton. Room to room I track the familiar slime of smalltime robbing. Any electrics, anything shiny—everything bust in the stupid belief that skint people stash away cash.

They've had Kellie's music. Her laptop—they must be hard up. They've had her medals. Her medals that got as much silver as them cartons out the Chinese. They vandalised Karen's room with especially adolescent disrespect. Don't bother checking mine—I got nothing.

Spilt letters all over the sitting room floor—Karen keeps 'em, ticking away: little timebombs of loss and missed payments. Old school reports of Kellie's—poor attendance, poor attention. Even letters telling Karen she ain't got the job. Takes special, resolute sadness to hoard those let–downs. Letter from the spine hospital. Sends a shiver. To The Parent Or Carer Of. Why can't they say Mum? 'Dear Ms… Your daughter Kellie's tests… Likely to recover but with diminished functionality.' Yeah. All that.

First shot cracks my knuckles but so worth it. Sledge stares, lip thickening then… Fuck it. Smack in… Get hold… Tangle. Fall. Roll him back. Ribs. Burn lines flaring hard. He stumbles up.

"What the fuck you doing?"

Half stand, butt his gut. He falls back on the wall. Get in and he's pushing me back, palms up.

"What are you doing?"

"Which of your shitheads trashed me?"

"What?"

"My base. Done over. Who?"

Shakes his head like it's very hard question. "Why would we do your place? Got nothing there."

"Got fucking less now."

"Listen to yourself." Sledge got a very small way of speaking, baldly at odds with untidy anatomy wrapped in tramp's rags that began as disguise and are part of him since he's gone native. The rare sound of his raised voice blows the length of the alley, freezes the twitch in my fist. "D'you know how much we made just from that street? We ain't even started them flats at the back. You think we'd drain that slum of yours for entertainment? Have a word. We're too busy dodging out filth and neighbourhood watch. We're too busy trying to get it all done before every inch from here to Stratford is one big fucking cop shop. You sure them bullets missed your brain?"

These afternoon hours are what I never got used to. Always, one way and another, I've had my time directed—never bothered by space in between or sticky hours that cling to my heels. Since I got back I seen more the afternoon people: old girls on their shuffling errands. Kids cutting school just kicking around, spinning love out a glance and a ringtone. Blokes who'll never work again, pushing pushchairs with this look of… this look of real pride. Pushing themselves to do a bit more, waiting on that same tomorrow when all our bills are paid. What we thought we was building in them cold mountains. When all the while we was just punishing empty space. Fighting wars to fill our days.

I'm sure there's people upset when we come calling. It's not personal—just nicking stuff. We got basement heads and tenth floor hearts—no wonder we can't earn it. We take without malice, without harm mostly. We're not driven by the promise of Kingdom Come. But for all of it, walking back in that door and Karen on her knees, face burned red, trying to tidy and losing her way in tears: I feel a weight of tragedy come down. Like a dust storm digs in your clothes, your skin; your heart, if you let it—I itch and burn, choke and got nothing, nothing to say. Keep turned from her—fix up the telly, straighten chairs, shift away what's broke without fuss, without chancing her swollen eyes. She sniffs, makes noise, asks what I can't answer. She ain't insured, she ain't called the law: what's the point? I shrug, like to say none.

She keeps asking and asking: "Who done this? Who would do this?" till I tell her straight on: "I dunno who done this but I swear it's the last they'll do," and mean it, right through. Never had such hate for a living person before. Out there, when you hit the switch, watch 'em fall in clouds of dust and turbans it's not like you hate 'em. You and them are doing a job. So you hit the switch. But this, seeing this and her face—I feel travelling hate, a hate that moves, seeks and finds and slips the catch from revenge. I'll render who did this, and enjoy it.

No sound from Kellie. No tunes no more. Ask: "How's Kellie?" and Karen looks up like: "How you think?"

Find stuff for a sandwich—leave it a little way from where she's sat in this mound of letters that gets no more tidy. I thought they was junk about debts long missed and jobs long gone. But they're not. They're what's her life. "Was she hurt bad?"

Karen sits, cried out.

Running round, that bargy with Sledge, patching this place: when I lay on my bed streaks of fire griddle my body. When I asked the doctor: "You get all the bullets?" he said: "The important bullets," and laughed. On their charts you're dead or you're dancing. I got my toes back on the floor, though with diminished functionality. Eight weeks later took the long cruise home. The pain will go, one day. Or I'll get more used to it. That's where they win, them blokes in the hills: whatever, they get more used to it. Them lads go off head first and wherever they fall find god. From here, god never happened.

Can't rest—go out on the landing, don't know to do what. Nothing to hear but a distant scratch of sirens chafing the night and, very faint, Karen snoring. Always fond of women who snore. Don't wanna make noise so I stand here, feel the empty dark swirl like hill weather. Clicks and thuds around the house: just night noise—don't jump like I used to. Footsteps outside grow and fade: some wet little coppers sent out on the beat maybe, for reassurance, for entertainment.

I cut my lines, left no way back, so I stand staring over the banisters as a door opens behind me. Don't pretend I'm going anywhere, coming back from anywhere. Don't say I was just passing. It's too quiet for alibis. A hiss, the toilet empties down. In silence emerging from the water's long drag through the pipes she's stood beside me. We look over the banister rail—two people on a stalled ship in some vagrant sea. "She told me."

Kellie leans into the rail. It creaks with her strength. "I should be there. Could have been there. My coach… everyone said."

"It's shit," I tell her, poor of words for sympathy and caring.

"Watched it when I was a kid: who won, what they did. Had plans for how I'd beat them. And here. Home town. Right in the faces of everyone told me I couldn't."

"She said."

"That equipment was bust."

I heard blokes say that exact same thing as I lay in bed with a drip one end and a drain bag the other.

"I did that move every day. Practised and practised. The pommel was unstable. Felt it go the second I put hand to it."

"And your fall split the crash mats?"

"Freak accident. Million to one. I had style. I had repertoire. Should be me going up them steps. Oh yeah: she skinted herself on a loan, to hear their lawyers tell us: 'You understand gymnastics is a dangerous sport'."

"And your lawyers?"

"Said it could go years without no one takes blame. Other people get compensation. But she has to lose. She always has to lose." She turns, leaning back to the rail. "Can't even pick a clean lodger."

A siren erupts close by, dies quick—as though they was waiting and got what they came for. Hear Karen snuffle, her snores reach up, drop back to regular bubbling breath. "Lot of law round lately."

"You'd know."

Seventeen or not her righteousness wears thin. "Smart move, your medals too."

"Worth nothing. Not like my old ones. But a thief just takes eh?"

"Won't you miss your tunes?"

"She'll be soaked with guilt and get new. Can get a loan now can't she?"

"Where is the medals?" Come around front to get a good look of her eyes. Useful, angry eyes.

"Mate's got 'em. Believe me: twirling medals ain't hard to get."

"Not for someone good as you."

She walks around me, that deliberate face–saving way I seen with lads who don't want to play interrogation no more. "Not Olympic gold is it?"

"You really think you was that good?"

She glances back—a hazy ghost in soft darkness. "I was the greatest gymnast there's ever been. Prove different."

Sledge offers up one of his smalltime crew who fancies doing the games en–suite at the Pentonville Hilton. He doesn't tell him how first I'm gonna put him in hospital and—to be fair—I don't beat the bloke half as bad as I could, and I do get him taken to casualty in a nice motor. A good habit I saw out east: when you can't beat on the real cause of something, give someone the hate in its place. Whoever he was, he's got the rest of the year on three meals a day and no hassle. I have to be a bit honest with Karen about how I found him, but Kellie's been lavishly honest for me so the worst of it stays in my kitbag.

I start sleeping with Karen and that—it's all quite friendly. She's got a nice way and some nights I just hold her and hear her sleep. Kellie's a bitch about it but it's what you expect and in a year or so her hormones'll settle; she really needs her mum. Opening ceremony's getting close and I'm every day walking with thieves. 'Course Rattner won't get his payday but I should worry: he's buying the drinks. Soon I'll have to move on. That's hard. This neighbourhood's robbed out. Without the games I'd be gone already. I move around with work, always have. Maybe go up north or Scotland way. I got a few connections. When heavy feet tramp down the hall I want nothing to come back on these two. But picking my time to go… That's hard.

Kellie's corps are doing some Olympic–theme display with their pom–poms. She cried off sick. Can't blame her. For them girls the dexterity, the precise pictures they make with their batons and bodies is as strong and together and beautiful as they'll ever be. But she had eyes on a place that's closed off to her now. Summer's gonna be hard for her. I'd like to stick around.

Telly's on while I do dinner. Always wars and bits of grief in them places short on rainfall. That's why we don't have wars in England: rains too much. Karen was shocked with the scars at first but she likes to be understanding. She said I was brave, she likes to think I am. But I've never done nothing that's made me think twice. Not really. Now it ain't even dark and I fancy an early night.

BD Feil

Men In Love

Apple

"RED-ASS DELICIOUS!"

And to accentuate his displeasure, he spits out the chunk of apple in a high and beautiful arc, like a rainbow's, and the old woman catches it in her napkin, her best linen napkin produced from her lap by no more than an involuntary spasm of the years.

The apples were on sale. The apples were fresh. The apples were pure and grown without much fooling with. She knew the orchard they came from. But they were Red Delicious, and the old man hated Red Delicious with a passion reserved for produce and baseball, a vehemence distinctly and loudly his. She knew of this hatred of Red Delicious, could hear his complaints as to their "goddamned cloying sweetness . . .", ". . . like old whores dressed up as baby dolls. . ." And their texture: "not exactly gritty . . . floury, floury . . . like they're full of powder . . . old whores wearing too much powder!" On what experience he based this analogy, she never asked, knowing it only fancy, his passion faithful. But so, too, were the apples and their integrity unimpeachable.

"Old whores" was the go-to. That and "ignorant." An "ignorant" move by the manager in sending the runners. Nothing more than "ignorant flailing-away" by swinging at a high pitch. But "ignorant," too, were raspberries obviously frozen and thawed and sold as fresh, no more than "ignorant mush." Or melon picked green and allowed to change color on the truck ride up north. Or worse, fruit gassed into losing its greenness. "Nothing goddamn ripe about it. Just ignorant."

"Loutish" was another. As was "pissant."

And lately he had been trying to work "child of god" into his stock criticism. But this was done sparingly and with some difficulty. And wasn't his all less criticism than eruption of passion? He spoke what he felt. He was a passionate man. This was why she put up with him. Truth and passion. This, her observation made near the beginning, 49 years ago, and turned and shaped since. And here for 49 years she had been accompanying him to baseball games, never bringing a book, never a crossword, never talking to children on a cell phone. And for 49 years she had been shagging the things that came flying over the kitchen table.

"Good catch! Like a child of god!"

Trombone

The prelude to the concert. A couple flashy solos while parents, friends, family grope for seats. The first, the Chopin *Tristesse Etude*, the soloist in a flowing prom dress. And what is not to like?

The second, a trombone solo, a show-off piece, schizophrenic, alternating between frenetic dance and great wringing of the heart. *Czardas.* On stage David dances with his slide, wearing the black tuxedo of the symphony, hair bountiful and bouncing to the piece's athletic demands. *Czardas.* The show-off piece, the piece where tumblers and dancers cavort to the side, plate spinners machinate on the wings, where Gypsies stand along the shadowed aisles honing the ends of their moustaches to fine points.

Later, when it is told, David will claim he didn't see that the woman coming down the aisle was partially blind. Yes, afterward when she found her seat, a darkness around the edge of the eyes, a darting back and forth at lines well-above the horizon, yes, blind. No matter, David will insist coolly. It would have made no matter. He will say it matter-of-factly, without any snide bravado, no cruelness, because he is a kind young man. But his hands were tied. His sense of timing too great, his showmanship too instinctive, the whole episode too visceral for any other gesture.

The woman approaches down the center aisle, closer the stage, closer. He throws his slide to and fro. Those with her fall back looking for seats. He wrings all he can out of the phrases. Down front in the orchestra, she spies seats. He stretches out of his tuxedo sleeves for a low note. She beelines for the seats, never seeing the one single shallow step that delineates the orchestra from the main floor seating. He nears the end of *Czardas*, the last bar. Was it his way of warning? He will only shrug his shoulders later in the telling.

David comes to his last note, and the woman at the end of his sighted trombone slide begins her dance over the shallow step, not an all-out sprawl or even a fall or a pratfall, not even a stumble, but an attempt at continuous motion as if nothing has happened, her chin and shoulders thrusting out ahead of her, a continuous glide, a vaudevillian kick and bounce.

And would it have been possible if any other instrument were in his hand? You see, it is the trombone that made him do it. His sense of timing, yes, the circumstances, yes, the woman, yes. But the trombone, that was it, that was the controlling thing. Under the spell of the thing in his hands, helpless, David adds a final flourish, off-score.

"WAH-Wahhhhhhh . . ."

Vibrato. End. Applause. The woman rights herself, her group up with her now, steadying her. Let the concert begin.

Moonlight

He had meant his last words to be a line from Kavanaugh's "Pegasus." Not the last line but the best line. *No more haggling with the world.* But the waters were warmer than he thought, a much earlier spring than anyone expected. And the jump from the bridge was from no height at all, a low level thing equal to the banks on either side, no more than a causeway really. Perhaps he should have left his clothes on to become sodden and heavy, weighed the pockets down with stones, rather than stripping completely and folding and laying out his things by the railing. And then only because he had read in multiple accounts that this was what jumpers did.

Instead, he blurted aloud, "Christ, they don't make this easy," and was sorry immediately he had. Now these could very well be his last words, and all hope for a final noble statement dashed.

He could now touch the bottom of the river with little effort. His toes were numb, but then his toes were always slightly numb. And unfortunately, the water on his bare skin was becoming invigorating. The moon was out, bright. Croakers in the reeds. Lone bird calls from the banks. The entire gesture, once thought successful, had now not only weakened, but had passed on, beyond hopeless, beyond gone.

"Christ. Christchristchrist . . ." He could not stop. And now he thought he saw a boatlight upriver and heard voices above on the low bridge. "Christ . . . "

This was not working. He would wade back, make for the croakers, struggle up the bank and scatter the birds, take his chances on the bridge above, back along the length of the bridge, stark and pink, naked. He rued his body now, his lapsed gym membership, age, genetics, gravity. At this point he could only hope for no audience.

But when the light upriver disappeared to nothing, and the voices overhead were realized into only breeze, breeze rustling litter, and breeze folding sound in on itself in the dark, he decided to linger a few minutes longer, stretch out on his back and dismiss circumstance, all gesture, and risk nothing more than falling deeper into the ideal of moonlit waters, into solitude, into romance.

Breakfast

In the morning, after he had dropped his bag at the door and gingerly entered the kitchen, and it was clear where he was to be seated, one place set with checkered napkin folded into a bishop's miter in the center of the plate, he sat but without saying a word, both hands resting lightly on the table, a little forward in the chair, up on the balls of his feet so that if he had to move quickly he could move quickly. She, too, said nothing, yet cooked away, at many things it seemed.

And then she was at his side, stealthily, as if meant to startle, with another platter, and he tensed because he'd been looking up at the wall clock opposite his chair, counting the petals of the daisy that made up the timepiece. She reached down, he flinched, and she snapped the napkin open and dropped it in his lap, taking his plate away, replacing it with the new plate, this warmed and arranged with food.

The potatoes were deep golden, slightly crisp, cut uniformly into half-moons. Eggs were fluffy, sprinkled with herbs from her window garden. He tasted thyme for certain, and was that tarragon as well? There were two slices of tomato to the side of the eggs, and dearly did he love a piece of tomato on the same forkful with some eggs.

Back at his side again like a spirit, she placed the original plate back before him and then was gone again, back to the stove and counter. On this other plate was sausage, almost blackened, with a few grilled onions, caramelized, and a separate cup of yogurt in the center, and around the other side strawberries and peaches, cut but connected still at one end so as to make a design of tiny colorful fans. A basil leaf laid whole on top of each.

Still, she said nothing. And he said nothing, only ate and watched the ticking daisy and worked out how long it would take to walk to the bus stop from her house, how long he had to make the transfer, how long he had to get to work. More than his usual route. Finally, when it became self-evident he could eat little and could only look at the beautiful breakfast before him, the one she had made just for him, he blurted aloud, "My god, you're a bitch."

He walked to the kitchen door and picked up his bag. She had not turned to him. She had not altered the busyness of her hands, the movements of her shoulders, the attention of her downturned eyes. He left, leaving her front door wide open. And it was not until he saw his bus pulling away and finally looked at his own wrist watch, did he realize that the daisy on her kitchen wall was ten minutes off.

Table

He left his shop doors open on to the street in case she returned, and he began cutting wood for the table. In the corner of the shop he kept an old saw, small, with a tapering jig set up to cut legs. Little if any re-adjustment was needed since the saw vibrated little, he never removed the jig, and all his legs were about the same length. In the opposite corner another small table saw sat, smaller, of the bench-top variety, and on this he cut tenons and only tenons. The fence was set to match the mortise width he always used, and this saw, like the other saw, was steady, little vibration, the settings rarely shimmying. And for these purposes only they existed for him: the one to cut tapered legs, the other to cut tenons. For all other cutting he used his big Powermatic in the middle of the floor.

The legs, from cherry, were set aside, and next he beveled the edges of the table top, also from cherry. And then in the exact center because it was still early in the day and the light was good and plentiful and because there was no evident reason, no saleable purpose in even starting a table today of all days, he drilled a shallow mortise, a small square in the exact center, chiseled out the bottom so it was flush and smooth, and then set about fitting and shaping a decorative insert from the small scrap of padauk that had been laying around the shop. He had considered purpleheart, but no, that was too gaudy, too clownish, too begging of attention. Something about using purpleheart in the wrong place and wrong time where you could make a fool of yourself. Not him.

The sides he cut and tenoned quickly, although, for that matter, there was no deadline with this table. Time was nothing. But assembly could not help but go quickly when all pieces and joinery were cut with precision.

And now as the sun set, and because when he had started, he meant to make this table in natural light, using only the sun that dropped through the two skylights and through the double doors that opened out on the street, he took advantage of the fading light and sanded by touch, by the feel of his hand over the cherry, running a damp cloth over the table to take away any dust that might cover the truth of the wood. And then he did the same with his fingertips and his palm and the sides of his hands so that the truth of his hands would not be hidden under dust, either.

And through it all, even as the sun thoroughly set, he left his shop door open in case she should come back. But she never did. And now it was night, and the table was done, and he liked the looks of it.

Tomek Dzido

Ya Get Me

MR FLANAGAN WAS DOIN' MY FUCKIN' head in goin' on about God and sin an' punishment an' hell an' all da uva fear da fuckin' saviour shit. Do what I say shit. Fuckin' foolish shit. So I start chattin' to Shavonne about da party dis evenin'. But he starts getting' all crazy. Starts goin' on about manners an' respec' and yoof and all da uva shit. So I just leave 'im to it an' try find out what time da party's gonna start. But he goes skyzo. Get's all het up and shit. Calls me a nuisance. A distruption to da class. A waster. So I tell 'im to go fuck himself, ya get me. Fuck him. Who is he to be sayin' dat shit about me. He don't know me. He don't know nuffin' about me. He don't know nuffin'. Standin' dere all fuckin' high and mighty wiv his butterz attitude getting' all fuckin' fresh and shit. Da manz a fuckin' fool and he gets all trippy cause he finks he can dis a school kid. Fuck 'im. He da one dat needs to learn some manners innit. He da one wyv no respec'. Fuckin' bare rude. But he sends me out da class. Tells me to go and see my form tootor. Tells me to fink about shit. Fink about what I said. I told him I already fought about it. I told him I fought about it a lot. I told him enjoyed *sayin'* it more dan I enjoyed *finkin'* about it. I told *him* to fink about it. Brapp.

Anway, School finally fuckin' finished and I shot out dem gates as soon as da fuckin' bell went. Ain't nuffin' betta dan getting' out dem gates, specially when it's da weekend, ya get me. Fuck dem tutors. Fuck dere lessons. Fuck dere oldskool shit and ancient fuckin' batty fings. It's all bullshit. S' fuckin' useless. True dat. Ain't no good to no one. Not where I'm from. What da fuck I gonna do wiv some fuckin' pyfagora's feorem or some *bull*shit? It gonna help me at da fuckin' checkout? 'M I gonna stand dere addin' ma potatoes an' peas an' chicken an' fink, ah, dat's five pound sixty. Boom. Na, I ain't. I ain't gonna use none dat shit. It's fuckin' whack. Na way. But history. Now history get me some ideas. History make me fink. History make me see fings dat mafs don't. It's different, ya understand. I don't like no fuckin' sums an' shit, but wid history I get me some knowledge of fings an' how dey used to be, an' how fings z changed an' why. For all a us. Everywhere. It's all different. We all different, an' Acton iz full a' us. Like me. I different. I different from da bruva next to me or da sista ova dere. Like dem poles, innit. I different from dem Poles dat come over an' eat dere kabanos an' saukraut cabbage an' shit. I don't look nuffin' like dem. But it don't matta. We da same. We all da fuckin' same. An' I know dey been froo some rough shit, ya get me. Dey seen bare ruff shit. True dat. Hitler an' his fuckin' Nazi bredrins and Stalin and his shit. All dem fuckers. Like Mao. Dey all evil. But dey ain't no different to all da uva fuckers dat still 'ere an' all da uva shit dat still goes on. I read da papers. I see it. History and all dat's happnin' now da same fuckin' fing, ya get me. Nuffin' changes. Nuffin'. Jus' people an' places. Same shit. Same shit all da fuckin' time. Ain't nuffin' gonna make a difference. Nuffin'. 'Cept dat stoopyd fuckin' Flanagan an' his dickshit lessons fink dere some better place. Fink dere's some greater meanin' an' higher power an' holy shit dat gonna help an' cure us. Dat dere be some way to change and make it betta froo God an' shit. So we gotta pray an' apologise an' den fank him for everyfin'. Fank 'im an' his family for all dey done an' do. Fank 'im. Fank 'im for what? Fank 'im for ma dickhead dad who jus' fuckin' drinks all day? Fank 'im for all dem times I got jacked and buss up? Fank 'im for ma mum da's dead? Fank him for ma sister dat say she ain't neva cumin' home? Fank him for dat shit? An' den when I'm dun I gotta fank 'im for Saddam an' Gadaffi an' Kim Jong an' Aferwerki an' Bashir an' dat fuckin' Cameron cunt? Fank 'im for dem cunts? For real? Ya gotta be jokin', ya get me. I ain't see no God in dat shit. I ain't see no fuckin' angels and saviours. I see hell on fuckin' erf, blud. But I got a brain. I read ma books. I watch dem documentries an' shit. I see da news. I educate. And I see uva fings, innit. I see it. But I don't let no motherfucka know. Ain't dere business, ya get me. Ain't no mans business. It's da way it is, innit. Da only way. I do what I do ta survive an' you do what you do. We all do whateva shit we fink'll make our lives betta *now*. Not in some future fuckin' bullshit in da sky. *But here. Now.* An' I don't give a fuck how yoo do it. *I don't give a fuck.* I don't come up in yo crib and judge yoo. I don't say my way's betta. I don't say nuffink, bruv, I just do ma fing and leave dem uva bitches be. Ya know what am sayin'. It's da troof. Gospel.

But da's long ting head fuck shit so now I gonna chillax. I gonna go an' have a joint wiv ma sister Michelle. She one ma friends. I mean propa friends. Like we propa tight an' shit. We grew up togeva. Been in same nursery and primary skool an' now in anuda fucked up skool. But she make it all okay. Cause we got each uva and no-one gonna take dat. Da's it. We sisters. For eva. An' now we gonna get mash up. Get *high*. We all got our ways to relax, an' dis is ours, ya get me. Dis da way we chill out an' fink bout nuffin' an' try an' forget all dat shit dat gets you down. Happens, but you get on wyv it. Happens to everyone, innit. It's always happenin'. You jus' gotta find ya means ta cotch an' enjoy da shit you got. Fuck. Dere's planty a fings dat'l' make ya cry and shit. But da's for pussies. Don't do nuffin'. Don't help. Never does. So we put on some choones an' smoke a bifta. Talk shit an' have bare jokes. Fuck da Flanagans. Fuck dem other cunts. They all fuckin' clowns. All a dem. Dey jus' angry an' shit cause dey forgot how ta *have* jokes. Dey all angry an' shit cause dey stuck in some fucked up marriage or dey *wanna* be stuck in some fucked up marriage. But dey neva happy. *Neva*. An' dey gotta let every uva fucka know it. Share it. Make 'em suffer too. Fuck 'em. Dey should puff on some weed. Get high. *Den* maybe dey'll see God. And den *he'll* tell 'em to *shut da fuck up*. Ha.

I breeze past some yutes an' dey try and churpse me but I ain't interested. I ain't interested in none dat shit. Even if dey were older an' had bare sterling I wouldn't give a fuck. Tings have changed. I ain't got time for dat shit no more. Not now. Dey jus' messin' an' dats da way I treat it, so I flash dem my teef an' bowl on. Dey'll find der laydee. Unless dey're batty. But den da's up to dem, innit. I don't give a fuck. Betta for me. I see Michelle cotchin' by our bench and head over. 'Hey girl, how's it goin'.'

'S' cool.' We greet each uva. 'Wha' happened wyv Ms. Shemal?' She arks me.

'Nuffin'. She jus' gave me a Saturday detention, innit.'

'She gonna call your dad?'

'I dunno.'

'Shit.'

'Fuck it.'

She pulls da spliff from her pocket and smiles. 'Le's get high.' She sparks up and takes a few tokes an' I watch da glow a da cherry as it changes colour an' get's bigga an' brighta. Da smell makes me feel betta. I fink about all dem fuckers dat smoked before us. All dem fuckers dat done shit an' achieved sumfin'. Made uva's feel betta. Helped people like me. An' despite da rest I know dat dere is dem uva betta bruvas and sistas dat make fings betta. Make de sadness lighter. Make us feel betta an' fink 'bout shit. Make us act like we should, like people, wyv hearts an' minds an' care an' love an' shit. Dey dere. Dey just harder ta find, ya get me. But dey dere. Dey waitin'. Trust me.

Michelle start's hummin' 'Survivor' an' I can't help but fink how fuckin' wicked it is. How wicked she is. She's ma girl. She always senses when I feelin' shit. She knows. 'Here.' She passes me da spliff an' I start tokin'.

'We goin' dis party tonight den?' She arks.

'Yeah, I fink so.'

'Aaron's gonna be there.'

'So?'

'You gonna chat wyv 'im?'

I take a long toke and close ma eyes. 'No.'

'Don't you fink yoo should?'

'No.'

We finish da spliif and sit dere. I feel high but dis time it's different. I can't stop finkin', ya get me. I can't switch off. I fink about what's gonna happen. How fings is gonna change. I fink about Michelle goin' uni and leavin'. She gonna go study English Lit cause she wants'a be a writer, and she fuckin' good at dat shit. She bare fuckin' good. Trust me. She gonna bust dat shit *up*. But it's up in Chester or sum shit and bare mileage from Acton. S' far innit. It's all good dough. She gonna get outta here. And dough it's scary dat she gonna duss, I'm happy for her, innit. She gonna have a betta life. She gonna be fucked up wyv debt an' shit, but she gonna be doin' somefin'. She gonna make a difference. And…more important dan all dat uva shit, she gonna be happy.

'I gotta go.' I say and get up.

'So we gonna meet at eight?'

'Yeah.'

'What you gonna wear?'

'Dunno.'

'It don't matter. You fine anyway.'

'Shut up.'

'Im serious, girl. Aaron stoppyd if he don't see it.'

'Yeah, well. Fanks. You too girl.'

'You know dat. See ya laterz den.'

'See ya.'

We separate and I bowl back to ma estate. But I don't wanna go back. I don't wanna go home cause I know he's gonna be dere. I know da fucker gonna be in an' I don't wanna see 'im. I don't wanna look at 'im. He's a fuckin' pussy'ole, ya get me. He's a propa fuckin' fool. But I have to get outta dis fuckin' skool shit, innit. I have ta get ma garms on an' get maself fresh. Do ma hair and nails and duss back out. As quick as fuckin' poss. Fuck 'im.

Da lift's still broke so I take da fuckin' stairs an' have ta step round dat fuckin' smackhead dat live's dere. He's mash up an' I step round him an' make sure ta look out for any a' his needles an' shit. Fuckin' sad. Ain't no way ta live, ya get me. But no one dere to save 'im. Not no Flanagan in dis fuckin' crib. Neva. S' fucked up. I get to ma floor an' every step I take's against ma every fuckin' wish. Against everyfin'. But it's gonna be over soon. I just gotta keep remindin' maself. Stay strong girl. Keep it tight. Finka about da bigga picture. Fink about da future.

I open da door an' dere he is. Waitin'. 'Where you been?' He says and knocks over de fuckin' coat rack. I try to get past 'im but he just stands dere swayin' like a fool.

'Nowhere.' I say and pick up da coats an' rack.

'Do you know what time it is?'

'Yeah.'

'So where have you been?'

'Nowhere, innit. Was jus' comin' home.'

'For this long?' He leans up on da wall cause he can't fuckin' stand straight.

'It's Friday, man. Wha's wrong wiv you.' I get froo da gap between his pissed up arse an' da wall an' head to da kitchen. I need a drink. I need ta get away from him an' his rank up stink. Da man's a bare disgrace, ya get me. Fuckin' embarassin'.

'Don't walk away from me, I'm talking to you.'

'Yeah, yeah, yeah.' I get me some Coke an' close ma eyes as da coldness makes me feel good an' helps ma dry mouf. But he bowls up behind me, innit, followin' me, wantin' somefin', always fuckin' wantin' somefin'.

'How was school?' He arks.

'Same, innit.' I go to wash ma glass an' see da man's been sick in da fuckin' sink again. 'S fuckin' mingin'. Always da same shit. Every fuckin' day.

'Nothing happened?'

'Na, nufin.' I turn da tap on an' close ma eyes as I push ma finga around da plug 'ole. Da smell makes me wanna fuckin' puke. You'd fink I'd be used ta it now. I pour some bleach down da drain an' turn to see 'im starin' at da bottle a whiskey he finks I can't see. He's so fuckin' stoopyd.

'Your school phoned.' He comes up to ma face an' starts swayin' an' shit, propa stoopyd like. An' he stinks like dem mans on da street so I turn ma face away. 'Told me you got detention.'

'So.'

'Saturday detention.'

'Yeah. And?' I push past an' try to get to ma room, innit, get away from 'im.

'And? And?' He follows me down da hall. 'Come back here. I'm talking to you.' Before I can open ma door he grips me by ma arm an' flings me round, all aggressive an' shit. So I stare at da motherfucka, ya get me. Fuck 'im. 'What did you do this time?'

'Nuffin'.'

'It ain't nothing. Tell me.'

'Why. Wha d'yoo care.'

'I *do* care.'

'Bullshit. You don't care bout shit cept yo fuckin' drink.'

'That's not true.' He let's go a ma arm. 'I…'

'What. You what?'

But he don't say nuffin' an' jus' stands dere like a fassy'ole. He's all pissed up an' shit. He's 'fucked up. Mans always da fuckin' same. Always. So I go in ma room an' close ma door. But I sit on ma bed an' straight away hear a can open in da kitchen. Fuck. Man, fuck dis shit. I can' take it no more, ya get me. Fuckin' all day every day. Cookin' an' makin' food an' shit an' washin' an' cleanin' an' takin' 'im ta hospital when he falls ova an' breaks his fuckin' arms an' shit. Pickin' 'im up an' tryin' ta carry 'im fuck to bed. Moppin' up his piss. Fuck dat shit. Fuck all dat shit. I ain't go da will no more. Ain't got da strenf. Not for dat shit. I don't care, ya understand. Not no more. I got uva fings on ma brain, ya get me. New fings. More important fings. Betta fings.

I start pickin' out some a my garms when I hear da fucker come up ta ma door again. He don't leve me alone, man. He don't let me be. Man, fuck. 'I'm… sorry.' He says froo da door. But I don't give a fuck, ya get me. He always fuckin' sorry bout some shit. I pick out ma spesh D&G dress an' try an' get it on, but it don't fit no more. I gettin' too big and I look at maself in da mirror. '…I'm… sorry…' I gettin' fat, innit, but it's all right. I still look good. Still got ma lips and hips. Boom. He finally fucks off an' I finish getttin' ready. Even do I got ma shit on I take a few uva dresses an' fings jus' in case, innit. I'll see what Michelle finks. When I look in da mirror again before dussin' an' I smile, damn girl, I look *good,* ya get me. I look *fuckin'* good. Fuck all da uva shit, I fine. Know dat shit. When I open da door an' walk back out into da hallway, I hear 'im cryin' in da kitchen an' mumblin' about how much he cares an' shit. It's bullshit. So I try ta be quiet, innit, try an' sneak da fuck out wivout him hearin'. But he does. 'Where you going?' He arks an' almost falls over as he gets up.

'Out.' I say an' put on ma jacket.

'What about dinner?'

'Get some chips or somefin'.' I'm about to open da front door when he pulls me back.

'You're not going out.'

Now he's all angry an' shit. One minute deres tears an' shit and da next he's all wexed and fucked up. He's a fuckin' mess, ya get me, proper fucked up. 'S da alcohol. Dat an' whateva fuckin' crazee shit's inside his head. But I been froo it too. All a it. An' now I had enough. I pull ma arm away. Fuck 'im. 'Why not?'

'Because I said so.'

'You gonna stop me?'

'Yes.' He stumbles in front a da door an' leans back on it. 'What's that?' He points at ma bag an' I see his eyes roll about his fuckin' head.

'S ma bag, innit.'

'What's in it?' He tries to take it off me but I move too quick. 'What's inside?'

'Ma clothes an' shit.'

'What? What do you mean your clothes? Where are you going?'

'I told you, blud, I'm going out, ya get me, out. Away.'

'Stop talking like that.'

'Like what?'

'You know what.'

'S da way I speak, shit.'

'Stop talking like that.'

'Man, fuck, get outta ma way.' I try to move him but he's a heavy fuck. He grabs me an' we push and pull each uva about in da hallway. Da fucker's crazy. 'You well pissed, jus' move.' He grips me by ma collar an' slams me against da fuckin' wall. I drop ma bag and he holds me back as he picks it up. He opens it an' looks inside.

'What's this?' He arks.

'Nufin'.'

'You leavin'?'

'What? Shut up.' I grab ma bag back an' try ta get past him again but he keeps grabbin' an' pullin' me, fuckin' up ma hair an' dress an' shit.

'You leavin' me?'

'You talkin' fraff.'

'No I'm not. Tell me.'

'You been in Red Lion an' got all pissed an' shit. You a fuckin' mess.'

'Stop it. How many times have I told you? How many times? Eh?'

'Whateva.'

'Don't fucking talk to me like that.'

'Chaaa.'

'Don't you dare talk like that.'

He starts shakin' me an' shit an' I stare straight at da fucker. He's all cryin' and dribblin' an' mumblin' an' shit. Trippin' out. He's fucked up. I mean propa fuckin' crazy, ya understand. For real. I can't remember da last time I saw him like dis. Cryin' an' shoutin' at da same fuckin' time. He's propa lost it. Shit. He's fuckin' mental. An' den I remember. I see it. I was like five or sumfin'. It was when mum died. An' den again a few years later when Jess left. But I was hurtin' too, ya get me. I ain't *stopped* fuckin' hurtin'. Ever. An' now I jus' wanna get out, ya understand. For good. 'Talk like what, blud, like what? What?'

'Like them.'

'Who? Who da fuck you talkin' about?'

'Like them niggers at your skool.'

'Shut up.'

'What d'you say?'

'I said shut up. You don't know shit.'

'You ain't a nigger.' He screams.

'You bare fuckin' racist.'

'Ain't no nigger in my house.'

'You sure bout dat?'

'No fuckin' way.'

'No?'

'NO!'

'What about a nigger baby?'

He jus' stands dere. I see his eyes. I see da hate. I see it all. Den I feel his fist on ma stomach. Once. Den twice more. Again and again. Da last one proper fuckin' hard. I can't see shit no more'. Everyfin' fucked up. I feel da blood in me eye. I crumple over on da ground. Fings started going hazy. I can't see shit. My nose is fucked. Everyfin's fucked. He spits and I feel it on ma face. Den da door shuts. I hold my stomach. I hold it tight. But I don't cry. I fink about…da flat I've applied for…

….but fings start get blurry……

…I start blackin' out…

…but I fink bout...

…da council...

…da government…

…helpin' me...

…helpin'…

…me an' ma baby…

…s' fucked up...

…s' all fucked up…

…but…

…we'll make it......

…I whisper….

…you an' me…

…………togeva...........

………we're………

………survivors...........

……………both a us................

……………we'll.................

…………………make it....................

….

………………………………….I promise………………………………….

………………………………….I………………………………….

………………………………….promise………………………………….

………………....I…………………...

…………………..

…………

Quenton Baker

Thirteen Ways of Looking at a Nigger

1.
A
new presence, the barely drawn edges of an
I, brown
gristle puffed with
griot soul, an
etched heart that will strain to imprint itself on
rough steel.

2.
Accelerated progress through elementary school,
no other child matches his dexterous
intelligence or his
ground cumin skin. Thank you
God for giving his mother the spirit of a hustler. She sought out the entrance
exam into the program that would tell the teachers:
relax, you can expect something out of *this* one.

3.
A
new girlfriend.
I love you, I say (right?),
girlfriend says: *I love you, too.*
Girlfriend says: *my dad is home, so you can just drop me off, it's*
easier. Word, I say. *He*
really isn't open-minded like me, she says.

4.
Ay
nigga:
I'm for real: every
gotdamn day this Chinese nigga be trippin on me

gettin on my fuckin nerves
eying me and shit thinkin I'm stealin his greezy-ass fried
rice— nigga, fuck your buffet.

5.
Abaddon. He's biblical.
Never got into mythology but
I'm cool with Abaddon.
Greek mythology, I mean;
Greek. It's pretty much the only one, right?
Except
Roman, right?

6.
Aaron S.;
nice kid.
I tutored him after school in math,
gave him my
graphing calculator at the
end of the semester.
Respect the polynomials, I said.

7.
Ambidextrous motherfucker,
nice with the rock.
Inside game mostly but would step out,
get you with the jumper or hesitate, head fake,
go to the rack smooth,
easy left-hand layup
ringing off the glass.

8.
Amazing Grace or
Nobody Knows the Trouble I've Seen or
I'm on My Way to Canaan or
Go Down Moses or
Get Away Jordan or
Every Time I Feel the Spirit or
Roll Jordan, Roll or

9.
"America land of opportunity mirages and camouflages" "speaking loudly sayin'
nothin' you confusin' me you losin' me your game
is twisted want me enlisted in your usury" "reflection rarely seen across the
surface of the lookin'
glass walkin' the street wondering who they be lookin' past lookin'
gassed with them imported designer shades on" "I find it distressin there's never
no inbetween we
either niggas or kings we either bitches or queens the daily
ritual seems immersed in the perverse full of short attention spans short tempers
and short skirts"

10.
At YMCA summer camp,
near Lake Chelan,
I won the watermelon eating contest; the
girls liked the way the hot-ass sun hit my skinny ten year-old sixpack, the
guys liked that I could
eat a huge fucking watermelon
really, really fast.

11.
Alcoholic.
Never met him but
I was told he held me once,
grinned, even, which was rare apparently. Only have the one picture of him,
got it restored and blown up last year around
Easter: he's young, sitting on the steps,
reading, his own son between his legs; I can't make out the title of his book.

12.
At least. At least. It's a mantra.
No hard feelings. I mean,
I loved him. I mean, I love him. Monday through Friday:
gone. Saturday and Sunday:
gone, but a different kind. Escaped?
No. Absent? No.
Reluctant, maybe, but flesh. At least.

13.
Ammunition is something I've hidden from but
never lacked. Out of habit, I thumb bullet after bullet
into my chest. My ribcage is a drum magazine
girding a heart of etched
glass. I am afraid,
every day, because I am also the barrel, the firing pin, the
reticle, the frame, the trigger.

Eamon Mahoney

Blood on the Moon

There is not a nation on the earth guilty of practices, more shocking
and bloody, than are the people of these United States, at this very hour.
—Frederick Douglass, July 5th, 1852

And the hour has not changed. The money is still in the cotton.
The cotton still woven into the money. The money still gained
through blood. The loss of blood raises a call for more cotton
for the printing of money. Never for cotton to bandage the wound.

What incentive is there against blood? Against the hour? It has not
changed. Every year since then until now. The hour is young.
Blood in the soil makes cotton grow strong, weigh heavy
on the scale, buy another field, diversify the crop. Only difference
between a field of cotton and oil is depth. Machines are built
by hand to reach what the hands cannot. They rise taller than
a church tower, a flag raised on a roof top, a hillside, the moon.

One time, blood became a flag. Then the flag became blood.
Money was printed from cotton with an image of the flag. The money
bought another field, built a church for the promise of the longest hour,
built machines, lifted oil from the deep, bought another field,
the moon, stuck a flag in it, even found water with a divining rod.
It still takes water to grow cotton. How easily, like the hour, we forget.

Kevin Conner

SKINNY

I.

We'd never say it,

but all us boys cheered the day
Roselyn
wore the sky-blue
two-piece
that hung down
just enough

between the legs,
wet.

We cheered when she ran,
her thighs
slapping,

hands clasped onto her chest.
Her lungs,
beating.

We cheered when she
jumped from the cliff
by the old airport—

fell screaming
into a creek named after
livestock,
Indians,
the buffalo.

We'll never say it,

but that day she climbed
to the top the tree,
to the rope.
We stood under her,
just staring—
Our stomachs
ached:
Come on.
Strip.

II.

We'd never say it,

but all us boys cheered the day you
climbed up the tree,
too.

Your brown skin,
shirtless
and sweating.

Your greasy black hair,
dripping water

over your shoulders.

You went up that tree.
You climbed.
One board,
after one board—
higher than any of us

white boys.

We cheered as a group
in waist-deep
water
as your short arms
hugged the trunk,

and the top of the tree
swayed back and forth
under your weight.

We shouted,
Mex! Mex! Mex!

as you grabbed for the rope,
just like Roselyn.

We screamed,
Mex-i-can! Mex-i-can!

as you lifted your feet,
tensed,
and began to swing.

Then,
we laughed in excitement,

for one brief second.

Until,
from free-fall,

with your hands slipping—

the rope tangling
around your ankles,
and your head
snapping down,

we just whispered to ourselves:
Oh, God.
Oh, fuck

as your
skinny body

struck the ground.

John Blair

Three Little Indians

RONNIE HAD BEEN WAITING ALL WEEK to shoot something. Jamie and June were already at the pit quarry, sitting on a rise of caliche limestone in the shadow at the bottom, Jamie with his father's rifle, June with her knees drawn up to her chin. June was small and slight and her hair was a coppery red that Ronnie would have thought was pretty if she'd ever brushed it, or if at twelve years old she wasn't such an annoying little kid.

"Hey," Jamie called out, "about time. I been having to listen to June whine for like a half hour now."

"No you hadn't," June said, "and it wasn't just me. You were saying stuff, too."

"Is that a gun you got?" Jamie asked, ignoring her. He hopped down off of the rock and Ronnie put the case down where he had been sitting, opened it and took out the Remington. Jamie whistled, took it from him. "Cool, man. Where'd you get it?"

"Birthday present," Ronnie said. He'd turned fourteen last Tuesday. They stood and admired the rifle until June couldn't stand it anymore and said, "Damn, come *on.*"

"Watch your mouth," Jamie told her, but he handed the rifle back to Ronnie, picked up his father's gun, and they started for the far end of the quarry, where the biggest trash dump was.

Trash was heaped everywhere in the quarry, piled high into the dead-end canyons that led off of the main pit, and stacked along the walls, much of it the large sort of stuff that costs money to have hauled off to the county dump—furniture, old appliances, a few rusted-out cars and trucks. Most of it was shot through with bullet holes large and small. They picked through the piles as they walked along, looking for unbroken bottles and whatever else might be interesting to shoot at. Ronnie hoped they might run across something really good. It was a like a treasure hunt, and the best finds were fragile and familiar—TV sets, car windshields, Mason jars filled with fruit or jam so old the color had faded to yellow-brown. Once, last summer, they had come across a toilet, intact and bone white, *American Standard* written across the front of the tank in tiny, light blue script. They had devoted nearly an hour and two boxes of shells to reducing the toilet, tank and bowl and base, to a heap of shattered porcelain.

This time, they didn't find much. Beer bottles, a couple of intact light bulbs buried in a rotted-out cardboard box like eggs in a nest. Jamie kicked open a fat plastic bag full of kitchen garbage and found an unopened bottle of RC cola, heavy edge-worn glass, the metal cap starting to rust around the crimp.

Jamie tossed the bottle a couple of times in his hand, considered its potential. "What do you think this bad boy'll do when the bullet hits it?"

Ronnie's first impulse was to say something about wasting the soda, but that was his mother's thinking. Nobody wanted to drink soda out of garbage dump, anyway, even if it hadn't been opened. "I don't know," he said, "nothing, maybe."

"Naw, man. I think it's gonna go up like a rocket. All that carbonation, it'll be like a bomb or something. One shot and *boom.*"

"It's probably been in that bag for like ten years. More likely it won't do anything except break."

Jamie shook the bottle a bit. "Naw, man, you're wrong. I can feel it. This one's gonna be something. You just watch."

June stood nearby with a light bulb in each hand, cradling three brown beer bottles against her chest with her forearms. "That's what you always say," she told him.

"And I'm always right," Jamie said, "so why don't you just shut the hell up."

"Why don't you?"

"Lord," Ronnie said, "ya'll just don't ever stop, do you?"

"Nope. If she wasn't being a pain in the ass, she'd dry up and blow away. It's all that keeps her breathing, I think."

June stuck her tongue out at him, and Jamie pitched one of the bottles he was carrying in her direction so that it hit the ground and shattered near her feet. She shrieked and skipped back, almost dropping her burden of bottles and bulbs.

"I'm gonna tell," she said.

"One of these days, I'm gonna stop caring, and then I won't miss. I'll crack open your little peanut head and let the ants have you."

June just stuck out her tongue again and made a face.

Ronnie kicked another plastic trash bag and the sun-faded plastic split open like a rotten melon. Something darted out from underneath the bag, and he jumped back. He saw brown-gray fur, a pinkish tail, and then the rat slipped under a broken fruit crate.

"Rat," he announced, and Jamie stooped and dropped his bottles in a pile and raised the rifle from where he had been carrying it in the crook of his arm. Ronnie saw him push the safety off.

"You go kick that crate," Jamie said, "and I'll pop the little son of a gun."

"What you want to shoot it for?"

"'Cause it's a rat, dumbass. You see a rat, you shoot it. They've got diseases and shit."

"All right, I guess so," Ronnie said.

"June, you get off behind me," Jamie said. He put the rifle to his shoulder, and Ronnie walked to the crate. He waited for Jamie to nod, then he kicked it and leapt back. The crate tumbled over and the rat bolted out from underneath it, headed for a pile of rusted and bullet-riddled washing machines and refrigerators. Jamie held his fire for so long that Ronnie thought the rat was going to make it, but three or four feet before the rat could make the safety of the appliances, the rifle cracked and the rat jerked, slewed sideways by the impact. It didn't stop, though; it scrabbled across the remaining few feet in a crippled and panicked flurry and disappeared under the stacked machines, leaving a streak of bright blood on the graveled floor of the quarry.

"Where'd I hit it?"

"Hindquarters, I think," Ronnie said. "I didn't think you were going to hit it at all. It was a pretty good shot."

"I've done better," Jamie said, but he grinned. They both knelt down by the blood smear and studied it for a long moment. Ronnie looked up at the place under a tilted-over washer where the rat had disappeared. He wondered how long it would take it to die, and he felt bad thinking about it.

"Yeah," Jamie said, "should have led him a little more. We see another one, I'll take his freakin' head off, you watch."

They lined up the bottles and light bulbs along the rail of a truck bed that someone long ago had turned into a trailer, and then abandoned here when the floor rusted out. The ground around it was blanketed with broken glass and spent brass shells, crunching like old snow under their feet. June sang a nursery rhyme under her breath as she set beer bottles in a row: *one little, two little, three little Indians.* Ronnie waited for Jamie to tell her to shut up, but he didn't.

"All right, then," Jaime said, placing the unopened RC bottle at the very end of the rail.

"Let me shoot first," June demanded.

"Like hell."

June started to open her mouth and Jamie stooped and picked up the top half of a broken mason jar. "Don't you say it," he told her, "or I'll pop you upside the head with this. I swear I will. You can just wait your turn."

June closed her mouth again. She gave him a hard look and crossed her arms, strode away a few yards and squatted down to wait. Ronnie moved back, checked the safety on his Remington, worked the bolt to load a shell into the chamber.

"Hold on, hold on," Jamie said. He looked at his sister. "Hey, June. You still want to go first?"

"Yeah," she said, sullen.

"Why don't you show Ronnie what you showed me."

She stared at him for a long moment. "No."

"C'mon," he said. "I'll even let you shoot the RC bottle, if you want. It's the best thing we got."

She considered, squatting on her heels, her legs skinny and white against the blue of her shorts. Ronnie waited, curious. "All right," she said. "But just for a minute."

Jaime grinned over in Ronnie's direction. "OK, then. Let's go over to the new Chevy." He leaned his rifle against the side of the trailer, and June stood up with a sigh that sounded put-out and irritable.

Jaime led the way through the stacks of junk, Ronnie following, June in between skipping every third step or so to keep up, since she was shorter. Ronnie watched the back of her neck as they walked, the bobbing scatter of freckles along the nape like someone had flicked a brush full of umber paint at her. The new Chevy was a wheel-less half-ton pickup that somebody had dragged out to the quarry in the last week or so. Someone had already shot out the side windows and a good deal of the windshield, but the doors still opened and closed and the bench seat was still mostly intact, just a few tears in the vinyl that let the foam cushion poke through. Jaime pulled the driver's side door open, and used a strip of cardboard he tore from the top of a rain-warped box in the truck's bed to brush the little cubes of broken safety glass off the seat.

"Get on in," he said to June.

She sighed again and rolled her eyes, but climbed on up into the truck's cab and scooted across to the passenger side of the seat. Fisher watched, starting, he thought, to understand a little of what June intended, and feeling a strange sort anticipation mixed with something very like panic. June turned around in the truck to face them where they stood outside the door, pulled her heels up onto the seat and shucked her tennis shoes off with the toes of first one foot and then the other. Her socks were white trimmed at the top in light blue thread, and there were faint outlines of her soles and toes marked on the bottoms with grime from the dusty caliche gravel they'd been walking through.

"Hey," Ronnie started to say, thinking he ought to tell her to just quit it. Before he could say anything else, she lifted her narrow hips off the seat and stripped her shorts and panties down and off in one quick motion, and then lay back on the seat with her knees up.

"Let's see," Jaime told her, and she parted her knees. She looked away, past her own shoulder, out through the broken windshield, uninvolved.

Ronnie slid his eyes away to the steep walls of the quarry, the mounds of junk and trash, the high cloudless sky. But he found he couldn't keep looking away. He felt hot and embarrassed. He was suddenly conscious of his hands hanging by his sides and stuck them in the pockets of his jeans, then that felt wrong and he pulled them back out. Jaime stood next to him, and Fisher could hear the sound of his breathing. Ronnie looked, and he thought about the soft, lacquered pink deep inside a cat's ear.

"That's enough," June said, and clamped her knees together, then pulled her panties and shorts back on, again both together at once, so quick that he didn't see much else, mostly just that her panties were the same pale blue as the thread edging her socks.

She pushed her feet into her shoes and scrambled out of the truck, pushing past her brother and Ronnie.

"C'mon, hurry up," she said. "It's my turn to shoot."

They followed her back to where they'd left the rifles, June skipping up ahead, weaving through the trash. She made a sort of pirouette around a set of rusty blue barrels and then started running in that loose, arms-out way that girls ran, and he watched her go, powerless not to. Something inside him went soft and strange, and he thought that he would do just about anything she asked him if it would make her run again just like that.

She snatched up Jaime's rifle from where it leaned against the truck-bed trailer.

"You be careful with that," Jamie ordered.

"You said I could shoot the soda bottle."

"Yeah, all right. Just hold on."

He picked up the bottle of RC Cola and shook it hard, then put it back in place. "All right, now," he said. "Don't miss, or I get to shoot it."

He came back to where Ronnie waited. June knelt carefully about twenty feet away from the targets, putting her knee down on a piece of cardboard on top of the layer of broken glass, brought the rifle to her shoulder and took aim. Ronnie held his breath, waiting for the shot.

June fired and the RC bottle shattered with a hollow *pop* as the bullet hit it, a foaming gout of soda splashing down over the rusty side of the truck bed. The bottle didn't collapse into itself as most bottles did when the little .22 bullets hit them; instead, the top two-thirds of the bottle simply disappeared. Ronnie heard the bullet ricochet off of the rock wall behind the truck bed with a high moaning twang like a stretched fence wire breaking.

And then June screamed.

It took Ronnie a couple of heartbeats to understand what the scream meant, but then he knew, and he dropped his own rifle in the dirt and ran to her where she lay, curled in on herself, both of her hands pressed to her right eye. He got down on his knees beside her in the broken glass and spent shells. She started to cry, a high-pitched keening that made Ronnie want to start crying, too, that made him feel awful inside, like someone had punched the air out of him.

"Let me see it, June," he told her. He felt Jamie come up behind him, stand over him. June just moaned, and Jamie said, "pull her hands away so we can see."

"Hold on," Ronnie told him. "June," he whispered, "June, let me take a look."

"What happened to her?" Jamie asked. His voice wavered with panic.

"I don't know. I heard a ricochet when she shot."

"You think she got hit by the bullet? In the eye?"

"I don't know," Ronnie told him. He hovered over June, reached and touched the back of one of her hands. She didn't flinch, she didn't move. She was curled tight in upon herself like a pill-bug. He could see blood, just a little, seeping from between her fingers, and he felt suddenly and deeply afraid.

A memory came to him, something he had forgotten until this moment, until he saw the blood: June when she was seven or eight years old, lying still in the dirt of her father's corral. He'd just met Jaime at school, was hanging out at their place. June was practicing dressage on a tired old mare, and it spooked when a coyote came out of the brush, crossing silently though the far end of the corral. The horse had bucked once sideways and June had flown off and hit the ground hard. He was amazed that he had forgotten it, how alarmed he was then, thinking for a moment that the little girl was dead. He had run to her along with everyone else, but she was already sitting up as they reached her, her nose bloody and her eyes wide. Her father had helped her wash her face in the mossy old bathtub they used for a trough, and that was the end of it, and the whole thing had slipped out of Ronnie's mind so completely that even now it was only a ghost of a memory: the coyote gliding under the corral fence like an apparition, a little girl lying still on the ground, red hair and blood, the smell of stagnant water in the blazing afternoon sun.

"June," he crooned to her, "you got to let us look, OK? Come on."

"I can't," she moaned.

"We got to make her," Jamie said, but it occurred to Ronnie that it might be better not to see. What could they really do if a bullet, or maybe a piece of a bullet, had gone into her eye? Nothing, really. But Jamie stooped down and took her hand and started to pull, and Ronnie took the wrist of her other hand and helped. June only struggled against them a little, and they got her hands away from her face far enough to see a bleeding groove in the skin just above her eyebrow, about an inch long. Ronnie let his breath out in a rush, almost overwhelmed with relief. Her eye was OK.

Something glistened at the end of the groove in June's skin, a piece of glass the size of an apple seed, buried just under the skin. Ronnie pushed at it with his thumbnail and June writhed and shrieked and tried to cover her face again with her hands, but the glass shard came out, stuck to his thumbnail by her blood. He showed to Jamie.

"Just glass," Jamie said, "shit, man. Wow."

"Let her go," Ronnie told him. They let go of her hands and she pressed them over the cut on her brow again. She looked up at Ronnie, her face flushed and wet with tears. "It'll be all right," he told her, "it's just a little cut. We'll take you home so your mom can fix it up."

"Our mom ain't home," Jamie said, but Ronnie ignored him. He reached an arm under June's shoulders, another under her knees, and picked her up and stood with her.

"Man, you don't have to do that. She can walk. You can walk, can't you, June?"

June didn't answer him; she was still crying, though not as hard. "Just get the guns. I can carry her."

"Whatever, man," Jamie said, and he gathered up the rifles, gave Ronnie a look, and then jogged over to get Ronnie's rifle case. Ronnie walked with June in his arms, careful not to bounce her too much as he went. She wasn't particularly heavy, a little more, maybe, than a sack of feed corn would weigh. He kind of wished that she were heavier, that it hurt to carry her, made his back ache and his arms cramp.

Jamie walked ahead of him, and they followed the road out of the caliche pit. At the top, where the rutted road curved up and out, June suddenly started to struggle in his arms and Ronnie had to put her down. She stood with both hands still pressed to her forehead and glared at him.

"I don't need you to carry me," she said. "You just leave me alone."

"All right," Ronnie told her, "I was just trying to help."

"I don't need no help from you." She took one of her hands away from her wound, looked at the blood on her fingers. "I'm gonna tell," she said to Jamie.

"Like anything in this world could stop you," Jamie told her.

"Daddy's gonna whoop your ass," June threw at him, and she turned and ran, loping off ahead of them down the road, one hand still pressed to her head. Ronnie stood beside Jamie and watched her go. There didn't seem to be much to say.

Finally, Jamie sighed and handed Ronnie his rifle. "I don't think we'll be shooting again for a while."

"Yeah, I figured," Ronnie said, and realized he was glad of it. "If you want, I'll tell your daddy I did it, let her shoot that bottle. He can't whoop me. Most that'll happen, I'll get grounded when my dad finds out."

Jamie seemed to consider it, shook his head. "Naw, that's all right," he said, "it won't matter, anyway. I always get blamed when shit happens to June. That's just how it is."

Far up ahead, June stopped, turned and looked back at them as if to dare them to try to catch her. "You don't know how damned lucky you are not having a sister," Jamie said mournfully, "you just can't even imagine."

"I know it," Ronnie told him, and he realized it was the kind of truth that could make him regret just about everything he might someday become.

Leslie Rodd

Las Manos Grandes

I WOKE UP ON MY EIGHTH BIRTHDAY to the sound of drums carrying across the mesquite and cottonwood trees, beating from the heart of the Mexican settlement to announce another soul crossing over. Later would come the wailing of the mothers, and then the funeral, where I, as altar boy, would play an important role for the last time.

Ears alert, I sat up in my dorm cot in the bare, empty room as I had all summer, alone, the only student not claimed by a family when the convent school year ended. The morning light—thin and yellow like my sheets—was stingy, of Texas, not the generous light of my home in Kansas, where all things were backlit by my grandparents' love.

Bong, bong, bong, I heard, imagining the men

pounding their drums in a circle, remembering the feel of the mallet on the drum skin, the parade of deep sounds I created the few times they let me take a try. Why did someone have to die on my birthday? And if someone had to die, why wasn't it one of the nuns, the blessed Sisters, my keepers, my jailers? At the thought of the nuns, their rough-and-tumble ranch, the insufficient light, my fists clenched and my rough knuckles were ready for a fight.

It was a rugged life I'd be leaving, and I felt the proof on my body: a gash on the ridge of my nose where I'd hit the hackberry tree running, scabby scratches from the sharp-edged milking pail where it brushed my arms each morning, aching bruises on my shins where the cows had kicked, and dead fingernails on both hands from hammering myself and not the fence posts. With each new injury, I was toughening up.

Walking between the rows of empty beds, I found my way, bed by bed, to the open window, felt a breeze, heard it riffle the branches of the old Chinese elms in the side yard of the Sisters' not-so-prosperous ranch. I looked out at the moving leaves, but they were no more distinct than a blurred fluttering to me; no matter how hard I stared, I could never make my eyes work. But never mind the blurriness, or the strange and limited way I saw my world: a prison-like room painted white against the heat and held in by strips of dark mahogany, the sun shining in on the rows of metal frame beds making shadows of regimented lines. The religious compound of dormitories, nuns' sleeping quarters, convent school, and church was a bear trap that my grandfather was coming to spring me from today.

It was with extra care that I washed up in the long basin meant for sixteen boys, not just one, with the same yellow piss soap Sister Aloysius used to wash out my mouth and felt the cool windmill-pumped water wake up my skin. Remembering how my grandfather always made such a fuss on my birthday, I whistled, note-perfect, *Casey Jones,* his favorite railroad song.

I dressed in a clean worn t-shirt and overalls, leaving my wide sun-browned feet bare in case he came early to the pasture rather than the train station. The minute I heard his voice again, I'd be ready to run over the crumbly red earth like a snake-bit coyote into his arms. My suitcase lay open on the floor by my bed. There wouldn't be much to pack, just a broken railroad watch, a spinning top, four pieces of good black flint, Apache arrowheads, pieces of congealed carbide, the broken magnifying glass Sister Mary Michael gave me, and the one marble I had for the winter tournament. I would be gone when the other boys returned to show off their new possessions and tell stories of the summer they'd spent at home with their families. I pictured the nuns describing my rescue to my classmates, grinned to think how they would be jealous of me for a change.

"Happy Birthday, Jaime," Sister Rita sang out, entering the room with a motion that rolled in and out of my splintered vision. She was the convent baker, one of the two nuns I liked, from the small Mexican community nearby. "I baked you a birthday cake. It's cooling on the kitchen windowsill. A special cake just for you. Eight candles, is that right, Jaime?"

I nodded and wished I could see her more clearly. From what I could gather I knew she was warm and mothering, with a smooth brown-skinned face, gentle, soft, fleshy, not like the other nuns, who stuck their pinched noses up close to me in class. Sister Aloysius was the worst, her red sores and flaky skin and strong hard hands hurting me with a punishing grasp, bony fingers digging deep into my shoulders as if she carried God in them.

"Thank you." Ever since the other children left for the summer there had been no cakes. It was a red-letter day, for sure.

"Qué Pasa, Jaime? Why the suitcase? Are you leaving us?" There was a lilting lift to her voice. "You can't run away again, pobrecito. Your eyes are so bad." I bent my head to one side to see the Mexican nun in the thin slice of light where things were more distinct. When she came closer to me, I squinted into focus her bushy eyebrows and the dark hair that escaped from her starched white headdress.

"My grandfather's coming for me today," I whispered with conviction, head still sideways, breathing in her smell of vanilla and cocoa, feeling my heart pound. "He'll be on the 3:15 train from Kansas. Don't tell the others."

"But Jaime, how do you know that?"

"My father told me."

"Did he call? We never hear from your family. They owe Mother Superior a year's tuition, a lot of money." She touched my head.

"My grandfather will be here on the god dumb train. I know it." I bristled, tensing back into the boy who yelled "fuck you" to the Mother Superior and Sister Aloysius every chance I got, their mouthwash no punishment any more. "He won't forget my birthday. He promised." *We'll come for you when it's time. Who will? Your grandfather will.* That made sense to me, so I waited, and instead of praying to God for good eyesight as the nuns instructed me, I prayed to the moon I couldn't see for my grandfather to hurry up and rescue me.

After crying my eyes out that first day of convent life, I heard the train whistle echoing over the Sisters' land and put another puzzle piece in place: I would be rescued by my grandfather by train!

"He'll be here, god dumb it," I said, staring as hard as I could into Sister Rita's face, where her blurred arrangement of lines gave no clue whether she believed me.

"Jaime, you shouldn't speak like that. God sees and hears all," she said.

Outside the window, closer to our ears than the Mexican mourning sounds, the mockingbird sang a repeating series of crystal clear notes—four long peeps, a short brrrup, four long peeps. I thought about the mockingbird and the day I had raided that very nest—ordered to by DeWitt, with the other convent kids watching—and had thrown the baby birds against the adobe walls, heard them splat one after another. It was a mean thing to do, killing baby birds. But I'd had no choice. Circumstances made me do it. Now, with Sister Rita standing there staring at me, I felt too warm. It would be another in a long string of stifling Texas days, but with one big difference: rescue! My grandfather would come in on a storm—I stuck my chin out at her—with rain to wash the thick Texas dust from my eyes.

"You hear the drums? You hear my sisters crying? Chuy left this earth last night, Jaime." Her voice was very soft, but my well-trained ears heard each word without straining. "We'll have the funeral later this morning, before it gets too hot. After you finish Mass and your chores, stay in shouting distance. I'll have your black robe ready."

"I'm sorry." I knew Chuy, two years old, had seen him just the week before grabbing his mother's twisted braid and necklaces, hanging on tight. I didn't remember anything unusual, didn't sense the fever hovering. In the Mexican settlement near the convent, where the nuns hired their workers and the settlers were parishioners in the convent church, they all made a big fuss about Chuy and Sister Rita told me why. His parents thought Chuy's birth meant a change in the luck of the Sandovals, who'd had five girls before him and lost three of them before they were old enough to walk.

"We have something special this time," Rita said, "for the cross, to show how much we loved this niño." I felt slightly cooler air from the open window, a cloud moving across the sun. My grandfather taught me how to follow the sun—not the well-defined orb that sighted people said they saw in their crowded sky, but the sun's diffuse rays, the sun's effect—so I would always know where I was. Alone this summer, outside on the Sisters' ranch, I got good at it, pretending I had been raised in the wild. "All of us Mexicans gave money to Chuy's father so he could buy decorations for the cross." The graves of the other Mexican children I had helped the priest bury that summer had all been marked with cheap plywood crosses, unadorned, as if the parents preferred God not notice so many children dying. I liked Chuy, his mother let me play with him when I visited, let me hold his hands up high and pretend walk him around inside the Sandoval's small shack.

"Don't be late for Mass today, Jaime. You know how angry Sister Aloysius gets. You don't want anything bad to happen on your birthday, do you?" She rested her hand softly on my shoulder. "If you really are leaving, don't forget to come say goodbye to us. After the funeral, yes?" I could tell from her voice that she didn't believe in my rescue, that if she thought I could see she would wink at me. I'd show her. I'd show them all.

Sister Rita left humming and I followed, down the steps and out into the warm air, walking slowly across the convent grounds and in no rush to get to the church, stopping to look for flints in the dry brown bushes by the porch. I ran my fingers through my uncombed hair, plentiful and thick like fur, making it stand straight up atop my wide-browed face, my square boy's body, the stocky body of a cinnamon bear cub. My wild red hair, the way I charged about, and my explosive attitude were all a livewire contrast to the sleepy browning fields of late summer and the whispered scurrying of the Sisters.

I made my way across the quadrangle and let Sister Aloysius pull centipede-like pieces of brush from my hair, straighten my shoulders, get me into my red cassock and white surplice, and put shoes on my feet. She had no idea what happy thoughts were running through my head, or that those thoughts stopped me from spitting on her hand.

"Morning, son," Father Gresham greeted me. I knew he didn't think I was his son and I didn't like it when he said it, but that morning nothing got to me. I took the glowing long-handled taper, found the three candles on the left of the altar and carefully lit them, knelt down and genuflected, then rose to light the three candles on the right, while the priest sprinkled holy water on the linen altar cloths and my mind was remembering my last birthday.

I'd been living with my grandparents for four years, since my mother died giving birth to my sister, the same year my eyes went bad and my family split up. My baby sister went to my father's family, the Catholics, and I went to my mother's parents, the heathens.

"Never forget you're not a Catholic, Jimmy," my grandfather had said to me on my seventh birthday as we walked down the broad tree-lined street toward the Topeka train depot, where he was a supervising conductor on the Atchison, Topeka, and Santa Fe railroad. "Your mother marrying a Catholic, that's what did her in." And then he made his promise. "Next year, on your eighth birthday, I'll let you come to work with me, ride the train all day, and punch the tickets for me."

"Dominus vobiscum," Father Gresham prayed with the congregation, kissing the altar. I stared at the pews and made out flashes of the brightly colored shawls of the Mexican mothers, knew that Sister Rita would be sitting there too. I couldn't really see them, but I felt their eyes, felt they might be praying not only for Chuy but for me, for my rescue.

I would miss Sister Rita and the Mexican mothers. Maybe, with my newfound praying power I could ask the moon to help them, too, once I was safely gone from that place.

I loved it there, in Mexican Town, where I could hear laughing, and their rich language, and singing as I traipsed from shack to shack, counting them, ten families in all. Just being there calmed me down, made me feel loved for that short time, gave me strength to go back to the convent and wait. Sister Rita had introduced me to all the Mexicans and they encouraged me to visit their shacks whenever I felt lonesome.

"Et cum spiritu tuo," I said for the last time in my life, taking the Bible from the stand and handing it to the priest, then taking my place to await my next duties: ringing the altar bells and hitting the four-bar chimes with a mallet. If my grandfather had come in right then and seen me performing those Catholic tasks he would have let loose with swear words. I had heard my grandfather curse many times before, heard him telling people to go to hell in his railroad conductor's voice. It stopped people in their tracks, made them pay attention. As the priest intoned, I called up the vivid memories of my grandfather—his fragrant pipe tobacco, the navy blue uniform with twelve buttons, the stiff-brimmed conductor's hat he let me wear on special occasions like my birthday—that had kept me company all year.

"No grandson of mine will be raised Catholic," my grandfather had said so many times. Take him! Mother Superior would soon say. Take the boy off our hands! Forget the money you owe us.

During communion, I worked by rote, did my thing at the altar, enjoyed making music with the bells and the chimes while the Father Gresham poured the wine without spilling a drop. Again my eyes found the colors of the Mexican mothers and I remembered my first visit to their homes, where I found Sister Rita hanging laundry outside on the line.

"Where have you been hiding, Jimmy?" she asked, calling me over, using a rag to brush the bits of broken stalks from my back. "In the sugar cane, I see." She laughed. Soon Sister Rita had me pulling wet clothes out of the laundry basket and handing them to her for hanging. As we worked, she hummed, happily, and soon we were surrounded by more Mexican women, with laundry baskets, chattering to each other in their own language.

"Our altar boy," Sister Rita pointed to me, "is very helpful. Jimmy, do you know..." and she went around the circle, introducing each of the Mexican mothers in turn, Sandoval, Aguirre, Sepulveda, Hinojoso, first names Dolores, Maria, Ponciana, Ofelia, and as each new woman introduced herself I followed the sound of her voice and stepped toward it, sticking out my hand the way my grandfather had taught me to do when I met someone for the first time.

"Jaime," they said, one after another, and instead of shaking my hand they gave me a big hug, some of them holding babies in one arm and me in the other. Jaime, the first time in my life I'd had a new name, and I liked it.

Our work went swiftly, me helping Rita and the others hang their wash out to dry. They knew enough English to ask about my family.

"Where is your mother, Jaime?" Dolores Sandoval asked, and then the others chimed in, voices so much sweeter than the voices of the nuns who had never asked me about my mother, not once.

"She died," I said simply, and went on pulling wet sheets from Sister Rita's basket, feeling funny, feeling shame. Mrs. Sandoval disappeared, taking her flower scent with her, and when she returned she handed me two warm, sweet Mexican pastries in a nest of newspaper. "Here. For you," she offered, and encouraged me to eat them right away. From that time on, I loved to hang out there, helping out, hearing them talk to each other, absorbing their good natures, eating the sweets they loved to give me, hearing them pray out loud for my family to find me soon. It wasn't until last month that I told them about my grandfather, keeping it from Sister Rita because, although I trusted her, I didn't want her to slip and give the other Sisters advance notice of my rescue.

Now, performing my last mass, reciting my part of the Latin prayers out loud, I heard the mothers murmuring in unison, clicking their rosary beads in prayer in a regular rhythm like metal wheels hitting the tracks, click, click, click, on the train ride that had brought me to the convent almost one year ago. Suddenly I felt dizzy with the heat, my hunger, the close air and heavy robe, and the light in the church that was always too dim for me.

My grandparents had to make an emergency trip back to Germany to see a brother who was very ill, with no choice but to leave me with my religious father and stepmother, who wasted no time. We were on the train barreling to Texas and Catholic-land before the sun went down.

My stepmother, dark-haired, small, and wearing a perfume that made me sneeze, sat next to me praying for my soul and my father dozed in the seat ahead of us. Whenever I nodded off to sleep, she would wake me up and push me off her lap. I had no idea where we were going. Or that I was being dumped. I could never have imagined that these adults, my own father, would turn around without me and take the next train back to Kansas. Why did they do that? When I finally realized what was happening and got an inkling of where I was, I made a big screaming fuss. That's when my father told me my grandfather would come get me when it was time.

In the pews, the Mexican mothers' prayers clicked off my woes: Jimmy, the only kid in the convent who came from far away, the only one who had to work for his room and board, the only one whose family didn't come for him that summer. Click, click, click. Two more weeks and the other boys would be back. Click, click. The games would begin. Click, click. They would choose sides for baseball, stickball, marbles and I wouldn't be there to feel lesser, to come in last, to have no ammunition, no ball, no bat, no good marbles, not a thing of all the things a boy should have. I would never have to face that sadness again. My heathen grandfather was coming that afternoon to take me home! I wished that the priest and every last god dumb nun could be at the train station to witness my rescue.

When the mass was over I ate my breakfast of buttered bread and fresh milk by myself in the kitchen, then went to milk the cows and tell them goodbye. I was saving my other farewells for later, after the funeral, before my grandfather's train arrived to take me back to Kansas.

Midmorning, I retrieved my birthday cake from the windowsill and marched with it to my special hiding place in the sugar cane field in a daze of happiness, holding it in its pan ahead of me, trophy-like. As I walked I felt ants climbing my fingers and arms and I shook them off hard. I would eat my fill of cake and wait for Sister Rita's summons. The cows I'd just milked were feeding in the pasture now, life buzzing around their slippery udders. Insects hopped in the already hot grass, and a light breeze disturbed the crowd of mesquite trees. The nodding heads of sunflowers covered a nearby field, bright and distinct enough for me to see in swatches, and still the ants found my arms and made me give first one, then the other, a good shake. I took a path between the rows of sugar cane and sat down in my usual spot. The minute I lifted the cake out of the pan, I felt the piss ants all over, swarming on my cake where they'd been all along, riding the cake like a train from the windowsill out to the pasture and the sugar cane field. I blew with all my breath on the cake and got rid of some, shook my hands once more until they were ant-free, then bit into the cake and took greedy mouthfuls, not minding the bitter taste I had to eat to get at the sweetness, determined to let nothing spoil my day.

When I felt full enough, and not so full of cake as to slow myself down on this day of rescue, I left the rest of the dessert to the ants. I wiped my mouth of crumbs and ants, took my shirt off, and lay on the ground with the cool earth and sharp pieces of stalk against my skin. I heard the sound of blackbirds rustling the cane as they escaped through the roof of fragrant stalks. I closed my eyes, breathed in the smell of sun-scorched sugar, and dreamed I was back in Kansas, telling them stories of my life in Texas. The party flag was hanging outside our small frame house and the neighbors were celebrating my homecoming with my grandfather's home-made beer and Maw's applesauce cake. I stood on the dining room table so they all could hear.

"The cane grows in big long stalks reaching up to the sky and tastes like sweet sugar. The earth between the rows of cane is cool even on the hottest days," I shouted, "and I would go there every day after my chores." What chores, they asked anxiously, knowing my visual limitations. "Helping, as altar boy, at every mass and funeral, milking eight cows, mending fences, fetching the bull three times a year, shelling peas..." the list went on and on. I left nothing out. Maw sniffled into her white embroidered handkerchief and my grandfather growled his curses about the mass.

"We're so sorry, Jimmy," my grandmother cried. "We love you more than anyone in this world."

"I rescued him in the nick of time," my grandfather declared. "Before they made a god dumb priest out of him!"

"Sorry, sorry, sorry," everyone was saying, smothering me with hugs and kisses.

An hour later, back to being convent altar boy but in a black robe this time, I walked along the dirt path in step to the music of cow bells, ukuleles and drums in a procession to the Mexican cemetery on the outskirts of town. Clenching the censer chains and swinging the pan of hot coals high in the air, trying hard to spill them, I was well aware of Sister Hawkeye Aloysius trailing behind me, watching my every move, hissing at my purposeful missteps.

Every one of the Mexicans had an instrument, begging God to listen, and I wanted their god to notice me, too, orchestrating the holy incense, keeping Aloysius on edge until we reached the outcast cemetery with its so-called fence—one single wire strung between posts—that kept no one out, where another cheap board cross waited to mark another baby's grave. It was my fifth Mexican funeral that summer, so it was a routine I was familiar with, I knew my cues, the prayers, the shovelful of dirt, the wailing of my friends, the Mexican mothers. The sad unadorned crosses always reminded me of myself.

I spoke out my short responses as the men dug, heard the clang of shovel on rock, like the sound of the rocks I'd thrown hitting the iron convent gate, or the shovel pitching coal in the boiler room on my grandfather's train. When the last shovelful of dirt fell on the small unvarnished casket, the wailing of the Mexican mothers began again. I had heard them cry up close before at other funerals, but this time I was pierced by the sound.

How different from the hearty laughter that greeted me when I visited their humble shacks, the laughter I stayed and listened to long after the convent lights had gone down and the nuns were deep into their evening prayers.

I felt bad for the grieving Mexican fathers, who were happy when they wrestled with me, and worked the Sisters' ranch, riding the railroad handcars, burning off the brush, dirtying their clothes.

But the grieving of the Mexican mothers was unbearable. I wanted to rush to their big soft bosoms, against dresses that were torn under the arms, into their thick braided hair that smelled like corn. I wanted them to stop wailing, start laughing and call me their special nickname, "las manos grandes."

"Why are your hands so big, pobrecito?" They had teased me.

"From fighting," I had showed them my fists, "and milking cows." They had laughed and told me I was a bear cub, osezno, with my ample paws and boxy body and face.

Chuy's father picked up the wooden cross, crying "aaiieee, aaiiee," and in my usual blur I saw him place it in the ground at the head of his baby son's grave. What did this new cross look like?

The crying stopped. Everyone gathered around the cross and ooh-ed and aah-ed. It was as if Chuy had come back to life. I pushed through them to get close enough to see just a blurred glimmer of color up and down the flat boards of the cross.

"Ojo de Dios! Ojo de Dios!" the mothers exclaimed with excitement. I backed out of the circle. Eye of God, I knew those few words from Sister Rita. The Eye of God! If crosses were on the graves to protect los niños, to keep El Diablo far away, as the mothers had explained to me, then this cross with God's eye would protect better than all the others.

The families backed away from the grave and Father Gresham and I went on with the funeral. I knew the rest of the routine, heard the baby's mother bless the colorful cross and throw empty perfume bottles onto the fresh grave bed scattered with flowers where the glass delicately clinked. I had a handful of petals, sprinkled some on the earth over Chuy with a standard prayer and stuck the rest under my black robe in the bib pocket of my overalls, a souvenir of my last day at the convent.

One day last year Maw took me and two bouquets of sweet peas, one for me and one for her, to my mother's grave in Topeka's city cemetery. The spring smell of the flowers had filled my whole face. Maw was sad we couldn't afford a proper marble gravestone, she told me.

Sweat dripped down my back under my robe; my face, wet all over, stung around my mouth where I'd been bitten by the piss ants crawling on my birthday cake.

Hours later I made my way to the train station, almost too excited to breathe. I had done the practice trip many times before, knew the landmarks and the feel of the roads that led out from the convent compound. My suitcase was light, my feet were bare to better feel the terrain, my face was freshly washed of the sticky sugar cane residue.

The sound of the whistle of the approaching train shook my taut-muscled body. As I waited on the train platform with a few townspeople for the train from Kansas I wondered, did people bawl from happiness? Soon the train would rumble to a stop and my grandfather would step down without luggage, in uniform, tip his hat to his fellow conductors, tell them to hold the train while he swept me up in his strong arms, let me smell his cherry tobacco, and helped me climb up the metal steps to the train, which would turn around in El Paso and head back to Kansas. What would be the first words out of my grandfather's mouth?

"Jaime! Jaime! Hey amigo Jaime! Las manos grandes!" Several of the Mexican fathers called to me, good-naturedly. I waved them away as if they were already part of my past. When the train stopped, one long whistle, a few passengers disembarked, and as I waited, heart jumping like a frog in my chest, the apparitions began: one too tall, one too short, one white-haired, one who yelled, "I have a present for you," in a voice that wasn't my grandfather's and walked right past me in a hurry. I picked up sounds of happiness and greeting, and even tears. And then there was a hush; I heard and saw no more. Suddenly alone on the platform, I refused to acknowledge the soft parting whistle, two long sounds, or look at the back of the train—indistinct but obviously moving away—as it left the station, fixing my weak eyes on the wooden slats of the station platform instead, trying to calm my breath. But maybe, with my eyesight…I had missed…When I looked up, there was still no one there for me. I fingered the petals in my pocket and felt a grown-up arm reach around my shoulders.

"Jaime, are you crying for baby Chuy?" It was one of the gentle-voiced Mexican fathers. "He'll go to Heaven. We put up that magnifico cross to chase away evil spirits. Go home now, Jaime. Get out of the hot sun." I turned away and, rather than go back to the god dumb convent, made my way to the sugar cane field again, carrying my suitcase, wanting to fling it to the empty heavens. The usual blurry scene was swaying this way and that as I charted my way by the sun, stumbling back to my hiding place, not wanting to see another person, nun or Mexican, friend or foe. If my father were to have appeared right then, I would have punched him in the mouth. I blamed him for dumping me there in the first place and then lying to me, not my grandfather for missing the train.

I sat down on the sweet earth, crying, hurting, and dumped the suitcase, scattering my few pitiful possessions; my tears soaked my face, my neck, my once-clean t-shirt. In the distance, I heard the Mexican mothers picking up again, wailing for Chuy the way no one had ever wailed for me but me, and I was drawn to them. Getting right back up, re-packing my suitcase, going straight to the sound of the crying, falling once or twice on the way, distracted, eyesight worse than ever, I went to the Sandoval shack where all the mothers had congregated. I didn't say a word, just went from brightly colored shawl to brightly colored shawl, looking for hugs, looking for someone to say they were sorry my grandfather had forgotten his promise.

"Sister Rita tells us…" Maria Aguirre began. "Feliz cumpleaños, Jimmy. Feliz cumpleaños." They all echoed my birthday greeting, in flat exhausted tones, then went back to their crying circle and there I stood with my suitcase.

"My grandfather…" I began and then I stopped.

"Poor Chuy," they moaned to each other, barely seeing me and my suffering, giving me loose hugs when I inserted myself into the circle with my head, butting like a friendly calf, but their pretend hugs were worse than no hugs at all.

"Jaime," Sister Rita whispered, handing me a folded piece of paper. "Could you take this note back to the Mother Superior, right now?" She waited. "Did you have a nice birthday, Jaime? Did you like your cake?"

That evening back at the convent I spoke to no one, gave Mother Superior the note from Sister Rita, and when the nuns gathered round after dinner and gave me a present wrapped in cloth I opened it without enthusiasm. Three bars of crummy soap carved in the shape of fish. That was the best anyone could do for me.

"Can you see them, Jimmy?" Sister Aloysius asked. "Can you see the fish shapes?"

"No." I was the only person I knew who had bad eyes. Eyes like mine weren't normal, were a bad thing, gave everyone in the world an advantage over me. The facts of my situation, one leading to another as the nuns stood around being quiet and separate, finally made some sense. My blindness was the reason my father had dumped me at the convent where I would stay for the rest of my life. He thought I wasn't fit for any other place, or anything more than three bars of yellow soap. I felt like kicking every one of those nuns but just nodded to them instead, and ran up to bed.

I cried myself to sleep and woke up before dawn, a small piece of sugar cane stuck on my chest, my tears dry. I sat bolt upright awake, brushed myself off, heard echoes of the god dumb wailing still, and a thought flew from my mind like a blackbird: I had to go back to the Mexican cemetery to see the Eye of God up close.

When I reached my destination I found the newly turned earth with my bare feet and sat down on Chuy's grave. Inspecting the decorated marker, the baby's protection and proof of his family's love, my eyes up close so my nose almost touched the plywood, I discovered what my mind had suspected without me seeing them. Stuck in the holes drilled in the spine of the board cross were brand new black beauties, cat's eyes, blood rubies, swirled glass *marbles*! Here right in front of me were marbles that only rich Henry Horace Reynolds, winter boarder, could afford, marbles we'd all gaped at in the toy store in downtown Stanton! Looking closer, there it was, what I had come for, in the center of the cross above the nail where the two thin pieces of plywood met, a huge red marble staring at me like God's eye. I waited.

When the sun came up I was still sitting in the same position on the freshly turned earth, in front of the cross heavy with marbles, right over poor Chuy's dead head. I heard Sister Rita calling for me, and the other nun's voices pursuing me over the ranchland, but I paid them no mind.

The Eye of God had no power over me. Crouching astride the delicate mesquite flowers and fragrant perfume bottles, no longer hearing the Mexican mothers' wailing, I carefully tapped the marbles out of the cross into my hands, *las manos grandes,* and filled the pockets of my overalls.

Kristen Hay

Hazard Ratios

Dear Dr. Little,

It has been exactly ten days since I received the notification that I failed your Statistics 203 class, and today I am packing up my belongings in old cardboard boxes. I am moving out of this sorority house, which has been my home for 1.5 years. And all I have to say to you, Dr. Little, is thank you. For while I may not have learned much in the way of statistics, your lectures allowed me to discover the textures, the sounds, even the colors of words. I know that sounds strange, but please, allow me to explain.

When I walked into class that first day surrounded by four other girls in my sorority, we were gossiping about something. I don't remember what, but I do remember how Lucy fell momentarily silent when she saw you. She, like the rest of us, was struck by your small stature, 3 ft 11, you later told us. She recovered quickly and pretended that she didn't notice. We'd been trained to ignore our differences, so we masked our surprise and continued chattering. We, or perhaps I should say I, secretly congratulated ourselves on our maturity.

Then you introduced yourself, Dr. Little, and I hope you enjoyed our reactions. I could feel the tension spike as we assessed your name. Was it a joke? A few people chuckled, but then became unsure of their responses and covered their laughs with coughs. Once the coughing became ridiculous, some of us threw in sneezes for good measure. You just stood there, looking at us intently until you smiled and made a comment about stating the obvious. The ice broke, the class thawed, and statistics began.

My classmates took notes on your lectures, and I tried to keep up, honestly I did, but frequently I found myself drifting off somewhere far from statistics. I often wondered about you. Please don't take that the wrong way. I was simply curious. Did you like your name? Did it amuse you, or did you get annoyed making the same joke, over and over?

I've always found my name to be ridiculous. My father christened me Kentucky, wanting to pass along some part of his childhood home on to me. Really though, who names his kid after a state? But that's my dad. He nicknamed me Tucker, but that's not much better, only reminding each of us how he'd wanted a boy, and instead got stuck with me. So while my name doesn't illicit quite the same response as yours, Dr. Little, it does get its own special set of looks.

But forgive me, I'm digressing. I signed up to take your class at my father's urging. He's a financial advisor who likes to tell people how he built his business from the ground up. He's always enjoyed statistics and I was eager to find out why. I thought that maybe the next time I saw him we could avoid the silences that had become so familiar, yet never comfortable, and instead have an intellectual discussion about equations and chance. I even thought that if I excelled in your class, Dr. Little, that maybe, just maybe my father might come to respect me.

For the first few weeks of class I maintained focus and for the most part took diligent notes during your lectures. Yet every now and then I found my mind wandering. Please don't be offended by that. Your enthusiasm was, or should've been, contagious. But instead of catching it, I wondered about it. How did you sustain it, seem so happy to be where you were? What did you see that I didn't? Then my mind was off. Please Dr. Little, excuse my ignorance, but I found myself thinking about what the world looked like from your point of view, day in and day out. Did you see things that I missed? When I spoke with you after class one day, I noted that the top of your head came up to my ribs. For the next week I looked at people's ribs, their curves, the way clothes clung to them. I saw the familiar, almost careless way the woman in front of me at the grocery store ran her hands down her husband's torso, straightening his wrinkled shirt. I also saw him pull back slightly from her touch. When my friend's sister, eight months pregnant, visited for the weekend I noticed that her hands trembled slightly when she touched them to her swollen belly. Are those things that you see, Dr. Little? If so, what do you make of them—the things right there, so obvious from a different vantage point that most people never take the time to notice?

Despite my occasional daydreaming in class, I still managed to get an A on the first test. When I called home later that day, I was surprised to hear my dad answer. He usually avoids the phone, saying he doesn't like talking to people when he can't see their expression. Really, he's just not much of a talker, not to me at least.

Yet in that conversation, and this is the kicker, when I told him that I had gotten an A on the exam, he actually said "Well, I'm mighty proud of you Kentucky. You must take after your old man." Now Dr. Little, I know it sounds cliché but my when I heard those words my heart actually leapt a bit, filling my throat. I couldn't speak.

"You still there Tucker?" he asked. I squeaked a response and we said our goodbyes. This happened Friday evening. Saturday morning I threw my duffel bag in the car and drove the four hours home. I couldn't wait to see my dad, to maybe even discuss some of the problems on the exam with him. I knew my mom would be happy to see me too. She'd been asking me to visit. I probably should have told them I was coming, but honestly it didn't even occur to me. I mean, it was still my home, right? So, almost giddy I burst through the front door and the first thing I saw was that sparkly red high heel, its buckle undone. It just lay there, strewn lazily on its side in the middle of the hallway, as if it had a right to be there. I knew that ridiculous shoe was not my mothers. No, it belonged to Mrs. McAnderson, the floozy. She'd worn those very shoes to our high school's fundraising banquet just three days after my mom had found out about her and kicked my father out of the house. She'd smiled at me (can you believe the audacity) and all I could manage to do was to look away, to look down, where her fleshy feet spilled out between the red straps of her high heels.

Later that night I'd returned home to find my mom curled on the couch, hollowed. She spent weeks like that, not even getting up to go to work. My dad came over frequently and begged her to let him move back in, giving up all precedent of trying to shield me from the ordeal. And my mom eventually relented. You'd think this would've made me hate my father right? See him as the bastard he is. Instead I felt sorry for him, ousted from his home. Please, don't think me a simpleton, but somehow thought that if I helped convince my mom to let my dad to move back in, he'd see that I was someone who he could trust and depend on. I imagined him and my mother, back in the same household, happy, and me being a part of that. By the time I left for college, things between them had seemed not perfect, but better.

Yet there I stood in the hallway with that ugly red shoe and the door to my parents' bedroom, down the hall, closed. Anger pulsed through me, gathering strength as it flooded my fingertips, and before I could think I grabbed shoe's strap and yanked it from the floor. Operating purely on instinct I made my way back into the truck, shoved the shoe in the glove compartment, and sped away. It rattled the whole way back to school. No matter what position I arranged it, it shook, like it was trying to escape, to make its way back to the familiarity of where it came from.

Dr. Little, I apologize if this is more than you ever wanted to know. You barely knew me, so I'm sure you're not eager to learn my family secrets. But you must understand how my head was still spinning when I returned to your class that next week. How eager I was to grasp at anything to make sense of what was happening. You provided the words for me to do so.

I began to write poetry in your class. I know, I know. I should've been taking notes on your lectures, studying them to pass the tests, to learn how to analyze numbers. Instead I wrote. The day I returned to your class after I found the shoe, you spoke of hazard ratios, but I misheard you. I wondered instead about haphazard ratios—how one event casually gets thrown a top another, and that somehow, god knows how, we're supposed to make some sort sense out of them—analyze them in a way that will hopefully find significance. But how can we make sense of things for which there is no apparent reason?

At first I tried to bury the knowledge of my father's infidelity, hide it deep within my blood, muscles, skin. Yet it kept fighting its way out, showing up again and again as I sat in your lectures. I would be listening, even following the concept you were explaining, but then you would say a simple word, such as probability, and my façade would crumble. For what were the chances, I could not help but wonder, of me coming home to find my father fucking Mrs. McAnderson? Had that become his normal weekend behavior? Or did I just walk in at an unlucky moment?

I wanted that pain out of me, strewn across the paper in a tangible way. So my notes became poems. I used your words, your equations, simply your presence, and tried to make some sort of sense of it all.

I knew I was failing your class, Dr. Little. But I didn't care. And when class ended and I received an F, I felt dread tinged with elation. This was new. This was a problem I had created, and I would be the one to find a solution.

I called home, and once again my dad answered. I could picture him sitting on the couch, his bulk engulfing the cushions. He liked to rest both hands on his rounded belly and cross his feet on the coffee table as he watched the news. When they spoke of stocks and bonds, he often grumbled to himself, issuing sounds that never amounted to full words much less sentences. As a child I used to pretend I understood the meanings of those noises, and reply with my own strange sounds. For years I believed it was our secret language.

"Tucker," he said. "You picked a bad day to call. Did you see what the stock market did? My clients are calling left and right looking for advice. They just don't understand how sometimes you just need to sit tight and weather the storm. You know?"

"Sure," I responded, surprised by the length of his greeting.

"One day, if you take the same path as your old man, become a financial advisor yourself, you'll see. You have a good head for numbers. Hell, you might even be better at this than me." He laughed.

It was the sound of that laugh, throaty and smug, that made me do it. I swear Dr. Little, I had no plan of confronting my father about his infidelity. I didn't know what purpose it would serve. Yet he sounded so damn full of himself, so proud that I would turn out to be like him, I felt the words bubble to the surface.

"I am not like you," I said.

He still laughed, thinking I was joking around.

"I came home last month. I saw Mrs. McAnderson's shoes in the hallway of *our* home. I'd forgiven you. Mom had forgiven you! And then you go and do the same fucking thing!"

"Whoa Tucker, be careful there. You don't know what you saw." His breathing had quickened into the phone.

"Yes I do. And it's bullshit. But that's not the reason I called." Dr. Little, I know it may seem strange. But I didn't want to hear excuses, justifications, or told that I imagined the whole thing. At that moment I simply wanted my father to know that he had not gotten away with it. That I knew. So before he could say anything else, I proceeded.

"I called to let you know that I failed statistics," I said.

You should have heard him, the anger in his voice. He became unhinged, yelling that he wouldn't pay for college anymore, that I would have to figure my own damn way out in the world. That after all he'd done for me, all the sacrifices he made, he couldn't believe I was throwing it all away. How I had no right to fail your class on his dime. Then he hung up.

And what did I do next? Well, you might be pleased to know that I dug my statistics book out from under my bed. I know it's strange, but that book comforts me. I appreciate the curves and bars of the graphs, and the numbers all there in a concrete, logical way. Everything laid out, explanations included, for an analysis.

A few days later my dad left me a message saying that he'd send me a check for next semester's tuition. He said he might've been a bit too hasty, but added that he expects me to retake your class, to complete it with nothing less than an A. But you know what Dr. Little? I've decided that I don't want his money.

So what am I going to do? Well, I am happy to say that I do in fact have a plan. You know that huge house on the outskirts of campus—the one with peeling paint on one side and murals of nude women on the other? Well, I'm moving in. They have cheap rent and I was lucky enough to see an ad that they were looking for a roommate. I called and they invited me over for an interview. Now, imagine this: I entered the house to find four people sprawled in various spots throughout their oversized living room. One was asleep on the tattered couch, a book, I believe it was Kerouac, hung off his chest. The second person I saw perched by the window in a white tank top, with her friend painting vibrant orchids down her arms and shoulders. They were laughing. The fourth sat, scribbling into what looked like an old, worn journal, his fingers tapping the table, cigarette hanging from his lips. Murals decorated the walls, intense reds swirled with softer yellows, and I smelled incense, and what might have been peppermint tea. They looked up slowly when I pushed my way inside (the door had been partway open). Eventually their eight eyes looked towards me, taking me in.

I have never been so utterly conscious of my clothing, my jewelry, even my vaguely flowery scent. I felt the heaviness of my long blonde hair on my back, the weight of the gold and amethyst pulling the skin of my earlobes, and was acutely aware of the Greek letters, signifying my sorority, on my sweatshirt. I watched them exchange looks, dismissing me with a smirk. Their expression was one that I'd encountered from my father, time and time again, and this time I grew angry. I fell into a voice that I didn't know I had that demanded their attention. I spoke of poetry, told them of you, of my desire to live with people who created, that I too was an artist. And you know what Dr. Little? They're letting me move in.

Tomorrow I leave the sorority. I have not spoken to my father since our last conversation. I have not spoken with my mother either, but hope to soon. Dr. Little, I'm writing because I feel that I owe you an explanation. I would hate for you to think that I failed you, or that you failed me, or some sort of combination of the two.

I still keep my statistics book by my bedside and whenever I feel discouraged, I leaf through it. Its torn pages are littered with my words and sketches during the course of the semester. They chronicle my rationalizations and search for significance through the murkiness of chance, the unknowable of the haphazard.

Sincerely yours,
Kentucky Jones

Jenn Chan Lyman

The Natural

THE FIRST TIME I WAS DECLARED "UNFIT" was when I was eight, slouching in a too-tight tutu, pointing my right toe out and to the side in a poor attempt at the second position. Miss Lu, a woman composed entirely of lines: thin horizontal lips, long narrow eyes and a tailbone permanently tucked for a posture so vertical she'd tip over if somebody were to poke the mole between those eyes, pronounced the word in an unapologetic tone to my father.

"Unfit." She circled around me, elbows splayed, hands resting on non-existent hips. "She is completely unfit for ballet."

"Please, Comrade Lu. She just needs more practice."

Miss Lu reached out with her baton and rapped

twice on my tailbone. I held my slouch. The elastic waistband of my tutu pinched terribly but I fought the urge to tug or scratch. Through the mirror, I could see my father drawing back his sloped shoulders to stand taller.

"Look at her spine. Twisted. An ill-formed sapling will never stand tall. And her legs." Miss Lu hinged forward to tap my calves as if we didn't know what legs were. "Much too short." She snapped back to vertical.

"But she's only eight, surely we can—."

"Not everyone is meant for this art, Comrade Chen. Your daughter should find other pursuits. It would be criminal of me to take any more of your money."

With a tight one-eighty swivel, Miss Lu was off, her skinny rear twitching from side to side as she headed toward the practice barre across the room, where a girl from my preschool was gazing smugly at her own reflection as she stretched one unnaturally long leg up and over her head. I stared at my father staring. Eventually, he grabbed my hand and led me out of the studio and straight home without a word. My shell-pink ballet slippers turned the color of green mud as we trudged through the park. When we walked through the door, my mom noticed my slippers at once and began to chastise me for not changing into my walking shoes. A tear, wobbling free and dribbling down my face, stopped her mid-sentence. Father dropped my hand. He thrust the satchel with my walking shoes and regular clothes toward Mom, and, in a strange monotone that I would become accustomed to, said: "Don't fuss about the shoes. No more ballet. She's unfit. The teacher said so. Unfit." After a beat, he added: "Too fat." He went into their bedroom and closed the door on us both.

The last time I was declared "unfit" was nineteen years later, by Wade Hsu, my boyfriend for the past two years. We met at an alumni event on a private Napa Valley resort of some well off alumnus, two of a handful of Asians surrounded by mostly white people and two or three black people. Wade and I had attended the same California liberal arts college. In the two years we overlapped, we'd never met. Tall, handsome and Chinese-American, he was my mom's dream come true: college was where I was supposed to rise above the common flock, meet the most promising boys, and attain the kind of class my mom dreamed of as a little girl on a farm in Anhui, craning her head to squint at the blue between the clouds.

But Wade was rolling into his sixth month of unemployment post-Lehman and losing the swagger that had attracted me to him in the first place. It didn't help that I remained employed. If anyone should remain employed, it should be the American, hyphenated or not, not the Mainland Chinese FOB. He didn't state his opinion out loud; I sensed it in his tone when he asked how my department was doing, how many of my colleagues were afraid. My bank was China-focused and analysts like me who could interpret due diligence documents and legal contracts in Chinese were especially safe. As the months passed without change to either his or my employment status, Wade began to pick at whatever he could find: rinse more thoroughly before putting the dishes in the sink; don't use so much salt in the marinade; buy longer skirts; watch your gender-specific pronouns. The list compounded. So three days ago when we were getting ready for bed and he looked up from his magazine and said, "According to this article, you are totally unfit for motherhood," I wasn't completely taken aback.

I stopped massaging my cuticles. Cuticle dryness had become an obsession ever since Wade pointed out my hangnails the week before last. I capped the jar of overpriced Australian hand cream and placed it on the nightstand.

"Did you hear me?" he said, dropping the magazine to his lap, his voice taking on that edge I was coming to dread. "This says you're unfit."

I breathed in, trying to maintain my composure, but the heady scent of lavender hand cream tickled my sinuses and I sneezed violently. I reached over him for a tissue and my left breast brushed against his chest, which had become firmer from his post-layoff exercise regimen. I missed the warmth of his body. I was holding myself against him, still reaching for the tissue, when he plucked one out of the box and stuffed it into my outstretched hand. Face flushing, I settled back on my side. Months ago, we would have been doing something much more exciting in bed than massaging cuticles and reading magazines.

"Who says I want to be a mom anyway?"

"No, seriously. It's crazy how many of these apply to you." He picked up the magazine and pointed at the page. "Workaholic, check. Smoker, check. Underweight, check. High-stress lifestyle, check. Travels constantly, check. Puts career before everything else including boyfriend, check."

"Stop it, Wade."

"What? I'm just saying. It's something we should talk about. I want kids, I mean, not now, but eventually. Like two, or three, even. I've never heard you say a word about how many you want. I know your culture isn't all about popping out a soccer team or anything, but one kid just seems sad."

Your culture. Wade loved to point out our differences: his all-American, democratic upbringing versus my communist Chinese childhood; his integrated, bicultural salad versus my Chinese greens with American dressing. My delineation was much simpler: who could pronounce their own Chinese name correctly and who could not.

"I got a meeting early in the morning, Wade. Let's just go to sleep, okay?"

"I'm just saying, if we're thinking about getting married, we should talk about kids, and given the way you live and breathe your job and take such shitty care of yourself, I'm wondering if you're compromising how fit you'd be for motherhood if we were to, you know, in a few years or so."

I ignored his tepid half-proposal. Instead, I switched off the lamp on my side, slid under the cool covers, turned away from Wade and closed my eyes.

Right away I saw my mom's face, or I should say, a particular version of her face captured in a black and white portrait: she was smiling lopsided at the camera, forcing a dimple in her right cheek; her bobbed hair was parted down the middle, framing her face, a face that was shaped like an upside down teardrop. My father chose that portrait for her funeral, and ever since, that was the face that always floated up first when I thought of her. I inherited her teardrop face, her slender eyes, her petite, hazelnut nose, and the older I got, the more I saw her face in mine.

That day after Miss Lu's, after Father shut the door on the two of us, her delicate features had taken on a look of defiance. A tirade ensued: that bony Busybody Lu has no right to tell us what our daughter is fit or unfit for; women who don't get married become bitter hags; only a bony little nobody like Busybody Lu would call an eight year old "too fat." I didn't tell her that Father had come up with "too fat" himself. Nor did I remind her that Miss Lu was the third teacher in my three years of ballet to come to more or less the same conclusion.

"Don't worry, precious girl," Mom said, kneeling down to brush the tears from my face. "We'll find you something else. Ballet is stuck-up, anyway. Piano is much better. All the high-class girls play piano."

"But Xiao Zhen says my fingers are too short for the piano," I replied, wiping my runny nose on my bare forearm. Our downstairs neighbor's daughter Yang Zhen was half a year older than me, which meant that I followed her everywhere and believed everything she said. Twenty years later, Xiao Zhen was still my closest friend. "Xiao Zhen says girls with sausage fingers aren't made for classical piano. She says I should take up bean-planting."

Mom bit down on her lip, before replying, "Don't listen to that no-manners, stuck-up princess. I've heard her through the window and she's not very good at all, banging on those keys without any grace. She's just jealous of how good you're going to be. We'll find you the very best piano teacher, okay?"

I didn't believe her, because I'd heard Xiao Zhen enough times through the same window, and her piano prowess was something the whole neighborhood talked about. I also didn't want to quit ballet for piano, because even though

I hated the scratchy tutus and headache-inducing hair buns, hated feeling completely out of my element while skinny girls pranced effortlessly around me, ballet meant time with Father. He took me to every weekend lesson; he attended every quarterly recital. Some evenings we would sit together, watching dark and fuzzy VHS tapes of performances that he found from who knows where, or listening to a Tchaikovsky or Prokofiev record, where at some change in the music he'd say, "There, there he picks the wrong Swan!" or "That's where Romeo sees her for the first time!" and I would say, "Yes, of course!" with no idea what he was going on about, and he'd smile, pat me on the back, and say "Smart girl, smart girl." The man was obsessed with ballet. Piano would not be the same. I should have tried harder—couldn't I have ignored the discomfort like the rest of them? Couldn't I have stood straight like the others twigs in tutus?—but it was too late. He had given up. So I nodded to the piano idea and Mom's face lit up.

"Let's go tell Ayi to fry up some sticky rice cakes," she said, leading me by the hand toward the kitchen. "The sweet kind. You must be starving after all that nonsense. Piano will be great. You will be a natural. My little piano star."

I didn't become a piano star, or a chess star, or a calligraphy star, or a ribbon-dance star, or a Chinese-opera star that year, but not for lack of trying. At Mom's insistence, Father took me to practices and auditions and contests and recitals, but I was right: he had no interest in anything except ballet. There were no more afternoons with Tchaikovsky, no more evenings at the Shanghai Ballet. We descended into a habit of shared silence, going from lesson to lesson, hobby to hobby. And with every flop, my mom would say, "Don't worry, precious girl. You'll find your niche. It's just a matter of time."

I would nod and let her feed me another sticky rice cake, or crab apple, or dried plum, depending on the season. That's how it was with my mom: I was always a star.

On a rainy day in March, three days after our talk about kids, or I should say, Wade's little checklist on why I wasn't mothering material, I sat in the passenger seat of his SUV, stuck in Friday afternoon traffic between Newport Beach and LAX, worried that I'd miss my flight.

"I really don't understand why you have to go back so suddenly. You were just there for Christmas."

"I told you, it's Qingming. I've got to visit my mom. And Tom gave me time off since the Dalian deal died on Wednesday." What a lucky break. As soon as I heard the deal was dead, I asked my boss for leave. Wade was driving me nuts. I had to get away and the first place that came to mind was home.

"Well, like I said, I've never heard of this Qingming thing. I don't remember my parents ever going to the cemetery in April, of all random months. And my parents are totally Chinese."

I held my tongue from saying something I would regret, like, "What the hell would you know, just last year you thought Chinese New Year was a one-day thing," and replied with a line I'd learned in primary school: "Qingming is important, it's the official day for honoring ancestors and cleaning up their graves." I wasn't going to tell him that my own family had only honored Qingming once, when Mom was interred.

"Qingming. Is it the same 'ming' as your name, 'ming' as in 'bright'?"

"Yes."

He grunted. "Doesn't even make sense. Doesn't 'qing' mean 'clear,' or 'green,' or something? What does 'clear,' 'green' and 'bright' have to with graves? Visiting graves sounds more dark and depressing to me."

I was admittedly stumped. How did I know why the festival was called Qingming?

"And if it's so important, how come you didn't go last year?"

"Wade, just drop it. I have a ticket. I'm going." The words came out sharper than I'd intended. His hands tightened around the steering wheel and I eased my shoulders into the leather seat. "It's just ... I haven't seen my father in a while. I want to spend some time with him before we visit my mom. It just happens to be his birthday as well, the day after Qingming. He's turning sixty this year, so it's kind of a big deal." This last part was a convenient half-truth. It was my father's birthday, but he never celebrated. Mom explained to me once that he didn't like to throw a party the day after everyone was thinking about death.

"Well ... well, why didn't you say so? You didn't tell me it was your dad's sixtieth. I know that's a big deal in China. I could have gone with you, you know. I mean, I still could."

The injury in his voice made me reach over and put my hand on his. "I know, Wade. This was last minute. I want you to meet him when I've had a chance to tell him about us first. Next trip, okay? We'll have more time to plan."

He slipped his hand out from under mine to turn up the radio, a gesture Wade often resorted to when we were in the car and he didn't like what I was saying. I looked out at the blue-gray buildings, blending into each other in the downpour. Big cities looked the same in the rain. Shanghai would be in its short window of fair weather right now, before the mugginess of late April took over. Father and my crazy uncle were probably sitting on the curb in front of our house, muttering in the spring light. I had not called him since I made the rather sudden decision to go home three days ago; I'd have to call him from the airport. Last time I spoke to him was during our bi-weekly call four days ago; the conversation had gone as usual: me talking while he breathed on the other end. After my father sent me to boarding school in the U.S. after Mom died, our phone conversations had pretty much been that way: he didn't ask any questions and I filled the dead air—nothing more awkward than Trans-Pacific dead air for a dollar a minute, or however much it cost back then.

When the sign appeared up ahead for Departures, Wade clicked off the radio and, without taking his eyes off the road, said, "I'm sorry about what I said the other day. I don't really think you're unfit to be a mom. I was being stupid. This layoff, the frickin' markets ... I think I'm just nervous. I know we haven't talked about marriage and stuff, and I know it's important to girls and all, but I don't think I can offer you anything concrete right now since I don't even know when these headhunters will pull through–"

"Wade, it's okay. Let's talk about it when I get back."

"I'm just trying to say—."

"Let's talk when I get back."

I looked over at the profile of his tanned face, his high cheekbones, his angular jaw now clenched. His eyes were tired, his lips were chapped and the dimple that appeared beneath the outside corner of his right eye when he smiled was absent. This was the guy who had replaced the cocksure wisecracker, the man on a mission to prove himself, the one I'd fallen in love with over Pacific oysters and Napa Valley wine. What would Mom think of post-layoff Wade? He was not the first to deteriorate in my presence. In fact, all the guys I'd dated before Wade had somehow gone from impressive to depressive in a matter of months. Wade had taken longer, sure, but here he was, drawn, defeated, and truth be told, kind of a dick. Then again, Mom was all about perseverance. She'd probably dust me off with one of her encouraging smiles and say, "Try, and try again."

Wade pulled up in front of the terminal and said, "Make it quick, okay? Cops are getting trigger-happy these days with curbside citations. Especially with Asians. Have a good trip and SMS me when you land."

I pulled my baggage out of his trunk and watched him drive away.

Even though business class took much of the edge off of the fourteen-hour flight, I felt grimy and sluggish when I landed the next morning. I'd spent the entire flight lost in movies, one after another, and thinking about my mom. The anniversary of her death was in a few days: March 30th. It seemed appropriate that I was going home, although for the past thirteen years I'd never been home for the anniversary. I'd always been in school or at work. I could actually go to her grave this year, if I wanted. But would I? What difference would a slab of stone with her name on it make? And Father. I wasn't even sure that he'd want me around. The more I thought about it the more I wondered if going home was a good idea. I should have picked somewhere else to escape, somewhere else to indulge in my usual March 30th rituals: eating a ton of Chinese food and wearing her perfume, Chanel No. 5. Although my last memory of her smelled of the TB ward at People's Hospital No. 6.

As the taxi driver loaded my bags into the trunk, he asked me in Mandarin where I wanted to go. I responded in Shanghainese, "Shyü'wae, K'angb'ing Lu," the only address I'd ever had in Shanghai. He immediately peppered me with questions: Shanghainese, eh? Coming home? For Qingming? Living overseas? Oh, America! So prosperous, but not so prosperous lately, yeah? What's it like living around foreigners all the time? At first, the gritty timbre of Shanghainese was comforting, but after a while I pretended to fall asleep. As my head rested on the chilly glass of the car window and my skull took in every bump along the road, I watched the city go by, its gray buildings fading in the distance into an equally gray haze, thicker and more opaque than L.A.'s smog. Rumbling along the outskirts of Shanghai was a dismal way to see the city. There was nothing of the neighborhoods, the trees, the curving side streets that represented home. At some point, the cab driver pointed out the upcoming site for next year's Expo, a massive grid riddled with cranes and scaffolding, and I remained quiet, though I could sense his eyes on me in the rearview mirror, trying to reconnect.

Soon we were honking down Heng Shan Lu, passing familiar spots like Jo Jo's Fun Bar, Sasha's, Thousand and One Nights. I was about to ask the driver why he'd taken the long way, when I suddenly realized that I hadn't called my father yet. Shoot. It would be weird to show up unannounced and I was in no mood to deal with his silence. Just as we were about to make a right onto my street, I asked the driver turn around, redirecting him to the first hotel that came to mind, half an hour away in Pudong. He glanced at me but kept his muttering to himself, and I went back to feigning sleep.

By the time the driver announced that we'd arrived at the Grand Hyatt, I had fallen asleep for real. When at last I slipped into the cool sheets of the hotel bed, I felt a freedom that I had not felt in a long time. Tom, my boss, had signed me off for ten days, given my twenty yet unclaimed vacation days. Wade thought I was home with my father. Father had no clue I was even in the city. No one knew where to find me. I was everywhere and anywhere and nowhere. And I promptly fell asleep.

The next day, I went out to meet Xiao Zhen for a late Sunday brunch at a new brasserie tucked in a courtyard full of magnolias. She was with Wang Lei, a tall, twiggy girl we'd known since we were kids. It had only been a few months since I'd last seen them, so the updates were few, confirming no significant changes (still employed; still not engaged). I listened to the two of them gossip, interjecting here and there for clarification (which guy? what new club?), though most of the gossip was about people I'd never met.

Between the entrée and dessert, Wang Lei turned to me and said, "Ming, your Shanghainese is getting worse. You better come home before you forget altogether."

I didn't answer right away; Wang Lei had a way of irritating me. Sometimes I wondered if it was because she was actually annoying, or because she reminded me of my ballet days, with her perfect posture and unnaturally long legs. I'd grown out of my chubby phase by the time I was thirteen, and was even taller than Wang Lei now, but still, she irked.

"What's the point of Shanghainese?" Xiao Zhen interjected. "Most everyone speaks Mandarin these days. Shanghainese is dying."

"No it's not," said a voice from behind. I turned to see a woman, heavily made up and decked out in orange and lime Kate Spade, a woman who the other girls obviously knew. They introduced me to Catherine, who had just finished lunch in the restaurant's back patio.

Catherine sat down at our table and continued, "Shanghainese is not dying. It's our heritage. When Robert and I have kids, I'm only going to speak to them in Shanghainese; they can always learn Mandarin later." Only then did I notice the huge diamond on her ring finger. My eyes flickered to Xiao Zhen and Wang Lei's ring fingers, even though I already knew that they were bare like my own.

"What does Robert think of that?" Xiao Zhen asked, leaning toward this Catherine woman in a manner I'd never seen in her before: not quite admiration, but something like it.

Catherine shrugged. "Doesn't matter. We'll be in Melbourne then, and I'll be the one with the kids at home. It's not up to him. Anyway, I'd love to stay, girls, but my driver is waiting."

After Catherine left, Xiao Zhen turned to me and asked, "You still dating that ABC?"

It took me a second to respond. Watching Xiao Zhen with Catherine reminded me of something my mom told me at the hospital, a few days before she died. With no shame and some defiance even, she'd said that when she first laid eyes on my father in the commune town hall with a knapsack on his back and a lost but resolute expression on his face, she'd decided that he would be her husband. It took a few years, but she persisted, because she knew that he, a self-possessed, educated youth sent to her village from Shanghai, would be her ticket out of the countryside. For me, she wanted even more: a ticket out of the country. A life with no limits. Wade was one such ticket: an ABC with a passport. I'd forgotten to SMS him last night, and when I did this morning his response was: "Good. At gym. Ttyl."

I finished taking a sip of tea and replied, "Nah." My stomach curled.

"How come? Too ABC? You're pretty much an ABC now anyway," she said without laughing. My jaw clenched involuntarily. Wang Lei shifted in her chair. There it was, the usual barb about my non-Chineseness. I'd been away too long; every year I didn't come home the barbs got worse. Perhaps they were justified, perhaps I was more American now than Chinese.

I was about to laugh it off when a petite, well-dressed but fragile-looking woman with a beak-like nose came up to the table. This was how it was with Xiao Zhen and Wang Lei, constantly running into people they knew, people in the scene. The other girls immediately began speaking in English in her presence and it turned out that the woman, Ruth, was Chinese-American, also from Los Angeles. We both thought the other looked familiar, but neither of us could place where we might have met. Her cheerful West Coast accent made me feel at ease, despite Xiao Zhen's pointed looks: she had this way of glancing at me sideways whenever she spoke English around me, or vice versa.

After brunch, Xiao Zhen and I stepped into a cab together out of habit; we had, after all, lived in the same place for most of our childhood. She told the taxi driver the address and I corrected her.

"Why are you at the Grand Hyatt?" she asked, face twitching. "That seems a bit much."

"I don't know. I heard it was nice."

"So have you even seen your dad yet?"

"No. I'll go see him tomorrow."

"He knows that you're back, right?"

I didn't answer. She raised her eyebrows for half a second. Then said, "Okay, well, you drop me off first then. I'm not going all the way to Pudong and back."

When I got to my hotel, I picked up the phone to call my father, but ended up calling room service instead. I didn't have any concrete reason to avoid him. Given that the anniversary of Mom's death was the next day, really, I should have called. Maybe I was tired from jetlag. Or maybe I was simply tired of keeping up my lies, lies that had been compounding for years. One after another.

They began in the summer of 2004, after university and after I took a position in San Francisco as a financial analyst, the lowest on the totem pole of corporate grunt work. Not that it was anything to be ashamed of. It was honest, well-paid work that plenty of graduates would have died for. But when I called my father to tell him, when I heard his voice on the other line, tired, distant, I realized that I could tell him anything and it wouldn't make a difference. For all of boarding school and college, I dutifully repeated every grade, every acceptance, every distinction or commendation on our bi-weekly calls and he would respond to one and all with a murmur: "Oh, yes? Mmm." It wasn't that he didn't care. Of course he cared. He was my father. He had to care. But the details, well, who cared about details? Maybe if I made up something ridiculous he would actually give me more than an "Mmm." So I told him that I was moving to London to work in sales at a large insurance firm. It was a double-edged ploy: he loved London; he hated insurance salesmen. (He once said that they were the worst kind of professionals, preying on people's fears.) But neither detail riled him. "Mmm. Be careful in a new country." The next time I called, I recited to him a U.K. address as my own; it was the listed address of a London shrink. I gave him a +44 number to reach me at home; it was the number to a bar in Covent Garden. I even told him that I'd taken an English name: Juliet. Juliet Chen. "Mmm. Sounds professional."

As the months passed, I fabricated other details of Juliet's life while he breathed on the other end, asking no questions. The lies slipped out. One after another. A dog. A convertible. A British boyfriend. I was a natural. I even developed an accent. I described the London fog while staring out from my office at the mist obscuring Coit Tower, Alcatraz, the Golden Gate Bridge. I flew to Brazil, South Africa, and all over Europe for big ticket insurance deals, rather than to run financial models and explain Chinese contracts. When I transferred to L.A., Juliet transferred to Manchester, then, after a few months, back to London, because I ran out of things to say about Manchester. According to the Internet, Manchester is boring, boring, boring. And as I'd predicted, the details didn't matter. He absorbed them all with no question.

I guess part of me thought he'd catch on eventually. One phone call to that pub in Covent Garden would have done it. But he never called. I thought at least the white boyfriend would have gotten a rise out of him, but not really: "British, huh? Hmm." Over the years the lies piled one on top of the other; unexposed, they didn't matter. And whether I was really in Shanghai for Mom's anniversary, or London, or Los Angeles, didn't matter either. It was probably better, anyway, to spend it apart.

Xiao Zhen would not accept another "no" for an answer, so I met her at some hot new hotel bar the Monday after Qingming. I'd spent the week in bed, dodging Wade and Xiao Zhen's calls, watching movies, and trying every dish on the room service menu.

The bar was as swanky as the other places she'd taken me to. Xiao Zhen had done well in Shanghai; she was an executive at a public relations firm specializing in luxury hotels, restaurants, and bars. Every manager in town seemed to know her; there was free champagne, vodka, or Scotch, any night of the week. She led me up to the rooftop and we sat at the Jacuzzi, which was the centerpiece of the circular patio. It was only 8:30 p.m. so the patio and its unobstructed view of the Bund were completely ours. Xiao Zhen kicked off her heels, pulled aside her hair, drew her legs over the skirting of the hot tub and dipped them in. I did the same, shedding my ballet flats and gathering my long skirt into my lap, even though the water was much too hot for the weather. The sky wanted to rain. I could feel it in the oppressive heat, the lack of oxygen. The mugginess had come early this year. I thought about the clean, clear air of Newport Beach. A waiter, long and lean with the face of a twelve-year-old, came upstairs with champagne. I watched as he popped the cork and filled the glasses, tilting each to minimize the froth. He left without a word.

"So tell me for real, what happened with that last ABC?" Xiao Zhen asked, flicking her cigarette ash on the patio floor.

"I don't know. He just isn't right, kind of boring. Not a big deal." I fought the urge to pluck a cigarette from the pack beside me. I'd been avoiding cigarettes since I'd arrived, but it would be good to light up, inhale, and push the memory of Wade and his "two or three kids" through my nostrils and out of my head.

"That's the thing with you, Ming. It's never a big deal. I wish I had your attitude with guys. For me, it's always too big a deal." She took a long drag from her cigarette before exhaling slowly. The smoke sidled over the railing and down to the black expanse of the Huangpu River, outlined in glittering lights on either side like a runway. I thought about Wade, about how at first I thought he was the one, as with Aaron, Gilbert, Duane, and the other American Born Morons I'd dated, and how that feeling always spoiled in the end, like rotten meat.

"You and Patrick okay?"

Xiao Zhen didn't answer at first and took another puff instead. Patrick was a good-looking Australian, a hotel marketing executive she'd met on the job. Every time I saw him he would marvel at how perfect my English was, how much better it was than Cassie's. He called her Cassie. She'd taken on "Cassandra" in high school. I don't think he even knew what her real name was, or ever bothered to ask. They'd been dating for three years and Xiao Zhen grew more anxious each year, though she'd die before admitting it.

"We're fine. Busy." She plucked her feet out of the tub. "You talked to your dad yet?"

"Nah." I suddenly realized that it was his birthday. Today. It was also exactly two weeks since we last spoke, which meant he had two reasons to expect my call.

"Why not? I thought you came here for Qingming."

For a moment, I wanted to tell her everything: about Wade and the fact that I hadn't really come for Qingming, about London and my lies, about my week in bed missing my mom. But I just shrugged. I lifted the heavy champagne bottle to refill her glass. Then mine.

"Is that Chanel No. 5?" she said, wrinkling her nose.

"Yeah," I replied, my face and neck flushing red.

"That's vintage of you."

I downed my glass and refilled it. Hers was still untouched.

"It's not true you know."

"What isn't?" Xiao Zhen's eyes flitted toward me.

"That I don't think it's a big deal. With guys, I mean." I looked away from her and into the glowing swirl of aquamarine bubbles around my legs. "I find these guys, and then ... they just turn out different. They get worse. I don't know, maybe it's me. Something about me makes them worse, and then after a while, I don't want to be with them anymore."

Xiao Zhen was quiet. Other than the bubbling of the Jacuzzi, the only sound around us was the medley of car horns from far below. Then, she reached out and squeezed my hand.

"It's not you, Ming. You haven't met the right one. When you do, you won't let go."

For a while we sat there, my hand in hers, listening to the bubbles and the distant horns.

"Hey, let's go dancing. There's this Mexican restaurant that has salsa tonight. Don't make that face. It's a lot of fun, lot of cute guys. Foreigners, mostly. No ABCs. Come on."

I followed her downstairs. She spoke briefly with the manager, and then we left, our half-filled champagne glasses still in our hands. In the cab, she yelled, "Fuck Wade!" out the window and I laughed harder than I had in a long time. My forehead was numb; I felt wonderful about everything. We stumbled out of the cab and up the stairs to the main floor of Agave, where salsa was in full swing. A whirling disco ball flung colors into every corner. Bartenders handed out tequila shots nonstop. A man, handsome in an intense sort of way, pulled up a chair beside me. He was foreign. Not white, though. Maybe Brazilian.

"Are you a friend of Cassandra's?" he yelled with an accent I couldn't place.

"Yeah!" I yelled back. I was still hanging on to the champagne glass, now empty. He took it from my hand and set it down.

"Good. Let's go." He grabbed my arm with one hand and lifted me out of the chair by the waist with the other. "Wow, you are really tall for a Chinese." He was in a suit, but even through the layers I could feel his heat. I pressed my body against his and felt a charge that I'd forgotten since Wade shut down. The nape of the man's neck was soft, downy. In all my years away, I had never dated, not even made out with a guy who wasn't at least ethnically Chinese. Xiao Zhen had always found it strange; I'd always thought it was the right thing to do.

"Are you a teacher here?" I asked as he dragged me to the center of the floor.

"*Si.* Ramon." He twirled me, dipped me, and twirled me again. I fought my nausea.

"You are a natural," he said too loudly into my ear. He pointed to my ballet flats. "Did you dance when you were young?"

I started to laugh, and laugh, and then the laughter took over so completely that soon I was doubled at the waist, tears streaming down my face. He leaned over to ask if I was okay and his animated caterpillar brows made me laugh even harder, until I was a heap on the dance floor, laughing amongst the flurry of legs. He knelt down beside me and grinned.

"You are *loca*," he said. "Super crazy. I love it."

He lifted me onto my feet and part of me wanted to pull him closer, feel his heat on me, but instead, I slipped from his grasp and out the French doors that led to the balcony. The air outside was weightless. The moon, dented, hung high in the sky. I drew my phone out of my purse and the screen lit up: 9:44. Father was a night owl. The phone purred in my palm and I held my breath, wondering what I would say. Happy birthday would be a start. The phone rang and rang, until finally, I switched it off.

Tomorrow. I'd try again tomorrow.

That day, after Miss Lu's verdict and my muddy green slippers and my father's storming into the bedroom and my mom's kind words, I saw something I shouldn't have. On my way to my room, I passed by my parents' room and the door was slightly ajar. I don't know what possessed me, given the smacking that I'd have coming had I been caught, but I crept up and put my eye to the crack. My father, half-silhouetted against the window and half-lit by the afternoon sun, was sitting on his side of the bed, holding a photo to the light. His face and the photo were too far away for me to see, but I knew that he was weeping. I backed away, a lump forming in my throat. When I heard him leaving the apartment an hour later, I stole into their bedroom, walked around to my father's side of the bed and opened his drawer for the very first time. Inside was a stack of photos. I pulled out the one on top. In the fading afternoon light, I took in the small portrait of a slim girl, younger than I was then, in a pink pancake tutu, her right arm arced effortlessly overhead while the left floated parallel to the floor, her right foot crossed in front of the left with the heel rotated inward, in a near-perfect rendering of the fourth position. The girl's hair was twisted into two neat buns behind her ears. Not one stray hair, not one roll of fat above the waistband. Not "too fat" at all. Her face, tilted slightly toward the light and gazing eternally at the palm of her raised right hand, radiated with a quality I had come to recognize on the faces of other girls my age, in preschool, in ballet, in Xiao Zhen: pride. My own face burned. I knew at once that she was the reason behind my father's obsession and my three years of balletic misery. She was his ballet star. Faint handwriting in blue-black ink on the back of the photograph said "April 1981." I put the photo back, eased the drawer shut, and never spoke of it with anyone, not even Mom. Years later, when Mom told me the story of Cousin Tingting, my crazy uncle's daughter, who had died before I was even born, and whose death drove my uncle to madness, I knew she was the one in the photo, the girl I could never be.

I learned her full name when we brought my mom's urn to the niche in the columbarium where all the Chens were kept. It was my first time at the columbarium. I stood beside my father, my shoulders almost level with his because by then I'd grown tall and lean. Father grasped my hand in his clammy palm, but he wouldn't look at me. The last time he'd held my hand was that day at Miss Lu's; even at the hospital, as we watched my mom's heartbeat count down to zero, he'd held only hers. Since Mom died a week before Qingming, by the time the crematory gave her back to us, it was the weekend of the festival. So there we were, amongst throngs of pious descendants honoring the dead like we never had before. I had never seen so many people weeping out in the open. The two of us were not. I could have stood there forever, just to keep holding his hand. He stared at my mom's name, Hu Jinglin, freshly carved in stone, while I stared at my cousin's name, Chen Xianting, three slender characters in a vertical line, until it was time to go home.

It's noon. The sun is half hidden behind the clouds. Here on the eighty-second floor, I am so high up that the people walking around Lujiazui below look like ants. Xiao Zhen is still asleep beside me; we'd stumbled back drunk last night, craving twenty-four hour room service. Despite the pounding in my head from too much champagne and tequila, one clear thought has persisted since I woke up an hour ago: today I will call my father. After Xiao Zhen wakes up and goes home, I will call my father and tell him the truth about his daughter.

I will tell him that she does not live in London, and never has; that she does not go around the world selling insurance, preying on people's fear; that she does not own a Yorkshire terrier named Mimi who rides beside her in her convertible when she vacations in Devon in the summer; that she never dated that English banker, nor the Irish football player, nor the Scot with his own band; and that her name has never been Juliet.

I will tell him that I work at a bank in L.A., with data and numbers; that I don't like dogs and never take vacations, other than to come home; that I have dated thirteen Chinese guys over twelve years and none of them could pronounce his Chinese name right, and none of them was the one; and that although I might be Ming Chen there, instead of Chen Ming here, I have always and only been Ming.

I will tell him that two times a year, on March 30th and on Mom's birthday, I put on Chanel No. 5 and go to a Chinese restaurant to eat seven courses, stuffing myself until I puke. I will tell him that when I look in the mirror, sometimes the face I see is not mine at all, but my mother's, or that other, perfect face, tilted eternally toward the light.

Today I will call my father. I will answer the questions he's never asked. And I will not call room service instead.

Wulf Losee

IN A SEASON OF RAIN

"Others will enter the gates of the ferry, and cross from shore to shore;
Others will watch the run of the flood-tide..."
—Walt Whitman

i.

I lived through the season of rains in Hong Kong,
when monsoon storms blew in with a daily rhythm.
They bathed the glass stalagmites of Central
with layers of rippling water that washed
the diesel soot from the smooth planes of skyscrapers.

The dislodged soot gathered in carbon back-flows
where leaves and garbage slowed the storm water
until gutter-dams burst or overflowed to join the outwash.
The city is a vast organism, and these were the excretions of
this mechanical reef that rises from the mucus sea.

In the harbor, the oily ash of Hong Kong's metabolism
clotted in slicks behind breakwaters and under piers.
It grasped the sargasso mats of trash with rainbow fingers,
gripping the floating cups and plastic bags and bottles
until tides and harbor traffic washed them free.

ii.

The ferry gate buzzed open, and I was swept aboard—
part of the human river—and as I stepped on deck
the wind changed and I smelled the city's breath
of flowers and mist, rancid cooking oil, the exhaust of lorries—
all in an single exhalation between the storm-fronts.

As the ferry plowed across the harbor to the Kowloon side, the
grumble of diesel engines shook the benches.
I picked out words *Guangdonghua* above the noise,
the gossip shouted into phones, the arguments and
oaths and endless negotiations of Hong Kong *yan.*

Looking across the harbor I could see myself there joining
the flood-tides of people pulled by the gravities of
commerce—I project myself and I return—always
I am separated from the flow, yet I am a part of the flow. I
am both disintegrated and integrated into the scheme.

iii.

Neon light curdled in the puddles of the Kowloon streets and
shop-fronts billowed chilled air upon the sidewalks— cold-
fronts blew through the hanging plastic strips
into the living clouds of the human storms beneath
the random jostlings and multicolored battles of umbrellas.

Waterfalls of monsoon water poured off the awnings— they
bounced off the pavement in waves of spray— splashed again
and again into fountains by the traffic— until each drop was
shattered into molecules of mugginess that become the sweat
of the city that soaked my clothes.

As the storm paused to regather its energies, I could hear
the trickling rivulets and the stale dribbles of dehumidifiers. The
chorus roar of air conditioners echoed in the alleyways from the
rising stories of apartment windows they sounded like ghosts of
distant jets leaving the runways of old Kai Tak.

iv.

In Tsuen Wan I caught a red-roofed minibus before it fled
up the shoreline road—it took me through the hybrid landscapes of

wilderness and city that battled for the hillside slopes—
it meandered up the sharp curves of jungle roads—
then down again to the urban strips between the peaks and sea.

Above the concrete facings, camphor, bamboo and orchid trees
clung to sliding hillsides, waving in the storm-pulse winds.
From beneath the New Territories, the pressure of granite aquifers
pushed against the crust of the retaining walls, leaked through
algae-stained cracks, and spewed plumes of water out seepage pipes.

A troop of wet macaques, their gray fur matted with rain,
picked through the scattered spreadings of a garbage bag.
A bulky male stared at us and paced the roadside as we passed, and
then, our challenge having driven on, he bowed and cringed like that
wet tiger in Rousseau's painting of a jungle storm.

v.

I am the messenger of tides who speaks in alien codes.
I am the flotsam traveler who whirls on the influx and outflows of
identities as I drift through the slow histories of time—washed up
on this spit of land where the Pearl River's
muddy clouds join the currents of a sovereign River Ocean.

I call out my stop to the driver, and the man beside me
compliments me on my Cantonese in perfect English. My
umbrella is useless in this downpour. I am soaked. I try
to skirt the deeper puddles and gutter-waves,
and I bow into the rain like that gray-furred macaque.

The sun pokes through as I slog back to my rooms. Sometimes
the clouds break, and we wallow for a moment in the hot sky-
light of a day as it angles across a road.
I pause and breathe deeply as I enjoy my body's identity, and
I exhale before I wade back into the flood.

Doris Ferleger

Now the Smoke Bushes

We had no more to say, we agreed
as we sat face to face, your left ear
pointed heavenward. Left equals language,

I bring myself to recall how *round*
meant *hard*, how I was the only one
who could decipher

aphasia's lexicon
when you said,
The egg is cold and round,

and finally I said,
I think you mean cold and hard,
though I did not move

to make a soft and hot egg,
So it was like that.
How the round sad hard

soft-boiled egg lay
stuck to the bottom of the pot
brought upstairs

by the hired help who
had been trying to re-heat it,
or maybe she was tired

of trying, as I was,
to do anything more
to please a dying man.

~

Now seven months after your body
was sung into the earth
I think of the afternoon I put the spoon

in your mouth too quickly
wanting only to catch the last
rays of sun and you smiled and whispered,

Five more minutes
and so I blew on the broth
for what I foolishly hoped was

enough time
to spare me
from regrets.

~

Three a.m. snack. I swear I hear you
call my name from upstairs.
But I dismiss it

not because you are dead
but because you would never
be up at this hour.

~

Rib cage like wire, like balsa, like tabla.
Breaths, ten per minute. I thought it would be
easier for me once you were gone

to wake and write and breathe
to let the sun fill the earth and me give off
its loamy essence from our hillside.

Instead, I make you alive though I do not
picture us reliving anything—
not swimming side by side

in the turquoise sea year after year,
not planting the purple smoke bushes
months before your diagnosis. They are now

eight feet high and you are missing
the tufts that look like billowing filigree
smoke. They dazzle and burn the living.

Gregg Schroeder

Apartment 6D

SAYING GOODBYE TO MY FRIENDS in San Luis Obispo didn't take long. Summer is quiet on the Central California coast. Graduates disperse and everyone else who can gets out of town. I had just finished college and decided to put an ocean between the familiar and myself. Where I went didn't matter, but I chose Hong Kong—a straight line southwest from Avila Beach.

I landed in the sticky heat with a fresh passport, a one-year contract at a PR firm and not much else. I needed a place to live. That's what led me to Apartment 6D.

I'd been in town a week when I found the rooms in Sheung Wan. The block of flats was considered old—built in the 1950s' post-war rush to house the masses escaping revolution in China—and it was basic. Fifty-odd years later, it was also crumbling and life stained. It was hard to imagine it ever looking new.

The flat was small. Just a sparsely furnished bedroom and sitting room on the sixth floor, with a grubby bathroom that had a hose for showering, and an impromptu kitchen with a gas ring, metal sink and no fridge.

The main gate downstairs was more obstacle than entrance. Just past that, the rusted iron door was pulled permanently to the side exposing rows of tin mailboxes like crooked teeth. A few steps into the gloom, then the stairs curved to the left, up six floors to Flats A and B on one side, C and D on the other.

The building was close to downtown but off in a cheaper corner, where colonial Hong Kong began and now, well over a century-and-a-half later, was a run-down part of the city with slummy buildings, moldering temples, a neglected park and streets of wholesalers stocking everything from shark's fins and dried shellfish to herbs, snakes, bird cages and coffins.

And I loved it. I looked forward to diving into a new culture; the taste of different foods, the sound of an unknown language. After far too long doing what was expected of me, I was going to live for myself. I was going to have an adventure. I was going to get to know people and create my own future.

The property agent had taken care of the details and given me the key. So I was surprised that the first neighbor I met was my landlady.

"This building is very good. Very clean. The neighbors are quiet," Mrs. Chan declared, standing in my doorway, peering past me. "You need anything, you just come upstairs. I live on the roof." She stood for a moment, looking me up and down. Then, apparently approving, she nodded and left.

What a nice old lady, I thought as I closed the door after her.

Life in the new building was quiet, as Mrs. Chan had said. I never saw any other neighbors, though I'd see evidence of them: the red lights of a household shrine glowing like eyes, through blinds; burnt paper offerings outside a doorway; the scent of incense everywhere.

In the first few days, Mrs. Chan appeared again and again, late in the evening or early in the morning before I was up.

"Here's a chair!" she called, lugging a cast-off down the stairs. "Here's a better table!" and "That mattress on the floor is terrible!" She said it as if she'd never seen it before. "You come up on Saturday and I'll give you a newer one."

I was in no position to turn down free furniture. I'd arrived with one suitcase and not much money. And I was increasingly curious to see how she lived, on the roof.

Saturday morning I headed up the narrow stairs to the rooftop. Certainly Mrs. Chan was up, but I tapped quietly on the door just in case.

"Bin go leih ga?!" she whispered hoarsely. She opened the wooden door,

just a crack. I could see her eyes in the shadows, through the iron grating. She brightened and stood straight. "Oh! It's you."

She let me in and told me to wait. Her apartment was a jumbled mass of shapes. I made out old furniture, television sets and boxes; the kitchen area was piled with pans, a wok, dishes—some clean, some dirty. A pot of something burbled on the stove. When my eyes adjusted to the half-light I could see that the walls were made of scrap wood and the ceiling of corrugated iron. A hatch led out of the main room and onto an open area of the roof.

"Pick a frame," she told me, waving a hand lightly toward the shadowy end of the room. A row of metal bedsteads leaned against the wall. "I'll get a mattress." She opened a door and out came the sound of light snoring. Mrs. Chan closed the door behind her but re-emerged a moment later, tugging an upended mattress into the main room. When the far end came through the doorway, a girl of about twelve was holding onto it. She had long hair and wore striped pajamas. Her face, shyly averted.

"Oh! Really, I don't want to take your ..." I paused to guess, "... *daughter's* mattress."

"It's fine," the old lady said. "Her room is full of them."

Mrs. Chan passed the mattress off to me and I bent and tugged and yanked it through her front door, down the stairs and into my flat. Soon my new bed was set up and the old mattress thrown over the railing onto the rubbish heap below.

The bed spruced up my narrow bedroom, but I felt odd taking it out from under the girl. *A second-hand mattress is better when you don't know who slept on it last,* I thought.

In the following weeks, I focused my attention on work. Although I had a degree in graphic design, the PR agency hired me as an account executive for English-speaking clients overseas. It wasn't the most direct route to a design career, but it was a crack in the doorway to the business world, in a new place, and would be a good way to learn about running my own company someday, without falling back on my parents and the family business. It was a sharp climb: learning about regional markets and rice bowl industries; looking for signs of emerging sectors and calculating market share; studying the competition and understanding the internal power structure; making friends and alliances; finding the best cheap lunch.

The party neighborhood of Lan Kwai Fong was on the way home, so drinks after work were common. These often stretched into long evenings of laughing and eating, too. The narrow streets were packed every sundown with revelers—bankers, brokers, teachers, journalists—all celebrating as if it were a never-ending Friday night. These young, beautiful people clearly had jobs that paid well—better than mine—and well enough to give them unbelievable amounts of money for cocktails and for delicacies flown in from Canada, New Zealand and France, prepared by chefs trained in China, India, Italy and beyond.

My colleagues and I rooted out the lower-brow dishes—local-style Chinese, Thai, Malay, Vietnamese—in greasy-chopsticks restaurants squeezed into upstairs flats and alleyways down below. Affordable Hong Kong may not have always been strictly above board, but it was not hard to find even in the high-rent district of Central, once you knew where to look.

Despite our ingenuity, it got to be expensive. I didn't manage to save any money, but it was early days and I needed to invest in a social life. And it was beginning to pay off. I found a group of guys to go running with on the weekends, and I'd been invited by a couple of girls in the office to a boat party on the Dragon Boat Festival holiday.

The day of the holiday, squally showers cleared just as about twenty of us assembled at the pier to wait for the trim white cruiser that would take us around the island to the main event, just off the beach at Stanley.

"Is this your first time to watch the races?" one of the girls asked, when we were gathered on board. Carol had a pretty smile. Her bobbed hair was pushed back behind her ears.

I told her it was. "It's a lot of fun," she said. "You don't even have to watch the dragon boats. There's plenty of food and beer—we usually just lie in the sun and relax."

It was a beautiful day to be out on the water. Everyone was up on the roof of the boat, laughing and playing cards in the steamy sunshine. Victoria Harbour was choppy with ferries and the flotilla of junks and cruisers heading to the races on the south side. On both shores, skyscrapers glinted in the June sun, green hills behind them.

We sailed past the heart of the city, skirted Green Island with its defunct lighthouse and headed past suburban Pok Fu Lam, the university, Queen Mary Hospital and the luxury housing estates. These were the neighborhoods our company managers called home and the staff aspired to, but from what I could see they were simply collections of bigger blocks of flats, with better views. My flat looked out on the blank wall of a school, but theirs faced the sea, peaceful-looking Lamma Island with its joss stick power plant chimneys, and the mist-shrouded peak of Lantau Island.

Entering busy Lamma Channel, container ships passed our starboard side as we hugged the coastline. At Aberdeen, we waved to the fishing boats, then to the rollercoaster riders at Ocean Park, perched on the hill. I was taken by the contrast to my gritty parts of town: green hills, mansions on cliffs overlooking sandy coves, peaceful inlets, a waterfall. In my neighborhood, I had to look straight up to see the sky.

Repulse Bay water-skiers came into view before we rounded the Stanley peninsula and entered the bay. Party boats were already lined up, jostling in two rows along the race lanes, but we found a slot. Competing teams dressed in bright colors shouted and laughed. No matter that we didn't know the team names. The spectacle was enough. The sleek boats, each brought to life with a dragon head, pounded through the waves powered by twenty paddlers; a leader at the front banging a drum to set the rhythm; a sweep at the back to keep the course. The crowd on the beach and the partiers on the bobbing junks were one big extended family—one that I was suddenly a part of—all eating, drinking, cheering and having a good time.

I could almost have been back in California, though if I were, I wouldn't have been out on the water in the middle of the action. Back then—only a few weeks earlier—I spent every weekend, every holiday, behind a pile of textbooks or the handle of a broom, just keeping things going until I could finish school and get out on my own; get far from family interference.

Despite the distance I'd put between my old home and me, one dream recurred: *I'm at the bottom of an empty swimming pool, the one in our backyard when I was a boy. High above sticking his nose over the edge is Buddy, alive again and cocking his mongrel head to one side. I want to get out, to be with my dog. I claw with bare hands and feet—scratching away at the smooth inside of the pool's dry shell, as Buddy did when he wanted to run after a car or another dog but was held fast on his leash. That little dog would fire like a bullet if let go, as he did the day he was struck down. Just the same, I'd rocket out of this pool if I could only get a grip.*

I opened my eyes and saw the lush green escarpment above Stanley, not the low dry hills of California. My thoughts were interrupted by shouts from the crowd as the heartbeat of the dragon boats—*dum-dum-dum*—rang louder and louder through the air.

"I've always wanted to join in," a colleague said, also swept up in the excitement. Nick's face was already rosy with the sun and the beer.

"It would be great, wouldn't it?" I replied. "Looks like a pretty hard workout."

"Yeah. And the serious teams practice a lot—mornings before work and at night as long as it's light. You wouldn't get soft like most office jockeys."

We decided, then and there, to join a team.

Through the rest of the summer I got up early on paddling days and met my new friends at Deep Water Bay. The mornings were bright and hot, and the humidity lay like a sopping blanket over the island. It was good to get away from the stifling city and out onto the water, where there might be a breeze. We worked hard to follow the beat of the drum and build our paddling muscles, but we laughed a lot, too. We would meet up after work and I stayed out later and later drinking and planning with my teammates. Bleary-eyed by evening's end, I enjoyed coming home to 6D. The place wasn't much to look at, but as soon as I hit the mattress I was in sweet dreamland. Each sunrise, I woke up surprisingly refreshed and ready for another morning on the water or long hours in the office, the day's demands ahead.

One evening, on my way up the stairs to my rooms, I saw a longhaired girl. I was sure it was Mrs. Chan's daughter, in her thin pajamas and bare feet. "Hey, there!" I called. The girl must have been as surprised as I was because she didn't even turn around. She ran up the stairs to the rooftop flat. I didn't see her face; just a flick of her black hair trailing behind.

My new Hong Kong life was going well, but as autumn approached I began to think about my apartment. Colleagues teased me, asking, "When's the flat-warming?" We all lived in cramped quarters and knew that inviting friends over wasn't really expected, but it got me thinking. My place was certainly too shabby to reveal to friends. I didn't even have a television or any music. No wonder I was staying out so much.

And the early mornings and late nights were catching up with me. I realized I felt tired.

So I decided to spend more time at home, fixing up the place. I hadn't seen Mrs. Chan since she gave me the mattress; her free "upgrades" were practical, but not aesthetically pleasing. I tried rearranging the furniture, but that didn't help: the dining table was too big; the folding stools around it were—well, they were folding stools. The lacquered sideboard was chipped and gouged. There was no comfortable place to sit so I bought a reading chair from a discount store and lugged it up the stairs and squeezed it next to the kitchen door. I plugged MP3 speakers into the niche where the household altar was meant to go. Early on I'd found a second-hand fridge through the "Expat Sale" section of the newspaper, and now bought a few Chinese-painted tea mugs that came with lids, some bowls and basic cutlery. The bedroom was all bed, so there wasn't much I could do, other than to find bedding that looked better than the grandmother-ish pastels that I had purchased with the limited cash I'd brought to Hong Kong.

No matter what I did, the apartment didn't seem to improve. So I resolved to spend the upcoming long weekend tackling the problem. I could paint the sitting room—maybe that would help—and I could look for a bright rug to distract from the putty-colored linoleum covering the floor.

It meant begging off a couple of outings, though. My dragon boat team had planned a barbecue in the New Territories, and some friends from work were going to Macau for a weekend of gambling.

"Come on," one of the guys from the paddling team said to me. "We've been talking about this for weeks. The weather is great. It's too nice to stay indoors. Some girls are coming. Remember Carol? The promotions manager we met at the Dragon Boat Festival? She asked if you'd be there. What are you going to do at home anyway?"

Of course he was right. It would be good to get out into the countryside. I would skip the overnighter to Macau, but I could go to the Thursday night barbecue. It would only be a few hours.

We took taxis out to Sai Kung Country Park—about fifteen of us—right after work. It took almost an hour to get there. The barbecue pits were crowded and it was well after dark, with the moon just rising above the trees, reflecting off the water at Tai Long Wan.

There was loads to eat: chicken, pork chops, corn-on-the-cob and even roast bananas. But I wasn't very hungry.

Carol sat next to me, tucked her hair behind her ears, and asked me to hand her a drink from the cooler. I passed her a San Miguel and we thudded beer cans. "Cheers."

I looked away to the curls of smoke. *Maybe if I rearrange the furniture,* I thought. *I can fold up the dining table and get it out of the way—use a coffee table for eating.*

"Hey, you're burning that chicken wing," Nick told me, nudging my barbecue fork out of the flames.

"Sorry. I must have drifted off."

"Here," Carol said, taking the fork from my hand and putting the wing onto a paper plate. "It's not too bad. Let's just pull off some of that burned skin and it will be OK."

I must have been out of shape, despite the all paddling and climbing those stairs to 6D every day, because after my weekend of painting and domestic chores, I was exhausted. Or maybe I was coming down with a cold. Anyway, Monday night after work I went straight home to rest. The apartment, in the gloaming, was depressing—the fresh white paint didn't help the sitting room at all, besides making the other rooms look shabbier by comparison—but it was good to be home. I switched on the fan, got into my soft bed to read, and fell asleep for the night.

The next morning, like all mornings then, I dragged myself to the office. By mid-afternoon I was out of energy. It felt as though I'd lost half of myself. All I could think about was getting into my sweet-smelling bed. Just thinking of it was a balm.

A week later—it was mid-week—I needed to wait for the delivery of the coffee table I'd ordered, so I convinced my boss to let me work from home for the morning. The delivery guy was late and didn't come until the afternoon, so my boss grudgingly let me stay away all day. I got a lot done, including finishing up a report early and emailing it to my boss well before he needed it.

That got me thinking: *Why not work at home more often? Regularly.* I had my laptop—I could get a lot more done than in the office, without all the distractions.

While I was considering ways to approach my boss, I decided to see a doctor. She said I had glandular fever—whatever that was. I went back to the office, but didn't feel well at all. Turns out, glandular fever is another name for mononucleosis. I ended up staying home for ten days.

It felt so good to sleep in that bed.

After a few days, I was well enough to be bored. And then I realized, if I could show my boss I could get work done while I was sick, he might let me work at home a few days a week, after I recovered.

I finished reports, I started new ones; I caught up on back correspondence, I initiated leads. My boss was reluctant to give me any work, but after three days I had run out of routine tasks, so told him I could help with anything urgent. I ended up writing a PowerPoint presentation for him and doing background research on potential customers.

When I was back in the office, he took me to lunch.

"You did a great job while you were off," he told me when the plates were cleared away and the coffee arrived. "I think you got more done than you do when you're at your desk." He grinned. "But seriously, I wanted to thank you for stepping up, even when you weren't feeling well."

I expressed my gratitude. "I didn't really feel that bad after a while. I was just contagious." I paused. "But I do think I can accomplish more if I work from home—a day or so a week. There are fewer distractions."

I had prepared my speech at home. We could do it on a trial basis, I said, a day here and there. If it didn't work, there'd be no loss. If it did, I'd bring in more business.

I sipped my coffee, to stall and gauge his reaction. "What do you think?"

It took some negotiation, but he agreed. I started working at home, one day a week. It seemed like a good thing at first, because I was still very tired—the thought of dragging myself to the office five days a week was unbearable. I could just manage to get up and work using my laptop, at the coffee table. Once I got started, though, I felt stronger and could be extremely productive.

One day per week turned into two, and occasionally three. I didn't want to push it—aside from Nick, my other colleagues had stopped socializing with me. I had the sense they thought the boss preferred me, gave me special treatment. But I didn't care. It suited me just fine. They were always planning get-togethers and I'd had enough of that. I was just so tired; I'd close my eyes and feel as though I melted into the walls of 6D. All I cared about was being home as much as possible, where I could crawl into bed and have a quick nap whenever exhaustion overcame me.

Around this time my phone stopped ringing. I'd quit going to dragon boat practice. I had only been answering work email—nothing from friends—so those friends gave up trying to reach me and I didn't contact them. No Facebook. My parents, who still wrote letters, continued to write but I didn't bother collecting the mail except to clear out my mailbox when it got full. I dumped the contents onto the sideboard without looking through them.

Nick noticed the change and asked me if everything was OK. When I was working at home, he called several times, saying Carol had asked about me. He'd suggest we meet up after work. I always told him it wasn't convenient. After a while, I didn't answer when I saw Nick's number. He sent text messages but eventually that, too, stopped altogether.

I didn't feel isolated. The more time I spent at home, the more I noticed flickers of life around my apartment building. At first, I felt I was being watched, but when I'd look out the window or peek through the metal gate in my front doorway, I saw no one.

But gradually I did start to see the neighbors. They were mostly old folks, and I suspected they weren't comfortable talking with me because they didn't acknowledge me on the stairs. I tried to set them at ease by using a basic Cantonese greeting Carol taught me: *"Jou sahn! Sihk jo faahn meih a?"* They walked right past. I never saw Mrs. Chan. And though I was sleeping in her daughter's old bed, I hadn't thought of the girl since the evening I glimpsed her on the stairs. That is, not until I ran into her outside my door.

"Hi," I said, startled. She was so close I wanted to touch her long black hair, falling around her shoulders. Like the two earlier times, she was wearing pajamas. I felt like I was intruding, even though I was on the common landing.

She said nothing. She just gazed downward.

"H-how is your mother?" I didn't know what to say, but I wanted to keep looking at her. There was something familiar, comforting about her. "I've not spoken to her in a long time." She hung her head so I couldn't see her eyes. She tugged nervously at her pajama top. All of a sudden, the girl turned and went up the stairs.

"Don't bother about her." The voice came from behind me and made me jump.

"What?" I said, looking around.

"She doesn't socialize," the old man was standing right behind me. I don't know where he could have come from. "Come have a cup of tea. It's time we got to know you."

I'd been living there for months and had never seen this man. And suddenly after all the silence, a neighbor was being friendly.

"Thank you. That would be nice."

It turned out his apartment was just across the landing from mine. He pushed aside the gate with a rolling clunk. "Let me introduce my wife," he said, just as an old lady came out from the kitchen. "Hello, young man," she said with a flame of recognition in her eye. "It's nice to finally see you."

I sat down. Their apartment was the mirror image of 6D. Different furniture, but the overall feel was the same: tired and worn out. It was crammed to the ceiling with stuff: books, papers, an electric fan, child-sized stools around a small table, an ancestral shrine. The blinds were rolled up and the gray sunlight was streaming in. The lady—I didn't catch her name—brought me a steaming cup of tea.

"Have you lived here a long time?" I asked the husband.

"Oh, yes," he said, glancing at his wife. "We have been here a very long time. Since we first came to Hong Kong, in fact."

"Then you must know everyone in the building," I said. "I've only spoken to Mrs. Chan, upstairs."

"We know everyone in the building," the old lady said. "We used to know everyone in the neighborhood. But we don't get out like we used to."

After that, I would see the old couple more often, then nearly every day. We'd exchange *Good mornings*; they'd bring me treats: moon cakes, slow-cooked soup, sesame paste buns or rice balls wrapped in lotus leaves. They looked after me like doting grandparents.

The best thing about working at home was being able to sleep. I now spent most of my time in my bedroom, working on my laptop in bed. The light there was just right; it was the most comfortable spot. Also there was this fragrance. It was sharp and sweet. I didn't know what it was, or where it came from. The freshly-laundered sheets? Incense through the window? Chinese medicine on a stove somewhere? But it was always there and it calmed me. When I got tired, I could set my computer aside and take a catnap. I found I needed this more and more. I wasn't getting enough exercise. Once I caught up on sleep, I would go out for a run. If only I could get enough sleep.

Chilled by the winter monsoon, I would wake up several times throughout the night. My eyes would pop open suddenly. I wouldn't be tired; in fact, I'd feel refreshed in the cool dry stillness of my room. I'd pull the covers around me and work for a few hours until my eyelids began to droop. Then I'd set things aside and curl up for another nap.

I spent more time with the old couple across the landing, and with their tea guests. It was from them that I learned Mrs. Chan was landlady for the whole building. Several old couples would come to call, a few middle-aged people and younger ones, too; even children. The adults all dressed like they were out of an old photograph: women in simple tops and dark trousers, men in black or gray. The children wore one of the perennially out-of-date school uniforms seen everywhere in Hong Kong. We would be introduced, but I never caught anyone's name, and after the first few meetings it was awkward to confess I didn't know, so I let it pass, addressing everyone as Uncle, Auntie, Grandmother or Little Brother.

One evening, I went out into the corridor to leave my garbage for pickup. Mrs. Chan's daughter passed me, walking up the stairs to her apartment. I didn't say anything, but this time she turned and looked me in the eye with a strange half-smile. Then, she ran up the stairs and into her flat. I heard the clunk of the iron gate.

Curious, I followed her up. Through the gate, I caught a whiff of a mixture of Chinese medicine, steamed rice and roast chicken.

"Don't worry, Ga-jie," I heard Mrs. Chan say, over the clatter of a pot lid. "It won't be long now. We have almost enough." She turned off the stove. "Soon you will feel strong enough to go outside. Soon you can play. Soon you will be perfectly fine." She put a serving of chicken on a plate and a mound of rice in a bowl. "Now, come and have your dinner."

But instead of setting the chicken and rice on the table, Mrs. Chan walked to the altar. I craned my neck and peered through the window. She bowed her head to the black-and-white photo at the center, with the red lights above, and placed the food between two candles. Then she bowed three more times. When she stepped aside, I could see the photo clearly. It was a picture of the girl.

Sweat was running down my arms and legs. Mrs. Chan came toward the window and I didn't want to get caught spying. I rushed down the stairs and into my flat.

As soon as I closed the door, I was startled by the sound of the bell. I was even more alarmed when I opened the door to see my landlady standing calmly outside.

"Mrs. Chan!" She must have seen me at her window. I didn't know what to say. "It's ... nice to see you."

She didn't acknowledge me. In fact, she didn't even seem to see me.

"This building is very good. Very clean," she said. "The neighbors are quiet."

She appeared to be looking past me, over my shoulder.

"Er, yes," I stumbled. "You're right."

"You need anything, you just come upstairs. I live on the roof." Mrs. Chan nodded and left.

I reached to close the door after her. But the door shut before I could touch it. I stepped back. Then I turned. And I saw him. He was young, fresh and well dressed. He was standing in the middle of my apartment, turning back to boxes I had never seen before—unpacking.

Leslie Munnelly

Tonic Immobility

"IT'S CALLED 'TONIC IMMOBILITY'," I say, wrestling the young bonnethead onto its back. The shark resists, thrashing its tail as it tries to escape my firm grasp on its pectoral and dorsal fins. Above me, on cleaning detail, Katie drops her scrub brush and swims to the bottom. Gabe follows a few seconds later although I know he disapproves. It's my first time leading the dive show, and I'm supposed to stick to protocol; demonstrating tonic immobility on a two foot shark is not in the program. He shakes his head, avoiding the teeth of the struggling fish as I manage to flip it over. Immediately, the shark ceases to move. It lies completely still, resting atop Katie and Gabe's arms as I turn back to the crowd and resume my lecture. "Tonic immobility," I repeat. "Does anyone know what it means?"

Margaret waves her microphone at the shadowed faces of the crowd gathered before the tank. "Anyone?" she says. "Come on…take a guess."

"Is it dead?" asks a little girl. She's no more than four or five years old, and, from the tremble in her voice, I'm sure she's about to cry.

"No," I say hastily; "she's actually in a state of temporary paralysis. Once I've turned her over, she'll resume her normal behavior, but for now, while she's on her back, she can't move; she's immobile." I look beyond the glass of the big tank, over the sea of uncomprehending faces to Margaret who's shaking her head. "Scientists believe that it's a defense tactic that sharks use in high-stress situations; but don't worry, she's okay. See?" I grab the bonnethead by the fins and flip her back onto her belly. With a powerful thrust of her tail, she shoots away to resume her endless circling of the tank, avoiding me, and Katie, and Gabe like the intruders we are. The three of us are swimming in the Cape Fear Shoals Tank, her pristine, utopian, 235,000 gallon prison.

A kid in the front row with scraggly hair and an orange t-shirt, pokes the girl standing beside him, a blonde about ten years old who's probably his sister. He whispers something I can't hear and she gives him a dirty look. "You," I say, pointing directly at him. "What's your name?"

He startles like I've caught him stealing penny candy. "Who, me?"

I smile from behind my mask. It's a helmet actually, a helmet that pumps in air, allowing me to free-breath without using a mouthpiece. It's also equipped with a microphone and ear piece so that I can interact with my audience from within the tank - with the help of Margaret and her microphone on the outside, that is. Now, Margaret holds the mic up to the boy I've singled out. "Tell everyone your name, honey," she says, helpfully.

Contrary to her kindly appearance, Margaret's anything *but* a sweet little old lady. Gabe, Katie, and I've had a summer's worth of experience with the woman, so we know the truth, but the audience sees what she wants them to see: a nice elderly grandmother who volunteers her spare time at Fort Fisher solely for the love of fish and children.

"Cooper," he says, falling for her act.

"Cooper, what?"'

"Cooper Scully."

I turn to the left and then the right, a showman's trick that Jason showed me, intended to incorporate the entire audience. That done, I wink at a little girl and her mother before I turn back to young Cooper. "Where're you from, Coop?"

The boy regards me through the glass of the aquarium and shrugs. "Nowhere that you've ever heard of," he says, solemnly.

"Let me take a wild guess," I say. "North Carolina."

He shakes his head.

"Come on," I coax. "I've been around. Tell me…where're you from?"

"Don't ask," he responds.

"If you tell me, I'll take you on a tour of the pump room." I wait but get no response. "Come on, Coop, your very own tour of the aquarium. Now tell me…where're you from?"

Cooper Scully stares at the floor and shuffles his feet. I can see indecision in his eyes when he looks up again. "Onondaga," he says, finally.

"*Onondaga*?" I repeat. "Onondaga, New York?"

He nods. The girl beside him shirks away like he's diseased.

"Wow! The Empire State!" I'm excited. I can't help myself. I, too, am a transplant from New York, albeit five years ago.

"My daddy doesn't call it the Empire State," he says, his mouth close to Margaret's microphone.

She's not smiling as broadly now that she knows he's a Yankee, but she fights to maintain appearances, nodding her encouragement. It's tourist season and there are certainly plenty of people from north of the Mason-Dixon Line in this morning's crowd. She knows she can't afford to alienate them. "What does he call it, Cooper?" she says. "The Big Apple?"

He shakes his head.

She tries again. "The Great State of New York?"

"No," he says. "He calls it 'The State of Northern Aggression'."

I laugh along with the rest of the crowd, and, before my helmet, one hundred bubbles dissipate in the aquamarine water. "The State of Northern Aggression," I repeat, shaking my head. I've heard the term before in one of my undergraduate classes…Appalachian history, I think it was.

The boy named Cooper shrugs. His shoulders are thin to the point of scrawny. The orange t-shirt hangs loose on his small frame. "Alright, Coop from Onondaga," I say, getting down to business, "do you have any questions for me?"

He looks puzzled. "About what?"

"Anything," I say. "Anything you want to know about the fish or the tank."

He thinks on it a moment. "That thing you did with the shark… can people do it?"

"Tonic immobility? Nope. It's a special trick for fish. If a person tried it, he'd drown." I sweep my eyes across the crowd of kids and their parents, my voice grave. "So make sure you all take swimming lessons, okay?"

I get a few appreciative nods from the adults in the audience and open my mouth to continue my presentation just as a heavy-set woman in shorts and an orange T-shirt, identical to Cooper's, pushes her way through to the front. "There you are," she says, grabbing my young protégé by the collar. "Didn't I tell you to stay with the group?"

I watch through the glass as Cooper plants his feet, resisting her attempts to uproot him. "They're doing the dive show," he protests.

His captor squints at the tank, noticing me for the first time. I wave half-heartedly. Katie and Gabe wave, too, before retrieving their scrub brushes from the sandy bottom to resume cleaning. Not falling for my charm, she scowls and propels Cooper away. With my back-ups on the upper level, and my biggest fan gone, I'm left alone on the bottom of the tank before a lackluster crowd.

A few people wander off, toward the jellyfish and I realize that I'm failing to keep their attention, distracted as I am by Cooper Scully's drama. Kicking myself into gear, I swim toward the coral outcropping where the moray eel hides, resuming my spiel. When I turn to face the crowd, Cooper is gone. I can just make out his orange t-shirt as his chaperone steers him into the conservatory where the rest of his group, undoubtedly, are crowded around the alligator exhibit, another favorite of the facility.

Margaret smiles but her mouth is tense. I can almost hear her thoughts through the glass: *Good going, jackass. You really fucked this one up!*

Ignoring her pursed lips and narrowed eyes, I continue my speech, completing the rest of the presentation without a hitch. When the demonstration winds down, I wave goodbye with a few last words of encouragement to all of my budding young marine biologist fans. "Work hard in school and ask your parents to donate a few dollars to the North Carolina Aquarium at Fort Fisher! It takes *your* help to maintain this lovely facility." Then, I kick to the top of the tank and follow Katie and Gabe up the ladder to await the tongue-lashing that's sure to come from everyone's not-so-favorite grandma.

Katie rinses our wetsuits and drapes them over the pumps. With luck, they'll be dry enough to squeeze into by the time we suit up for the second show. "Do you want to eat lunch at the beach?" she says.

Gabe nods. He pulls his shirt over his stomach, his folds of flab creased by the seams of the wetsuit he'd worn into the tank. For some reason, God knows why, he insists on picking one that's a size or two too small. Katie says he probably thinks it makes him look slimmer, but we're agreed that he'd have to lose 40 pounds to pull that off. The three of us grab our coolers and head down the stairs. I unlock the deadbolt on the side entrance and we exit the building, crossing the parking lot to the path that leads to the ocean.

It was raining hard when I arrived at the aquarium two hours ago, but now the clouds have disappeared and the sun is blinding. It's hot; hot like only North Carolina can be in the middle of August, with humidity high enough to drown a cat out of water. Katie's wearing shorts, her bikini top, and yellow flip-flops. She's walking two steps ahead of me, but close enough that I could touch her back if I wanted to, freckled and pink from the burn that she got last week. I restrain the urge to reach out and peel the wafer-thin skin between her shoulder blades where it flakes.

Katie's Irish—Ireland Irish—and too fair to go outside without sunscreen; but we have a second show this afternoon and sunscreen is a big no-no in the tank. "I can't believe you tried the tonic immobility thing," she says now, swatting a mosquito away as she negotiates the last yards of the trail.

"It wasn't too hard." I hope I sound modest. Katie's a graduate student, focused on fisheries biology. I'm a year behind, just beginning grad school when classes start next week. I'd planned to attend Scripts Institute out in San Diego, but changed my mind when UNCW offered me a great financial aid package complete with an assistantship and stipend. It was an offer I couldn't refuse; an offer made sweeter by the fact that Katie still has a year and a half to go before she graduates.

Katie's full name is Katroina Brigid McDermott. We met in the Benthic Ecology Lab where I volunteer a few days a week. She didn't pay much attention to me at first, not until this summer, when we took a research diving class together. After getting our certifications, she told me that she'd offered to volunteer at the aquarium, so I did too. She's a year older than me, and, to tell you the truth, I'm kind of crazy about her. And I think she knows it.

Behind me, Gabe pants as he struggles to keep up. Katie walks fast, with the natural gait of an athlete, which Gabe is not. He's the kid who spent his childhood playing Halo on the computer; the kid picked last in gym class. We reach the sand and walk to the waterline kicking off our shoes. The ocean's warm, almost like bathwater. Katie puts her cooler down and strips off her shorts. "Last one in's shark bait," she calls over her shoulder, sprinting into the surf.

Gabe picks up her things and moves them back a few feet, away from the incoming tide. He sits in the sand and opens his lunch box. Gabe never goes swimming. Katie says it's because he's embarrassed to take his shirt off. She's probably right…I would be, too, if I were that fat. "Don't eat my sandwich," I tell him, pulling my North Carolina Aquarium t-shirt over my head and tossing it onto the sand. Gabe gives a disgusted snort. "I mean it," I say. "If you eat my sandwich, you're dead."

Following Katie's footsteps in the sand, I run down the beach and dive in as she ducks beneath another wave. Her hair is long and dark red. It floats in the water like seaweed. *Rhodophyceae.* Another breaker rolls toward shore. Katie's hair disappears beneath the froth. Down the beach, there's a group of kids in orange t-shirts. They're playing at the waterline, but none of them are swimming. I duck beneath another wave and then a third. When I surface, Katie's gone, back on the beach next to Gabe. A boy with scraggly hair stands beside her. I leave the water and walk to where they sit, eating their lunch. As I get closer, I read the back of his t-shirt: *SES! The Summer Experience!* It's Cooper, I'm sure.

"Hey, Coop," I say, shaking water on Gabe's head.

"Aw, Jeese," he whines. "You got my sandwich wet."

"It's just water and salt."

Cooper snickers. I give the kid points for his sense of humor.

"Look at all those little brats," Gabe says, pointing at Cooper's compatriots, 100 yards away; "they probably peed in the water and now it's all over my lunch."

"We're not allowed to go in the water," Coop tells him.

"Why not?" Katie says. She's got an apple in one hand and a Diet Pepsi in the other. I offer up my bag of potato chips and she takes a handful, passing it to Coop who does the same and gives the bag back to me without passing it on to Gabe. He gives us all a dirty look.

"Why can't you go in the water?" Katie repeats. "Can't you swim?"

"I can swim," Coop says, a little too quickly; "we're just not allowed to. Camp rules."

"Pretty lame summer camp," I say.

He nods.

Gabe wrinkles his nose and takes a bite of his ham and cheese. Mayonnaise squirts out the side. It makes me want to gag. I turn back to Cooper. "SES; what's that stand for?"

"Southport Elementary School," he says, his eyes glued to Gabe's mouth as he chews and swallows.

"Southport?" I frown. "Southport, North Carolina? I thought you said you're from New York."

"I am." Coop extends his hand for more chips. I give him the bag and offer him half my sandwich. He takes it without asking what it is. "My dad grew up in Southport. He met my mom in New York. We moved here last year after he lost his job. We're living with my grandma and grandpa."

"How do you like it?" Katie asks.

"How the hell do you think I like it? I hate it here…I want to go home."

Katie shakes her head. "What a mouth you've got on you, lad; how old are you now, seven?"

"Eight. Almost."

She offers him a mini Milky Way from her private stash. I'm amazed. Chocolate is Katie's biggest vice; she guards her Milky Ways with the fanaticism of a zealot. She pats the sand next to her and Coop sits down. When she speaks again, her accent is thick and kind, and, well, Irish. "Come now, don't be blaspheming God and the wee baby Jaysus," she says. "Southport can't be all that bad; it's right on the water! Don't you like the beach?"

Coop never gets a chance to answer. From one hundred yards away, there's the sound of a whistle as the camp leaders gather up their young charges. The fat woman in shorts waves her arms overhead and begins to march in our direction. "I've gotta go," he says, jumping to his feet.

"But you never got your private tour," I protest. I like the kid. He reminds me of my nephew; my sister's son.

"Maybe next time," he says. "We're catching the 2 o'clock ferry."

The ferry, a twenty minute ride that covers four miles, is a lifeline that connects the peninsula of Fort Fisher State Park to the town of Southport. Carrying pedestrians as well as vehicles, it crosses the mouth of the Cape Fear River where it empties into the Atlantic, saving over an hour of driving time and allowing easy access to the park, aquarium, and Kure and Carolina Beaches from points south. Close enough to walk to, the water between here and Southport turns a few miles into a million for a boy Cooper's age. Unless his mom or dad agrees to bring him over he'll never be back. He knows it, and we know it. I strip off my T-shirt and toss it to him. "This is yours."

"Don't you need it?" he says. "I mean…for your job?"

"It's okay; I've got an extra in my truck." I look down the beach. The fat lady's moving quicker now. Her face is as red as a plum tomato. "Hurry up; run…your class is leaving. You don't want to get in trouble."

Cooper Scully hides his disappointment behind a quick wave and trots down the beach saving me, Katie, and Gabe the trouble of voicing our worthless words of consolation.

"I guess we should head back, too," Gabe says, eyeing his watch. He struggles to his feet and begins to retrace his steps. Reluctantly, Katie and I follow his lead.

"You've got quite a way with kids," I say, walking beside her to the brush where the trail begins.

She laughs, her face pink although we've scarcely been outside for half an hour. "I should…I've got six of them back home."

Ahead of us, Gabe stops dead in his tracks. "You've got six kids?!"

"Brothers, Gabriel. Six brothers and two sisters. I'm the oldest of nine."

"Nine kids?" Gabe frowns. "Who the hell has nine kids these days?"

Katie shrugs. "Half the families in Tralee, that's who." She waits a moment as Gabe scratches his head and adds, "What do you expect, Gabriel? We're good Catholics, after all, aren't we? We're supposed to procreate!"

Back inside the aquarium, the three of us spread out among the smaller exhibits to scrub glass and clean coral. There're a few other volunteers around by this time, mostly students from the university, split between the two areas of the building: marine biologists with us in the marine area, and botanists and zoologists in the Cape Fear Conservatory. Gabe disappears to straighten up the pump room while Katie mans the touch pool. I'm stationed off the main room with the stingrays and sand sharks. Around us, heavy streams of visitors crowd the exhibits.

At two-fifteen, I take the stairs to the third floor where Gabe and Katie are already suited up and ready to dive. Katie's sulking because I get to do the demonstration again. I point out the fact that she still has four dives to complete before she's finished with her probationary period. Gabe, who started volunteering in mid-July, has eight dives to go.

We enter the tank and begin to clean, this time by the bottom, until Margaret appears with a group of people. She dims the lights and clears her throat. On cue, I drop my scrub brush and take my position in the front center of the tank as she begins her introduction. Katie tugs at my arm and motions to the shark that I'd demonstrated tonic immobility on earlier. I shake my head; after the first show, Margaret had been extremely clear about how much she liked my stunt with the immature bonnethead: she didn't. Instead, I begin my discourse with a few facts about the tank: how many gallons it holds, that the "coral" formations are actually made from a plastic compound that's simulated to look like a reef, and that the kelp and sea fans are mostly made of rubber.

After destroying the aquarium's illusion of a perfectly contained ecosystem, I move on, switching the crowd's focus to some of the authentic characters within the tank: the triggerfish and the African pompano. I'm mid-way through an anecdote starring the triggerfish (a feisty female that a former diver dubbed SallyAnn in dubious honor of his psycho girlfriend), when the lights come on, full-strength. Marie Clarke, the manager du jour, takes Margaret aside and holds a whispered conversation. When she's finished, Margaret turns back to the crowd. "Ladies and gentlemen, we have a situation that requires the temporary evacuation of the building. There is no emergency, so please take the time to collect your family and your belongings, then, if you could please follow me, I'll escort you outside to the snack bar where you'll receive chips and a drink, complements of the aquarium staff." She shakes her head in apology and gives her audience a winning smile. "I'm very sorry for the inconvenience, but I've been assured that full access to the facility will resume within the hour."

Katie and Gabe regard me through worried eyes. I shrug and wait for Margaret to fill us in. "We've got a lost kid," she says, her voice low. "A boy; about seven years old. The police have been called. They want to search the building."

"Should we leave?" Gabe asks.

Margaret shakes her head. "The staff can stay. Marie thinks we might be helpful."

Climbing from the tank, I strip off my wetsuit. This has happened once before in my tenure at the aquarium, and by the time the building was checked out and given the all clear, almost all of the visitors had left. Even if Marie decides to re-open, the dive show will not resume.

"Are you guys going to stick around?" Gabe says.

"I don't have anything else planned for the afternoon and I'm on feeding detail," I say. "I might as well." I turn to Katie. She's just emerged from the ladies room, a towel wrapped, turban-like, around her head. "What about you? Are you going to hang?"

She shrugs. "I've got a meeting with Dr. Margolis at six, but nothing until then. If you're staying, I will, too, at least for a little while. How about you, Gabe?"

Gabe drums his fingers against the metal of his scuba tank. "I think I'll take off. If the cops need help, you guys can handle it."

Gabe doesn't like cops, especially not the locals. He's been stopped between Carolina and Kure Beach three times in the last month for speeding. "Suit yourself," I say. I can't imagine Gabe being much help, anyway. Besides, with him gone, I'll have Katie all to myself for the rest of the afternoon.

The three of us go downstairs. The main room looks huge without the crowds to fill it.

"I wonder where he is?" Katie says, looking around. "Seven is pretty young to be on your own in this place."

I shake my head. "I bet he's outside somewhere. Probably, at the beach."

She frowns. "What makes you think so?"

"It's a perfect beach day. I'd be at the beach too, if I wasn't working."

Katie's frown deepens. "Maybe our little runaway doesn't like the beach," she says, carefully. "Maybe he likes it in here better."

Her words send a chill down my spine. *A runaway boy who doesn't like the beach. A seven year old boy who wants his private tour of the building.* I get a sick feeling in the pit of my stomach.

"If I were the kid, I'd be at the SharkBites," Gabe says, heading for the side door. "They should check there, first. Lock up after me, okay?" He puts his hand on the deadbolt and turns to me, surprised. "It's open. Did you forget to lock it after lunch?"

"Shit," I say. "Don't tell Margaret."

"You owe me, dude." Gabe slips outside. I secure the deadbolt after him as Katie puts voice to my fears. "A little boy, about seven years old. Jaysus, Will, I hope it's not Cooper."

"Me, too," I mutter, as Margaret heads towards us across the room, leading two uniformed officers.

But it *is* Cooper Scully who's missing. The fat woman from SES stands outside, peering through the main entrance doors, while we search the building. When that proves fruitless, the cops collect the disks from the surveillance equipment and head outside to begin a search of the state park and the beach. Katie and I offer to help. We have a personal interest in the results.

At five-thirty, she calls Dr. Margolis and reschedules their appointment. At six, we gather by the ocean for another sweep of the beach. The word of the missing kid's gotten out and there are twenty of us now, standing glumly in the dissipating heat, anticipating disaster. Katie walks to the water's edge and gazes out to sea. The waves are small and the breeze slight in the still hour before dark. I stand behind her and place one hand on her shoulder. She doesn't shrug me away like usual.

At seven-thirty, the sun sinks below the horizon and the shadows of twilight become the permanence of night. There's still no sign of Coop and the chances of finding him in the dark are slim. We decide to call it quits with a promise to return first thing in the morning. Katie and I walk back to the aquarium building and use our staff keys to let ourselves in. I have to feed the tank fish before I can leave.

"I'll help," she says.

It's quiet inside, with just the trickle of water in the exhibits and the whir of pumps to interrupt the silence. I'm seldom in the building when it's empty and find the stillness unnerving. Katie and I walk through the conservatory and into the marine area. Ahead of us, the Cape Fear Shoal tank is brightly lit, the fish inside circling endlessly. We bypass it without pausing and take the steps to the top floor.

On auto-pilot, I retrieve fish from the freezer while Katie moves through the offices and bathrooms, turning off lights and closing doors. She stops before a stack of wetsuits and frowns. "Did you move these?" she says, pointing at four or five neoprene shorties that have fallen from the top of the pile. In a jumble at her feet, they lie inches from the lip of the tank. She stoops to gather them and I shake my head as I continue to load my bucket. The next time I look at her, she's standing, head bowed, behind me, tears running down her cheeks. She wipes her face with the back of her arm and smiles briefly before they begin to flow again.

"It's okay," I tell her, reaching out to grasp her shoulder. "They'll find him; he'll be alright."

"I know," she whispers, stepping toward me.

She's so close I can feel the heat from her sunburn. Without thinking, I slip my arms around her waist and draw her tight against my chest. She looks at me without a word, an indication I interpret as encouragement. Tilting her chin toward me, I kiss her. One, two, three, four, five…her heart beats light and fast against mine as I explore this strange and wonderful new territory. For a moment, I'm euphoric. Then Katie pulls away abruptly and I realize that I've fucked up.

My face grows hot. "I'm sorry," I say; a lame attempt to undo the damage. Katie doesn't reply. Without a word, she lifts a trembling arm and points at the floor behind me. I turn, take a step forward, and stop abruptly as she reaches for my hand. Protruding from the middle of the stack of wetsuits is a piece of white fabric. I step forward slowly and pull it free. It's a t-shirt. A neatly folded white t-shirt, size large…with Fort Fisher Aquarium printed in aqua letters across the front.

"Oh, no," Katie says. She peels the wetsuits from the pile and heaves them aside until she finds what she's searching for: a pair of khaki shorts, dirty sneakers, and another t-shirt…this one, bright orange. "He's in the tank," she says softly.

I whirl toward the water and peer into its depths, shielding my eyes against the reflection of the overhead lights. Below me, the false coral is alive with color. Artificial sea fans and anemones sway in the current; blue tangs and parrotfish school around mock outcroppings of fire coral. A blue tip shark slides by, just below the surface, followed by a small stingray. Katie points a shaking finger at the water. "There," she says.

I lean closer, squinting into the depths. At first I don't see it, then my breath catches in my throat. Halfway down the simulated reef, around the twelve foot mark, is a wetsuit. I blink. From this angle, it's hard to tell, but I think I see a foot emerging from one of its legs. I'm rooted in place for an instant, and then I'm moving, running past the neatly stacked wetsuits, the bathrooms and shower area, the dive office, and the bridge.

I'm down the ladder and in the tank before Katie reacts. "Wait!" she screams, throwing a mask into the water.

Pulling the strap over my head, I swim to the far side of the tank where she stands, pointing downward. Then I take a deep breath and dive. Schools of fish part before me as I slice through the water. Flashes of color blur in my peripheral vision. Below me, the body of a boy, a small boy in a wetsuit, rests wedged against the plastic. He looks straight at me as I swim, his eyes unblinking, one small hand entwined in a strand of rubber kelp. His fingers and the seaweed wave in the current with perfect synchronization. My heart pounds against my ribs as my mind tells me what I don't want to believe: the boy in the wetsuit is Cooper Scully and he's dead. I'm sure of it. So sure, in fact, that I almost fail to notice the lone bubble that rises from his lips.

I push deeper through the water. A second later, there's another one. My ears pop, throbbing from the pressure. My lungs strain, aching for breath. Above me, I know that Katie's praying. Below me Coop's lips are parted, as though he's smiling. A third bubble rises, weaving its way skyward toward the surface, twelve feet above.

Tonic immobility. Hope consumes me as I pry his limp body from the faux coral. *Tonic immobility*. I turn him onto his stomach and wrap one arm around his chest. *Tonic immobility.* I chant the words over and over as I shoot toward the top of the tank.

Please God, I beg, *let me be wrong about the drowning thing.*

Breaking the surface, I see Katie waiting for us on the diving platform. I drag Coop to the edge and lift him into her waiting arms. As I take breath after breath of sweet clean air, Katie kneels and begins to pump his chest. Below her, in the pool, I can still feel her warm lips against mine, and the promise they hold of love and precious life.

Leslie Jill Patterson

Catch and Release

I WON'T SAY I LOVED JENNY. I won't say I didn't. But every year, in the early weeks of spring, when the skaters ditch the rink at Millennium Park and the sun starts to dress everything in glad rags again, my memories of the Animas River and our afternoons on its shore return, as keen as hunger. The fresh air warms your face in a way winter let you forget it could, but then the wind kicks in from the north, down Michigan Avenue, and sobers you right back up, exactly like a mountain gust scuffing across the river.

I work hard, then, to hide my memories from the wife, keep them out of our home, but at the office, I'll find myself closing my eyes, and if the phone shuts it for two minutes, I can mistake the sound of the El running the Loop for the river, fat on snowmelt and galloping high and wild. I can almost hear Jenny's voice then. I can almost hear her line whisk across the water.

A fishing guide lives a life of beginnings and spots THE END long before it happens. Jenny chooses her job for just this reason. She knows that her clients, all green, won't need her when they turn veteran, and she watches for their metamorphosis from rookie to crackerjack as vigilantly as she anticipates the lift of a caddis hatch off the river. She knows new clients can't hear the ruckus of their gear—tackle boxes or shoulder bags jangling at their hips, filled with strike indicators, weights, containers of dressing, tools they have no idea how to use. They expect trout to hit their flies hard, exploding from the river like rocks through a window. Trophy fish clever enough to jack open their mouths and, without any fanfare, simply swallow nymphs that float their way confuse her clients. They don't know to drop flies in a seam near a logjam or deep in the zone where these fish tread water. And when they discover a trout silently snagged on the end of their lines, they call it an "accidental" catch, something that doesn't count, like trash sunk in a game of eight ball.

As long as her clients are enamored with large, bushy flies a novice can easily see—Royal Wulffs, Stimulators, Humpies—they'll keep booking day trips. But the morning a student's eye latches onto the nymphs, hare's ear and pheasant tail, so tiny and intricate, that she hides like secrets in her vest pocket, a smart guide starts looking for new clients.

At night, I swim the Animas River, upstream, to the old spawning grounds—a homeland so ingrained I find it in my sleep. My hair, fine and blonde, stiffens into spines that slice through the crosscurrents. My belly bumps against rock. My legs turn to scales and narrow to one ankle, a caudal fin that slaps fierce and heavy. In the right mood, I can knock unconscious the largest of men.

Jenny and I, honest, we didn't argue much. But there were little things, and they added up. Like the way my mother called late at night when we were in bed, and I answered though it was sometimes an interruption—and then, for reasons I can't fully explain, I pretended to be alone, motioning Jenny to lie still and quiet so my mother wouldn't hear her. Or how I kept my flat screen parked on ESPN twenty-four/seven, and Jenny razzed me, nonstop, about the remote control apparently being broken. But a guy can scroll through the guide for hours, never landing on a good thing, missing the ends of ball games, catching only the middles of movies.

Jenny: she murmured in her sleep, flopped about whenever we camped, soaking our bedroll with her night-sweats. In the mornings, I'd ask what the hell she dreamed the night before, but she always said she couldn't remember. Sometimes, on weekends when the current outran my line, continually trawling my Adams across the river, she'd pretend she couldn't catch anything either, though we both knew better. All day, my flies dragged and sank. The fish bumped them but rolled away. Finally—and this irritated me most—Jenny would give advice.

"Maybe try a dropper rig," she'd suggest.

I'd cock an eyebrow at her. I wasn't one of her day-trippers; I hadn't paid for a tour. "I don't see you nymphing the river."

She'd shrug but apologize.

Then one of us, she or I, we'd count to ten and repeat the adage Jenny told me the night we first met at The Yankee Girl: "A man sinks a fly deep in the river, then he's daring the stones to fool him." We'd both smile then, content again, remembering.

That one line—it's the reason I asked her out after: how she spoke about the river, her words like a fortune cookie that made no real sense but sounded exactly like a prophecy you could count on. For the rest of the evening at The Yankee Girl, as we finished off not one, not two or even three, but four rounds of tequila, what I heard while I listened to her story was a mountain stream: one minute, her attitude chilled and all her secrets running below the icy surface, and the next, her eyes fiery and her regrets enraged. So different from the uptight Midwest. No one back home talked in public about failed marriages, affairs, children lost at birth.

The next day, on the phone, I asked my twin brother Rusty, "You remember that counselor from camp?"

"The blonde with long legs we wanted to knot ourselves in?" he asked.

Our parents had sent us away for entire summers to the Rockies, and we didn't mind. What kid would? Fishing and swimming at the reservoir, junk food and sodas between every meal, and a counselor at the girl's camp who went rogue occasionally and rowed out to the middle of the lake by herself, with a rod and reel. She wore cut-off Oshkosh overalls and, underneath, a tank the color of cotton candy. The ball cap on her head couldn't contain her hair, all curly and feral. She'd lean to the left when she cast her line then cock her head, simply chaperoning the fly's arc but nonetheless looking for all this world like the one aloof girl you could never catch.

"Jenny looks like her," I said.

Rusty snorted, and did so again when I told him Jenny kept pace for pace with each shot, what she said about a man sinking a fly deep in the river, how it cinched the deal.

"Aaron," he said, "a man who dips his stick in that girl's river, you bet, he comes out the fool. She's the type who shafts our type into marriage. You're a meal ticket."

Over the next weeks, I argued, talked her up, dared him to come meet her and prove me wrong. I said the way the trout crushed Jenny's hoppers when there was no hatch to speak of was a thing of mystery to me. I swore she was a magician with fire and a skillet, too. She'd sizzle a pair of trout in lemon and Parmesan, so down-home, but it was the best freshwater fish he'd ever taste.

On the river, Jenny and I ate under the stars, without a lantern, which was our way. She'd tell me the constellations overhead would forever remind her of my handmade flies, a galaxy, countless and splendid, pricking the interior roof of my SUV. It wasn't useful, this flattery, but every time she said it, I forgot all the bad news chasing WorldCom like a pit bull. I forgot my brother, the golden egg who would never start an investment firm that fell prey to get-rich-quick flimflam. He'd sure never attempt it in the West, where everyone simply poured their money into glasses and drank it to endure the winters. I even forgot my parents, the both of them pressing me to settle down—but with a nice girl, an educated girl.

After dinner, Jenny and I crawled inside our Coleman, unrolled our bags, and zipped them together. I was usually worn out, deflated after so many hours unplugging clients from one dot-bomb after another, but when Jenny nuzzled the crook of my neck, I'd feel sorry at the thought of missing the opportunity with her, and I'd manage to screw around until I at least got her off. We'd lay awake after, listening to the tumble of the Animas. Less than two months into the summer, late June, the runoff would slow, the river turn lenient and fertile, and what we'd hear along the shore was the drone of a fisherman's victory: pale morning duns and golden stones and caddis flies thick as snow.

There are secrets a guide reveals only by example because she rarely speaks on the river. In upper elevations, the feeding season is swift and savage, and Jenny knows if she skates a fly across the water, stripping her line unevenly, a freestone trout will convince itself what it sees is a mayfly at the mercy of the current, and it will strike when instinct warns that it shouldn't. She knows if she catches the timing of a hatch just precisely, she can raise the tip of her rod as her pheasant tail skulks downstream, so it resembles a nymph emerging in the liftoff of new insects. And while an inexperienced fisherman gives up when a fish taps his fly but spins away, a seasoned guide knows trout will thump a minnow once to stun it then come back a second time for the kill. She'll withdraw her line and cast again, quickly, into the same spot.

A guide's know-how on the river translates easily into con-artist skill far from shore. When a man on the make in a bar pats Jenny's rump then pretends he didn't, she can predict he'll come by a half-hour later with a drink he's decided she's thirsty enough to accept. Some nights, she saves herself the tab and lets the player crack open his wallet, again and again. Other nights, she convinces an admirer, earnest in his attraction, that he's snagged her, but when he wakes near noon, dragging his mind from murky night into clear morning, he finds she's gone. Afterward, the idea of her haunts his bed: the whiff of her skin, the shadow of her shampoo, the faint scent of citrus.

In early May, Jenny thought this story—the one between two fisher people in love with the river—might end differently. She thought she would see this tale through to the end. She thought, maybe, Happy Ever After.

Deep in the river, where the silt is centuries black, I move through schools of razorback suckers, Colorado squawfish, bonytail chubs—the native, the endangered, the trash no sporting man wants. They flicker in smaller and smaller numbers and portend things to come. Their scales flake. Their fins tatter. In amazement, they watch strange fish—familiar but foreign, like kin from exotic waters they think they remember but have never seen—seize their habitat and feast on their algae and crickets. Soon, these relatives, so sleek and muscular and grand, will become their bitter enemies.

Usually, my ability at restaurants to order in a flash, even off menus thick as a Bible, impressed Jenny. It was G for grouper over S for salmon, L for linguini over R for rigatoni, whatever came first alphabetically. When the meal hit the table, I was content. I didn't fork morsels off Jenny's plate, steal what wasn't mine. She also admired the way I picked, toot sweet, which movie we'd see Friday night (by the lead actress, blondes before brunettes) and which river we'd fish Saturday morning (the Dolores on the first and third weekends, the Animas on the others, the San Juan after rain).

Sometimes, though, she complained I lived my days on autopilot. Without emotional consideration—her phrase, not mine—I shaped conversations about our relationship into Harvard outlines and arguments about money around Robert's Rules of Order. She exaggerated, but I heard the message.

Still, even though I wanted to make her happy, tried hard to open up, it was a sure bet on failure when Jenny unknowingly raised the question of cohabitation mere hours after Rusty warned me that talk of religion or shared quarters was a woman's method of debating her way into marriage. His last words before he hung up the phone: "Get ready. It's coming." So that night, over dinner, when she asked about getting a place for the two of us, I was primed to give the wrong answer. I told her the choice was obvious: efficiency with an E before two-bedroom with a T. "Be logical," I said, then filled her glass with more Merlot.

"It'd be cheaper," she said. "What's more logical than money?" She dropped an ice cube into her wine, a quirk I ought to have made peace with by then, but it wasn't Welch's grape juice; it wasn't Kool-Aid.

"If you depart from the map of habit," I argued, "be prepared for dead ends." And I knew, even as the words tumbled from my mouth, I sounded exactly like Rusty.

Jenny stared at me for a minute then kept scanning the rent ads in the paper. She circled the apartments big enough for two but cheap enough to justify the merge—none of them anywhere near the neighborhoods I preferred. We finished our meal in silence, just the chatter of silverware. After she washed the dishes, she left *The Herald* on the counter. But the beautiful thing about Jenny: she recovered quickly after we argued. No sulking. No little revenges. Sure enough, a day later, the paper was gone.

If I'd been honest, I would have admitted Jenny and I slept at my studio most nights anyway. Her efficiency was on the old side of town, where all the river-rats lived and the apartments were carved out of dilapidated Victorians, two or three units on each floor. It was small and dark and cluttered with GO GREEN pamphlets and pickets. A bucket crowded the shower to catch the runoff spray she used to water the plants outside, and empty milk cartons and cereal boxes stacked up in the kitchen, ready for a trip to the recycle bins. She and her landlord talked about getting a compost toilet, which ought to have lowered Jenny's rent, but her landlord called it an amenity, said she had to charge for updates, especially eco-friendly ones.

Jenny's crush on global warming—that was my first reason for keeping separate apartments. The second: I liked knowing Jenny had a place to go just in case things between us turned ugly. When my brother came to visit late in May, Jenny wouldn't give the environment a rest already but instead fought with Rusty over light bulbs and paper towels and the bucket she'd set outside my own shower, hoping I'd move it inside the stall. When the two of them sat in the same vicinity—in my car at a stoplight, at a restaurant for dinner, or in my living room for a nightcap—I panicked. Seeing them side by side, it was hard not to. Imagine Jenny—just how I loved her—in her white tank and jeans and river sandals with quick-release Velcro straps, and her hair as wind-ruffled and white as the rapids, versus Rusty in his cargo pants, Dri-Fit workout shirt, and L.L. Bean hiking boots—some city dude's high-dollar outdoor costume, reminding me of all the expectations for my future. I knew immediately, I'd weighted the idea of Rusty's trip there with too much hope; it wasn't Jenny's magic he'd see but instead her principles, her scruffy clothes like some sort of accusation. He'd go home and tell our parents all the wrong things.

One night, after a clash over laundry detergent, Rusty told Jenny our dad always warned us how a woman's shadow on the water spelled ruination for the fish. "I've never understood that advice—" he smiled at her, "—until now. Thank you for clearing it up." Then he let his silence bury that little gem deep into her hard drive.

That day, her sermons had worn me out, too, and I couldn't sleep in the same bed with her—by that point, all of her nightmares, the tossing, the kicking, had tailed us from the river back to town. So, at eleven o'clock, I said, "You must be tired." For a minute, she misunderstood and moved toward my bedroom. Seeing her face drowsy and content with the idea of sleeping side by side, I almost stood down. But then I blocked her path with a hug, rubbed her back. "I hate you have to go home," I said, "but we'll get an early start in the morning." Her brow wrinkled, then she looked over her shoulder at Rusty, lounging on the sofa, his L.L. Beans propped on the coffee table, the remote control in his hand, the sound of the TV bouncing through all those premium channels she and I never watched. He wore a smile that could sell dog shit, and she opened her mouth as if she might say something but instead headed for the door.

The next morning, because I was still trying to impress Rusty, to justify my refusal to come home and settle on some downtown girl, all avenues and steel buildings and family money, Jenny and I took him south to Purple Cliffs, where the Animas is regulated and accessible by foot and makes her run toward the San Juan. "Gold Medal Water," that's what Jenny called it, because some lucky duck, decades ago, pulled the state record brown, all thirty pounds of it, from this leg. And it was a trophy of a morning. The cliffs shouldered up to the river. The sun, a bright orange, hung in the sky.

We geared up on the banks, everything fine until Jenny handed me some twist-on weights and felt the need to explain they were non-toxic so the fish wouldn't inhale any lead. Rusty stiffened, but before the argument could flare up, Jenny put on her wading boots and headed for the shallows. Rusty and I, we pulled on full waders and trekked upstream, away from her.

I gave Rusty a matuka and took a woolly bugger for myself. The choice to use streamers wasn't alphabetical or even a toss of the coin; simply put, large flies appeal to large fish, and anything short of a keeper was going to disappoint both of us. Rusty cast across the river and upstream, let the fly loaf in the current, a dead-drift, exactly like I'd shown him. But he wasn't watching his strike indicator. Instead, he stared at Jenny downstream. Her left hand mended her line, like a harpist thrumming her instrument.

"That little mermaid," he said, nodding in her direction, "is nothing but a pain and a nice piece of tail."

Yes, Rusty was the one who nicknamed Jenny, and I hated how she snuggled up to me in our tent later that night when I swiped the idea and called her my little mermaid. I hated how she wanted it slow and moaning afterward, though Rusty lay stashed in a tent right next to ours, listening and figuring he'd been right about her all along.

That morning on the river, I watched Jenny, too. A fresh hatch of midges, like the loft of a dandelion, ascended around her. She raised her rod tip, guiding her fly, then withdrew the line and cast again. Her wrist, so white, caught the sun—like a flash of fin, the blink of belly. For a moment, I longed so badly to have the river to ourselves, her and me, that I almost waded her direction and said, "Let's send Rusty home. Now."

"Look at her wrist," I said instead to Rusty, because, even still, I wanted him to see.

"Man—" he shook his head, "—no one's looking at her wrist. Not even you."

Here's Jenny's weekend costume, all woman and no guide: cut-off Levi's, Neoprene boots like school-girl knee-socks pulled to her thighs, and that heavenly wink of skin between rubber and denim.

"Quit staring," I said.

Rusty laughed then, as if we were two men sharing a dirty joke. "I'll admit, you won't find a chick back home who manages a rod as skillfully as Jenny. She's the little bang for your buck on a business trip that makes married life bearable."

And I wondered if that was an example of what my mother meant when she said Rusty was the blue-eyed half with all the charm.

"Aaron," he added, his face suddenly stern, "picture the mother of your children. Seriously, does she even remotely look like Jenny?"

What I pictured, right away, was me looking over the shoulder of a brunette, a lady who wore skirts and blouses and bras, not cut-offs and bikini tops, and she and I, not me and Jenny, were cuddling a kid. A for accountant or attorney—sound and sensible—before G for guide or T for tree-hugger. Because it wasn't pretend; it wasn't a fairy tale.

At dusk, a cool breeze along the river will put the fish down early, and an efficient guide packs her gear and goes home. Some afternoons, a cloudbank, a gift from the gods, will cause newly hatched midges to linger on the water, their neonate wings slow to dry, but by two o'clock, leisurely weather can fire into a storm. The wind shifts, and clouds explode over the mountains. In her legs, the guide feels the pressure drop before the front moves in. She feels the tug of earth drawing rain and thunder from the sky. And she knows water rises two feet every fifteen minutes where the rock walls cinch the riverbed to the skinniest of trickles.

Jenny hustles her crew uphill but keeps her voice calm. She imagines explaining nothing more than how to season a filet, how to heat the oil so it pops but won't scald dinner. When everyone's parked on a ledge safe above the river, she sings the themes from childhood TV shows. Eventually, the gang of city slickers joins in, hesitant at first but then loud enough to drown the storm. They watch the water rise. They sing: *The Brady Bunch, The Monkees, Gilligan's Island.*

Oddly, these are the afternoons Jenny feels most at home. Men, typically leery of a female guide, lean a little closer and heed her words. If they were back on the shore and fishing at that moment, she could stop faking; she could catch and release as many trout as she wanted. First and last take. Most and largest. The men would keep quiet, and not the way some of them do before unraveling in anger, but the way the first sight of the river hushes them for all the promise she offers.

The wives—tagging along, wearing their Liz Claiborne sportswear and Lee jeans, and their hair in obedient ponytails—usually sneer at Jenny's quick-dry Jackson pants and her shirt that buttons like a man's because it is a man's and her hair wild and tangled, the appearance of a tomboy, a half-woman. Now, though, in the storm, they sense her knowledge is something more like seduction. They huddle together in the rain, soaked and frightened. They sense trouble but don't know it's their cotton clothing, which fails to wick moisture off your skin and leaves you trembling at death's door. Afterward, back in town at the checkout, when the men turn once again toward their wives, shadows on their heels now, Jenny smells the hint of disdain.

Still, Jenny feels broken around other women. It's not simply her costume, but also her limbs, long and muscular, that set her apart. And the absence of children. A maternal instinct injured years ago and lately ignored.

But one spring morning, in early June, less than twelve hours after the first squall of the season, a headache snaps Jenny's eyes open. The memory of the river, turbulent still, roils in her stomach. It heaves up her throat, a hard current. Her legs throb; her skin is clammy. Then comes the exhaustion in the daylight, insomnia in the dark. In a week, maybe two, she fails to bleed.

Suddenly, it's a different type of secret she thinks she's keeping—a heartbeat she hears in the river that a fisherman might mistake for a trap.

Lately, in the riffs and shallow runs, razorback suckers pulse beside me. They flutter between my breasts and around the tender crooks of my elbows. My caudal fin, sharply forked and powerful as that of any fish, confuses the males. They paint their bellies orange then wait for me at the gravel bars where they believe I will deposit eggs. The females, though, sense the mistake of my torso. My pale skin is blinding; my arms are illogical and awkward as tree limbs. They chitter to one another in fear then turn away from me in shame.

The males, who would wait for me to bury a nest of eggs in the gravel, fret about their diminishing numbers, the migrants crowding their streams. If their species will not survive, they will fertilize the spawn of women not their own. The shadow of their features will haunt other fish; they'll pass on their keel-edged hump, their large head, their yellow throat. When they spot any eggs lying unguarded, they flit from the shadows and dance above the nest. Clouds of semen billow like exhaust in the water. Afterward, the men peer over their shoulders, wink at me, then dart away.

After Jenny said she might be pregnant, I heard a clock ticking behind all our conversations, and it wasn't her biological timer, but instead those precious hours of the early trimester slipping away, until it'd be too distasteful for options.

I told her not to bother with some plastic-strip do-it-yourself evidence. I said, "See a doctor."

The next weekend, which turned out to be our last, Jenny and I drove to Rockwood then hopped the train and headed north into the gorge, where the river is a water trap. Jenny didn't like fishing the sterile headwaters of the upper Animas. She resented the old mines that filled the river with ore and sulfur, and dyed it the color of egg yolks. She didn't like the roar of water that time of year either, how the snowmelt pumped it so full of fury it yanked your feet from beneath you. She made me tie a rope from one tree across to the other bank and a second tree, a handrail in case the runoff doubled during the afternoon and made treacherous the wade back to camp at the end of the day. In the beginning, Jenny's fear of rowdy rivers made me tender of her. Because it was the only time I ever saw her afraid; it was the only time she needed me.

But at that altitude, trout, though tiny, are feisty and hungry. The top-water action they guaranteed was what I wanted after another long week watching my investors' venture capital go up in smoke, the burn rates blazing like wildfires across the Internet.

I spent Saturday at a distance from Jenny, avoiding conversation, even keeping my sleeping bag separate from hers. When I climbed inside mine, I felt her staring at the back of my head, but I didn't roll over or put an arm around her. I kept quiet.

Sunday morning, early, Jenny baked biscuits in our Dutch oven, fried eggs in the grease from the bacon. I made coffee and took the mugs back into the tent. Jenny followed, with full plates, and zipped the canvas shut. It was chilly still in first light, and there was always something sorrowful about Sundays on the river. The workweek gloomed around the bend—the sound of traffic, the jam of stoplights, my briefcase versus her rallies, the two of us back in town where all our troubles lay. Whatever connection we'd made fishing the day before, it would thin like steam and rise off the water, unraveling in the sunlight.

Jenny winced when she took the first sip of her coffee—as she always did. She preferred her Joe with a scoop of Blue Bunny vanilla. But it wasn't daycare; we weren't first graders. Another quirk of hers: she thought she was a mind reader, but her hunches invariably missed the mark. Sure, watching her cringe as she nursed her coffee, I was thinking about kids, recess, those little cardboard cups of ice cream with the wooden spoons, flat as tongue depressors, that they give out to kindergarteners after naptime. I was thinking about playgrounds and Red Rover, not nurseries and diapers, an infant, ours, but Jenny looked me right in the face, said she had medical confirmation, and asked how badly I wanted kids.

I was barely thirty-two. My hands went numb; my stomach tumbled.

Sometimes, I tell myself what I'd been picturing was a school of fish, mine, swimming upstream, and Jenny's egg, mid-river, rooted and lying in wait in the mud—the swindle my brother Rusty had predicted from the get-go. I'd like to say what troubled me was the idea of Jenny kicked back and smoking a cigar, all satisfied with her fertility—the shakedown my parents expected from a woman like her, not yet thirty but already divorced.

Honestly though, days before, my head had settled on an image of Jenny and Rusty. In the kitchen one night, I overheard the two of them arguing in my living room, a debate about landfills and garbage and what effort, large or small, it took to recycle. As I came back into the room, with drinks for the three of us, Rusty reached out and grabbed Jenny's hand. She jerked hard, her eyes fierce, but Rusty held tight. He entwined his fingers in hers and smiled. He wasn't quarreling so much as proposing something he thought a girl like Jenny might warm to. She tugged free and stayed near me the rest of the night, one of her hands always resting on my shoulder or hooked between my hip and elbow.

Still … during those last weeks, and on that final morning on the Animas, what I couldn't quit picturing was a little girl with Jenny's wild hair, white and furious as the river, and eyes the color of the Atlantic, just like Rusty's.

So when she asked how badly I wanted kids, I couldn't help it: my eyebrows flickered before I got them under control, and what came from my mouth, without much emotional consideration, was something I'd thought a million times but never planned on saying: "A for abortion over B for baby."

Jenny's hand immediately cupped the curve of her belly, the way pregnant women sometimes feel for a kick or protect the womb. She unzipped our Coleman, made like she was going to leave. I called her my little mermaid, reached for her hand, tried to drag her butt back to bed.

"Don't," she said.

Right then, the sight of her so beautiful—her hair tousled; her skin damp, as if she'd just risen from a hot bath; even her brow knitted with anger—all of it made me think maybe I could accept fatherhood. I wouldn't hate Jenny for snarling the outline, so orderly, that relationships are meant to follow. I wouldn't feel duped, the old king trout who's always escaped the lure but now falls for a woolly-bugger streaking through the water. And when my parents halted my trust fund, and they surely would, maybe I wouldn't care.

If we could have stayed on the river, it might have been true.

There are summers when every guide witnesses death. A couple hikes above the timberline and gets caught unaware in a storm. Lightning strikes the man, buckles his knees, short-circuits his brain then snakes through the scree and plugs into the woman's feet. From the river, the guide and her outfit hear the crack of thunder and see the smoke bloom, two mushrooms overhead.

Occasionally, and some summers as rampant as a virus, she'll hear the squeal of brakes far away in the canyon. Trees splinter, and metal crumples against rock. It's eerily quiet then, for twenty, maybe thirty, minutes. Finally, a siren, thin as a mosquito buzz, starts from the south, crescendos as it winds through the mountains, drawing nearer, until the wail of it zips shut when the ambulance reaches the scene. If the tourists survived the accident, the ambulance revs up again and fades away. Usually, the guide hears nothing. Because there isn't any rush hauling the dead back to town.

Some years, drought and heat smother the landscape. The lakes dry out then turn fetid, and dead fish litter the beaches. You can't row a boat from one shore to the other, but you can drive across. Meanwhile, the rivers choke on their dams and bleed at their gates. The current dwindles and turns as meager as the winter flow. When the fish reach their spawning grounds, they panic. The skimpy cloak of water can't protect their tender scales from the sun's rays. The river stews; the fish drag, breathe slow, stall out. They rise to the surface like loaves of moldy bread.

Five years ago, Jenny herself experienced death, how it reaches from heaven like an arm turned to gaff at the wrist. She remembers, first, waking in a hospital to find her child delivered but gone and, later, returning to her and her husband's house, the baby carriage, changing table, and crib like junk crowding a landfill, and yet the emptiness so breathtaking, like the sharp edge of cold air in a mortuary. They had planned to fill their home with laughter, even the howls of an infant crying for milk, but afterward, the weight of loss buried the rooms in silence.

Her husband left a year later, with another woman, running from the sorrow Jenny could neither contain nor utter. The only solace she found came from the bustle of protests, crowds clashing over issues she cared little for then—just voices, so many voices she could join, raised in an outcry she had been unable to make otherwise.

She told herself she'd never again be caught short by the dead-end punch line of a story. She'd sleep half-awake. She'd eat looking over her shoulder. The next time, she'd hear The End creeping up on her, its footsteps like a wristwatch ticking, a bit of Morse code, or the smallest flutter in the undercurrent of her bloodstream.

Nights after a storm, I swim close to the surface of my dreams, where moonlight penetrates the water and I can glimpse the sky—a black velvet carpet pricked by the shiniest plugs you'll ever see. The turbid water seduces chubs and razorbacks away from the river bottom, too. Their eyes flip open and clap shut. Occasionally, one of them, unwise to the lure, nabs a grasshopper then bucks and thrashes and vanishes overhead. There's a beat of silence, then all of us flick around, glance over our shoulders, flick back, and carry on.

Even so, I can tell you that underwater, fear smells as tart as lemons.

Here's my last image of Jenny: her hands, those long, slender fingers, palmed against my chest and shoving hard. Here's the last thing she said: "You're so god-damned selfish." Then she flicked her coffee from its mug, dropped it in a shatter on the ground, and took off walking.

Jenny's resolve surprised me. For days, I'd told myself I'd be the one between the two of us who decided not to set the hook but rather cast again elsewhere. And afterward, Jenny, she'd get the abortion or she wouldn't, but either way, I'd be long gone, back to Chicago, where my parents and Rusty would fill me up with We told you so, but it wouldn't matter anymore.

That morning, I figured Jenny would walk it off, hike up the river a ways, watch the sun climb out of the well of mountains and brighten the sky. She'd return by lunch. Because how far could she get on foot? We were thirty-two miles from Durango and 2,500 feet higher.

I washed the breakfast dishes in the river, put on clean jeans, a shirt, a vest pricked with my best lures—all hand-crafted, my own work—a get-up that always softened Jenny's heart. For a couple of hours, I didn't notice that she took her Scott rig with her—the one possession she would never leave behind. When I finally gave up and hiked back alone to catch the last train, I still expected to find her sitting on the hood of my car at Rockwood, waiting for me, put out and tired of my ways but willing to make up. But she wasn't, and back at my apartment in Durango, all of her belongings had vanished. The little drawer where I let her keep some clean panties, a hairbrush, toothpaste—empty. That annoying bucket she kept outside my shower—gone.

I phoned Rusty, and he guessed things from the tone of my voice when I told him I was closing shop in the mountains. "Man," he said, "it's your lucky day. That little cherry was gonna turn up plump as a pie, and you'd never know who popped it in the oven." Then he rambled on about the firm he and I would set up, how we'd rake in the dough, live in some high-rise on Michigan.

I've always wondered if he could hear it over the phone—my heart hammering in my chest, my lungs shuttered tight, and me, shaking my head: no, no, no.

In mid-June, the guide goes to a doctor, who draws her blood to verify the news, whether joyful or unwelcome. He comes back to the examination room, in his precise white coat, his arms laden with line graphs and books and talk about hormones Jenny doesn't understand. He uses a pencil to point at facts on the page. He avoids looking at her face when he says she's young, yes, only twenty-nine, but part of her is already dying. Her hormones are that of a sixty-year-old; her body, hot and sweaty and senescent, is laboring to pump out an egg that isn't there. Only when she says, "What?" does he lock his eyes on hers and whisper, "No, no baby."

Next, silent and wounded, she drifts to a fertility clinic, a new-fangled spawning ground, tucked inside a bank and surrounded by investors. She wonders if she's come to bet on stock or ask for a loan. Up the elevator and in the waiting room, she can't help but notice the parenting magazines, even gossip rags, with cover photos of movie starlets, the search for the baby bump—all the literature like guarantees—lined up on the coffee tables. Other women sitting near her are plump as pumpkins, heavy gourds. When she starts crying, the nurse shoos her into an office, one with a plastic chair, no over-stuffed sofas that say family, kids, mom and dad.

When the specialist snakes a camera up to her headwaters, his face goes blank. He keeps the ultrasound monitor turned from her sight. Only after she's dressed again does he tell her what he found in the seams where her ovaries should be were two black holes, the quiet pockets where eggs once rested in numbers but where only failure lies now. If any hope remains, a straggler egg or two, they are tattered and worn and thin. Nothing of consequence.

The doctor holds her hand, tight, when he tells her this, and Jenny can't focus. She feels the heft of a storm gathering inside her. Her legs throb. She pictures her clients' wives sitting beside the doctor, their mouths stitched with pity but also contempt. She hears the doctor's voice, calm and kind, explaining the prospect of borrowing another woman's eggs, but tangled in his words is the rant of her fisherman's brother, railing against the practice of salvaging garbage. She saw possibility in recyclables; he saw useless detritus. And just in case his voice more ablaze than hers, and his face more ferocious, didn't prove he'd won the debate, he'd locked his palm against hers, latched their fingers together, and whispered he'd tell his brother as many times as it took: "A man can't catch a keeper when he's holding on to trash." Then, behind him, carrying a tray of shot glasses but also, in Jenny's imagination, a tackle box of useless gear, stood Aaron, smiling and relieved but already calculating how he'd find another nest, one ready and ripe for him.

Do not think I will forget the ghosts of fresh-water fishermen I have known. Even tonight, when I am not yet gone, I see the one who calls me his mermaid, standing along the shore of my dream he mistakes for a river. For my benefit, he wears shiny waders and sunshades the color of ocean water. He hopes to snag me with the pretty flies, like flowers, he stitches with his hands. His face, white and hopeful as a full moon, peers into the current. His reel, like the mating call of a cricket, violins through the air.

Where I once smelled fear in the locomotion of water, now I hear the surf, taste salt, feel the tide that tows me away. Tonight, I'll swim the Animas River, downstream from its headwaters, through the canyons, toward Utah. There, I will fork into the Colorado. By morning, I'll reach the sea. And when I think of my fishermen, when I pause and listen carefully, they'll be nothing more than the sound of the river running away.

Back in Chicago, this time every spring, people still wear their coats but stop looking overhead, no longer edgy about icicles lancing off the skyscrapers. In late afternoons, heading home, they glance at the bench under the heat lamps at the El stations, but they don't palm the power button or gather there for comfort; they're anxious for summer now and don't want to jinx its arrival by hanging on to the arm of winter.

Me, I still pump gas at the Conoco every Saturday morning. Always the right nozzle—high or low octane, either way. And now that winter's over, I purchase a car wash—rain or shine—if my purchase is divisible by two. Rusty, well, he still isn't married, and rarely works, but Mom clings to the promise she sees in him. She finds comfort in the fact that my wife is the ice queen everyone thought I needed: a journalist, all facts and names and take-charge skirts.

Weekday afternoons, haunted by Jenny and the Animas and the possibility of a little girl who looks like her, I linger at the office I'm inheriting from Dad, stall the trip home. Sometimes, when Rusty's killing time around there, he sees it in my eyes. Maybe he feels it himself. I'll give him this: Jenny rattled him, too. So come the first sunny weekend, he'll talk me into taking a boat onto the lake, my son and him and I. We bring our rods and tackle but don't catch anything. We don't talk much either. Definitely no bull session about work and the downturn even more brutal than the dot-com bust back then. We drink beer, sodas for Nate, and we might mention how a simple sandwich—turkey, Swiss, soft white bread—just tastes better when you're eating it under the sky. We'll make plans for a trip into Wisconsin where we fish every summer off Lake Winnebago.

Rusty will preach to my son the same lesson he delivers every spring, though I'm fairly certain he's directing it at me. He'll say, "It's a lucky life a man leads when he faces tough choices." Most decisions, they're a snap. But every once in a while, a man pulls something too good to be true from the river, and he's got a decision to make. He'll take pause on the shore, spin that gold medal brown in the sunshine, the light reflecting off its silver scales, its caudal fin still thrashing, its eyes glassy as pearls. Then, if he's wise, and generous, he'll unsnag the hook, hold the trout in his hands, gently, underwater, till it catches it breath, then let it go.

There was a time Rusty's story enraged me, but now, waiting for the early weeks of spring to pass, I find some comfort in it. On really bad days, I try hard to believe it.

Marge Piercy

The Next Evolutionary Step

In the Herring River, the mummichog
lives along with eels, alewives, green
and bullfrogs, snapping turtles
and muskrats. Of all these
the mummichog is the smallest

but the hardiest. It can withstand
heat and cold. Polluted waters
do not sicken it. It survives most
poisons and is predicted to outlive
us all in a nuclear disaster.

It schools with hundreds of kin
that move as one through muddy
waters, feeling their way. On
the full moon it releases its eggs
and on the new moon too making

sure there will always be multitudes
of mummichogs. I, who am far
less sure of my survival, salute
you, for in spite of all we do to
destroy, you'll repopulate earth.

Marge Piercy

The Solstice Looms

The gardens ploughed for the winter
look like rough wooden tables
from which the brightly patterned
tablecloths have been yanked.

The oaks cling to dull brown leaves
the wind tears off a few at a time.
All the other hardwoods are display
manniquins stripped of clothing.

The pine needles are tipped with
frost. The birds fluff their feathers,
jostle at the feeders. The hawk
circles overhead, hungry

for them. The coywolves trot
from the marsh before four,
hungry too. Even the moon
is lean tonight as a nail paring.

I long for more light. I wake
in the morning night. I dine
with darkness pushing against
the windows. What sun we get

is golden, then ruddy, slanting
so it hits the bottoms of the great
frigates of cloud that threaten
snow, sailing at us across the Bay.

Marge Piercy

All Those Pesky Night Questions

When friends grow ill, when friends begin
to fail, even when enemies and tabloid
strangers die, you begin to wonder:
which door will open and then close

on me? At seventeen I imagined dying
at thirty-eight or –nine, intact, glowing
and then banging out like a roman candle
leaving a fiery trail of brilliant sparks.

Who hasn't comforted herself
imagining her funeral, well attended
of course, old lovers weeping: that
will show them not to be good

to me. But time thins the crowd.
You wonder if it will hurt and how
much. Maybe you think that white
light leads to a resort in heaven.

Maybe you think it's a neural
mirage. But I know some little
beast is stirring in my heart
or liver, waiting to gnaw through.

At night sometimes I rehearse
it pointlessly. It is, as they say,
just a matter of time. Death
is the answer to every question.

Bruce Bond

Sea of Trees

Silence is half the music. The song breathes.
Winter chimes go still inside the trees.

And the hole in the music is musical,
because, oddly, it lets in what music

is not. Not alone. The stray cough,
the closing door. Silence is one half

merciful, the other the careless snowfall
of the world. I do not feel what you feel.

I cannot sing my way into your child's
suffering. I try. And the music of trying

goes speechless in the woods between us.
Let me try again. Once there was a girl

who climbed a tree to end her misery,
to hang among the branches like a bell.

Pain is pain. It is not beautiful.
What we do not know about her life

fills the forest with a light blue mist.
So why look, you ask. Is it her there.

Or is it your heartbreak that is a shade
cruel, not knowing what it is you break for.

Pain is not the music of pain. Not love.
Though it may find comfort in the light

blue distance, I know from experience,
this is not always true. Nerves go raw.

Too raw for the quietest of breezes.
Would it have mattered if the song were sad,

if it were less the theater of sadness.
The sandal that slipped her dangling foot,

its needle of endearment, does it charm,
does it paralyze love's will a little.

Half a girl in pain is our deafness to pain.
Unlike the deafness of the trees in winter,

we pretend. We try. We commit
our gaffs at the funeral reception,

and the mother crumples into tears.
It is our innocence that makes mistakes,

that makes us feel more cautious and ashamed.
Is it better to look or not look.

Or to desecrate the season. True.
In turning away, we turn into something.

What would comfort a lost innocent more.
Or is that the question. Is it not

the mother we should worry about now.
Is it not the blue gem of love she offered.

Is it not the sweet song she sang her child,
to make night safe for sleeping, once again.

Ed Madden

ADRIFT OFF THE ISLETS OF LANGERHANS

Sails down, we drift. Hospital time, fluid.
The room feels unmoored, floating world.

The horizon is a flotilla of hospitals:
Aunt Mary Etta names them one by one.

One night the moon loomed over them, a cold sun.
One day, a hawk pursued by two crows.

Signals flicker the inlets, like lightning that night,
followed by floods, followed by darkness.

Pancreas, meaning sweetbread, from the Greek
pan for all, from the Greek *kreas*, flesh.

The sign in the hall says: *Quiet, Please, Healing in Progress.*

An island of silence, like the quiet we've tended
for years, cultivating the rift between us.

Adeno, meaning gland, derived from the Greek for acorn.
All flesh meaning without cartilage or bone.

We sail beneath the sign of the crab,
though the sky says otherwise: ram and bull.

Cindy St. Onge

Egyptians

Suppose there is no Summerland,
no Valhalla, no Avalon.
Imagine, after an age of piety
and Christian sacrament
that the Sky World hasn't changed
since the gods ruled Thebes.

Maybe our enlightened dead
find an afterlife of dizzying mazes and
narrow corridors, the very world for
which Egyptians provided amply; an
eternity attained only after
seventy days of meticulous preparation.

Tell me, how would you feel
staggering the stony passage toward
the Hall of the Two Truths,
heckled and accused its entire length?
Would you still be straining
to recognize anything of
a cloud-carpeted heaven?

Shouldn't there be a scroll
tucked under your arm?
No less than forty-two gods will
expect you to know them by name.
How will you negate your sins without
carefully worded scripture?

What if your family, so removed
from those papyrus clues,
doesn't know to bring you food?

They could recite you a feast.
Or they could carve or paint
for you sustenance, never-depleting,
if only they knew about the *ka*
and its hunger.

That you'll die but once, you'd
implore Thoth, "Judge me!"
But he'll not soil the holy scales
of Ma'at with the likes of your heart—
still slick with gore, it stinks of
the living.

You'll remember that moment:
your blood and breath gone still, thinking,
"I'll never need or want again,"
that death afforded you
the leisure of a king.

But you didn't die a king.
And in this world
of kohl-eyed pharaohs,
empty-handed, you are a beggar.

It is here, you'll wait,
in the liminal breath between
the ever-living and oblivion, watching
perfect creatures of regal bone
and raisin skin proceed, judged
and blessed, into Duat.

Across rivers of water and sand,
these ferried souls become
themselves suns, and peers of Ra.
They are done with sorrow.

And when you've counted
a thousand ferries that have sailed
without you, seventy days
won't seem so very long a time.

Upon discovering that your shadow is
most cumbersome a burden,
you will understand that it was never
your body that hungered, or hurt,
or lived.

You would cry out, wouldn't you?
You would explain that you didn't know,
that your family didn't know,
that there has been an awful mistake—
if only someone east of here
would pray your mouth open.

Quenton Baker

Nude Transformation

—after Yusef Komunyakaa

Is this how you imagined
it? Cecile smiles at my silence.
She walks to my bed,
vanilla scent in a purple blouse
and a knee-length black skirt
sculpted by her thighs.
Lamplight turns to moonlight
when it spills on her
unbuttoning fingers;
her blouse falls behind her.

Do you think my breasts are made of ether?
She brings the sea and the dusk
in the switch of her hips.
I look at the floor.
Her slow walk toward my bed
turns the hardwood to sand
that her skirt litters like seaweed.

Is this where my I keep my voodoo?
She slides her violet panties
halfway down her hips.
I avoid her eyes.
The rain outside is turning
from high hats to kick drums.

What is a bed but a sea to drown in?
I hear waves at my back.
She drops her unhooked bra
where the water meets the shore.

Tell me, what is it that you think I have?
That you want so badly now?
Her fingers are at my chest.

There are dark waters in me too, I say.
There's a setting sun in me, too,
and I want to wear my skin
as well as you wear yours.
She smiles again.

But you're afraid of me, aren't you?
She flicks off the moon.

Erica Vega

An Open Window

Yesterday, when the window was left open
and the weatherman predicted the rain
to spark the violence
of growing

Yesterday, when the weatherman looked
into the screen and said,
tomorrow is a day
of relief

Yesterday, when the weatherman looked
into that electronic screen,
with eyes belonging to centuries not yours:
when he stood taller than you saw him before
and he said,
tomorrow, it will rain

I wondered if the crack in the window
you left open would wet the inside.
If it would sound like the day
wine replaced your voice
and you thought you loved me.

It is only water.
It is only water.

John Johnson

California Knockdown

"...life... the most fragile thing in the world."
—Blaise Pascal

Half awake, I lose my way
in bed, bump into
old friends, puzzle over
simple things: muddy
boots, ragged buffalo,
insects
pinned in life-like positions,
shattered continents, melting
ice floes, desire
luffed by headwind.

God of doorways, I am that jellyfish
acting out of character, aging in both directions.

Here in the Valley of Heart's
Delight, where a freeway is
never far, it's raining: slab
foundations crack, carpets
darken, garage floors
flood. Everywhere
families are pulling up stakes,
cutting guy-wires, piling into circus
cars. Big top walls are wafting.

Beneath the gold horizon,
among roots of "thinking reeds,"
flatworms,
in the mushroom bodies
inside their heads,

dream delectable
stenches,
meter in the motions of waves.

It's true what they say,
the brain has a mind all
its own.

Jenny Molberg

MATRYOSHKA

For some reason, the early nesting dolls depicted what appears to be a family without a father. —The Mendeleyev Journal

I.

When you take away the children
the mother is empty. Her round head
shrouded in red, her lips thick
and pursed, her cheeks rouged
with big circles of flush. And her eyes—
she is keeping her inside secret.
The matryoshka's arms, creased
with plump, hug
a glossed rose. Sprigs
of cornflower and baby's breath. If
you look closer, a thin line
cuts the rose. This is where t
he mother is broken.

II.

I have discovered the mother
inside the mother. Her eyes
are dark like mine. She doesn't want
what is inside her. Her arms:
thin. Her collar: drab, her lashes: straight.
Her flower is not a rose. This mother
fits better in my hand. When I pull
her open, she creaks.

III.

The last mother has no arms,
no dress, no collar.
But she is smiling.
She breaks willingly.
I turn her open
and find myself. Each daughter
becomes my mother and I become
each mother. I hold myself
in my hand. This is my secret—
I have seen how small
I can be. I will put
the wooden child back inside me.
And the woman inside me. And the woman
inside me. And the woman inside me.

Vincent M. Basso

On the Death of Poets

I.

A man loses his job, and for what reason he cannot tell.

Over the cartons of Lo Mein and Peppered Beef, he tries to explain to his son
what this will mean.

He goes to the welfare office, and the woman at the desk stares at him as if he is sick.
Is it my spleen? He asks. He is a clever man.
She slides the forms across the counter.

Everyone in the lobby looks worn out and sad.
The security guard tinkers with his portable TV, then eyes the room with suspicion.

The man feels small and alone. He stares at the forms and thinks he can feel the earth
turn slowly in its orbit.

He senses that this is the mark of his failure, and that soon he will be undone.

After supper the man reads his son a bedtime story.
He seems distracted, sometimes losing his place. Later, after the boy is asleep,

he thinks of what it might be like to end his life.

II.

There had been a country, and a war in the country.
The poets sang, *Verde que te quiero verde. Verde viento. Verdes ramas*[1]
The poets sang, until the army rounded them up, and killed them.

There were many small bands of refugees in the forest then.
The people everywhere were very hungry. Very hungry, and very afraid.

They spoke of the poets, and sang near the small fires of their encampments,
Our lives no longer feel ground under them. At ten paces you can't hear our words.[2]

III.

The man slowly pronounces the word ar-bor-vit-ae, then pauses to make certain his son understands how to repeat it.

In the story that is told, there is a man and a boy and a crow,
who wandered the earth for generations, and through the wars of generations.

Who believed there was a wisdom existent before the autumnal forest,
and so walked amid the palsied leaves, bowing their heads

in deference to whatever animal rustled from the underbrush.

Mosses concealing the rotting stumps of trees; while ivy vined further
into the crevices of battered limestone, sheer above the icy light of the creek.

Always the wasted forms of rapture—the occasional animal skull, or scrap
of the made world to lure them,

further into the mouth of it, where a deer might startle and bolt,
not expecting the three to be watching it root

amid the fungi that would burst into purple or rose powders
if brushed with a hoof.

IV.

In the story that is not told the boy grew into a man, and grew old.
Most nights he sat in his house and waited for it—waited

for death to come screaming through the rafters, or to wash over his old stubbled face
with the promise of a final dawn.

Countertops strewn with dishes and stacks of yellow newspapers.
Flypaper hung in ribbons.

In his dreams there was a boy, who he would offer water in a filthy glass,
only to make a sound, as if it quenched his thirst.

In the story that is not told the man lived in squalor, and without teeth,
and believed the hard clawing and yowl that came from the ceiling each night

belonged to that of the archangel, with whom he'd try to bargain,
If you would forgive me, I would come.

V.

The man and the boy and the crow wandered the forest for generations,
and through the wars of generations.

They entered the clearing of oak and elm—a mosaic of red, yellow, brown—
sweet rot coating the ground.
Where is the tree you promised us? Asked the boy.
Nothing lives, or dies, anymore. Said the man.

In the forest where the people had lied down to grieve, and bury themselves in snow,
if you kept very quiet, and very still, you could still discern
their sad reverie among the trees.

VI.

The man holds his son, and promises that he will not suffer,
and, yet, the boy loves him still.
The no-see-ums flew their last furious carousels.

He closes the book and goes to the mirror and studies the man,
who looks back at him—the crow cawed madly against the failing sun.

The man thinks of what it might be like to end his life, then of the boy—

Deep in the forest the ragged survivors talked of a time
when they might sit at table with so many of the dead and living again.

The language of the fathers curled inward to its trace—
and the boy rubbed the bullet casing the man had given him,
like a talisman or river stone to ease back the chill.

It sweat in his palm—the smell of residual powder, a taste
like bitter earth.

The man promises his son that he will not suffer—

and the vast wilderness again takes shape, where the tree lay hewn to root,
and the chill wind lends a sheen to the creek, like a sorrow.

---

[1]Quoted from *Romance Sonámbulo*, Federico García Lorca

[2]Quoted from *The Stalin Epigram*, Osip Mandelstam

Brian Beard

Merci Jesus

NINE YEAR OLD MATU SAT on the first of many rows of narrow benches in the dim classroom, her flip-flops resting lightly on the dirt floor. The teacher had his back turned to the class, and the sound of his chalk on the board as he wrote a math problem sounded like bones being rubbed together. Instead of copying in her notebook, Matu turned her gaze outside beyond the field of pineapples and watched the flashes of bush taxis passing on the highway. Once Matu had looked up from sweeping hair from the cement floor of her mother's hair salon and asked where the highway went and her mother had told her it went to the city of Cotonou.

"And what is beyond Cotonou?" Matu had asked.

"The ocean," her mother had said. "Only water."

Ever since, Matu had wanted to see this "only water,"

but her mother would never take her to Cotonou on her monthly shopping trips. The day before her mother had gone to the city again and of course again she had not taken Matu. Matu knew if she were a boy, it would be different. If she were a boy, her father would not have left her mother. If she were a boy, her mother would not wake her before her older sisters to sweep the courtyard of the compound and to start the fire, would not whip her when things sometimes spilled and broke because her mind had again wandered off the task at hand. If she were a boy, she would have been to Cotonou, if only once.

Suddenly Matu felt the knuckles of the teacher descending on the top of her skull. He was a young man in a drab green suit who rode to the school from another town on a blue motorbike. He asked her for the answer to the problem on the board and she drew a breath as if to speak and held it as she stared at the indecipherable numbers on the board. Sika, Matu's friend beside her, raised her hand ever so slowly, as if reaching towards a fly and not wanting to startle it before she swatted it. The teacher nodded and Sika said "zero" and Matu exhaled, equally relieved and humiliated.

At noon Matu headed down the side of the highway with Sika for the shade of Sika's mother's market stall, where the two friends would eat beans mixed with manioc flour out of ceramic bowls. They kept their hands by their sides and walked in a straight line, as the bicycle, motorbike, and automobile traffic passed beside them, no more than a meter away.

The girls passed a lame beggar who got around on a wood plank with wheels attached to it; a stand of whisky bottles full of black market gasoline; a stack of firewood; and a stand of pineapples, their sticky, sugary insides oozing in the heat through the pores of their rough skin. At last they came to the market. Across the highway they could see the salon with its name stenciled on the front, MERCI JESUS, and a metal sign with a painting of three women's faces with coquettish smiles featuring three different hairstyles.

Matu saw a taxi parked along the highway in front of the salon with her mother standing behind it, waiting for the driver to unload her mother's things. Perhaps if Matu had been a year older, she would have gone straight into the market and avoided her mother altogether. But despite Matu's cool treatment of her, Matu still craved her mother's affection, still hoped there was something in her mother which loved something in her, and so she called out: "Mama!"

Her mother did not turn her head. Whether she heard Matu over the sound of the highway traffic and the voices of the people in the market Matu did not know, so she called again: "Mama!", but her mother seemed fixated on the objects accumulating at her feet—hair products, soap opera photo magazines, beignets and sweet bread, cool yogurt in plastic sacks.

Matu knew the highway was murderous. She had heard the collisions of metal on metal, had come running out of the salon with the customers, combs still stuck in their half-braided hair, had witnessed the wreckage, the broken bodies, the groans of the dying. Perhaps in that moment she forgot, or perhaps she was blinded by her need for her mother's acknowledgement, but in any case she felt the urge for action, and she broke free of Sika's grip and took just one step in the direction of her mother, and—too late—turned and saw through the windshield of an oncoming taxi.

It was like peering into a forbidden, secret room. She saw the driver first, his bleary eyes void of expression; a beautiful young woman in the passenger seat blinking at the market; an old man in the back with an unshaven beard, his eyes closed as if he were asleep or praying; chickens on the ledge behind the backseat lost among the inaudible clucking of their chicken dreams. The taxi came to an abrupt halt and Matu's spirit rose to the height of the trees, leaving her body on the highway, its hands flexed upon the asphalt. A crowd from the market spilled onto the highway, one part of it circling around the body, another part around the taxi.

Matu watched as her mother, one hand clutched to the shoulder of Matu's body, one raised in the direction of the taxi, shook her head and mouthed expressions of grief. A policeman on a motorbike hollered at everyone to clear off the highway; when people did not seem to hear him he began striking the highway with a whip; the crowd dispersed, but just as soon regrouped, like ants when water is poured on their mound.

Not yet knowing how to move in her spirit form, Matu hung in the air above the crowd for a moment before finding herself moving along the highway as if carried by a breeze. Soon she came to where no one had heard about the accident and the day was normal and large and pleasant. She passed a boy walking with a bundle of firewood on his head; she passed pineapple farmers in their fields; and everywhere she heard the voices of people calling to each other, greeting, joking, teasing. From time to time she would say something to one of them, but they did not seem to hear her, and she did not herself understand the words which came from her own mouth: already language had lost its meaning to her.

Cotonou at dusk was a bustle of traffic swirling in a cloud of dust and pollution. Matu stared in wonder at the kaleidoscope of fabrics on the people on the motorbikes racing around a roundabout below. She passed the terraces of restaurants and marveled at people of various colors of skin eating strange foods; she peered over the metal gates before enormous two-story houses at the light seeping around the edges of curtains on windows.

Floating over cinderblock compounds and dirt courtyards she came to the beach, where a line of fishermen stood before nets bursting with fish, their scales shimmering silver feathers. When it grew dark she headed out into the sky above the ocean, a tetherless place swallowing up and disposing of all manner of problems before they could be mentioned or even conceived, the waves below her swelling with brine and phosphorescence, as insistent, as fugitive, as breath.

Sara Patton

The Bull Rider

THE BULL HADN'T BEEN POLITE. The contractor had said the Brahma would turn right, but Blackjack spun quick out of the chute to the left, did a series of twisted cocky bucks, not sure which way he wanted to unload the cowboy. The result was a bluish red hoof print on his right calf.

Waking with a jolt, for a second he doesn't know where he is. The familiar comes in slowly, white ceiling of the trailer moist with condensation, cowboy hat resting on a hook, sweats, long handles. He sure as hell knows he's not at a rodeo. He has kept the propane going all night with the oven door open for some warmth, but he can still see his breath. Throwing off the blankets, he places his feet on the floor and sits a moment staring at his legs. He can barely see the imprint, just a faint outline. He got off easy that time, far cry from a broken leg, wrist or ribs, places he's been before. Nothing a few Canadian aspirins couldn't cure. Putting on his long handles he walks the two steps to the kitchen, grabs a beer out of the mini-fridge, takes a dip of Copenhagen and stares out at the falling snow, the snow piling up.

"Shit."

The boys called him "lost and found." He may have started out without a clue, trying to find the airport in Phoenix to catch a plane to the rodeo, but then he'd just look skyward for descending planes and put the dually in high gear, sometimes arriving minutes before his ride. The boys, laughing, having already placed bets.

He spits chew into an empty beer can and thinks now they'd call him "stuck." He'd got the Skid-steer stuck yesterday trying to level out the area by the barn, got too close to an edge which he couldn't see anyway with all the snow. He liked driving the Skid-steer, scraping snow, clearing the road to the barn. In the cab he could be in control and the sound of the engine kept his many minds at bay. Out of the cab and the agitation takes hold. The separation, kids, no money, all slap him in the face like a harsh wind. More beer sounds good, but he makes himself some toast instead. Seems like lately all he's seeing is the bottom of a Coors can. Although he thought yesterday's meeting with the bankruptcy attorney went fairly well despite the secretary's hiccup with his name.

"Okay, Mr. Waterstin, you can go in now."

"Waterston, like waters a ton."

"Okay, Mr. Waterstone, you can go in now."

The attorney was probably ten years younger than him but pudgy with acres of balding on the top of his head. Walker had vowed he would never let his waist hang over his belt, like his father's. At forty-nine he still had six pack abs, despite all the beer. Maybe he was just lucky, but he doubted that.

"I'll need to ask you a few questions. Any outstanding warrants?"

"No."

"Any felonies?"

"No."

"Child abuse?"

"No."

"Spousal abuse?"

"No. Ask me a yes question."

"Excuse me?"

"Do I like to fish, ask me if I like to fish, I can answer yes to that question."

He layers on the long handles, wool pants, fleeces, laces up the Schnee's and heads out. It's a half mile from his trailer to the barn where the temporary phone line has been put in. This far north cell phones are a joke.

Growing up the South Dakota, winters were brutal. His family lived two miles off the highway. The oldest of four, his job was to harness Bessy. He'd ride Bessy and she would pull the toboggan with his brothers and sister wrapped in sleeping bags, to the highway where they'd meet the school bus. He was in fourth grade. He can't remember how Bessy got home.

Punching through knee deep snow, he's annoyed by the surprise of it. The soon to be ex told him she wants a divorce on the airplane back from vacationing in Mexico. The kids were sitting across the aisle. What kind of a person does that. A bitch. Never thought he'd marry one. He tried to break it off once, but then she started crying. He walks faster using his boots as a snow plow, flinging snow plumes,

"Damn."

His German shepherd, Sheba, comes bounding out of the pine trees heavy with snow, her tail wagging.

"Where the hell have you been? You don't have to answer that. C'mon, let's go call the pretty girl."

The first time she came up here to help him pull the dually out, he could tell she was nervous by how tight she gripped the wheel of her truck. When his buddy from Arizona came up here to get him lined out on the job, they would eat at the cafe where she works. She was nice to talk to, not like the other girls who seemed to be looking for something. He sure as hell didn't need something right now.

"Mary, Miss Mary, How em ya? Where em ya?"

"It would be called work."

"Really, I don't know what that is. Ha."

"Let me guess, you're stuck?"

"Bingo."

She had come to the village in the spring when the sand hill cranes flew in to mate on their journey south. Walking by the lake she was amazed that the cranes

didn't need massive pillars to stand, that their long skinny legs were enough to hold up their bulbous bodies. The villagers welcomed her. They didn't examine her as if part of a husband, as if part of a missing link. They never asked about her ex and she was glad not to have to regurgitate a story that was over. She loved the mountains, loved the harshness that comes with remoteness. And they accepted her for loving that.

Driving up the snow packed road with her yellow lab Molly in the cab, she can't deny she enjoys his liveliness. Her ex was such a bore. Walker came into the cafe with smiles, humor and an interesting take on the English language. She told him she loved swimming and swam at least three times a week. On his second cup of coffee he'd ask her how her "swimmage" was. If it was raining or snowing out he'd tell her it was "participating." She guessed in a sense it was. But under the surface she can see the heaviness around his heart. She knows she can't own it. She had her own frozen water and had to claw her way to the surface. Under the ice she could swim freely in her own private world but she knew she would never have a relationship again if she wasn't willing to come up to the surface and breath the same air.

Waiting for Mary, he shovels snow around the Skid-steer. There's way too much snow. He knows this is stupid but if he stops he'll explode.

"Fuck it."

He grabs a beer that he stuck in his fleece leaving the trailer, and heads back over to the phone. Calling his buddy Walt Grimes isn't the smart thing to do but he misses the bulls. He misses the boys.

"Mr. Grimmus, how em ya?"

"Walker Lee. I've been wonderin' how you're getting along."

"So how'd you and the boys do?"

"I rode like a fat girl."

"Did you pee down your leg, too?"

"Just about."

"What about Kevin, Chris, Ricardo?"

"Nah, everybody just came to look."

"Ugh, so nobody rode?"

"Sam got one jumped, knocked the sap right out of him."

"Serves that squeaky little Texan right."

"Riiight. Ya hanging in there?"

"Oh yeah, I'm in debt up to my hat brim, live in a trailer with mold on the walls, but I'm thinkin when it warms up I'll wash it down with Clorox and it'll be good to go."

When he was three years old his father put him on the palomino, strapped a dog chain around his waist and tied it around the horn of the saddle so he wouldn't fall off. He rode in the parade. Later the palomino decided to race alongside a train moving through town. He never fell off.

When Mary arrives the snow is coming straight down in big gentle flakes, landing softly, as if no one will notice. She sees how buried the Skid-steer is and laughs,

"You've got to be kidding me, there's no way."

He really wants this to work. "Never say whoa in a mud hole. Ya know why?"

She's smiling, "No why?"

"Cause ya might get stuck! Who dee who!"

Shaking her head, "You ready, let's do this."

"I was born ready."

For over an hour they try to pull the Skid-steer out, changing the angles on the tow rope. Reluctantly, he calls it quits.

Wading through knee deep snow with the dogs who have become instant buddies, "This is beautiful."

"Yeah, the logs are all hand peeled. It's for a guy in the oil business. He's a *bizznessman.* I use to be a *bizznessman."*

She laughs, "Yeah, well I used to be a wife."

"It's kinda funny."

"Thanks a lot."

"No, I mean the way you and I came here, not knowing anybody, all miscombobulated and whatnot."

"I think it's discombobulated."

"Mis, dis, all the same."

"Destiny."

"Yeah, well I'm not afraid, are you? I'm not afraid of anything." He Kung-fu kicks a snow bank,

"Whoo wa!"

After he has showed her the barn, they trudge up the hillside scattered with leafless aspen trees like needles on a pin cushion. He shows her the log home that was started last spring, all the while telling her about the good life he thought he once had. The job managing a linen company for all the fancy resorts and hotels. Eighty grand a year. The log home which backed up to forest service land. He had his horses, snowmobiles, a speed boat with a fish finder. He could saddle up his horse and just ride out or hunt deer and elk. That was before they sold the place so he could rodeo. He told Mary that his wife encouraged it. She bought his rodeo card for a Christmas present. Maybe there was something going on. He was so busy working. Working at being a husband. Working at being a father. He thinks he may have talked too much but Mary looks him in the eye like she's listening, listening to all of it.

He started riding bulls at sixteen. Saddle broncs were no longer a challenge. He didn't tell his mother. The ride didn't last eight seconds. He went home without his front teeth. She wasn't upset about the bulls. He had had such pretty teeth.

Work is all he knows, so the next morning he is determined to shovel the Skid-steer out. He's methodical about shoveling and gets a rhythm going using his back and knees. He just wishes he wasn't so angry. An anger that festers in the pit of his stomach every time he fills up the shovel. "Shit," he tosses the snow back over his shoulder. "Shit," why couldn't he'd seen it coming. Seventeen years younger than him, how did he ever think it would work in the first place. His best friend's sister. His eyes well up with tears, and he shovels faster, glad to be alone with his vulnerability. He shovels faster as if he's the one buried. Try is all he has, try is all he knows.

It's a small community, more like a village, Mary is the only person he thinks he knows. But in this remoteness words travel on snowflakes and trees have eyes. So he doesn't have to shovel very long when a rancher comes chugging down his road in a monster sized blue tractor plow. They have the Skid-steer out in less than ten minutes. Wearing a wool natty cap with ear flaps down, the rancher looks a bit goofy. Walker shakes his hand and the rancher asks him if he likes to ice fish. They should go out on the lake someday, "before it melts." It's snowing again and they both laugh.

When Mary came to the village in the spring, she would take long walks in the grasses that were beginning to weave their way in and out of the snow patches like frayed stitches on a blanket. In the meadows she would look for pieces of cow skeletons, discarded antlers, bones. Once she found a horse head skeleton that the ants had cleaned white. She hung it on her wall, a skeleton of what was once so alive. Her marriage had been reduced to a skeleton. They had gotten under each other's skin to the point that there was nothing left to pick apart. She thought she must learn to love a person for what she saw and not dig too deep. Not get to the point where she wanted to rip their skin off and rebuild them.

Walker tells himself he's not looking for something and he's not. It's just that he misses talking to her. He invites her to his trailer for spaghetti dinner and a "picture show," a thank you for helping him out, for being his friend. After dinner they watch the movie sitting next to each other on his bed. He speaks again of his kids and she gently touches his face with her hand.

"My mother died when I was young. Leaving my kids wasn't an option. I wanted to give them what I never had, maybe it wasn't fair to my husband but it was the way I had to do it."

"Wish mine were in college."

"Don't worry when they're teenagers, she'll be begging you to take em."

"She's living with a guy. She wants me to walk away. Not gonna happen. I'm their father, he's not gone."

"They're not babies. They know who their father is."

"But I'm so"

"Angry?"

"Fuck."

After work she drives the snowy four miles to his trailer. So much snow filling up the bed of her pick up, like a giant snow cone. Sometimes they drink wine and play dice. He likes the way her eyes light up like fire flies every time she blinks. Her smile is a mile wide when she laughs and he likes to make her laugh with his silly child- like jokes just so she keeps that smile. And sometimes they cry, as they open their hearts, as they lay bare thoughts that have been buried deep.

"Were you scared?"

"Yeah, I thought I would die, like I wouldn't be able to make it on my own."

"I'm glad you didn't. I think we were brought together for a reason."

"I was more scared of not taking the risk, deep down I was really unhappy. I just felt like, don't laugh, that at the end, whenever that is, god would say I don't know you, you've lived a lie, no bed for you at the inn."

"Your husband, what was he—"

"Oh no."

"You know what I think, that he didn't appreciate you. You're smart, pretty-"

"I dunno, I think he found a comfy place on the couch and stopped doing stuff."

"Well no worries here, cause I don't own a couch."

The first time they have sex it surprises them. So they do it again. Under layers of blankets he sings,

"Oh it's 40 below, heaters broke, my truck won't start and I don't give a damn cause I'm off to the rodeo."

Under layers of blankets they wrestle and giggle and he shouts out,

"Who dee who, who dee fuckin' who."

Under layers of blankets they begin exploring each other's bodies like new found continents. He's amazed that making love to her is all he wants and she amazed by his unending desire.

When they come up for air spring has arrived. They take a road trip to Montana to retrieve the leftovers from his marriage out of a storage unit. While he drives she kicks off her shoes and puts her feet up on the dash. She has the most beautiful feet, slender, high arches, toes all lined up in the correct receding order, toenails painted cream color. Walker would rather be massaging her feet and about drives off the road. They stop along the way and make love on a blanket in a pine forest. Afterwards he fishes the creek and she sits half naked dangling her feet.

"This is my happy place."

"Mine's swimming. I swim so much I could sprout gills."

"Really?"

"Really."

"I'd notice."

This was true. He knew the topography of her body better than her ex of twenty years. His fingers tracing the outline of her birthmark. His hands finding relief in the contours where her legs joined her hips, where her neck joined her shoulders. As if paying attention to the details of her body he was putting together a puzzle that would unlock his own unhappiness. He thinks, maybe, maybe there is a god who hooked him on to a preciousness that he can finally grasp.

Every day he tells her, "Have I told you that I love you?"

"Yes, this morning."

"Well, I'm telling you again."

Come June his bankruptcy and divorce are final and he gets his kids for a whole month. Ten-year-olds, a boy and a girl arrive wearing t-shirts and smiles. Walker shows them how to dangle salami on fishing line to catch crayfish, they fish for trout in the lake, and swim. Lying on the shore in the sun, they wrestle and giggle. He makes fires at night where they cook hot dogs and roast marshmallows. They sleep with him every night and although he doesn't get much sleep with all the knees and elbows jabbing him, he doesn't care. There are tears when they have to go back. Being a good father was never the issue.

He's itching to ride bulls again. He wants to share this with Mary. Share the smell of rosin, leather bull ropes, bullshit on the boots. Share the sounds of spurs jangling, chutes opening and an eight second buzzer. He wants to make a ride and he wants her to see it, live, not just in all his pictures.

Bouncing around like a ball on a tether, he throws his gear bag in the bed of the truck and they hop in the cab. Mary had forgotten what it was like to be around a twelve-year-old.

The bull riders have a nefarious way of greeting each other,

"Hey, shit head."

"Asshole."

"Bone head."

"Bitch," followed by hugs and pats on the back. When Walker introduces her, they shake Mary's hand and tip the brims of their cowboy hats. She leaves them to their talk and wanders back to the stock pens to look at the bulls. Fifteen to twenty bulls standing around, some laying down chewing on bits of hay, staring at her with big brown eyes. One so close to the metal gate she can reach her hand in and scratch his forehead.

She's seen all his pictures; the one where he's riding with a cast on his leg; the one where his hand is hung up in the bull rope and he's flipped over the bull's head, airborne, parallel to the bull's body. If you didn't know better the picture looks comical.

On the drive down she had asked him, "Why ride bulls?"

"Because I can."

"Anybody can say that. You're an adrenaline junkie."

"Maybe."

"Why not saddle broncs?"

"They're scary."

"Right."

"Love."

"Love?"

"Yeah, love. I love the sport, it's exciting, broken ribs, jaws, legs, doesn't matter. I ride because I love to ride, doesn't matter, if I get stomped to death, then I died doing something I love. How many people can say that?"

They spend two days at this rodeo and he gets on three bulls. He doesn't "ride," he only makes three or four seconds. But each time he gets on Mary holds her breath and when he's bucked off and walking back to the chute, she lets the air out. Mary is surprised by Walker's buddies. She had thought they would all be ride the range cowboys, not businessmen, teachers and chemists. She likes hanging out with the boys listening to their stories. She likes how driven they are. Eight seconds of pure love. Growing up a motherless girl, driven is a concept she's wrapped herself around. In college, she climbed mountains, living in Hawaii she ocean kayaked, at forty she earned a Black Belt in Tae Kwon Do. And her friend, her boyfriend Walker Lee Waterston, woke up every morning like a rolling ball of butcher knives.

Mary has to get back to work. Her feelings for Walker have surprised her. It's like some invisible force plucked them out of the universe and said, "Okay you two need to meet. How about in a pine forest with clear mountain air." Still in back of her mind is that little voice saying, "Don't fall, don't fall safety nets are good." Walker goes on with his buddies, a couple more rodeos. He promises he'll call her after every ride. He just wants in on it all. Wants to have those eight seconds where there is no ex, no money problems. But his mind hasn't made dust of them, they're still blowing around, finding comfortable corners, waiting.

The bull stood quiet in the chute. Stood quiet as the bull rope wrapped around behind his front shoulder blades. Stood quiet as the cowboy got on and flipped his chaps around as he settled in on the bull's back. The bull let him get his glove hand secured in the handle, make the wrap. He stood quiet as the cowboy moved around with his knees and thighs getting a firm grip on the Brahma's back; he twitched slightly as the cowboy touched his shoulder blades with the rowels of the spurs. When the chute opened the Brahma moved out giving the cowboy some bucks he could ride, constantly spinning to the right the way the cowboy liked to ride. He gave the cowboy six seconds, enough to let him think he'd made the ride. Then the Brahma lowered his head, kicked out high with his hind legs, twisted to the left and tossed the cowboy in the air like a stuffed toy. When the cowboy came down he was under the bull and the bull was ready to be done with him. Ready to head to the gate and be turned back out with the other bulls. In a final hurrah, the bull bowed his head, took a whiff of the cowboy under him, and with both his hind legs pushed off the cowboy like a stepping stone on his way to the gate, head held high.

His buddies run out and help him get up. They walk him behind the chutes, leaning against a gate, a trickle of blood makes a line down his chin, slowly his body slides down the gate. Walker feels as though he's drifting off to a place, a place he can't control. "Boys", he says, then nothing. There is no hospital in this rural town, so the ambulance takes him to the family clinic. His injuries are beyond the scope of the family doctor whose specialties are ear infections and sprained ankles. A call is made for a helicopter to transport Walker to the closest trauma center an hour away. With all the blood coming from Walker's mouth, the doctor knows he's going to have to try to get a chest tube inserted. And try he does, three times. He makes a slit along the side of the rib cage and each time he thrusts the foot long tube into the chest, Walker jerks, open his eyes, comes back from the place he thought he was going to. As the doctor is attempting this, two young nurses are preparing to put in a catheter. As they begin cutting off his pants, Walker tries to make light,

"Be prepared ladies, what you're about to see is huuuge."

Mary is lying in bed reading when her cellphone rings, lights up his number, but it's not his voice on the other end.

When she walks into his hospital room the first thing she sees is the chest tube coming out of his side, watered down blood flowing into a clear plastic box with chambers. It reminds her of those plastic containers kids buy to fill with dirt for ant farms. The suctioning machine, in a steady rhythm, sounds like air being pulled through teeth. A constant sound she'll hear for five days. A locked box with morphine is next to the chest tube, hooked into his forearm with a needle. Walker is sitting up in his bed, looking out the window. When he hears Mary enter the room he turns to face her. For a second the gravity of his accident takes hold and she'd like to back out of the room. Put the movie frame in reverse, back down the hall, down the stairs, out the door, get in the truck. Do overs.

Walker lights up, looks happy to see her, in an opiate sort of way,

"Hi hon."

She goes to him and kisses his forehead. Now she knows where they came up with the word *ashen.* His cheeks are sunken and he's lost weight. Weight he doesn't have to lose. There are no visible wounds. She knows this is the bad part, they're all internal. Her dad was a doctor. On busy days he'd ask her to come over to the hospital so he could visit with her. The smell of chipped beef and antiseptic comes wafting back. Smiling she kisses him again, "Back at ya, you look like shit."

"Ya well, you look beautiful."

In an uncomfortable chair she sits next to his bed. Once in a while Walker will want her to lay beside him and she'll do so, gingerly, trying not to disturb the tubes coming out of his arm and his chest. When the bull was doing his final coup de grace one of his hind legs got caught inside Walker's protective vest. The result is seven ribs broken twice on his left side. Broken off at the vertebra and broken again in half. He's chest x-ray looks like a game of pick- up sticks. Then there's the punctured lung.

Ten days later, Walker is discharged. The doctor shows Mary how to insert a Bic pen into the chest tube opening, "Just in case he has trouble breathing, going over those mountain passes."

Exhausted, she starts crying and Walker wraps himself around her, "Fuck it, let's go home."

Mary drives the eight hours, constantly turning her head to watch Walker's breathing. Bottles of juice, aspirin, pain killers, all his losses like scraps of paper fill the cab of the truck. As the sun descends into a watercolor on the distant mountains, Walker wakes from napping, "Are you in or are you out?"

"What?"

"With me, with this."

"I think I'm in."

"No, you're either all in or all out, there's no thinkin."

Mary pauses, heart and mind fusing into one truth, "I'm in."

"Okay, then."

The gift of grace entered Walker's life like the first drop of snow melting in a spring thaw, the first flicker of light dawning over the mountains, barely visible but integral. Hope would follow even though Walker wouldn't be able to put a name on either of them. Within a year the ribs found their mates and rejoined. His muscles worked became strong. Never say whoa in a mud hole.

There is a black and white photograph. He is on the palomino. His two brothers are sitting behind him. He is five years old and they are three years old. The palomino's left leg is bent to the ground, the right leg stretched out in front. The palomino's head is tucked down and back, bowing.

In the fall as the aspens wake to new colors, he works on the barn while she walks the woods with the dogs. They gather for lunch around a fire he's built from scrap wood, drink Coronas and eat elk meat that sizzles in a wok over the fire. They sit in lawn chairs and talk about the garden they'll have or the bed he'll make them out of fallen logs.

Carol Kanter

Carriers

> "…to be a discoverer you hold close whatever you find, and after a while you decide what it is." —William Stafford, *Security*

Suddenly this autumn—The
urge to collect feathers shed
out of the blue here and
there.

Never before have I noticed
such talismans
from birds.

I hesitated yesterday,
but bent to pluck
a feather off the sidewalk.

A variegated blue gray,
two fingers wide and longer
than an octave,
smooth, flat,
let go
maybe by a jay.

But, truth is, I barely glanced,
just slipped it in a pocket
of my purse
not knowing why.

Today, another.
Short, smoky white, fluffy, it
beckoned in the breeze from
a tuft of grass.

I do not search for them;
each surprises.

*   *   *   *

I am surprised
that none appeared
yesterday along my route. I
still don't search
but today chance upon
five all together
under a tree in my back yard.

Who knows
what I'm to make of them?

*   *   *   *

Six days in Boston;
four of them feathered.

In Logan Airport Wednesday's
plume stuck out of my hanging
bag's pouch
as it rode
the luggage carousel.
Hard to figure, but
there it was—
One side thin and smooth;
the other, triangular— two
inches wide at its top black
band that tapers gray
below,
and half way to the point
divided
by a v-shaped gap,
as though this unnatural,
cooped up ride unzipped
its tiny barbs.

Thursday's feather—
a blend of taupes flank
its long spine curved
gentle, awaiting ink
for replicating scroll-
work and archaic smiles.

Nothing Friday;
followed by a specimen
chewed ragged at the top,
its stem crushed flat,
but in between a long stripe
the iridescent brown
of serendipity.

Sunday's white feather—
miniature ostrich down
below rivulets of tan—
could do honor
to any hat.

Then nothing more.
At least, I do not count

the small, pure black wisp
on my pillow
when I woke up on Monday.
Already processed,
its source so clear,
how could it hold magic?

*   *   *   *

A featherless two days
after flying home,

followed by this challenge:
a giant clone
of my pillow sample,

this one aflutter at the curb
by my parked car,
impossible to disregard.
(So who said
not to count the omen
of that small, black wisp?)

*   *   *   *

A walk along the beach.
Feathers everywhere.
From gulls.
Mostly rumpled, ravaged
by the lake, the wind.
I choose three light
gray, pristine.

How comforting to know
that when in need
I can find more than plenty
along this shore.

Meanwhile, inklings
flap their fledgling wing.

Taylor Brown

The Vizsla

HIS FATHER WAS A BREEDER of gun dogs. Pointers, wire-haired, enlivened the fields before him like some vanguard of old. The dogs stepped lightly through the tall grasses. Their ears were flung outward like small wings, their heads cocked. Their noses ever-twitching, telling them secrets he would never know. He cradled his shotgun close against his chest. He watched them work. He was 16 years old.

They flushed a covey of game-birds, doves, from a tall thicket of scrub-grass. The birds exploded from the roost, panicked and whistling, and he shot two of them black against the blue sky. Their wings folded against their bodies and they tumbled from the air. The dogs retrieved them, soft-jawed and light-eyed. One of the birds was still alive, twitching. He twisted its neck until it cracked.

The light was dying when they crested the last hill toward home. The dogs were slinking a little, tired and hungry. Him too. He put them in their kennels and fed them. They each ate separate. He slid the bowls through slots in the chain-link. He called them *boy* or *girl,* depending. He rarely called them by their names. He was not the one who named them.

The last light retreated into the horizon. He leaned against the old willow and smoked a cigarette. From here he could see the yellow rectangle of light, the kitchen window. He could see his father in there, in his overalls. He could see him fishing in the fridge for a new beer. When he stood up straight, bottle in hand, his head was right in the crosshairs of the windowpanes.

The screen door banged shut behind him. His father was sitting in his recliner, as always. A bottle of Budweiser sweating in his palm. He did not turn around to look.

"You feed em?"

"Yes sir."

"Drizzle on some of that fish oil, like I told you?"

"Yes sir."

"You get dinner?"

The boy set his game-bag on the kitchen table.

"Good," said his father. "Better get cooking. I'm starving."

The boy cut a block of butter into a glass dish and turned on the oven.

"Yes sir," he said.

They ate oven-fried dove on white plates with sautéed peas. His father did not look at his dinner. He looked at the television set. The dark pearls of lead shot from the meat, he set them in a tight grouping on the oilcloth table setting. The boy spit his into a wastebasket he'd set near his foot. They ate in silence. On TV, Clint Eastwood sat his horse, squinting. The old set made his skin look orange, the mountains purple.

"Can I borrow the truck tonight?"

The old man sniffed.

"What for?"

"Just to get out."

"Skylarking. Waste of time and money."

The boy said nothing. He looked at the television set and spit a nugget of lead into the wastebasket.

His father was asleep in his recliner, his mouth a black vent that dribbled moisture. On TV, Clint peeled away his poncho, revealing an iron shield. The boy wondered why nobody had aimed for his head. He slipped out the backdoor and opened the truck door and set the gearshift into neutral. He began rolling the truck down the gravel drive, toward the road.

He cranked the engine a safe distance from the house and headed for the old railroad bridge. The moon was puddled in the dark slink of the river. The stars were out. No clouds. The boys were already on the bridge. Ricco and Troy, Danny and Sal. He could see them sitting up there, their silhouettes huddled against the night sky like dark and enormous birds. They had a case of beer, begged or stolen. The cans were silver. They threw him one as he approached.

"You're just in time," said Ricco.

"For what?"

Ricco handed him a rifle. "You know what."

He sat down next to Troy. He propped the rifle on his thigh, barrel skyward.

"You're dead," said Troy.

Ricco pointed at him. "You ready?"

"Sure am."

Ricco pointed at Whit. "And you?"

Whit nodded.

"One, two, three, go!"

Whit and Troy popped their beers and started chugging. Troy finished first. He jumped up, hopped the railroad tracks, and hurled the empty can over the far side of the bridge. Then he jumped back, propped his rifle against one of the bridge's steel trusses, and thumbed off the safety. He had a fancy autoloader chambered for .308. When the can appeared from under the bridge, sliding downstream, he started shooting. Geysers shot up around it.

"Shit," he said. "Shit."

Whit was right behind him. He was slower, smoother. The rifle they'd given him was an old bolt-action .30-06. When his own empty can appeared, he shot once. It sank below the surface.

"Shit," said Troy, differently this time. He sat back down and groped in the box for another beer.

Whit sat down next to Ricco, handed him back the rifle.

Ricco leaned over and bumped him, shoulder to shoulder.

"What'd you get into today, bud?"

Whit cracked a new beer and shrugged. "Went out running a couple of the old man's dogs is all."

Troy leaned forward.

"You run that dog for my Daddy?"

"Maybe."

"He says he didn't pay for no dog trained by you. Says your Daddy better make sure she's good-to-go, or he ain't paying."

"He'll pay," said Whit.

"You sound pretty sure," said Troy.

"I am."

Whit felt his way back to the truck. Clouds had moved in; he could hardly see. His feet were unsteady, his vision liquid. The other boys were staying longer. It was Friday. He had to be up early tomorrow for chores.

The first beer can hit him dead in the gut as he came through the backdoor. It was full. He dropped to his knees and covered his face. The second beer, a Budweiser, busted his hand against his head. He turned and scrambled through the screen door and rolled down the back stoop.

"I told you not to take my truck, you little son of a bitch!"

A third beer struck the doorframe, hemorrhaging foam.

"Out drinking, that it? Here, have another!"

The last beer tore the screen from the door. Whit was already clawing his way up the back slope toward the kennels, clutching his bruised hand to his chest. He got to the chain-link door of the first one. A wire-haired Vizsla, Sarah. He fumbled for his keys. He looked over his shoulder. His father's shadow filled the rectangular light of the backdoor a moment, then started down the back steps, a case of beer under his arm. Whit got the padlock undone and crawled through the dog-sized door in the chain-link.

The Vizsla had been curled in a ball; she had her head up now, watching him. Her eyes were almond, white-rimmed with alarm. Her ears were perked. She jumped up and came to him, sniffing him, her nose light against his skin. Inspecting him for wounds, for blood.

His father stood lopsidedly at the fence. Whit could smell him.

"Come out of there, you little son of a bitch!"

Whit held his hand to his chest, said nothing. The dog stood looking at the old man, rigid. His father grabbed hold of the chain-link and rattled it, violently.

"You hear me, you little—"

The dog exploded with fury, snarling, her wolf-teeth bared, her ears back.

"No!" said Whit.

He reached out to the dog, to pull her to safety. She was whelmed with power, quivering. He got her by the haunches. He was afraid what his father might do. But when he looked up, his father had stepped back from the fence. There was something strange in the old man's face: surprise. He turned and staggered slowly back to the house.

Dawn. The sky was red, like a fire just over the horizon. He rose stiffly from the concrete floor. The Vizsla looked up from her bed. Her head was cocked at him, her eyes wide, as if asking him a question.

"Good girl," he told her.

He ruffled the scruff under her chin. Then he unlocked the padlock from inside the kennel and crawled through the door. The lights in the house were already on. He could see his father moving in the kitchen. He walked through the backdoor. His father's hair was slicked back, clean. His overalls were pressed. He was cooking breakfast.

"Morning," said Whit.

His father nodded. "I'm cooking breakfast."

"I saw."

They sat at the table. Eggs, sunny-sided, and microwave sausage patties. Whit was hungry but forked his food around the plate.

"Last night—" said his father.

"Let's not talk about it," said Whit.

This was not the first time, not the last.

"But this time—" said his father.

Whit got up and walked to the bathroom and turned on the shower.

The phone rang. Whit was just in from feeding the dogs. The sun had just cleared the trees. His father answered.

"Parker's Gun Dogs," he said. He listened.

"Sarah, you say?" He shot a quick glance at Whit. Whit gave him no indication. "Sure," said his father. "She's ready."

They pulled up an hour later, Troy and his father. They drove a big Dodge, black, with camouflaged rocker trim. It had metal dog-boxes in the bed and a whip antenna steadied with a tennis ball. Troy had on his hunting bib, blaze orange. He had a dip in. He spit in the driveway while his father rubbed his hands together and asked to see his new Vizsla.

"We wanna run her this morning," he said. "Get us some quail."

"You won't be disappointed," said Whit's father.

When they left, Whit went to clean out the empty kennel. He removed the plaid bed and dog bowls. He swept it out and hosed it down. The other dogs watched him, nervous. When he went inside his father was depositing the cash in the small safe in his office. Whit went to the freezer and got a frozen pack of peas. He needed to ice his hand.

It was noon when the Dodge returned, rattling down their drive at speed. It bounced over the red ruts and skidded to a stop. Whit was standing on the jump-dock, launching deadfowl dummies for a pair of German short-hairs they were training. He quickly ordered them back to their pens. He locked them up and turned around in time to see Troy jump from the truck on one side, his father from the other. They left the doors open. His father dropped the tailgate and grabbed a dog by its collar and slid it out of the bed. It dropped slackly to the dirt. It was the Vizsla, Sarah. Troy's father stood over the body, hands on his hips. Looking at the house. Troy reached in through the passenger side and honked. Whit wanted for something scoped. He would have used it.

His father came ambling out of the house. His face was red. Whit started down the hill, fast. The shouting had started, the finger-pointing. He went straight to the dog. Her front leg was bent strangely, like it had an extra joint. A red shard was visible at the break. Blood pooled on the ground. Her head lay on the ground, her one eye watching all this. Whit looked into it. In its wet orb he saw the shadowy violence reflected, the boot-stamping and black-mouthed curses. He turned around.

"Goddamn bitch bit me," said Troy's father. He held out his arm. It was neatly vented at the forearm, red punctures crowned in bruise. The man's mouth was wet.

"How'd she break that arm?" asked Whit's father.

Troy sniffed. "Daddy kicked the bitch for biting him," he said. "That's how."

"You're damn right I did. Put her down is what I should of done."

Whit's father looked at the two men. Then he looked at Whit, sideways. Something flickered in his eyes: light.

"Well," he said. "She never did like assholes."

Troy's father hit him in the jaw with a closed fist. You could hear the crack. Whit's father went down to his knees, and the man hit him again, again. He held him by his shirt so he couldn't go down. Whit's father turned his head. His mouth and chin were messy and wet, his face bright-bearded with blood. His nose bubbled. His teeth were red. Troy's father hit him again.

Whit looked at Troy. The boy leaned and spat. Smirked. Whit leapt across and feinted a punch. Troy covered. Whit kneed him in the groin. The boy dropped, face twisted with pain. Troy's father had a pistol holstered at the small of his back. A fancy nickel-plated Colt with trick grips. It wiggled when he punched. Whit looked at it a long moment. Then he looked at his father, his face purpled and leaking. His jaw slack, like he was laughing. Beaten. Punished. This man beating him, he was not going to stop. He was breathing hard. His face was flushed. But you could see it in his eyes. He wanted blood. Whit reached over and ripped the gun from its holster. He worked the slide and fired a round off into the sky.

Everything stopped.

"Get off him."

The man dropped Whit's father. He pulled his son off the ground. The two of them walked backwards to their truck, slowly.

"You little son of a bitch," he said. "You'll pay for this. The both of you will."

"Maybe," said Whit.

They tore off down the drive in a fit of smoke. Whit watched them a long time. He wanted to make sure they were gone. The truck disappeared down the far bend. He un-cocked the pistol and turned around. His father was not where he'd been. The ground was red-streaked where he'd crawled. He was curled next to the whimpering dog. He was whispering to her. Petting her.

"Good girl," he was telling her. "You're a good girl. We'll get you fixed up, I promise."

Whit stood over them. Their blood was mixed in the dirt. His father's. The dog's. The red earth darkened like molasses. His father looked up. The old man's face was monstrous, misshapen, a storm of bruise and blood. But his eyes, they rose wide and quivering from the damaged flesh. Hoping. Pleading. Not for help. For something else. Something harder to give.

Whit looked down at him a long moment. He worked his jaws. Blinked. He looked away. He started inside to call the vet. To get his father the bag of peas.

Joan Lee Hunter

The Dog

MRS. WARD ASKED WOULD I STAY HERE and look after the dog while they visit her mother in New York. She said Mr. Ward and her wanted me because the dog knows me good, being as how I clean here every week.

It's the dog fur's the reason they need me so much. Them two, they make no mess at all. Everything in its place, lined up just so. No spit in the bathroom sink; no grease spills on the stove.

Mr. Ward—Todd, he says to call him—used to be some kind of lawyer in New York. He told me he retired young, four years ago. When he said it, I had to bite my tongue because to me he looks like he should of retired a long time ago. All them wrinkles and lines, that worried look.

He got himself a young body, though. It's because

he don't eat much, don't sit down to lunch. He grazes, he calls it, all day long with them protein bars and nuts and such. And every day—he says he never misses a one—he gets his cardio going, either walking the dog or using one of them machines down cellar when the weather ain't good.

I guess he knows a lot about lawyer work, but he don't know much more. Nothing of any use, far's anybody can tell. Him and Mrs. Ward—Jean—just pick up the phone when they need something done. They got a lot of folks around here working for them.

Me, I'm in charge of dust and fur. I'd say their dust runs about the same as everybody else, but that dog fur is worse, the way it sticks to them scatter rugs and don't budge. And the central vac they got's good for nothing, the hose so long there ain't hardly any suction. The deep plush rugs, I gotta go back and forth this way and then that, and sometimes—good thing I'm still young—I have to bend over and pick that fur out with my finger and thumb.

Summertime is the worst.

My Galen used to plow and sand for them winters, but no more. Mrs. Ward told me she made a note to herself to call him to say they won't be needing him anymore. She's doing this on my account. How did she say it? In *deference* to me after I told her how he's been bothering me with all them phone calls ever since we broke up. He misses me, he says in his sweetest voice, but now I know better. He shows his nice side when I ain't there to do what he wants. Those other times I went back to him after we broke up, he was hisself again in no time at all, bossing me around or else acting like I wasn't even in the room.

The other day I told Mrs. Ward I tell him I've had it up to here whenever he calls. When I said it, Mrs. Ward asked did I have caller ID? I told her I did, and she smiled and cocked her head to one side like I'm telling a joke. Then why, she wanted to know, do I answer the phone?

I ain't finished thinking about that, but I don't have to just yet. I'm here at Wards' now instead of at home. And in case Galen calls there, I left a message on my machine saying I'm away for a while. I made it mysterious on purpose. Let him wonder where I am. Let him think I've gone somewhere far off, not just down the road to babysit a dog.

Lou Ellen is what Wards call the dog; funny name for a boy. He's a German Shepherd with real shiny fur Mrs. Ward says is because of the cod liver oil. He's young still, only two years old. His favorite thing to do? He charges like he's planning to rip out your throat, then stops right when he gets up close. Scared the bejesus out of me at first.

He keeps the wrong people away, says Mrs. Ward. That's important because they got a lot of good stuff. My daughter Tammy asked me what was I going to do with myself here, and I said, Ha, you're kidding me, right? They got a big-screen TV and about a hundred DVD's. They got a stereo and every CD you can think of. Books galore on any subject I want. And if I feel like doing nothing at all, I can just sit on one of them matching pieces of furniture and look at them paintings on the walls.

This house, they built it where the old Milton farm stood. Mrs. Ward said they bought way out here because they wanted a simple life and a view of the mountains. I hate to tell them, but this house they built ain't simple at all. It looks like one of them resorts, with big glass windows and decks all around, the lawn and shrubs just so. May as well have a sign out front says, Rich Folks Live Here.

But it's their money; they do what they want. They're paying me $500 to look out for the dog, and on top of that I can still take care of my regular cleaning customers. Mrs. Ward says all's I have to do for the dog is cook him his two meals with his chicken and carrots. Sneak in the cod liver oil. Put on the electric collar when he wants to go out. Walk him on the leash afternoons when I get home from work. That last thing—the walk—I already know I won't. I did it once before, and he like to pulled out my arm. What it is, is—I don't walk fast enough.

Even if I wanted, it'd be dangerous to walk that dog, it being hunting season and all. Me and him are like to get our heads blown off. Right before they left, Mrs. Ward made a big show of putting that orange vest for me on the hook by the door and right next to it, Lou Ellen's orange snap-on coat. She told me that when I take him for his walk to stay out of the woods, just walk alongside the road. As if that were safer; what does she know? Hunting season, you're not safe anywhere outdoors with all them stray bullets missing their targets and keeping right on going. Not to mention all them drivers going too fast on that skinny road. Walk that dog alongside the road? No sir.

Anyway, I don't know why she worries so about his exercise, with that invisible dog fence running all around the house. On his own the dog gets what exercise he wants. He needs to run; he runs. He needs to walk; he walks. He's smart enough, that dog. He knows how to take care of hisself. They just baby him because they never had a baby theirselves. And because Mrs. Ward told me once walking fast is one of them things she does for fun. Not me, I told her. I get all my walking done on the job.

You want my opinion, she walks too much. All them veins of hers showing, no flesh on her bones. She stand sideways, you can't see her, is what Galen says about her.

Galen, he likes a woman round and short. Likes my big boobies and jiggly rump. He used to say he liked having something to hold onto when he was loving me up. Hair, he favors long and blonde, and that's what I got. Down to my waist and straight out of a bottle.

I've never been here at night before. There's no shades to pull, no curtains to close. Everywhere I look, I see myself in the windows of this great big room that's the living room and dining room and kitchen all in one. It gives me the creeps to think I could be watching TV and out there someone could be watching me.

At least I have the dog. As long as he's here, no one's bothering us, no sir. He is sitting here beside me, watching American Idol.

The phone rings, and I get up to see if it's Mrs. Ward, but it's Galen's name that's on the caller ID. How did he find out this was where I was at? Nobody knows I'm here but Tammy, and she wouldn't tell him, I'm sure of that.

The ringing stops and in a few seconds the red blinker comes on. I can't listen to the message because I don't know Wards' secret code.

I wonder what he wants.

I start to worry, will he try to come over? He should know better than that. I got this big German Shepherd right beside me on the couch. If he were sitting any closer he'd be in my lap. The dog wouldn't take to Galen coming round, no sir. For one thing, he don't know Galen. When Galen does his plowing he don't get out of the truck; he mails Wards their bill once a month. And for another thing, Galen can seem kind of gruff at first. It's because he don't say much and because he's tall and wide and has those eyebrows that run right together above his nose.

I been sitting here awhile half waiting for the sound of Galen's truck, but he ain't coming; I'm sure of it now. American Idol gets done. I turn off the TV, put on the electric collar, let out the dog. Go into Wards' bedroom where they said to sleep. That bed, so big you could fit five people acrost it. I pull back the comforter, and there I see that Mrs. Ward changed the sheets for me. There they are, all crispy tight and smelling good. Wasn't that nice?

I open my suitcase and put on my pajamas. Go into the bathroom, brush my teeth. The dog barks at the front door; I go let him in and take off the collar. I get into bed, and so does he. I don't mean he's at the foot of the bed or nothing.

He's right here up against me with his head on my pillow—mouth open, eyes shut. I push at him a little, but he don't budge.

You have to wonder about Wards' sex life with the dog around. Or maybe they don't even have sex anymore. I don't suppose that would surprise me one bit. As hard as I try, I can't imagine them two doing it. All them bones knocking up against each other, all the mess it can make. And her so fussy about every little thing—her who, after walking Lou Ellen, takes off her shoes at the door, then takes a towel and wipes each foot of the dog.

Morning, first thing, the dog has to go. I put his electric collar on and open the door. Out he goes. There's a little bit of snow on the ground; the hunters, they're happy about that, I know. I watch the dog lift his leg, then chase a squirrel over the stone wall. Close the door.

Today is my usual day to clean Wards', but first I got to have me some coffee. I look high and low—inside the refrigerator, every shelf and drawer. I check everything again, but there's no coffee at all. All's they've got is tea with herbs. Mrs. Ward offers me some of that sometimes. She says, Would you like a cup of tea before you get to work? I do when she says she's going to have some herself. That's when we get to talk to each other. I've tried the peppermint and the ginger, and I suppose they was alright, but mornings I got to have me something with bite. Something to wake me up and move my bowels.

I call in the dog, and he comes running because he knows he's getting fed. I make him his grilled chicken and shaved carrots the way she said, then I get in the car to go get me some coffee.

I'm on the Canaan Road, heading for my house, when I see Galen's truck headed in my direction. I'd know that truck anywhere, that big old silver Dodge Ram with the black plow on the front. On the door it says *Galen Milliken, Property Maintenance*, I know, but I ain't looking at that. I'm looking at Galen himself as he passes on by. He's got on his orange hunting jacket and cap; his hunting rifle's in the rack.

I know where he's going. He's going hunting up to Blueberry Mountain. He sees me, I know it, but he passes looking straight ahead. I don't know what to make of that. Those other times we were broke up, he at least lifted his fingers up off of the steering wheel or nodded his head. No sir, he just drives by this morning as if he don't know who I am.

I wonder why he wants to go and act like that; both of us got to live in this here small town. It makes me wonder all the more what that phone message says.

Mrs. Ward said I need anything, to call her cell. Well, I do. I need her to check that message Galen left on her phone.

I get back to Wards', the dog barking to beat hell even though he can see it's me through the glass door. Once I let myself in, he shuts right up and rubs against my leg. I dial Mrs. Ward's cell phone, but she don't answer. I leave a message asking her to check Galen's message and let me know what it said.

I make myself a cup of coffee, drink it standing up. Right away quick, I got to do my business, but I forget to shut the bathroom door. Across the living room I see the dog watching me pull down my sweat pants and sit on the pot. He looks at me funny, then crouches low and pins back his ears. Next thing I know, he's running straight at me like he's going to tear off my head. Stops at my knees just like that and hangs out his tongue. I'd a been some scared if I didn't know better.

Again, he wants to go outdoors. I take the collar off the hook, put it on him and open the door. I watch him jump and roll around on his back in the snow. It's a good thing someone's enjoying theirself.

I call to check my messages at home, but I don't have none. Tammy, she's not home and not answering her cell.

There's just one thing I want to know from Galen. Why after all these years of us knowing each other does he decide this morning to pretend that we don't? Tammy would say, Good riddance, Mom. Mrs. Ward would ask me—as she did once before—why I give a darn after all those years of him treating me like dirt. What I never tried to explain to either of them is, for a long time it was real good between us before it got worse. Galen ain't a bad person; it's just that between us, things don't always work so good.

I call him at home, now I know he's out. I leave him a message, explain myself. Tell him that the part on my message machine about being away for a while was just me being smart. That I'm not really away; I'm only a mile from home. All's I'm doing is babysitting Wards' dog; nothing for him to upset himself about. I tell him to leave a message on my phone if he wants to talk.

This is one of those times I wish I had a cell. Now I have to wait until he gets done with his hunting to see what he has to say for himself.

My hands are sweating when I hang up the phone. Cleaning will calm me down. I always feel good when I clean at Wards' because I pretend it's my own house and everything in it I picked out myself. Even the dog. Look at him, sound asleep smack dab in the middle of the big white rug. Bless his heart.

Four hours, and I finish up. I'm hungry, but I can't eat nothing the way my stomach churns. I watch a movie called *Tender Mercies* about a drunken country singer who falls in love and cleans himself up. He looks a little like Galen when Galen was younger.

The snow has stopped, but it's got that cold look outdoors. I look across to the clearing on the next ridge over and see three hunters in blaze orange come out of them woods. They huddle and smoke, their rifles under their arms. Galen always hunts alone. Always did, he says, since he was a young'un. Likes getting off by himself and away from folks and work and who knows what all. There's a quiet side to Galen I don't dare interrupt. Me, I have to talk things out, but he pulls in like a turtle when he's got something on his mind. Mrs. Ward says maybe he's the silent type, but I tell her I wouldn't go that far. Most of the time he's cussing at this or that, making a fuss about nothing I care about.

The sun has come out. It's kind of pretty looking out through those big glass windows toward the mountains. Right above the left peak of Pleasant Mountain there's a dark cloud looks like a dead guppy floating on its back. I'm watching how it ain't moving at all, neither sideways nor up and down, when who do you suppose drives up Wards' driveway?

It's Galen and a dead buck, its antlers showing up over the bed of the truck. I watch him get out and slam the door. The dog gets up, and he's got his lips pulled back so's you can see all his teeth. The minute he sees Galen walk up to the glass door he starts in barking and twirling hisself.

I'm wondering what Galen wants.

We're looking right straight at each other through the door.

There's blood on his jeans from field dressing the deer. He's got on his blaze orange jacket and tie-up boots. His hair's a little tousled from taking off his hat. He looks pretty good, I have to admit.

Open up, he is saying through the door.

I can't think what to do. The dog is jumping against me and then against the door. I open it a crack, but no more.

I want to know something, he says.

Uh, oh, here goes. What?

I want to know what Mrs. Ward was calling me about. She left a message to call her back and I did, but she hasn't returned my call. I figured you might know.

How did you know I was here?

Because this is your usual day to clean Wards'.

Oh, right you are. Well, I don't know nothing about nothing, I say to him. I don't want to be the one to tell him she wants him to get done.

The dog is making that growling sound in his throat with some whimpers like he's going to die if he don't get around to killing somebody, and I'm keeping my body between him and Galen on the other side of the door. Galen's eyebrows are wrinkled into a frown. I watch him unzip his jacket real slow and rest his hand on the knife that's hanging off of his belt. He takes a big step back.

The dog is jumping up and down. I tell Galen I got to shut the door.

Alright then, he says.

He turns and walks back towards his truck, but I ain't done. I crack open the door. Wait, I got to ask you something.

He's about halfway between here and his truck. I watch him turn his whole body around and plant his feet wide apart.

Our eyes lock, and I feel that feeling that sometimes happens between us.

How come you pretended you didn't see me this morning?

Because it still hurts.

Just like that, he said it. Without a second thought. What hurts? I ask him, just to be sure.

You and me not together anymore.

I start to ask him *where* does it hurt when the dog jumps, gives a yelp, and he's out the door. I watch him run past Galen, take a leak on the back wheel of the truck, then get up on his hind legs and sniff at the buck.

Grab him! I yell at Galen. Grab him quick by the fur. He ain't got his fence collar on.

Galen runs towards him. Ho, boy. Ho, boy, he's yelling.

But Lou Ellen snarls at Galen and then he's off. He's running hard, leaving paw prints in the snow as he runs across the yard and the driveway and into them woods. A howl comes out of him I ain't never heard.

I run outdoors. Lou Ellen, Lou Ellen, I call out over and over.

That dog is gone, says Galen.

I have a sick feeling in my stomach. Galen and me, we're standing side by side looking out at the woods. Everything's quiet all of a sudden. The dog ain't howling, Galen and I ain't talking, and that buck sure ain't making any noise. I ain't got nothing on but my sweat pants and scoop-neck tee, and I feel cold all of a sudden. I rub my arms.

Next thing I know, Galen reaches over, slips his arm around my shoulders and pulls me close. I lean my head up against his chest, and that feels good.

Don't worry, he says. He'll be back soon enough. He says it like he knows something I don't. What time, he asks, are Wards due home?

Next week, I tell him. I'm here babysitting the dog.

He didn't know that before, and I feel his whole body stiffen a little as he thinks things over. He don't say nothing, though.

Me, I don't want to think about anything at all except the feel of Galen making me warm. I look at the sky; my guppy cloud is all gone. It's all broke up into little pieces that don't look like nothing at all. It makes me think about how something that's one thing one minute can change just like that into something else.

Well, standing here don't do nobody any good, Galen says.

I ask him does he want to come indoors, and he says yes.

Soon's he walks in the door he gives a long, low whistle as he looks around. He takes off his orange hunting jacket and hangs it on the hook by the door, right alongside Lou Ellen's little snap-on coat. I start to cry when I see them hanging side by side.

Galen says, Stop your worrying now.

He reaches for me and holds me so tight it's like he wants to squeeze out all my breath. I let him do that just a little while, then I push him back and point to his feet. You need to take off your boots and leave them here by the door.

Who says?

I do because I'm in charge of keeping this place clean. He stares at me a minute, sees I mean what I said. He leans over and unties his laces. Pulls off each boot while dancing on just one foot. We look at down at his stocking feet and then up at each other. Three distant rifle shots ring out in them woods, and both of us act like we don't hear nothing.

Chris Connolly

Rabbit

AS HIS WIFE ZIG-ZAGGED BACK AND FORTH across the kitchen, beads of sweat hanging from her brow as if glued to it, he enquired about her day. Not because he was interested—though it wasn't disinterest he felt—but because that was what he had always done.

He found it difficult to concentrate on what she was saying, but gathered that her day had been a busy one. Their youngest son had phoned from her from college to say hello. Following this she had spent much of the morning queuing in the bank to wire him money for 'books and things', the primary reason for his call, he suspected, though he elected not to mention these suspicions to his wife who seemed buoyed by their conversation. He was settling in well, she told him.

As they sat down for dinner he made a mental note

to give him a call in a day or two, to make sure that he was in fact settling in well, but also—possibly more so—to relive some of the debauchery-filled memories of his own college days.

As his wife continued to recount to him the minutiae of her day, his mind drifted back to the rabbit. She was telling him something about a friend of hers she had met in the supermarket, but thoughts of the rabbit, which he had encountered on his way home from work, continued to distract him.

He had come across it by chance when he happened to notice some movement in the corner of his eye while driving along the quiet, grass-lined road that led to their home. Curious, he stopped when he realised that it was an animal of some kind. Having decided that he was in no rush to get home—and with the vague feeling that some sort of disruption or distraction to his daily routine could only be a good thing—he got out of the car and saw the rabbit lying there, trembling and immobilized.

The rabbit was a grey-brown colour and of medium size, or what he thought was medium-sized for such an animal, though he couldn't be sure and couldn't remember the last time he had seen one up-close. It was probably at a petting zoo when the boys were of petting zoo age, he thought, and it was probably when he himself was that age that he had last seen a wild one at such proximity. He approached it slowly, not wanting to frighten it. As he got closer he saw that one of its hind legs was splayed at an unnatural angle to the rest of its body, lying there limp as if not belonging to the rabbit itself, and saw that it was bleeding from some unseen wound. It had been hit by a car, he guessed, and by the looks of it wouldn't recover.

It was the image of the incorrectly angled limb that was caught in his mind as his wife began to discuss their elder son and what seemed to her his overly-demanding workload in his new job. She was worried, naturally, that he was working too hard, and hoped that his girlfriend was looking after him properly.

Her husband hoped too, with a grin, that his son was being sufficiently looked after by his girlfriend, but as he toyed with the last piece of chicken on his plate he found himself worrying. Not about the latest girlfriend, but about whether his eldest son was following in his father's tired footsteps, getting into a career that might not turn out to sustain his interest past a few years. He wasn't quite sure what investment banking was, but he had an idea that it wasn't the kind of thing that his son—or anyone else's son for that matter—had dreamed about doing as a child.

He had worked for over thirty years himself, steadily climbing the ladder and gaining promotion while at the same time—and at roughly the same rate—losing any enthusiasm for the work that he did. He had counted himself lucky to be offered the job straight out of college. Nevertheless, he often wondered now what might have been had he only put a little more thought into what working as an insurance broker for the rest of his life would actually entail and a little less thought into the financial compensation he would receive for it.

Back then he had been filled with the excitement of finally beginning to make his own way in the world, filled with hopes and fantasies about all the things he was going to do, but somewhere along the way everything had seemed to fizzle, and he had become content to roll slowly along, eventually drifting into what had become his life.

He had a few years left before retirement—a prospect that frightened him in some way, though he wasn't sure why—and there would be no more promotions, demotions, or surprises of any kind. He arrived punctually each day, going through the motions until he departed again, no longer striving for distinction. He had started to think with increasing regularity about this job that had been the basic focus of his life for so many years, and about how that fact really made him feel when he allowed himself to think deeply about it.

He didn't share these thoughts with his wife. He often wondered whether she had the same thoughts about her choices—the same *regrets*—but thought it best not to ask. He hoped that she didn't.

Despite some troubles midway through—troubles to be expected in any marriage as long as theirs—their partnership had been a successful one. Naturally by now, much like in his career, the excitement had faded and routine had taken over. Over the years they had become companions more than anything else, but wasn't that the way things were supposed to go for people of their age? They had settled into their lives rather than actively shaping them, but essentially they were happy.

He was thinking about this as she finished her monologue on the importance of a steady relationship in a young man's life, but again the memory of the rabbit forced its way into his mind.

He had stood on the side of the road watching it for a few minutes, unsure of what to do. Eventually, not knowing how to proceed but feeling foolish at his inaction, he knelt down beside it and attempted to pet it. Immediately the animal tried to flee but managed only to lurch forward a few inches, the dead limb dragging behind it and its breathing becoming more rapid, its trembling more frenzied.

He stepped back and leaned against the bonnet of the car, feeling useless, looking up and down the quiet road and hoping at first to see another vehicle coming his way containing someone who could assist him, before realising that anyone who did pass would simply drive by unless he flagged them down, in which case they would probably think he was either mad or a fool when he told them he needed assistance—what type of assistance he didn't know—with a dying rabbit.

He had been in a similar situation as a child, finding a bird lying prone on the ground with a broken wing. He had stood there watching it for a long time, as unsure of what to do back then as he was now, until finally he had worked up the courage and found a large rock with which to put the bird out of its misery. Even as a child—was he 9, maybe 10?—he had realised it was the right thing to do. It was an easy decision, but the act itself proved more difficult. It had taken three attempts back then.

A combination of lack of coordination, lack of strength and last-second doubts resulted in the first two attempts merely injuring the bird even further until finally, crying like the child that he was, he finished the deed. He could still remember the bulging eyes of the magpie, almost-but-not-quite dead after the first and second attempts. He looked at the rabbit's eyes now, wondering how long they would stay etched into his mind if things went the same way.

He hadn't thought about that magpie in years. Standing on the side of the road looking at the rabbit he remembered, as if from nowhere, a night many years before when he and his wife—both still in college, and still in the throes of youthful passion—had lain together in the small single bed of his dorm room. They had been exchanging stories—talking, making love, excited by each other's secrets and hungry for each other. He had told her then about the magpie, about his botched attempts at killing it and how he had cried all the way home, knowing he hadn't had a choice but faced for the first time in his young life with the incomprehensible feelings of sadness and guilt that could arise from doing the right thing.

He hadn't cried when he told his wife the story—he was no longer a child, nor was he a man of many tears—but she sensed his sadness and kissed him, he remembered, kissed both him and that little boy, letting her lips rest on his neck for a few moments. It was a moment he recalled intimately as he looked at the rabbit. He stood there faced with the same dilemma now, a full half-century later, somehow feeling even less sure of what to do.

The thought of moving the rabbit was as daunting as anything else. He squirmed in his skin at the image of the limb dropping off, or some unseen laceration gushing organs and innards all over him.

He stayed standing there, just looking at it, wondering what the rabbit was thinking about this strange two-legged creature that was looming menacingly over it. He wished he hadn't stopped. He cursed his curiosity.

His wife had finally run out of things to say, eventually asking how his day at work had been. As usual, he replied that it had been fine, that there had been no major excitements or disappointments and that—to her mild but obvious disappointment—there was no scandal to report or gossip to pass on.

He didn't mention the rabbit, or the rabbit's broken hind leg, or the blood on the rabbit's body. He didn't mention the way the rabbit's leg had trailed after it when he tried to pet it, or how he couldn't get the image out of his head of it lying there as he got back into his car and drove home, having finally decided to put it out of its misery with a tyre iron. And he didn't mention that, having failed in the end to muster the courage to kill the rabbit, he had put the tyre iron back into the boot and driven away, or that he had felt close to tears for the first time in years as he resisted the urge to look back at the rabbit in the rear-view mirror.

He didn't mention that he was still thinking about all of this right then, over dessert, and that he was wondering whether it was still there; whether it was dead or alive, whether it had been eaten, or if someone else had found it after him and done what he had wanted and willed himself to do but wasn't, in the end, strong enough to go through with.

And he didn't mention either that, being honest with himself, the thing that he was really thinking about, as his wife cleared the dishes from the table and kissed him on the cheek, was that little crying boy holding the rock in his hands all those years ago, and where that little boy had disappeared to.

And how, exactly, it had happened without him noticing.

Sarah Gerkensmeyer

Vanishing Point

IT'S AGAINST THE RULES. Glenn slips into my sleeping bag in the middle of the night. We have to be quiet, which I don't mind. We've been told that the sleeping bags are meant to help us feel like we are back inside our mothers' wombs again. But I think were given sleeping bags because this place used to be a camping outfitters and why waste supplies that are already on hand, no matter how old and musty they are. The first time Glenn came to me in the dark, I unzipped my bag as slowly and as quietly as possible and he just stood there and watched without a single trace of anticipation on his shadowed face. In the mornings, he passes me the dented kettle of coffee or the tin plate loaded with thick cut bacon without saying a word, and no one else pressed together at the old pine table seems to notice a thing. The whole point of being here is to detach ourselves from what we have lost and what we need to grieve. And here Glenn and I are, attaching ourselves to each other every night, over and over again. Totally against the rules. He is lean and slow and so good at being quiet, and when we are pressed together in the stale heat of my sleeping bag I run through some of the mantra we've been taught to hammer into ourselves.

I love myself.

I accept myself.

I'm important.

I deserve good things.

I forgive myself.

Over and over again, every night, Glenn comes to me and I forgive myself.

Before coming out here, I knew to expect the lakes scattered everywhere and the mosquitoes and the huge pieces of rock jutting up out of the earth. I had stared at Arthur's little pamphlet for hours and had gone on-line to search "wilderness" and "Minnesota Boundary Waters." But what I didn't expect was the disorientating floating feeling I'd have being surrounded by so many bodies of dark, connected water. I didn't expect the mosquitoes to attack in swarms, the whinny of their multitudinous approach like the screaming of banshees. I didn't expect the orange and green lichen to cling to the jutting rocks like bright beards. I didn't expect the loon's call to sound lonely and lovely all at once. I didn't know I'd love or even notice the people who live in this pocket of the world, the ones who have lived here for a lifetime. If I lived here, I think I'd drive to the nearest town every day, which is an hour from camp, and fill myself with the thick malts and fried cheese curds that they serve in the tiny restaurants there. Then I would sit back and wait to feel it—a slow takeover of the introverted good cheer that people like Arthur possess. The mysterious thing that must keep them insulated and safe during the blind, cold winters that they have out here. I'm envious of all of it. And I'm surprised by this, how my mouth waters.

Here at camp, it's the ones without any kind of substantial proof of a lost twin who seem so certain and who buy into all of Arthur's theories without hesitation. Cathy says that she's had a strange numbness in her limbs each morning since as far back as she can remember, and that's all the proof she needs. For Frank, it's his eczema. Sheila has bad breath and Nancy has an extra pinky toe. Dan has a mole exactly on the center of his left knee cap. They look at these random, insignificant things and wholeheartedly grant them all the significance in the world. Look at this here. See this? This is the reason for my loneliness. My depression. My anxiety and anger and fear. This is the reason for the empty hole sloshing around inside of my soul.

When I was eighteen months old, I started falling whenever I walked. I'd land on my bottom and cry and cry, my face red with pain in spite of the padding of my thick diaper and the shag carpeting in my parents' home. My mother noticed a redness above my spine, just the faintest hint of something tough and swollen beneath my skin. Of course she was full of a sudden, vicious worry that only mothers can possess, the kind of worry that is sharper and more exact than intuition. She demanded tests, and there were tests. There was a biopsy and surgery. But it wasn't cancer, the darkest thing huddled there in the hot pocket of my mother's worry. It was something she never could have imagined, a benign cyst made up of a jumbled mess of hair and teeth and skin. The surgeons who removed the tumor told my mother that she had been pregnant with twins. That things had gotten a bit "complicated" very early in the pregnancy and I had absorbed the other fetus into my own body before it could finish developing into anything near human. It fused to the bottom of my spine, a mess of cells. Not really a twin, they told her. Just the makings of one. On the second day of camp, Arthur asked us to choose a body part and imagine that's where the absorption of our twin occurred when we were fetuses. I chose my right elbow instead of my lower back. I don't know why. Maybe because my elbow is easier to see. All of us campers catch each other glancing at these random parts of ourselves, trying to visualize and believe.

I don't know what body part Glenn chose as his lost twin's point of absorption. Maybe one of his bony wrists or the soft, delicate point where his hair trails into a V on the back of his neck. When I touch him, I feel like I'm intruding. I want to know which part of himself he has chosen to be secret and sacred. I would never touch it.

Arthur has told us that there is something swimming beneath the threshold of our memory, a primordial kind of awareness where our earliest experiences have been logged and stored permanently. Of course none of us remember floating around inside of the warm viscous-ness of our mother's womb, but the experience is there nonetheless, tucked deep into the folds of our psyche. Arthur says that some of us might claim to remember, but we are lying to ourselves. It's about something altogether different from remembering. And that's what we are supposed to get at while we are here at Vanishing Point, way out in the middle of the Minnesota Boundary Waters Wilderness. One of the rivers that my shuttle from the Minneapolis Airport crossed during the day-long drive to camp was called Baptism River. Sometimes Arthur seems like a preacher, no matter how quiet he gets. No matter the fact that he has taken our money for two weeks of crazy jibber jabber about the Primal Wound of the Womb and Emotional Freedom Technique and Conception Guilt and Womb Twin Survivor. He does seem tapped into something that I don't think any of us could ever recognize, no matter how long we stayed or how much money we shelled over.

The first project Arthur had us do when we arrived—before we were assigned an old sleeping bag or given time to unpack our things—was cut a photo of a person out of a magazine. He had a random collection piled up on the table where we take our meals, and many of the issues of *Vogue* and *Good Housekeeping* and *People* and *Self* had already been picked over by previous campers. Arthur asked us to cut out a face that embodied some quality of our lost twin. The other campers took their time, agonizing over issues of *Time* and *Maxim* as they tried to narrow down their choices. I chose the first person I saw when I opened up a worn issue of *Ladies Home Journal,* a plus-sized model smiling bravely in a simple black bra and panty set. We wear the pictures around our necks, slipped into waterproof plastic sleeves. Glenn was the only other camper who made his choice quickly, and when I saw the picture in his badge—a teenaged Goth-looking model who is all skin and bones—I thought maybe he was joking. I thought there might be the relief of whispering with him at the campfire about how outrageous this all is, who could ever believe it. But he's serious about all of this, I've realized. Just like everyone else here, he's got his reasons to believe. He's left handed. He had a stutter as a kid. He's miserable without the companionship of recreational drug use.

I've started slipping into my sleeping bag naked each night. I tell myself that I'm trying to give Arthur's theories a fair shot, that maybe I'll better be able to imagine my return to the primordial womb if I don't have a stitch on me. Really it just makes things easier when Glenn comes. Trying to wriggle out of my clothing with both of us pressed in there is a bit awkward and jerky, nothing at all like the sex itself. There are only two sleeping cabins. When Glenn comes over from his, he's not too careful about keeping the door from creaking and whining. He shuffles over to my cot, and it sounds like someone is trying to sweep away dead leaves. But no one else ever seems to be awake but me. Maybe everyone else's sleeping bag has some kind of spell on it that places them into an unconscious state much deeper than sleep, a place where Arthur's therapeutic work can continue in the farthest reaches of the brain. Maybe my sleeping bag is defunct. And Glenn's. The two of us are quiet, but I don't know that we need to be. Frank snores aggressively just across from us. Cathy is stiff as a corpse in the bunk above me. And here I am with a stranger pressed into my sleeping bag, feeling just as sleepy and lost as everyone else in this tiny cabin. When Glenn arrives in the middle of the night, a cloud of mosquitoes comes in with him. We disappear completely inside of my sleeping bag, pulling the top all the way over our heads. Still, we can hear the solid, patient whine of anticipation just above us.

Arthur is small and wizened and decades and decades old. He runs the place like the tightest of ships. There is no questioning the schedule that is posted next to the front door of each sleeping cabin. We move together in a herd from skin diving sessions in the little lake to breakfast to group therapy to quiet journaling time to lunch to arts and crafts to individual sessions and on and on and on. Although the property is well over three hundred years old (it used to be a French fur trading camp), everything has been kept in working order. Arthur runs a single crank generator for the radio and the refrigerator and the few bare light bulbs scattered about the shack-like buildings. He is religious about it and says the place has never run out of power. You would expect him to have huge, bulging muscles from all the time he spends turning the little wheel of that generator, but he's so small. None of us understand it. And we don't understand why a man like Arthur would choose to run a camp like Vanishing Point. During therapy sessions and workshops he pulls stories out of us like easy, silk threads, but he has never said a word about himself in any deep, personal regard. Maybe this is because that kind of information would be too distracting from our own work here. But the mystery surrounding Arthur is what's most distracting of all. We sit around the dying campfire after Arthur has left, no longer swatting at the mosquitoes because of the warm buzz of the whiskey that Sheila smuggled in. Glenn glares at us with a hard smile of abstinence on his face, and we try to piece together what Arthur's story might be. Maybe he was married once, and he lost his wife when they were young. Maybe he was a secret operative for the CIA and he retired out here in the wilderness to try to escape the horrible things he had done and seen. Most of the campers are certain that Arthur himself must have lost a twin before he was born. But I don't buy into that. I think that this entire program that Arthur has put together out here is a random obsession for him and it's as easy as that. Maybe he came across an old issue of *National Geographic* at the dentist's office and opened it up to a story about us, survivors of a vanished womb twin. Maybe he was taking a series of old fashioned correspondence courses through the mail and the one on Vanishing Twin Syndrome caught his eye, the sketches on the front of the pamphlet of the kidney-bean-sized fetuses floating in a ghost womb. Yes, Arthur could have made up all of the theories and techniques that he teaches us here. But I think all of this is something that he himself bought into. Something that he studied up on and then chose to believe in. And if he was ever lonely in his life, how can he be now? We send in our deposits and take flights from all over the country to get here and sit with him in old aluminum chairs on the dock, trying to shoo the ungodly bugs away as nonchalantly as possible because Arthur here just sits and takes it without the slightest flinch.

On the first day of camp we were all issued t-shirts with the Vanishing Point logo, a rough sketch of an empty road viewed head on, so that the two yellow lines in the center of the road seem to come together and merge into one single line that shoots off into the horizon. Arthur says that's the vanishing point, where two separate things have the illusion of coming together. But why name the camp Vanishing Point when Arthur asks us to discover the opposite of that union, to learn how to push our invisible twins out in a gentle kind of exorcism? What would you call that? I couldn't begin to design a t-shirt logo for that.

During group therapy sessions, I often find myself staring out the old, billowed screen windows at the rocks and trees and water that make up this landscape. Sometimes I panic at the thought of being in a place where I could get lost so easily. What if I tried to turn this whole experience into a fairytale? I could fill a little pack with a few smart provisions and then set out into the thick fingers of pine and birch. I'd drop little crumbs from the hard, waxy biscuits that Arthur sets out each morning and none of us touch. The moose and the black bears and the wolves and the foxes and the otters would eat those crumbs and no one, not even Arthur, would be able to track me. The open darkness that must rest at the center of all of this forest would swallow me whole.

During art therapy, Bill tells us how he has two separate wardrobes. One for his fat, masculine self and one for his thin, feminine self. Genie describes the telepathy she shares with her dead twin. Frank tells us about his issues with money. We are supposed to be drawing two pictures of our mother's womb. The first one of before the loss of our twin and the second one of after. The crayons are broken and old and smell like a school library. Sheila shades her mother's womb (the after) a deep, furious purple and says that she suspects that she is electrically sensitive. She says her watches always stop working soon after she buys them and that streetlights often go out when she walks beneath them. Tom tells us that he lost a sister in the womb. He is quiet and gentle, with long, beautiful hair that all of the female campers envy. Tom says he wants to give birth to his lost sister. And during this loaded, intensely personal moment I stare out the screen windows and watch the ripples on the black lake. I've seen campers paddling past in their canoes. Most of the people who camp out here in this wilderness know what to expect. They come with only one or two tight packs and a lot of good sense. But I've seen some clueless people paddle by, fumbling with the folds of big maps, their canoes weighted down with huge coolers and too much expensive, useless gear. Arthur tells us stories of people who have gotten lost after going too far out for their level of experience. They lose track of the portages—the little, rugged paths that connect the endless web of lakes. The smart ones don't panic. They stay put and patiently wait days, or even weeks, for another camper to appear. Or they set fire to the scraggly trees on one of the little rock islands that dot this country and wait for a fishing guide or a Department of Natural Resources officer to fly overhead and see the thin, desperate trail of smoke. But what about the ones who aren't smart? The ones who panic?

We were issued a mask for skin diving when we arrived. The dives in the lake take place early each morning, well before breakfast. When I hold my breath and peer beneath the surface of the lake for that first shocking glimpse of the day, I'm so hungry and cold that my vision is sharp and precise. I'm able to focus in on each tiny bit of silt that's been stirred up from the lake's mucky bottom. Arthur has been training us to hold our breath for longer and longer chunks of time each morning. The goal is to be able to hold our breath long enough to dive down to an old wrecked car at the bottom of the lake. Arthur has no idea how long the car has been down there or how it got there, but he uses it for the Final Ritual of Letting Go at the end of camp. He says that the breathing techniques we've been learning during our morning dives will allow us to push our twins out of us during that final, difficult dive down to the bottom of the lake. In the mornings I slip off of the dock into the cold water and gasp and sputter while placing the big mask over my eyes and nose. We tread water and stare at each other before beginning the breathing exercises. We look like a swarm of silly insects. Everything down there is brown and yellow and green and strange. There isn't much to see. The endless hulk of rocks piled solidly together. The quick golden-silver flash of a bony northern pike turning away. A dead frog floating with its limbs spread wide in surprise. Magda can't swim and she has been at Vanishing Point for years, watching group after group of campers go through the two week program and then finish their final dive. There are rumors that she came as a camper and then stayed on as Arthur's lover and that this is why she has become a permanent fixture. But she seems nothing like a secret lover. She goes through all the groups sessions and workshops right alongside us. She's just as clueless about Arthur as we are. She watches us each morning from one of the aluminum chairs on top of the warped dock, bobbing there above us with endless longing and envy.

Glenn and I are out picking blueberries and dodging black flies before this afternoon's workshop on The Healing Fetus. We kneel next to the little shrubs behind the canoe racks and collect the tiny berries in plastic baggies, hoping our pitiful offering will somehow spruce up Arthur's horrible cooking. He insists on making all of the meals and won't allow any of us to volunteer in the cramped kitchen. He enjoys feeding us, his strange flock.

"These are so tiny," Glenn says. "It would take years to pick enough for one single pie."

Glenn and I have exchanged very few words over the past couple weeks. Nothing is said when he crawls into my sleeping bag at night. He wants to be nonchalant out here in the open. He wants some small talk beneath the hard sun. But he's jumpy and wired. I wish I could wrap him up in a sleeping bag right now. Glenn says little during group therapy sessions. When he does talk, he refers to his drug use as if it's such an ordinary task—doing the dishes, sorting the mail, shooting up. I don't know the exact kind of detox he is facing. He should go somewhere legit that is designed to handle that kind of thing. The setting out here is too severe and wild and haunting with its crisp air and water, the land rolling and spiking away from us in every direction like something completely un-mappable and un-nameable.

I wish I could tell Glenn something about myself, even something tiny and trivial. I've been holding back from everyone here, including Arthur. During therapy, I've lied and made up an alcoholic, verbally abusive father. I've given myself two evil step mothers and a horrible bout of meningitis in middle school. I've survived earth quakes and car jackings and botched liposuction. All of it lies. I want to tell Glenn something real, because he is so shaky and uncertain. Because he deserves it. Instead I lie.

"I'm here because of my dreams," I say. "They have always felt like someone else's. They have never felt like my own."

Instead of looking at me like I'm crazy, Glenn stares at his little baggy of blueberries and nods.

Besides Magda, who was born alongside the mummified, shriveled body of her undeveloped twin, I'm the only one here who has any kind of legitimate proof of a lost twin. But I've told no one about the cyst that was removed when I was a toddler, not even Arthur. That experience doesn't feel real enough. I think telling that story would be more false than the lies I've been telling since the day I arrived here. Somehow, it would seem more false than the way the other campers lie to themselves during therapy, willing a lost soul mate into their empty lives. And then there would be the jealousy. If the other campers knew about my tumor, they would eye me with something like hate. I'm sure of it.

It isn't true that I haven't thought about my lost twin. Sure, I'm obsessed in my own way. What's it like when I do think about it? It's like when you are going about something ordinary and trivial and you hear a siren off in the distance—too far off to know if it's a fire truck or an ambulance or a cop car. And you catch yourself closing your eyes and saying something like a prayer. For a split second, before the sting of self-consciousness takes over, you feel connected to everyone in this world.

My cyst could have been on my face. Or up in my nasal cavity. Or tucked inside my brain like a grotesque egg. My cyst could have lodged itself in my ovaries and waited there for years and years, dormant until it finally ruptured and insisted that I give birth, in some kind of bloody fashion, to my own unformed sibling. All of that hair and skin and bits of bone and teeth without an ounce of soul, why would I want to feel any connection to that? Sometimes I wonder if I have been living my twin's life all along. We've all heard those stories about twins separated at birth who are reunited as adults and realize they have the same husbands and the same dogs and the same sweaters. What if my life, all of the good and all of the bad, isn't my own? Sometimes I feel territorial of all of it, even the mistakes and the mundane.

It's the morning of the Final Ceremony of Letting Go, and Arthur asks us to name our womb twins. He doesn't make us share our names or talk about it with each other. He simply suggests that we think of a name and hold it in our minds and our hearts. I stare at the face of the plus-sized underwear model that's sealed in the waterproof pouch around my neck and try to think of a name. I try to give her Connie or Bess or Sandy. Amy or Rachel. But she won't take any of those names. She just smiles back at me, dumb and defiant. A lot of the other campers start to cry. I can see the exact moment when they think of the right name. Something shifts in their faces. Arthur is somber. He stands at the end of the dock and tells us that the womb is an unsafe and unstable environment. He tells us that we weren't alone and that our twin was there to support us. "Wombs can carry grief and fear older than time," Arthur tells us. "You were not alone."

The final dive isn't hard. Arthur's intense training has taught us well. He takes small groups of us out to the spot above the sunken car in an aluminum boat with a sputtering outboard motor, and after he drops the anchor we take turns going down. I suck in one succinct pull of air and then go. The rusty hulk of the car is hard to make out in the endless brown water, but it doesn't take long to spot the orange piece of plastic flag that Arthur tied to the antenna who knows how long ago. I do as I've been told and let go of my plastic badge just above the driver's seat so that my twin can drive away to somewhere else, away from me and into her own life. The badge just floats there and then starts to drift away from the wreck. But I like to imagine that all of the badges end up sinking into the driver's seat. I like to believe that they are piled up there, all of those ghost faces wilted and silted over with time. I don't get a chance to linger and wait for some kind of change to occur down there in the abyss of the lake. My lungs ache and sting and I can't help rushing back up to the surreal looking surface.

Tonight Glenn and I get high. When he comes to me, he pulls me out of my sleeping bag and we walk out to the dock. He places two or three tiny pills in the palm of my hand. I can barely see them because it's so dark. They feel like nothing when I swallow. Glenn is already somewhere else, rigid and loose at the same time. I hold onto his arm while I wait to feel whatever it is that he is feeling. The quiet, economical sex we've been having has not been nearly enough to distract Glenn from this. My head starts to contract and expand and I can't stand it. It's not the high—a sweetly sick, sharp soaring—that I mind. It's watching Glenn betray himself. Watching him give in to what he came all the way out here to fight against and avoid. And here I am dipping my hand in right next to his. Glenn is one of the mark-less ones with no tangible proof of a lost twin. He's got a miserable life. That's all. Standing next to him on the dock, my head swirls away from us and I wish that I could make him my lost twin. I hate how forced I've let so many things in my life feel, and I wonder if that forced feeling is a true symptom of all of this bullshit that I've paid two thousand dollars to swallow out here in the middle of this wild bit of country.

I'm in the water and it takes me a few moments to realize this. I'm not panicking and sputtering and drowning. My legs and arms maintain a confident, efficient stroke. I let myself disappear beneath the surface and I hold my breath for a very long time. When I come up, I see Arthur holding a lantern and peering out at the dock. He sees Glenn standing there, just at the edge, and he sees me treading water and he knows. I'm high on something. Who knows what. And I want Arthur's vision to be altered for a moment, too.

We had to fill out a survey and send it in with our deposit in order to register for camp. We had to rate our loneliness on a scale of one to ten. We had to remember and count the number of stuffed animals that we slept with as children. Broken bones and break ups. Sexual identity. Posture. Suicide attempts. Loss. Rate your loss on a scale of one to ten.

When I get out of the water, I'm still treading and floating. I don't strip naked. I don't change into dry clothes. I find Arthur in the tiny shack that houses the crank generator, not much bigger than the Porta-Potties. "I'm here," I say. My voice comes from somewhere outside of me. I want Arthur to know that I'm okay. I didn't drown. Who knows about Glenn. For all I know he's still standing there at the end of the dock right at the edge of the world. Arthur is cranking the generator and the little wheel spins silently and efficiently. My head slices into everything. There's a mosquito on my calf, piercing me over and over again. It takes me so long to realize what that stinging could be. "Sorry," I say. Because there are no drugs allowed at Vanishing Point. No sex. Just healing and coming to terms and casting aside. Arthur keeps cranking, and I shiver and wonder if I could shake off this high, if it might evaporate. But until it does, I feel brave. And so I ask, "Why do you do all of this?" Arthur keeps cranking, but he looks at me. His face is dried up and kind as always.

I know that he used to run this place as a camping outfitters. He used to send people out into this wilderness with powdered milk and sleeping bags and slabs of bacon and cheese that had been smoked for so long they wouldn't need to be refrigerated for years. He sent people out with top secret tips on the best fishing spots for walleye, and pulleys and long pieces of rope to suspend food packs high in the air between two trees, away from snooping bears. Now he runs Vanishing Point and keeps us here, tucked in safe and tight at base camp, doing all the searching and exploring on the inside. And so when I ask him about why he does all of this, I expect him to go off on one of his old song and dances about the Trauma of the Womb or Detachment Narratives. But he doesn't. He tells me about the ama divers, women who live on islands off of the coast of Japan. Since at least the third century, these women have been skin diving for shellfish and edible seaweed. They hold their breath and swim to the bottom of the sea, placing whatever they bring back up with them in wooden tubs that float on the surface of the water. Most of the women dive topless. They are better divers than the men because of the extra layer of fat that women have. Arthur tells me all of this, and I sort and file the story in my head in a panic, because it feels like something important. It's a story I could never make up, no matter how high or lost I ever got myself.

"I want to go dive with them someday," Arthur says.

His eyes are wet. He has told me a secret. This is the old issue of *National Geographic* that he must have smuggled out of a dentist waiting room and tucked away somewhere, coveted and worn.

When Arthur found me out in the lake tonight, did I look like one of those Japanese divers? When I surfaced and he saw me in the flickering light of his lantern, did I look like I could fit into the grainy, out of focus photographs of an old *National Geographic*? I am thin, but maybe the moonlight gave me the illusion of extra padding on my shoulders and arms. Arthur is more than thin. He is tiny. I wish I could imagine him in the cold morning waters off of the coast of Japan, trying to hold his breath and shivering, thrown around by rough waves. Surrounded by full-busted women with thick voices and strong arms. Those other women would crowd him out with their competent strokes. Arthur is still cranking the generator. How much time he must spend out here in this little shack, spinning away so that this place has just enough electricity running through it to keep going.

Maybe he never sleeps. There's an old stationary bike set next to the generator. Arthur sees me staring at it and says, "I hook that up to the generator sometimes. When my arms get tired."

I am high and soaring and I can see it—Arthur pedaling furiously all night long, for an eternity. Arthur told us that something like one out of four natural pregnancies begin as twins. He told us that in some cases one of the twins bleeds out early on. Nothing alarming, just a little harmless spotting. Or else one fetus is absorbed by the other. Right now I think my head is light enough to believe almost anything. Maybe there is a tight pearl of what could have been tucked away inside of all of us. Maybe the craziest intuitions that some of the people here at Vanishing Point have are dead on, and maybe our twins are solid and real. Maybe there is a pocket of forest deep in this wilderness where all those twins that Arthur's campers expel from themselves end up. I can see them—furrier, happier versions of ourselves. Sleeping in tents and getting things to grow in the rocky soil. Harvesting armfuls of wild rice in the shallows of unmapped lakes. Maybe they never wanted to share our lives. They never wanted to haunt us. Arthur and I could form our own expedition, just the two of us, and try to track them down. But they don't want to be found. They are a content tribe, untouched. I don't want to find them. I don't think that's why I came out here anyway.

"My husband got sick," I say, and I feel like I am back in the lake again, sucked down by the weight of my clothes. "He didn't get better," I say. Arthur keeps cranking. My little story, what I have just told him, floats sharp and concise in the whirring silence. "He got sick," I say. "That is all." Arthur doesn't ask for more. I feel like I could sink with that bit of story alone. I could sink and drown. Future Vanishing Point campers would take deep breaths and dive down and try to pick bits of my bone out of the old wrecked car. They'd give the bones to Arthur and he would place them in a simple box made out of birch or just an old glass jar set on top of the crank generator. He would glance at the pieces of me every now and then while he turns turns turns.

I will tell you this. My husband and I had a simple story. No faded sleeping bags or mosquitoes or packs of sad, quiet adults doing arts and crafts together each afternoon. No patchwork of rock and water and forest in a wilderness as pure and heartbreaking as silence. It was our life, plain and simple. I would give her this story if I could. My twin. That gritty mass of tissue and mis-happened cells. She can have it.

Tracy DeBrincat

A Certain Fire

THERE IS A CERTAIN FIRE THAT PURIFIES, that makes you more beautiful the longer you burn. This is the flame that names you. It is a white heat—not scorching but alchemical—and manifests only to those gentle enough to suffer the powers of the cosmos. To some the conflagration bears no sound; to others it commingles all sounds as one: crackling tinder, ocean roar, serpentine hiss. Fear not the blaze—it is a joyful thing.

Marnie is toast and she knows it. She lowers the molded chicken product into a vat of bubbling oil and steps back to escape the splatter. She is in a sweat. Not just from the spreading heat, though that alone is enough to soak her uniform through both pits to the waist and across the small of her back. But because she was late to the Shithole. Third time, and she'd been warned, so it's nobody's fault etcetera. But her back hurt most of the night, and when she fell asleep she had that dream about the fire that she didn't want to leave. She woke up extra late and feeling out of sorts, as though she were still in the dream. She couldn't get the name "Kris" out of her head, then had an inexplicable case of big blubbery animal sobs in the shower. She missed her bus, punched in an hour past punch-in, and now her stomach ached like there was a monster in there. Probably from missing breakfast. Nothing to be done about it now. Not with the Bitch staring her down, just waiting for Mr. Williams to come in so she can gloat while Marnie gets canned. It's her own fault, really.

Mr. Williams' hands are the color of fried chicken product. He lays out the bills from the petty cash box. One, two, three. "I hate to do this, Marnie," he sighs. "You're a good girl. One of my best workers. But rules are rules."

Marnie smiles on the outside like her mother told her because if that's what she shows the world that's what people will see. But Marnie knows what people see. The muffler of flesh below her chin, bracelets of fat around her wrists, dimpled pudge-cakes where her legs bend in the middle despite her attempt to show the world something else.

"Merry Christmas," says Mr. Williams. "God bless."

Marnie pockets her cash and opens the door. Before she enters the brightness of day, turd-shaped objects bounce off her shoulders and the back of her head. They are not turds, but misshaped molded chicken products: rejects. She turns and sees the Bitch, who waves and smiles at Marnie. *"Mooooooo,"* says the Bitch.

Marnie closes the door behind her, and waits for the button to click into place. She wants a solid demarcation between the Shithole and the future, even if it is invisible.

Walking down the street during work hours is almost a joyous event. The display windows of the few shops that remain on the boulevard are draped in tinsel and painted with fake drifts of snow. It has never snowed here as long as Marnie's been alive and she's lived here her entire life. She cuts through the park, where children too young for school shriek in the playground. Babies wail as their mothers chat on phones or visit with girlfriends. Drivers in cars slow down at corners and wave for Marnie to cross even when there is no stop sign and they don't need to wait. Clouds part below the sun and the temperature ticks upward. December has been warm, practically like living in a desert. Her lower back aches, her thighs are sensitive from rubbing against the uniform, and her feet throb despite the ugly stand-all-day shoes she purchased to make her job bearable. But that is par etcetera. Marnie wriggles out of her sweater and turns her face up to the sky. Her hair is damp with sweat but at least she is able to walk. At least she has a sweater. At least she is able to look up.

Pansy sits on a cloudlike landscape of seat cushions, bed pillows and duffel bags on the small square of gravel outside her trailer. She is birdlike and bony, with a flat chest and angry, pocked skin. Kids at school used to give Pansy and Marnie the usual Jack Sprat crap for hanging out together. Unlike Marnie, Pansy was super talented at telling people to eff off.

"Come with me to the Red Barn," Marnie says. "I want to get Joe a present." She wants to be sure his gift is gotten before she forks over the rest of her pay to Einkorn.

"Can't," Pansy says. "I lost my you-know-what money." She is frantically inspecting the cushions and pillows: zipping and unzipping, tucking and un-tucking.

Marnie helps with the unzipping and un-tucking until she has to pee. She is tired when she returns outside, so she rests on the stair of the trailer.

Pansy looks up from a ripped-open bolster, feathers flying about her head. "Maybe the Asshole stole it." The Asshole is Pansy's husband. The Asshole is actually a really nice guy, the kind of guy Marnie would fall for if she didn't already have Joe, who is also a really nice guy, but whom Pansy also calls the Asshole. It's what Pansy does, in addition to losing things. But even friends have their faults and Pansy is Marnie's best friend. Since second grade. Through Marnie's weird older brother's suicide and her mom's drinking and then her parents' divorce. Through when Marnie's mother ran away with Marnie's little sister and that guy. They used to call that guy Super Asshole, but then decided it would be better if they just never talked about him at all.

"Here," Marnie says. She lays out the bills on her thigh. One, two. She keeps the last for herself. Well, for Einkorn. "Pay me back when you find your money."

"I can't take that," Pansy says, but she already has. It's in her hand, then her pocket, then Pansy's on the phone, then her cousin Spoot comes over in a green station wagon. Pansy buys her stuff and disappears into the bathroom.

Marnie knows who Spoot is but never knows what to say to him. He dropped out of their school after eighth grade. Now he's doing all right, with the station wagon and his designer sweat pants and blinding white sport shoes he wears with no socks. He has a weird blotchy mark on his cheek, like a fresh slap.

"I forget your name," Spoot says. He looks Marnie up and down with his hands on the wheel. "You got a boyfriend?"

"Marnie." She bares her small, vampiric teeth in a smartassy smile that not even her mother could complain about—it is one of Marnie's signature "show the people what they want to see" expressions. "And, yes, I'm taken."

Spoot lightly fingers the mark on his cheek. "When he breaks your heart, give me a call," he says.

"Sure," Marnie says. She is one hundred percent positive Joe will never break her heart.

Spoot smiles, winces, then catches himself and smiles again. The whole exercise looks painful. "Pansy give you a burner yet?"

Marnie doesn't know what a burner is. "No."

"Marnie, come here," Pansy yells from inside.

Marnie rises to her feet and reaches around to brush off the seat of her pants. It's mostly a gesture; she can't reach back that far and ends up waving her hand like she just farted.

"If she does give you one, I bet she'll tell you she invented it or something. But she didn't. She learned it from me." Spoot thumps himself on the chest, revs the sputtering engine, then palms the steering wheel round. The station wagon leaps forward, knocks a dirty cushion into the gutter, then careens into a dusty U-turn.

Pansy is one of the two ways she gets. Not mean, like shooting cats or picking fights with girls she doesn't even know at the Circle-K, but extra lovey-dovey. She hugs Marnie and promises she'll pay her back ASAP.

"Ouch," Marnie says to her friend's enthusiastic embrace. "I don't feel so good today."

Pansy boils hot water for tea and carries in some of the cushions. She arranges them so Marnie can lie down on the couch, then turns on the radio. Pansy knows the words to pretty much every song and can match her voice to whatever singer is singing. She used to talk about auditioning for *American Idol* after she won second place in the school talent contest, but then she stopped.

"Maaaaarnieeeee, you are so good to me," Pansy sings to the tune of a radio song. "So so so so good. What are you doing here anyway? Aren't you supposed to be at the Shithole?"

Marnie tells Pansy how she was so happy in the fiery dream that she never wanted to leave it.

Pansy lays her hand on Marnie's arm. "You don't want to croak off or anything, do you?"

"No, not like that," Marnie says. "I just felt so much better in the dream than I ever felt while I've been alive."

"I had a crazy dream like that, too!" Pansy's demeanor suddenly quiets. "Remember that time I was pregnant?"

Of course Marnie remembers. She and Pansy took jobs at an envelope factory that smelled like vomit and glue for two and a half months to earn enough money for Pansy's abortion before it was too late to have one.

Marnie continues her story, about the name "Kris" and crying in the shower blah blah blah. She leaves out the section about the chicken parts and the moo; she doesn't want to end up back at the Shithole watching Pansy beat the crap out of the Bitch.

When the water boils, Pansy stirs in the tea crystals and sugar. While Marnie warms her hands around the jelly jar, Pansy shoves her arm under the couch. "I want to give you your Christmas present early." She goes in deeper, then squirrels out a wire coat hanger. "It's really cool. It's called a burner. Spoot showed me how."

Marnie is proud of Pansy for not telling a lie like Spoot predicted she would. She watches Pansy hammer the thick wire with the heel of a shoe. The letter K appears, then an R, then I, then S.

Pansy's tongue finds its way to the corner of her mouth as she yanks another piece of wire into the shape of a six-pointed star. She lights an entire book of matches and holds it under the wire shaped like KRIS. "Where do you want it?"

"What are you going to do?" Marnie asks, but as she does, she pulls off the top of her mustard-colored uniform and rolls up the tank top beneath it, pushing down the waistband of her pants. She likes when that happens, when her brain doesn't know the answer but her body does.

The wire is a beautiful neon orange. Just before Pansy presses it onto Marnie's white skin, Marnie thinks she should probably wipe the spot with some antiseptic. Too late. It is already done.

"Damn," Pansy says, looking up from the mountain of Marnie's belly. "You got some righteous abs for a heavy girl. That shit is solid."

There is a microsecond when Marnie sees what Pansy has done and feels nothing. A millisecond second when she loves Pansy for calling her heavy and not fat. A full second before the white flash explodes across Marnie's forehead. Where she sees Joe smiling down at her like from heaven. She smiles on the outside and the inside too now. She concentrates on the smell of burning skin as the flesh below her navel is suddenly made vibrant and real. Beads of blood rise up red. The red of life and the planet Mars. The red of tomatoes. Marnie slides beneath a gray blanket of pain and thinks again of Joe.

He is very particular about tomatoes. He likes them in sauces but not cooked. In salads, but not cut into wedges. Never on sandwiches except BLTs. Don't even say "Campbell's" or he pales. Tomato juice makes him queasy, but he'll drink Bloody Mary's if he's already drunk. Dips his fries in Thousand Island, never catsup.

Marnie is thinking maybe when Pansy finishes the burner, they can go to the Garden Center and she'll get Joe some tomato seeds, when something *down there* seizes up like a mother. Marnie gasps; she can't tell if it's from the hunger, the hanger or something else. Something more mysterious and unnamable.

"Hang on," says Pansy, "I just gotta do the star."

The pain enters the jacket of Marnie's flesh and ties a black ribbon around her brain. To keep from crying out, Marnie shuts her eyes and tries to recapture the dream. She thinks about the last time Joe put his head *down there*. She laughed and she told him to stop but he told her to shut up or he would do the other thing, the thing that they had promised each other they were waiting to get married to do, so she stopped. It was beautiful the same way the fire was beautiful, the same way their promise was beautiful in spite of Joe's sometimes complaint that his balls were turning blue or his warning that if she didn't use it she would lose it. Beautiful in that she never wanted it to end. When she opens her eyes, she can breathe again, though the rhythm is ragged, uneven.

"Merry Christmas." Pansy holds up a little mirror so Marnie can see the burner. It says KRIS, just like in the dream, only backwards. The skin around it is pink and taut. A thread of blood slides from the star above the I, which brings her back to tomatoes, back to Joe.

Einkorn is watching *Golden Girls*. He thinks those old broads are hilarious. He has showered and shaved after a day on the site. A day that starts and ends much earlier than Marnie's. "I got fired today," she says.

Einkorn says nothing in response. Marnie doesn't expect him to. TV time is Einkorn's church time so there's no talking to him except during the commercials, which is now. He tosses Marnie a beer from the ice chest at his feet. "C'est la vie," he says. "You got a backup plan?"

"Not yet," Marnie says. She slips her hand into the pocket of her uniform, where her last bill, number three, is folded into tiny squares. She pops open the can and sinks into the depression on the sofa across from Einkorn. She is suddenly aware of her bare arms and neck and remembers she left her sweater at Pansy's.

"Horny bitch," Einkorn says to the TV as that naughty Rose buys ultra-sensitive King George condoms in black. He empties the can.

Marnie feels the comment is directed at her, but there is no reason for her to think that: Einkorn's eyes don't leave the screen. "Joe will be home in an hour," she says, and sips her beer. "We'll make a plan then."

Joe works part-time at an auto body shop a few blocks down. He and Marnie share a back room at Einkorn's. If Marnie hadn't screwed up *royale*, if it hadn't been for the dream, she and Joe would be arriving home at the same time. Joe doesn't like Marnie to be here when he's not.

During the next commercial break, Einkorn looks directly at Marnie from her eyes to her feet. She reaches for the crocheted afghan at the end of the couch.

"You don't have to do that," he says.

"I'm cold," she says. She rubs the tops of her arms with both hands, even though it is way hotter inside the house than the warm winter day outside. The afghan traps the stink of stale onion rings and chicken products and hamburger meat from her uniform and blasts it toward Marnie, who becomes mildly nauseous.

"Whose turn is it?" Einkorn asks.

"Joe's," Marnie says. She feels feverish and sharp pains shoot up from her crotch, but her mother made the afghan, and Marnie instinctively, if illogically, feels it will protect her. As Einkorn's gaze returns to the screen, she remembers the last time she woke up under the afghan. She wants to close her eyes, but she is afraid to without Joe.

"Rent's due in a week," Einkorn says. His tone is flat, light.

"So's Christmas." Marnie wishes Pansy were here. She would know what to say. But Pansy refuses to come over since she and Einkorn got into it in. Marnie never got the full story, but Joe called the cops. Pansy didn't press charges, being best friends and all, but she didn't see Marnie for a week and would never talk about it again. That was another of the ways Pansy got.

"I know plenty of people need a place to stay who can pay on time," Einkorn says. "Not like you two are anything special."

Marnie knows Joe won't be paid for two weeks. She pulls number three from her pocket and places it in her mother's crystal candy dish. The only thing the old lady left her, besides Einkorn.

That night Pansy and Joe won't talk about was Marnie's fifteenth birthday. Pansy made pink cupcakes; Joe brought beers; Einkorn, tequila. Marnie had dreams of roller coasters and Ferris wheels. Not really dreams, but a feeling as though she were riding on swoops and swirls, hair flying up or behind her, arms detached from her body, legs in a separate compartment, car rocking at the top as the electricity died down in a vortex hum. The view was beautiful up there, with tree tops and stars smiling back at her, but below was the inevitable fall into the void or worse, onto the people waiting on line, a crush of bones and scarves, down jackets and caps with knitted kitty ears.

When Marnie opened her eyes that time, Joe was in the kitchen making chuck roast in a plastic bag and mashed potatoes from a box. Einkorn was in his usual place in front of the TV. Pansy was gone.

Marnie's jeans were on the floor as though she had flown right out of them. Her panties were on the coffee table next to the crystal candy dish. She was horrified, but had no recollection, no idea, how they got there. Was she doing laundry? Had she fallen in mud? Then she saw the crumpled wrapping paper, the pink cupcake box, the empty bottles.

"The lady awakens," Einkorn said without waiting for the commercial break.

"What happened?" Marnie asked. Her entire body screamed as she leaned forward to swipe her panties out of sight onto the floor.

"Nothing bad," Einkorn said.

Joe looked at Einkorn, a hard look like Marnie had never seen.

"What's the matter, Joe?" Einkorn asked. That same tone, like with the rent.

"Nothing," Joe said.

"Birthday girl got tipsy and blacked out," Einkorn said. "If she's anything like her ma, it won't be the last time."

"Dinner will be ready soon," Joe said to Marnie. "Why don't you go take a bath?" His voice had a strange echo, like he was speaking into a vacuum.

Marnie thought her hearing had gone wacko, then realized it was because Joe was looking into the oven.

She stayed in the tub until her skin radiated bright pink from the waist down. Later at dinner, Joe and Einkorn refused to look at each other or at her as they passed the meat and potatoes around the table. But Marnie was ravenous. She finished off seconds of both dishes, savored the last cupcake for herself, then threw it all up before she went to bed.

"Taco time." Joe's voice is close to her ear.

Marnie instinctively feels for her pants; they're still on. The only item on the table is the candy dish, minus the bill. She covers the bandage on her belly with her hand, feels the throb of pain and magic beneath it.

"I'm not hungry," she whispers. She is starving, but the idea of food is revolting. Dull cramps embrace her lower regions. Maybe she's finally getting her period.

Einkorn sits alone at the kitchen table and pours an entire container of red tomato salsa on his pile of tortilla chips, being as Joe's preference for salsa is green.

Joe stretches out his hands. "Let's go for a walk," he says.

Marnie places her hands in his and focuses on the bulge of his muscles as he pulls her up. The blue veins beneath his skin are gnarled and ropy. They pulse with blood and tacos and love. As she slowly rises, she allows herself an "Oof!" and silently thanks him for his silence.

The sky is a dark winter bruise. Six in the evening looks like midnight, and the day's desert-like temperature has dropped to a steely chill. Marnie tells Joe everything. "How could such a beautiful dream lead to such a terrible day?" she asks.

He wraps his arm around her. "Why don't we go see what's happening down at the Red Barn?"

Joe and Marnie zigzag through the parking lot, which is loaded with cars going nowhere, waiting for spots to open. The tree at the entrance to the mall is decorated with tinsel and glittery balls and poinsettias. A golden light shines from within its branches as though a very special gift lay beneath.

Marnie veers them toward the Garden Center. She keeps her hand on her bandage and concentrates on breathing through the cramps. They pass through the cyclone gates, then the automatic glass doors. The fluorescent atmosphere feels serene; piped-in music soothes with violins and an occasional angelic chorus. Joe steers them toward the Christmas trees. Marnie smiles as she pulls away from Joe's hand and pushes him on ahead. He cocks his head—*are you sure?*—but she smiles even bigger.

The display at the end of the aisle has a cartoon graphic of laughing, dancing tomatoes. Bright red tomatoes in elf-like green caps, bursting with joy, good will and flavor. She looks over her shoulder as Pansy has taught her, then slips a pack of seeds into her sweatshirt pocket. She quickly moves past the display to catch up with Joe and feels a tightening in her stomach, as though something has hardened and softened at the same time. "Hey," she calls, as she steps outside and nears the small forest of trees.

Joe has put on a red-and-white furred Santa's cap, and is posing next to a tree, the only one there strung with white twinkle lights.

Marnie feels a gush of hot liquid between her legs. It keeps coming and coming and coming. She feels nothing below the waist. She looks down at herself as if through a telescope and the bottom half of her body is in a separate galaxy.

Far, far away, her jeans are drenched to her feet. Her knees buckle and she swoons to the floor, which takes a deliciously long time, as the floor is a thousand miles away.

Joe floats above her with both hands on her face. Twinkling lights and green tree tips form a wreath around his head. "What's happening?" he asks. His voice sounds strangled and dim, as though he's climbed inside Einkorn's oven and can't bear the heat.

"It's Kris," Marnie cries. Inside, she is delirious, golden. The dreadful pain of creation is unimaginable ecstasy. "It's the dream."

Conor Broughan

Move Forward, No Delays

BY JANUARY 27, 1967, NASA HAD DEVELOPED a case of go fever. A month before the first Apollo mission was scheduled to launch, everyone from the president down to the technicians had learned that a Russian cosmonaut had walked outside an orbiting capsule one hundred and fifty miles over Europe. He'd spent close to twenty minutes swiping cosmic dust and flipping through space, just so the Russians could say he did it first. The Soviets had done a few things first but Sam Bedford had assumed NASA would take the time to do it best. Sam stood behind the control boards in the pad 34 blockhouse, cleaning his glasses and listening to Gus Grissom ask if anyone was even listening. He and his crew, Roger Chafee and Ed White, sat in the Apollo capsule desperate to finish the plugs-out simulation test.

Sam leaned over the desk and grabbed the microphone.

"Loud and clear, Gus. Every word."

"Why are we still in here, Sam? There's a problem with the circuits."

Through the cloud of cigarette smoke, Sam couldn't see the quote painted on the blockhouse wall, but he knew it by heart: "It is man, not merely mechanics, in space that captures the imagination of the world." They'd all received that memorandum back in '61, when they were still trying to get NASA off the ground. Now they couldn't even get through a simple plugs-out test a month before the Apollo I launch. If they wanted to get to the moon by the end of the decade, Sam thought the mechanics had better get better, and quick.

Delays and inconsistencies had become standard for the Apollo I capsule as soon as Sam and his crew of technicians opened the box. North American Aviation had been contracted to put it together at their plant in Milwaukee, and by the time they sent it there were already over one hundred and thirteen engineering change orders. Sam, the lead engineer on the capsule, knew that some were based on poor design, but most were just lazy manufacturing. They'd built it fast, not well.

By six o'clock, Gus and Ed White and Roger Chaffee had been hatched-in for close to four hours. Sam watched them on the closed-circuit television, fed up with the poor communications and the mission in general. Most Fridays nights, Sam would've taken his wife Shelley to Wolfie's Deli in Cocoa Beach for pastrami-on-rye sandwiches and a pitcher of beer.

"How are we going to get to the moon if we can't speak between three buildings?" Gus asked no one in particular. Sam called Shelley and told her he wouldn't make it home for dinner, if he made it home at all. He told her it was the weather, the record low temperatures. Ever since the end of the Mercury mission Shelley had been trying to reason with Sam, asking him to work a few less hours and delegate some of the design work. He'd promised her that he would, though he never got any further than that promise. Sam stepped out of the blockhouse and pulled out a cigarette. The capsule looked like the wick of an unholy candle back-lit inside the gantry scaffolding.

January 1967 was brutal cold by South Florida standards. Up north citrus farmers hosed down their orchards to insulate the fruit in a layer of ice before a week of Arctic temperatures. When that kind of air blew down from Canada, a heavy fog would soup over the Gulf Stream, and the capsule at the top of launch 34 would disappear in mist. Sam listened to the chatter over the radio as the cold air stung his bare arms. He wanted to make Shelley happy, spend more time at home, but he couldn't delegate his designs. It was his work; lives were stake.

Maybe he'd lived in Florida too long, but it felt damn cold, almost as cold as the winter he and Shelley had spent in Ohio. After he'd graduated from North Carolina State with a degree in mechanical engineering, Sam trained to become an Air Force pilot at the Wright-Patterson base outside of Dayton. He met Gus Grissom a week after his physical, when the doctor told him he could see but not perfect, not good enough to be a pilot. The base ophthalmologist had confirmed his childhood diagnoses of keratoconus in both of his eyes, a degenerative eye disorder that had methodically thinned his cornea at a drastic rate. They found a spot for Sam in research and development. He'd been permanently grounded.

Flying airplanes had been his dream since the summer of 1938—the summer Sam turned ten years-old—when an unprecedented number of cutworms hatched and a pestilence of suck flies swarmed over North Carolina. On a Saturday in early June, Sam's father, a switchman for the Atlantic and Western Railway, walked Sam and his little sister to the edge of town. The Sanford town council had agreed to pay for a dusting over the tobacco fields to ensure a crop. Three biplanes circled the fields near their house and they sat on the gravel road with families from the block, watching the planes dip and turn at impossible angles; the spray from the wings shimmered in the sunlight over the bright green tobacco leaves. That's when Sam Bedford decided he wanted to be a pilot.

His father had liked the sound of that, so in early August he packed the truck and drove Sam to Winston-Salem to take in the air show at the Smith-Reynolds Aerodrome. Before interstates, the drive from Sanford to Winston-Salem took half the day on dusty roads. Sam had heard the planes before he saw them, as soon as they'd passed through Greensboro. He leaned out the truck's window and saw a small fleet of Douglas B-18 Bolo Bombers in formation, flying low over the airfield. Douglas bombers were his favorite. They had a glassed-in bombardier hatch below the nose of the plane, giving it a pug-nose he recognized from the library books he'd borrowed and packed in his father's leather overnight bag.

The tickets to the air show had been good for two days and they would sleep on the warped bed of the truck. By the time his father had parked the truck, there was only an hour of daylight left, and Sam grabbed his picture books and pushed his way through the small crowd lining the airfield. He wanted to watch the planes take off, a sight that thrilled him to no end. The rudimentary design of a fixed-wing aircraft made perfect sense to Sam—the lift of the wings and the thrust of the propellers—but there was still that terrifying moment when the plane took off and the dislocation between land and sky seemed impossible to reconcile.

Sam and Gus became friends when Sam started engineering the experimental aircraft, tinkering with the engines, dynamics, and pyrotechnics to get those birds flying faster than they ever had before. Once, after Sam had made a performance modification on an F-100, Gus asked him if he wanted to go up and see if the modifications felt right.

"Hell, Gus. You know better than me."

"A second opinion never hurt."

The F-100 was a two-seater and Sam sat behind Gus, looking across the flat expanse of cornfields wavering on the horizon and a string of cirrus clouds tumbling over the heart of the country. They flew west, following the dull winter sun, and only a few minutes into the flight Gus pointed out Mitchell, Indiana, his hometown. Sam squinted and thought he saw a single street cutting through rolling hills, pockmarked with limestone quarries. It looked as if God had scraped his fingernail across the green earth.

When they reached altitude, Gus told Sam to take over the controls, to feel them out. He made a few slight, but nervous maneuvers.

"Feels alright to me," Sam said, but Gus didn't answer. He was taking a nap 20,000 feet over the Kentucky border. He didn't need Sam to test the modifications; he'd just wanted to give a grounded pilot the chance to fly.

Sam rubbed the cigarette between his fingers, extinguishing the cherry before he flicked it into a stand of palms along the blockhouse wall. He heard yelling before he saw the smoke. It was blurry across the tarmac, but technicians were pouring down the stairs of the launch pad. Audio communications were delayed by close to a minute. Sam had already started running towards the gantry when he heard Roger Chafee yelling fire from the blockhouse speakers.

Under perfect conditions, it would take ninety seconds to open the capsule hatch and the conditions were less than perfect. A fierce wind preceded the cold front and dense smoke billowed across the low moon over the Atlantic. Sam had designed the hatch, given it three different release points and twelve separate bolts that had to be manually loosened, all because Gus had run into trouble back in '61 when he splashed into the Atlantic in the Mercury II capsule. The explosive hatch that Sam had outfitted for that capsule had blown before the rescue chopper picked it up. The whole country watched while the helicopter released the capsule back into the heaving ocean so they could save Gus. People in front of their televisions cheered as the Coast Guard picked Gus up like a drowning kitten, but NASA didn't celebrate. They watched the capsule, and all the money that went into building it, take on water before it sank to the bottom of the Atlantic. Gus claimed he didn't panic and he didn't blow the hatch manually, and Sam believed him. That didn't stop him from scrapping the explosive hatch from the Apollo capsule design plans. That way no one would get embarrassed—or dead—from another faulty hatch.

Firemen ran past Sam on the gantry stairs and more and more technicians streamed out of the white room, trying to cough out the toxins that had poured through the burn-holes in the capsule. On the top landing, Terry Gleason clung to the rail searching for a breath.

"The hell, Terry?"

"It happened so fast." Terry couldn't open his eyes. "The bolts were too hot to touch even before we saw the smoke."

It took close to nine minutes for the firemen to release the hatch and by then the fire had burned through the available oxygen in the capsule and extinguished itself. Fred Kelly, the NASA surgeon, was the first to step into the capsule. When he stepped out a few moments later, Sam knew it was too late. He walked up to the open hatch, but Fred stopped him. He put his hand across Sam's chest.

"Asphyxiation, Sam. No reason to look." He tried to turn Sam around and out of the white room. "It'll take a few hours to clear. Why don't you go home to Shelley?"

Sam adjusted his glasses, wiping the smudged lenses with his index finger. The inside of the capsule looked like the furnace of a burned out basement, the acrid smell of burnt hair and skin. Sam knew he probably should go home to Shelley. They needed to call Gus's wife Betty, but he pushed Fred against the wall and stepped into the hatch.

"Make your report, Fred. I need to make mine."

The metal around the hatch was still hot. Behind Sam, a firefighter trained his flashlight on the jump seats and Sam saw Roger Chaffee still strapped-in, his hands stuck to the instrument panels, a toddler waiting for his father to unbuckle the seat belt. Ed White had fallen on top of Gus, trying to release the hatch manually. Both of them had been standing on the seats and their boots had melted into the vinyl. The back of Ed's head had soldered to his helmet and Sam couldn't see Gus's face. He was glad for that. It was clear that Gus had been helping Ed with the door before the toxins had killed him, before the fire had stolen the oxygen from his lungs.

Technicians and emergency personnel stood stunned against the walls, wiping their eyes and coughing into their sleeves.

"No press, understand?" Sam yelled. "We need cameras, but nobody lets in the press. We document the interior and the exterior before anybody touches a thing."

"What about Gus?" Terry asked. "What about the bodies?"

"They're dead. We need to investigate. We need to move forward. No delays."

Sam never did stop thinking about the Mercury II mission in 1961, when the hatch had exploded in the middle of the Atlantic on live television. The investigation nearly drove Gus to the brink. Sam had spent most of that June at Langley Air Force base in Hampton, Virginia, building a simulator that would synchronize with the capsule designed in Florida.

Gus had taken July 4th off to spend some time with his family and he asked Sam and a few of the other astronauts and engineers to a barbeque at his house in Newport News. Sam arrived early. A chartered Air Force cargo plane was scheduled to fly down to the Cape that afternoon, and he was determined to get home and watch the fireworks explode over the Atlantic with Shelley.

Burning charcoal permeated the air of the housing development near the mouth of the Chesapeake Bay. Sam walked into the backyard, expecting the Grissoms to be outside, Gus tending to the fire, but the yard was empty. He dropped a sack of beer on the patio table. The grill was open and the charcoal recently lit. An off-shore breeze caught the billowing flames and it sounded like a sheaf of graph paper being ripped again and again and again. Betty, Gus's wife, stepped outside.

"You're early, Sam." She walked onto the grass in her bare feet and moved a cigarette from her left hand so she could hug Sam. She'd cut her hair short, but she looked tired. By design, NASA had kept Gus busy leading up to the mission, but Betty could only watch and wait.

"Shelley sends her best."

"I miss having Shelley around. I really do. She'd be a nice voice of reason in this madhouse." They'd been close friends at the Wright-Patterson base when Gus and Sam flew together. As close as two Air Force wives could be.

The Grissom's house was large and modern. It had an open floor plan that Sam had read about in magazines, where you could see the kitchen, the dining room, and the television room all from the same spot. Gus's two young sons were lying on their stomachs in front of the television, chins propped on their fists. Shelly had enjoyed babysitting the boys when they'd lived in Ohio, when the boys had still been in diapers. At that point, Sam and Shelley hadn't known they would never have any children of their own. Eventually a doctor told Shelley that there was no harm in trying, as long as they didn't expect too much.

"Don't tell me Gus is still at the base."

"He might as well be." Betty mixed a spoonful of mayonnaise into a bowl of cold potatoes and pointed at the garage door with the wooden spoon. "Couldn't have slept more than an hour last night, and he's down in the garage first thing this morning."

Gus stood at the workbench in the garage, sanding down a length of wood. The hull of small wooden boat took up the space where he would typically park his Corvette. He finished sanding down the long wooden mast, a mess of metal rigging and hemp rope was piled on the far end of the bench.

"Never took you for a Navy man, Gus."

"It's for the boys. Something before I leave for Florida." He handed Sam a blueprint that he'd ripped from the back pages of *Popular Mechanics.* "Anyone can build it, it says. But damn if this rigging isn't giving me hell." Gus wore his standard-issue khakis and a sweat stained V-neck undershirt. "Designed a goddamned space capsule but I can't figure out this shitty blueprint."

Gus sat on a metal stool against the workbench. His face looked tired, taut as an open parachute. He was exhausted and not because of the boat.

"You look tired, Gus. Have you been sleeping?"

"Sleep? There's no time. You know that."

Gus had been embarrassed—the whole company had—when in April of 1961, Yuri Gagarin and the Soviets beat us into space. Worse, the press had caught wind of Gagarin's orbit and called Colonel Powers, the NASA spokesman. Around four in the morning, the reporter had asked Powers for an official response from NASA after the Soviets had won the first leg of the space race. Powers had only yawned into the receiver and told the reporter the truth: he and the rest of NASA had been asleep when it happened.

"It's worth the risk though, right?" Gus worked the mast pole into the setting he'd drilled into the hull.

"What do you mean?"

"As I see it, I'm just a glorified test pilot, right? Anything happens to me, to us, there can't be any delays. Gagarin orbited for an hour—he saw the sun rise over Siberia twice—and we've been up there for what, fourteen minutes?" Gus screwed a hook to the top of the mast for the rigging. "But getting to the moon, that's worth the risk, right?"

"I don't know."

Gus crossed his arms, waiting for Sam to continue.

"Yes, it's worth it, but not just to beat the Soviets." Sam grabbed one of the hooks from Gus's hand and helped him screw it into the mast. "Our fathers couldn't have even imagined a man walking on the moon. They couldn't have even dreamed it up. And now, here we are," Sam said, holding his index finger and thumb an inch apart.

Gus wiped the sawdust from his face and hands with a dirty t-shirt he'd crumpled beneath the workbench. "No delays, Sam."

"No delays."

The kitchen door opened and Betty leaned against the doorjamb. The flames had burned off the coals and a few cars had just pulled into the drive.

Two weeks later, after an initial delay due to poor visibility from ground fog, Sam sat in the blockhouse and watched the Mercury-Redstone rocket carry Gus into orbit. He'd wished him luck from the elevator at the bottom of the gantry, but couldn't ride with Gus to the capsule. No one trusted the capsule more than Sam—he'd designed it. No matter how much he trusted the technology, he could never forget that the only thing separating Gus from all that space would be a few inches of metal.

Thinking of those astronauts out there in unspeakably cold space, with no hope for a return to Earth unless his designs worked, Sam would think about standing along the rope at the Smith-Reynolds Aerodrome in Winston-Salem. All of ten years old, Sam answered each of his father's questions about the planes as if he were an expert. Luscombe Phantoms flew in formation over the crowd, criss-crossing each other in figure eights. Four Stinson Reliants dodged each other in near-miss maneuvers right above their heads. At the time, Sam was already wearing half-inch thick lenses in wide framed glasses. The doctor described the hard contact lenses—rigid gas-permeable lenses—that could improve his vision even if they couldn't arrest the condition. On his father's switchman's salary, the contacts were just too expensive. And so Sam, wearing goggle-sized glasses, had to squint to see the planes.

When the sun began to set, the master of ceremonies announced the last act of the day, a stunt pilot who was also scheduled to perform the next morning, flying the world famous Wing Walkers in what he called the most dangerous flight the crowd would ever see. The pilot ran to the plane, a single-seat Curtiss Falcon that didn't look all that different from the old dusters Sam had seen over Sanford earlier that summer. The pilot jumped onto the wing and turned back to the crowd, waving before he clasped his goggles over his eyes. Sam pushed his glasses back to the bridge of the nose.

He lost sight of the plane when it dipped below the tree line, but could hear it turning back, lifting higher and higher above the airfield. The exhaust of the plane had been modified so that a dense, white contrail followed it.

At the apogee of the plane's ascent, it spun out violently and fell towards the earth in wide, lazy circles. Sam's father bent over, noticing how anxious it made Sam, and said, "All part of the show, son."

He pointed to the plane pulling out of the stall before the pilot made a loop that left an enormous "O" behind the plane.

A few hours after the smoke had cleared from the white room on that cold January night, one of the technicians told Sam that Gus had said there was a strange odor inside the Apollo I capsule when he'd first stepped in. Sour buttermilk, he'd said.

Why the hell would a sterile capsule smell like sour buttermilk? Maybe it didn't smell so different than the milk his mother had cooked with back in Indiana, and maybe that's why he hadn't been concerned. Being concerned shouldn't have been Gus's responsibility. It was on Sam's team; it was on Sam.

"You have to let the investigators do their job." Fred Kelly had found Sam chipping residue from the instrument panels into plastic bags. "Go home to Shelley. Take care of her. We'll take care of all this."

Sam turned back to the jump seat, unscrewing a panel from the console. Behind Fred, the NASA photographer had walked into the white room, his eyes wide and frightened because he'd only taken publicity photos of the men before, not their remains. Sam called him to the hatch of the capsule, making sure that he didn't touch anything until it was completely documented.

It took close to six hours to separate the bodies and peel them from the command module seats. The fire had started beneath Gus's control board and for the next twenty hours Sam worked with the investigation team to figure out why. By Sunday night, he was no closer to knowing what had started it. The muscles in his shoulders had started to give out, and a searing pain punctured his lower back every time he curled beneath the panels to disassemble the capsule piece-by-piece. Late that night, Terry Gleason walked into the white room and called Sam out of the capsule.

"Poor Shelley's been calling and leaving messages non-stop. Take a break for her at least."

"Let me just get the rest of the panels out and double-check the wiring."

"They scheduled the funerals up at Arlington for the 31st. That's less than two days. Get cleaned up and get on a flight to D.C. I told Shelley to pack you a suit and a warm coat."

The breeze from the open door was cool and the moonlight created a mess of shadows on the gantry scaffolding.

The blockhouse was empty save for the skeleton crew that Sam has asked to stay on. He sat down at his desk and leaned back in his chair, stretching before he dialed for Shelley.

"Sam, please come home."

"I'm sorry, Shell."

"It's been an awful couple of days."

"The investigation had to move forward."

"But you could've called."

Sam had rolled the capsule blueprints into the file boxes above his desk and he pulled out one of the sheets. "I know that machine better than anyone, honey. They needed me here."

"I called Betty this morning."

"Did you? How did she sound?"

"How do you think? She sounded like her husband had just died and it's all she hears about on the radio and television. Reporters have been peering in her windows and camping out on the porch."

"That's terrible. I'll give her a call."

"Do that. No one at NASA has explained anything to her. She wants to know what he said before he stepped in. She wants to know." Sam listened to her move around the kitchen, the long phone cord slapping against the counters and wooden chairs. "Do you want to know the worst part? What she said that made me cry the moment I hung up?"

"What's that?"

"She said that she wouldn't know how to miss him. She said that she'd miss his phone calls. That's mostly what she had of him. Phone calls."

Sam didn't respond, not right away. "I'll make it right," he finally said. "I promise. When this is all over, I'll take you up to North Carolina for a few weeks. We can stay with your brother on the farm. Okay?"

She asked him to come home, and he told her that he would. He hung up the phone and pushed his briefcase and car keys and accordion folders off the desk, unrolling the blueprints of the capsule he'd drawn over a year ago.

On that clear, hot August evening, Sam's ten year old eyes strained to watch the stunt plane fly higher and higher, back and forth over the crowd at the aerodrome surrounded by tobacco fields. The pilot flew for almost five minutes before he let out his engine and fell into another tailspin. Only this time no contrail followed him, and the plane flipped upside down, spinning in wider and wider circles, drifting away from the airfield like house sparrow in a hurricane.

Men ran beneath the rope and across the field—Sam's father included. The pilot tried to restart the engine above the trees, but a plume of dark, heavy smoke materialized from the woods beyond the airstrip. Sam stayed behind the rope, hugging his picture books and watching the fire truck speed across the tarmac.

He waited for his father at the truck. The sun had set and the firefighters worked hard to put out the blaze. Sam could smell cedar trees burning. His father returned with his shirt unbuttoned and his hat off. Sam was desperate for his father to tell him that the pilot was fine and that it had all been part of the show, but he knew that wasn't possible. Sam understood how the pilot had to have been killed, but he couldn't understand how that machine could look so perfect and still fail.

"Not much we could do," his father said, opening the tailgate of the truck.

"Is he dead?"

"Very much so." He reached into the cab and pulled out the blankets and pillows to make a pallet over the rotting wood of the truck bed. "I'm guessing you won't want to stay for the show tomorrow, but it's too late to start back now."

He lifted Sam onto the tailgate and took off his glasses, wiping Sam's damp cheeks with his scratchy thumb.

"I still want to see the show."

"After all that?"

"I want to see the Wing Walkers." He wanted to see all the planes they hadn't seen. He couldn't go home until he'd had a chance to sit in the cockpit of the Douglas Bolo when they were opened to ticket-holders in the morning.

His father helped him take off his boots. "Suit yourself, but I won't watch."

Sam put on his summer pajamas and tried to get comfortable on the hard pallet. His father didn't undress or even take off his boots. Sam could smell the loose McClintock tobacco leaves as his father stuffed the paper and licked the edges before rolling the cigarette between his stained, rutty fingers.

In the middle of the dark airfield and through Sam's tear-stained glasses, the stars were bright. There were stars behind the stars. The sky looked like the swirling oil-slicks that freight trucks left behind at the rail yard when Sam would take his father's lunch to the switchman's office.

"Still want to be a pilot?"

The smoke from the cigarette tickled the back of Sam's throat and he coughed. He didn't know how to tell his father that he needed to be pilot, now more than ever. He wanted to walk into the woods and pick up the pieces of that plane. Sam knew he could fix whatever had failed that pilot and make it better. He'd start the engine, pull up on the throttle and fly that plane higher than anyone could imagine. The airstrip would look like a patch of brittle grass huddled between the lights of Winston-Salem and the green tobacco fields. From that altitude, so close to heaven, the burning cherry of his father's cigarette would look like nothing more than the distant reflection of a single star. He could see it all with a startling clarity.

Wayne Lee

Just Like John Glenn

Look there's a guy
who looks just like Scott Glenn the actor
who doesn't look at all like John Glenn
the first American to orbit the Earth
even though he did co-star
in the Academy Award-winning 1983 film
"The Right Stuff" directed by Philip Kaufman

although he played Alan Shepard
the first American in space
who should actually have been
the first American to orbit the Earth
rather than John Glenn
who was played in the film by actor Ed Harris
who also played in "Apollo 13"
the 1995 film nominated for Best Picture
and directed by Ron Howard
about the aborted and near-tragic
1971 NASA lunar-landing mission
starring Tom Hanks and a fine ensemble cast
in which Ed Harris earned a
Best Supporting Actor nomination
for his performance as the commander
at Houston Flight Control
who kept his cool while everyone else
around him was losing theirs

so I guess Scott Glenn isn't in as much danger
of astronaut typecasting as is Ed Harris
although I've never actually met Scott Glenn

but I did meet John Glenn once
that's why I know what he looks like

it was at the Kennedy Center
not Cape Kennedy
a lot of people get those two confused
it was at the world premiere of the movie
"The Right Stuff" which was loosely based
on Tom Wolfe's 1975 book of the same name
which was written all about test pilot Chuck Yeager
and the birth of the U.S. space program
and I was there at the Kennedy Center
not Cape Kennedy
as a cub reporter to write about it
for *The Washington Times*
coincidentally known as the Moonie Paper
so I was interviewing all these astronauts
with really macho names like Gus Grissom
and Buzz Aldrin who seemed deeply offended
that I didn't recognize him
but who except maybe some space groupie
or something would actually recognize Buzz Aldrin
in a crowd without his space suit on

but anyway that was where I met John Glenn
and also Chuck Yeager the test pilot was there
and I did recognize him of course
because I'd interviewed him the year before
about the same time he was probably filming
his cameo appearance as a bartender
for the movie "The Right Stuff"
it was while I was covering the National Folk Life Festival
and Chuck Yeager was there giving a sparsely attended talk
on the Mall that day sitting in the shade
over behind the information booth
telling all about the X-15 and being the first man
to break the sound barrier and all
but since it was a year before the movie came out
no one on the Mall seemed to recognize him at all
except maybe a few old VFW fanatics
who lived and breathed war memorabilia
and it was just them and their indifferent wives

who looked like they would much rather have been
clapping along with some toothless Zydeco fiddler
across the Mall at the Louisiana Pavilion
so it was just these few older people
sitting around on a few rickety wooden benches
listening to Chuck Yeager the famous test pilot
telling how he was so rattled in space
the rivets just about popped off his fuselage

and while I was watching Chuck Yeager
I found myself thinking how when he was younger
he must have closely resembled
author actor director and playwright Sam Shepard
who should not to be confused with Dr. Sam Sheppard
the Cleveland osteopathic surgeon
who spelled his surname with two pees
and who was wrongfully tried and convicted in 1943
following a sensational trial for the beating death
of his pregnant wife Marilyn by a man
described by Dr. Sheppard as a bushy-haired intruder
and who spent 10 years in prison before winning
a federal appeal and eventually being acquitted in 1966
with the assistance of celebrity attorney F. Lee Bailey
and who later died of liver failure at the age of 46
and whose sad tale inspired the hit '60s television series
and 1996 movie remake of "The Fugitive" starring Harrison Ford
who also has enough Flash Gordon good looks to play an astronaut
and who in fact did play a mercenary intergalactic pilot
of a spacecraft that could actually travel at light speed
even though it looked as though it too might pop some rivets
and get blasted out of the sky by the dreaded Death Star
in the landmark 1976 George Lucas film "Star Wars"
which won seven Oscars that year but none of the major awards

but Sam Shepard the author actor director and playwright
actually did play Chuck Yeager in the movie "The Right Stuff"
and coincidentally he spells his last name with only one pee
exactly the same as astronaut Alan Shepard
and in real life the real Sam Shepard cohabits with and has

children by but is not married to Jessica Lange
the Oscar-winning blonde actress
whom some people get confused with Meryl Streep
who also is an Oscar-winning blonde actress
and who played Danish-born baroness Karen Blixen
in the film "Out of Africa"
which won Academy Awards in 1985 for Best Picture
and for Best Director for Sydney Pollack
and which also starred Robert Redford
as an English bush pilot and adventurer
who had that same kind of wild-blue-yonder good looks
but Karen Blixen who later changed her name
to Isak Dinesen and gained fame in 1937
by writing the book *Out of Africa*
should not be confused with fellow African
author and aviatrix Beryl Markham
who spells her Christian name almost exactly the same
as actress Meryl Streep and who wrote
the best-selling 1942 book *West with the Night*
and who was alluded to but never actually appeared in
the movie of "The Right Stuff"

and I also found myself thinking that day how much
Chuck Yeager looked like Frank Perdue the Chicken King
but his nose wasn't quite as beak-like
and anyway Chuck Yeager was probably never accused
of being a chicken

and this guy across the restaurant
the one who looks just like Scott Glenn the actor
I bet no one's ever accused him of being a chicken either
he's got that same right-angle jaw you know
and just enough of a receding hairline
to make him appear dangerously experienced
and then too some people
might look at him and mistakenly think he looks just like
John Glenn the one-time presidential hopeful
and first American to orbit the Earth
not because they think they remember

exactly what John Glenn looks like
but because they do recognize Scott Glenn the actor
who after all did play an important astronaut
in "The Right Stuff" the movie and you know
coincidentally both of them do have the same last name
and all so a person could understand the confusion
and it all just goes to show that on earth as it is
in heaven what goes around comes around.

Jose Padua

One Night at the Nuyorican

One night at the Nuyorican I opened the bathroom
door to see a poet whose work I didn't like
standing bare-assed, ass side facing me, while her left hand
was moving downward mid-wipe. Now I know there are
people who hide out in port-a-potties to see this sort
of thing, and I know that singer GG Allin, who
overdosed across the street from my apartment in

New York one night, had a strange appreciation for
fecal matter, and although I'm certainly weird I'm
not *that* weird, and the reality is that no one
looks good bent over the toilet and wiping, and I
have no idea why her ass was facing *away*
from the toilet while she wiped, and I can't
say that I'm at all curious about this, and if

somehow you knew why and were to try to tell me
I probably wouldn't believe you anyway and
my opinion of you would diminish so swiftly
you'd swear I'd just smacked you in the face. I'd seen some
horrible things in my New York days, and her "jazz"
poetry and her "in-the-moment" performances
were two of them, but the only thing I can say I

wished I'd never experienced was the sight of her
wiping her ass. Maybe if I'd liked her work my
reaction would have been different. Maybe I would
have remembered a line from one of her poems. Maybe
I would have gone right home, picked up one of her books and
just read madly and uncontrollably for the rest
of the night. Maybe I would have jumped up, raised my arms

in celebration and declared *I've seen Judy Woolworth*
wiping her ass, or I have been blessed or Is there no
one here to challenge me? Judy Woolworth, of course, was
not this poet's real name. I do not and have never
had any of her books. I don't remember if she
used my name when she turned toward the open bathroom
door and said "Sorry, Jose, I'll be out in a minute"

or just "Sorry, I'll be out in a minute" without any
name, which would mean, perhaps, that she didn't know
it was me. And maybe, for that matter, she didn't like
my work. I never told her that her readings made me cringe—
we never spoke about these things—I never asked her, "Did
you know it was me who saw you wiping your ass at
the Nuyorican the other night?" These were the days when

New York was taller and the rest of the world seemed farther
away, and a few days after I saw Judy Woolworth's ass
was when I spent a quiet night at home while GG Allin,
whose shows I never saw and never wanted to see, deep
fried his fucked up ass so close to where I was that I
probably heard the same sounds he did—the car alarms,
the drunks arguing on the corner—before everything went blank.

Christopher Bursk

UNTITLED—MARK ROTHKO—1969–/70

1

What I see is the world before God got cold feet and said, *Let there be light.* A sky that resists sharing the universe with anything as annoying as that old Cossack, the sun—or any star, for that matter. Cassiopeia? Sirius? Orion. Those self-aggrandizing, self-referential luminaries of no more use to us than fireflies invented so we'd have something to ooh and aah about. *The palpable obscure?* Genesis before it was turned into a soap opera. I see a sky that's uninterested in what we might say about it and that doesn't want anything to spoil its bad mood. That would not budge an inch. Not for Jesus or Buddha, Genghis Khan or Billy Graham, Emily Dickinson or Ella Fitzgerald, Sir Francis Bacon or John Coltrane, Bill Gates or Bill Shakespeare. A dark so dark it is nothing but supremely itself.

2

Let's visit the Guggenheim, my wife suggests. We've only been to New York once before, on our honeymoon, and we walk the fifteen blocks from the train station because we don't know how much to tip a taxi cab driver and still have enough left for souvenirs for the kids. It's becoming clear to me I'll never be more than meteorite debris in the galaxy, but my wife tells me to stop talking and enjoy the pictures. We stand the requisite 18 inches away from Rothko, but neither of us says what we're thinking. Because I keep being pulled closer till I fear I'll plunge into that fabulously expensive darkness and the guards will come running, I shove my hands in my pockets. It won't be the first time they've got me in trouble. *Go ahead,* I hear each Rothko whisper. *Your life will never be the same.* When I finally think to look at my wife, she's crying and won't say why. *Let's go*, I say because sometimes that's the only thing to do: pick up your coats and step into the light you know will solve nothing.

3

Years later, opening one of those Taschen books that do their best to reduce an artist to 100 pages, I find *Untitled (Black on Gray.)* Though it's been shrunk to 5 by 8 inches, it's colossal. Half of the darkness belongs to sky, the other half to ocean and just as vast as committed to staying as it is. Water uncontaminated by living organisms. Water that reflects nothing and upon which you detect God's thumbprint. The waters of Day Three with nothing on the horizon except a gray streak too smeared to illuminate anything. A sea not expecting to be crossed, even by light. A sea asking and hoping for nothing.

Meghan Dunn

GALILEO SEES HIS FUTURE

She hurried after him, hair falling
from its knot, one strand caught in her mouth.
Her leather slippers slid over stone, the stairs
he had climbed before, burdened with materials
for experiments. For him, the climb was different
at night, lighter; he felt pulled upward
by the moon, by his own tiny importance.
At the top, she waved good night to Pisa,
sunset cloaking the hills, a tapestry.

What do you know? she asked,
twisting a white silk scarf. *Tell me.*
He could see the stars
pricking their way through sky.
Everything, he said. He told her about gravity,
how the earth fought her desire to fly,
how, in the end, we all fall the same way.
She drew closer. Above them,
worlds smashed

and rubbed rough places smooth.
Show me, she said, already lifting her skirts
to his hesitant hands. Breath heavy
with the wine they'd drunk, lips stained,
parted, a rusty whisper
escaped her. Later, they stood side by side
and observed the houses below. She raised one arm
and dropped the scarf. It spiraled downward,
curling and unfurling like a circling bird.

He knew the tower's height, could calculate
the scarf's descent. In the arc of night,

he saw his future: discoveries, the Inquisition,
his defense, which he mouthed: *But it moves.*
The scarf wheeled toward the ground.
He could see the path it would take, the very spot
it would land, and sighing, fold into itself.

Kristina McDonald

My Brother Tries to Tell Me About the Zeno Effect

I'm in the bathtub when he calls, but
I don't tell him this. *The zero effect?* I ask
and he says, *No, Zeno. Weren't you listening?*
Just by staring at something,
we prevent it from changing.

A watched pot? I ask and he says, *No,*
that's too big. The bubbles around me
are quietly popping. *I don't get it,* I say
and he says, *The unstable particle never decays.*
I don't get it, I say, and he says, *Our eyes.*
Our eyes are always asking, Where are you?
and the electron has to answer, I am here.
It has to. It can't do anything
but answer. As long as someone
is looking. It doesn't have a choice.

*

Our mother disappeared when I was five
and my brother said, *Let it go*
like she was some doll
I left at the playground
who was discovered by
some other girl, went home
with some other family.
Maybe my brother
could put it behind him
but a daughter never stops
looking out the window
or checking the closet for clues.

My brother said, *Let it go*
so I held on harder
to the pencils and markers,
drew a whole army
of fairy godmothers, pretended
every picture was a portal,
a different version
of her face. I was afraid
of forgetting. Every night,
I'd look them in the eyes
and tell them all
about my day.

*

It freaks me out, he says.
How can they know
someone is watching?
And I say, *What?* And he says,
The electrons! It's like they can feel.
I poke the remaining bubbles
with my pinky. *Why do you care?*
I ask and he says, *Why don't you?*

*

Ever since I moved, my brother calls
with the latest news, and I tell him
all about my day. It's ten p.m.
and my bath is over, my phone call
is over, I'm tucked into bed
and my walls are still drowning
in drawings of godmothers.
Somewhere in a lab, there's an electron
that's been waiting its whole life
to move on. Even when there's no one left
to ask the question, it keeps repeating,
I am here. I am here.

Lones Seiber

FINCHES

FOR THREE MONTHS BEFORE she disappeared, Petey and I shared eighth grade classes. She had just moved to Newton, so she didn't enroll until four days after spring break, the same spring Kenny Smith drowned while tubing on the Little River. To honor his memory, no one used his desk that quarter. Despite their grief, compounded by his youth and the suddenness of his death, Kenny's parents spoke without bitterness at his funeral, thanking God for the twelve years they had been permitted to share with their only son. Above names and dates on the gleaming-faced, marble monument, the carved image of an angel, with veined wings and a pleated robe, hovered protectively. Suicide bombers and steroids in baseball quickly displaced news of his passing in the media. By summer's end Kenny's parents had quietly separated. His mother quit teaching French at the high school and moved to Florida. His father George continued selling Fords for Cunningham Motors. Whenever anyone needed a vehicle, they asked for George. It was also the spring the high school instituted parenting classes for the five girls who were showing.

Petey sauntered into the classroom that morning after the last bell. She wore a Superman tee, faded jeans with frayed cuffs, and deck shoes without laces or socks. Razor thin, she seemed to be all knees and elbows. She handed an admittance slip to our homeroom custodian and science teacher, Mrs. Carpenter. After reading the document through glasses with lenses so thick her eyes appeared the size of golf balls, she stood and placed a hand on Petey's shoulder. Petey flinched.

"Class. This is Patricia," she said cheerfully, as if hope resided within.

"Hello, Patricia," the class sang in ragged discord, and then someone belched anonymously like a frog.

Petey rolled her eyes and selected a desk on the last row, which was otherwise empty. She rested her temple on her hands, her fingers laced into a pillow on the desktop, and remained that way during class, during all her classes, trudging grimly from one to the other, head down, hands thrust into her jeans' pockets.

On the third day of her blatant inattention, Mrs. Carpenter, wearing an ocher blush that made her face look jaundiced, interrupted her lecture, a spiritless dissertation on gravitation and the solar system that seemed to elicit several audible yawns but little interest, and glared for several seconds at Petey, who continued to nap.

"Patricia. Perhaps you'd care to come forward and elaborate on what I've been discussing?" she said tersely, feeling shrewd, I'm sure.

It was a standard, and usually effective, weapon in each teacher's arsenal: public humiliation for some un-enterprising half-wit.

Petey pushed herself up, red, finger creases along her cheek, and strode to the front with an attitude of ease. She cocked her head, her frizzy, rust-colored hair matted from neglect, and twirled dangling curls around a finger as, for a long moment, she studied the greenboard. Mrs. Carpenter had used a string and chalk to draw nine, visually perfect, concentric circles around a solid white center the size of a soft ball.

"This isn't quite right, is it?" Petey said, without sounding impertinent. She picked up an eraser. "Do you mind?"

Mrs. Carpenter opened her mouth wordlessly, but then waved her hand, her smugness having fled. She crossed her arms and tucked her lips inside her mouth.

Petey vigorously erased the neatly constructed circular array, sparing the sun, and scrawled lop-sided, intersecting ellipses, each larger than the one previous.

"Each planet tracks around the sun in elliptical, not circular, orbits," she said, "so technically it's not the center of our solar system, but is actually located at the foci of the orbits." I had no idea what a foci was, and I doubt anyone else did. Silent but amused glances were exchanged, everyone suddenly attentive. "To stay in orbit, each planet's centrifugal force has to equal the gravitational pull of the sun, otherwise..." She slowly drew a curved line, the chalk chattering, from one of the outer orbits, sounding a descending whistle as she did, and went: "Boom," when it impacted the sun. Most everyone laughed. "It would burn up." She laid the chalk and eraser in the tray, dusted her hands, and faced the class. "The velocity necessary for planets to maintain their orbits decreases the farther they are from the sun. You see," she said, preparing to enumerate on her fingers, "gravity is inversely proportional to the square of a planet's distance..."

"Thank you, Patricia," Mrs. Carpenter said abruptly.

"You're welcome," Petey said politely and returned to her desk, scraping it against the floor as she sat. Mrs. Carpenter made a helpless gesture toward the board, seeming unable to hold her head steady. "While it is true that the planets' orbits are elliptical, the deviation is almost imperceptible, so for all practical purposes, they can be considered circular," she said gamely, but the class was either doodling, with heads propped on fists, or slouched in the desks, arms dangling, eyelids drooping.

She never challenged Petey again, but the next day our English teacher, Mr. Elliott, began discussing "To An Athlete Dying Young," his voice so monotonous and without inflection it would have lulled the most assiduous insomniac to sleep. He paused several times, glancing at Petey, until he stopped lecturing and, sounding annoyed, asked her to come forward and explain the author's intent. Mr. Elliott had a pale, pinched face, a square, black mustache that looked like a miniature boxwood, and reeked of Old Spice; he reminded me of a llama, with his long neck and the way he stared disdainfully along his bent nose, annunciating each word slowly, as if we were all simple-minded dullards. He always wore hiking boots, knock-offs for people who never venture into the woods; black polyester slacks; a white dress shirt with the cuffs rolled under, like some blockhead from *Happy Days*; and garish, but perfectly knotted, ties with academic themes, like the green silk with red punctuation marks floating at skewed angles. Petey shuffled her feet as she made her way to the front, and after reciting portions of the poem from memory, as if it were a nursery rhyme, declared its idealized concept of glorious death to be "palpable, pedantic nonsense."

Mr. Elliott grimaced and shoved the glasses up on his nose.

"If you're dead, you're dead," she said. "Death is amorphous." She turned and stroked a line on the chalkboard, which she made a show of erasing. "There!" She held her hands to each side, palms up. "Gone."

And then she compared the poem to one, which none of us had read or even heard of, called "Dulce et Decorum Est." Obviously the title wasn't English, but other than that, I hadn't a clue. Mr. Elliott appeared stunned. Petey recited lines describing war and its collateral, human toll in a most graphic, appalling manner to dispel Housman's theme as a "sophistic, archaic myth."

As she told me later, the title was Latin, taken from an ode by Horace, which translated meant: "It is sweet and right." The irony of her comparison, and of the poem's antithetic theme, contained in the final line: "Dulce et decorum est pro patria mori," which she translated dramatically: "The old lie: 'it is sweet and right to die for your country.'"

Mr. Elliott brusquely excused her.

Unabashed, she returned to her desk and resumed her nap. Someone blew his nose.

Obviously shaken, Mr. Elliott stammered and shuffled papers before changing the discussion to Chaucer.

I suppose the word spread between the teachers, because no one challenged her again. But there was no reason they should. She always completed her exams first and, more often than not, with a perfect score. She became a kind of pariah, but a respected if not feared one, even among the students. They made way when they met or passed her in the crowded hallways. She might have been a genius, but one without ambition; while most of our blissfully clueless classmates aspired to be rich or famous or both, hopefully without initiative, Petey showed interest in very little, except getting through the day and, with a withering zeal, humiliating those who tried unsuccessfully to belittle her.

Each day I walked to and from school along Jackson Boulevard, the shortest route. I began to notice Petey walking the same way, sometimes ahead, sometimes following, both in the afternoons and mornings. I could have ridden the bus, and had during rain or snow storms, but I preferred to walk alone. I hated the clamor; the cliques; and the gossipy exchanges, accompanied by mirthless laughter, I could never quite make out, imagining eyes fixed on me. Even in school my shyness was a burden. I diligently prepared for each day's assignments, but as I waited to be called on, the randomness added to my anxiety; my heart pounded; my stomach knotted.

When the teacher finally announced: "Wesley?" I would blush and stammer and stutter, eventually acquitting myself, but only in the teacher's eyes. The "very good" when I was finished did nothing to alleviate my shame or quiet the snickers that lingered, at least in my mind, well after the bell had sounded.

In the school cafeteria I always selected a table where I could eat alone. I began noticing Petey sitting by herself, her lunch spread atop a collapsed paper bag, her eyes inches from an opened book. She scanned the pages, flipping them quickly. She'd been in school about a week. I thought about joining her, but then I didn't. What if she ignored me? Or dismissed me with a sneer? Finally I summoned the courage to try. I walked from the checkout directly to where she sat.

"Mind if I join you?" I said. I felt my mouth twitch.

She gestured.

"Help yourself," she said with her mouth full, scanning and flipping pages.

"Are you reading?"

She looked up, marking her place with a finger. She had a sharp, wedged-shaped nose, and hard, ringed eyes, the irises almost as dark as the pupils, making her seem even more intimidating than by her intellect alone.

"Yeah. Why?" she said, the skin between her brows wrinkled.

"I never saw anyone read that fast."

"I know," she said, dog-eared a page, and closed the book. "It's like a disease."

"What is it?"

"John Updike. What do you read?"

"I like Peanuts," I said, trying to be funny.

"So do I," she said and smiled. "Charles Schultz was a genius."

I unfolded the spout on my milk carton and inserted a straw.

"Where did you go to school before?" I asked.

"Toledo," she said, biting into her sandwich. "We move around a lot. My mom's a barmaid at Feathers."

"Mine's a supervisor at Good Samaritan."

"Beats being a barmaid," she said, and we both laughed.

There were only two bars in town. All the fights and divorces broke out at Feathers. Its owner, Tony something, was Italian. I'd heard he was a prick, paying slave wages, deducting broken glasses from what little the rough-edged barmaids earned, and requiring them to drop tips in a jar by the register, which no one touched but him. He yelled at the help but greeted customers with a watermelon grin and a pat on the back. Rumors abounded that he had Mafia connections. Truck drivers, foundry workers, drunks, and those who had fallen from grace congregated there. Plant managers, salesmen, bankers, local politicians, the movers and shakers, and those aspiring to be, drank at Camelot. In addition to their sticky, red lips, its barmaids wore perilously, brief shorts, fishnet hose, tuxedo jackets, and black bow ties.

"She works six nights a week; she never knows which until the day before," Petey said. "You got brothers or sisters?"

"No."

"You're lucky. I've got a baby brother, a snot-nosed little pain-in-the-ass I have to baby sit when she works." And then she shrugged. "But I'm sure I was just as bad, maybe worse."

I offered her half an orange.

She shook her head.

"Gives me diarrhea," she said.

She offered me an Oreo.

"Thanks," I said. "What about your dad?"

"He was killed," she said, seemingly unaffected. "It was really a shame. He was a nice guy, better than my mom deserved. He just wasn't a go-getter, you know?" I nodded. "He sold insurance, worked for Mutual of this and that, nowhere for very long. He drove this beat up old Falcon. One morning he was stopped behind a crossing gate when this redneck in a loaded dump truck plowed into the back of the Falcon. By the time the train stopped, there wasn't much left of the car or my old man. My mom has his ashes at the house. Who knows where? She stays all to hell." She finished the Oreo and licked her fingers. "Now get this. The redneck worked for a construction company, blew over the limit, and had an open six-pack in the cab. My mom could have gotten an attorney for free and soaked their ass; instead, she took what the insurance company offered and bought this junker Oldsmobile, which she wrecked two weeks later, drunk on her ass. Lucky we weren't both killed. She had to wear an orange jumpsuit and pick up roadside trash on weekends for three months. She also lost her license for a year."

"My dad was killed in Iraq."

"That sucks. Bush is such a moron," she said loud enough that some kids at the closest table stopped talking, glanced at us, and leaned their heads together, whispering. Petey didn't seem to notice, and I doubt she would have cared if she had. "Did you know that after he graduated from Yale, the University of Texas law school wouldn't admit him?"

"I didn't," I said as I shoveled green peas onto a spoon.

"Bully for them. That's what I say. That's why he went to Harvard for an MBA." She shrugged and bit into another Oreo, smacking her lips. "Yale, Harvard, same fucking thing. Hell. If you have enough money you can get a cocker spaniel through an Ivy League school." She finished the cookie and leaned on her elbows. "So what happened to your dad?" she asked in a quieter voice.

"It was an accident. Friendly fire, they said."

"In other words, somebody fucked up."

"My mother believes it was God's will, him dying like he did, that it had a purpose."

Petey shook her head and folded her lunch bag.

"What do you believe?"

I thought about it, wondering, for the first time, if I should.

"You're probably right," I said, averting my eyes, feeling a bit disloyal, heretical, even, as the bell rang.

She followed me to a conveyor where rubber flaps sucked clattering trays and silverware from sight, and then we walked to English class. She wore baggy camouflage pants.

"See you after school?" I said hesitantly as I opened the door.

"Yeah."

"I'll meet you outside the parking lot door."

"Okay," she said. She found a desk on the back row and dropped her head on her hands.

We walked home together that afternoon and to school the next morning. As soon as we were off school property that first afternoon, she tugged a wrinkled pack of Newports from her front jeans' pocket and offered me one. I shook my head and glanced around. She lit up with impunity, smoke snaking over her shoulder. I lived on Madison. She lived on Harrison, a couple of blocks farther away. We agreed that the first one to my corner in the mornings or to the parking lot after school would wait. We'd sit on the curb in the afternoons and talk until we had to leave, not because we'd run out of things to say. I was amazed by her intelligence, and her vocabulary, when she chose to employ it, but never in a haughty or condescending manner. As we walked from one class to the other, I noticed a change in attitude toward me, as if Petey's presence made my own more noticeable, more important, even. I could never be sure if it was from respect or suspicion. Sometimes we'd meet at the corner on weekends, when she didn't have to baby-sit, and ride our bikes. We'd browse rummage sales, mostly looking, seldom buying.

"You want to do something Sunday?" she asked one Friday.

"Sure. What?"

"It'll be a surprise. I'll come by around one."

When we got home from church, I changed into a sweatshirt and jeans. My mother fixed lunch and, after wiping her hands in the folds of her apron, needlessly tidied a house that remained immaculate and organized. In a corner cabinet with glass doors, a picture of my father, young and smiling; on a lower shelf, the bulky, triangularly folded flag that had covered his casket. The Army had flown us to Dover when he came home. We stood with other families that night as an honor guard removed flag draped coffins from the belly of the aircraft, proceeding in step with a practiced, almost robotic precision that echoed decorum and respect. Some who waited, the women especially, wept silently, their cheeks dewy with tears that glistened in the faint light, but my mother remained stoic, standing erect, holding my hand. I can remember her crying only once. She had built a sheltered platform in her flower garden where robins nested each spring. The previous year, marauding starlings had ravaged the nest, shredding the featherless bodies. I found her on her knees, the remains cupped in her hands, the parents diving and scolding as if it had been her fault.

My father's coffin looked no different than others being removed, one of which might have contained the remains of a soldier who had thrown himself on a live grenade. The train of deceased soldiers, as well as the rows of identical stones scattered across a groomed field where he was buried, spoke of brotherhood and anonymity.

When she finished straightening, she kissed me on the forehead, telling me to be careful, and then lay down for a nap.

I sat on the front porch. Petey rode up a little after one.

"Ready?" she said.

"Yeah."

Before I rolled my bike onto the sidewalk, she was pedaling like a demon, reaching the end of the block before I got going. She turned away from town, taking several rights and lefts before cutting through some woods along a path with low, hanging limbs, our heads lowered to avoid being swatted. We emerged onto Holston River Drive, passing the country club, a sprawling collection of classic, stone buildings, the parking lot filled with Lincolns, Mercedes, Beemers and one Rolls. The links were overrun with golfers in knickers, plaid socks, and floppy, wool caps, their open buggies parked alongside. Most seemed to be leaning on their clubs, one foot crossed over the other, talking. Past the golf course we turned onto Boyd's Pike and crossed Lawson's Bridge, a narrow span with picturesque arches framing rusting metal ribs, which was no longer safe for traffic to cross, so we had to lift our bikes over the barriers. And then I followed Petey into the Holston Health and Rehabilitation Center parking lot. Beside the facility an open pasture of thick and silky grasses, banded by barbed wire sagging on broken posts, led down to the river. A female cardinal, her color robbed by gender, sat on a top strand, bobbing her tail for balance.

Petey dropped her bike into a hedge beside the front door.

"This is a nursing home," I said.

"I know. We're going to visit."

"Who?" I said, but she was already through the door.

The lobby was a spacious atrium with plush, leather chairs and fully leafed plants reaching the ceiling. Sunlight lay in thick, yellow bands across the floor from the glassed ceiling. A cage, as large as my bedroom, housed dozens of zebra finches trilling noisily. While some mature birds flitted from perch to perch, others squatted inside wicker nests incubating eggs. A number of fledglings awkwardly tested their wings.

"Who are we visiting?" I asked again as I followed her through double swinging doors, our footsteps echoing down the wide, entrance hallway, the floor polished to a reflective shine, the walls lined with pictures of sour-faced nuns.

"Her name is Grace," she said. "She's called a resident, not a patient." She shrugged. "A rose by any other name." A passing nurse smiled and nodded at Petey. "Some in here are clear-headed; they just can't do for themselves anymore, you know, like cripples? They always look pissed. And who can blame them? Now the ones who are always smiling? That's a dead giveaway they're out of touch."

Once we passed locked offices, the halls became narrow and bleak, seeming almost subterranean, the air suffused with the odors of urine and bleach and the ubiquitous sound of a piano and muted French horn playing movie themes I recognized but couldn't name. Occasionally a voice interrupted the music, paging a doctor with a foreign name to a nursing station. We passed haunted and ancient figures in baggy bedclothes huddled in wheelchairs, some rocking, others chattering nonsensically. Accompanying the music, the forlorn moaning of minds gone or going bad, and the thump, thump of walkers. We came to a wooden quadrangle at the intersection of four hallways. A Black woman, only her eyes, forehead, and white cap visible, sat inside. She spoke to Petey, who grabbed a couple of Hershey's Kisses from a bowl on top of the railing as she passed. She popped one in her mouth and tossed the other over her shoulder that I caught on the fly. We walked along one of the corridors, a lighted exit sign at the end, passing rooms, some with people dressed for church gathered around a bed, others, with the blinds closed, looking like shadowy caves. Petey stopped at a room with an old woman watching the Weather Channel from a scissored hospital bed.

"That's Grace," Petey said, "but she won't remember, so there's no reason to try and remind her."

Petey strode in smiling. The woman, who was emaciated, looked at us with milky eyes and smiled. Her arms, bearing needle bruises, were nothing more than translucent skin laced with purple veins sagging on withered bones that seemed as brittle as leaf stems. Her hair was thin and stringy like corn silk. Petey took her hand between her own and began talking about people neither of them knew. Occasionally the woman would speak, making sounds that weren't even words but had a cadence, like a sentence. Tremors prevented her from steadying her gaze. Sometimes she would frown, and seem frightened for no apparent reason, until she glanced at the television. She would stare at a colorful United States map, spotted with fake clouds spitting fake rain, and calm noticeably.

"Who is she?" I said as we left.

"Grace."

"Is she family?"

"Somebody's, but they never visit."

"How do you know?"

"I asked."

"Then why…?"

"You ask a lot of questions," she interrupted with uncharacteristic, at least with me, bluntness.

I shrugged.

"Sorry."

Then she smiled.

"No need. I get pissy sometimes."

She straddled her bike and raised her fist. I popped it, and we pedaled across the parking lot and stopped on the bridge, leaning over the railing and watching beer cans and trash floating in the brackish water swirl around pylons. A large willow hovered over the water, its twisted bangs swaying as if caressed by a breeze I couldn't feel. The sun was low; it was warm, and everything smelled of honeysuckle.

I had known Petey almost three months when she called one Saturday and asked me to come by the next day, which was unusual, since my house was on the way to the nursing home. I was glad she called, because I was concerned. The day before, she had been called out of class around one and never returned. I waited for her after school, but finally walked home alone.

I rode over after church. Her house, an old clapboard two-story, sat behind a waist high stone wall; without a latch, the wrought iron gate swung freely. On three sides, fluted pillars supported covered porches, the surrounding banister braced with adroitly crafted, filigreed corners. Beginning at the second story, where I assumed there was an additional fireplace, the brick, exterior chimney stepped gradually to half its width. Many of the wine-colored roof tiles were either broken or missing. At each peak, lighting rods, the pointed electrodes piercing blue, ceramic balls. They looked like miniature mosques. The house had been built with patience and a love of craft, but much of the paint had eroded; the yard was overrun with weeds and rotting leaves, and an upstairs shutter dangled precariously. Spooky and sinister looking, even during daylight, I knew kids would avoid it on Halloween.

Petey answered my knock. I followed her into the living room, the only illumination moted sunlight, filtered through dingy windows and mini-blinds with missing slats. With the exception of a large fireplace, a purple couch with threadbare arms, an end table with a shaded lamp, and a cabinet model television, the room was empty. An intricately flowered frieze banded the walls where they met the ceiling; cobwebs spanned the corners. The house smelled of stale tobacco.

"You want to go on an adventure?" Petey said.

"Sure," I said, as a woman appeared in the doorway to the kitchen, her face a mask of thick, blue eye shadow and mascara. She wore a pink slip, a white bulky robe, and bunny slippers that slapped her heels when she moved. She held a coffee cup in one hand, a lit cigarette in the other. Tall, plump, her brassy blond hair peek-a-boo styled, or perhaps it wasn't, she looked nothing like Petey. A toddler hid behind her, clinging to her robe, sucking his thumb, and peeking at me.

"This is my mom. Mom, Wesley."

"Hi," she said in a smoker's voice and coughed without covering her mouth.

"And the midget is Joey," Petey said and laughed.

"How are you?" I said, my hands clasped behind my back. She didn't respond. Joey disappeared behind her. I thought about speaking louder, in case she was hard of hearing, but then I figured I'd feel like a fool if she weren't.

"We're going bike riding," Petey said, but they'd already disappeared, her coughing from deeper in the house. "She's a little warped," Petey said in a confidential manner as she threaded on her jacket.

"Where are we going?" I said as she rolled her bike outside.

"To climb that." She pointed at the water tower, Newton lettered across the front and back, standing high on its metal legs atop Sharp's Ridge. A road, which became a lover's lane on Saturday nights, ran along the crest to a dead end at large, electrical transformers behind a chain link fence topped with triple strands of barbed wire. "Danger" signs prominently displayed were meant to discourage intruders.

"You're kidding," I said, but she was already speeding away down the broken sidewalk. We passed faded hopscotch grids, shuttered shops, the Lyric Theater that had closed before I was born (*Bonnie and Clyde* still posted on the marquee), and churches emptied until Sunday night, all except for the Primitive Baptist whose services would continue until mid-afternoon. At the edge of town, the rail yard where the trains used to pass, a dozen coupled boxcars, abandoned and rusting along a spur, the sides covered, like a canvas, with artful graffiti. Several dogs chased each other across the tracks and into a thick tangle of undergrowth.

Climbing the ridge was arduous, so Petey, who still led, slowed, but my legs began to ache as I pedaled to keep up. Trees with translucent, thick veined leaves crowded the shoulders, the ground laden with a chartreuse shade. Clouds of pollen glistened in narrow slants of sunlight. As the road leveled, clusters of pine thickets suffused the air with their sharp, minty fragrance. A shuffle of birdcalls, along with the ratcheting sound of insects, formed an unscripted, ubiquitous chorus. When she reached the base of the tower, Petey leaped from her bike, letting it careen and jackknife, and collapsed, spread-eagled on the ground. I lay beside her, both of us gasping. The sky was clear and a deep, cobalt blue, the sun inclined toward afternoon.

"Thirsty?" she said.

"Yeah," I said, in an exhausted whisper.

She crawled over to her bike and unwound the canteen she'd lashed to her handlebars. We both took a swig.

"Ready?" she said, capping the canteen and tossing it aside.

I cupped my hands around my eyes like a visor and squinted toward the top.

"I'm not sure."

"Come on. I've done it before." She pounded her chest like King Kong.

"Why?"

"It's a good place to think. Gives you perspective." She scurried up the metal ladder attached to one of the legs. She climbed effortlessly, like a squirrel scrambling up a tree.

"Don't look down," she yelled. "Keep your eyes on the tank."

I didn't tell her how uneasy I was about heights; acrophobia, I think. She would have known. I gripped each rung so tightly my knuckles turned pale.

It took about ten minutes for us to reach a metal grate catwalk with a plumbing pipe railing circling the bottom of the tank. The grate was made of thick, diamond shaped webs, everything below clearly visible between my feet. At first I felt dizzy, and then as if I were floating and, for a few minutes, gripped the railing with both hands. I think Petey pretended not to notice how frightened I was. She sat on the edge with her feet dangling, her wrists resting on the railing overhead. Eventually I sat beside her.

"Nothing to be afraid of," she said and smiled. "It's like being on top of the world."

"Yeah." I had begun to accommodate my fear and absorb the wonder of the view. The landscape had lost definition. Familiar features seemed oddly displaced, like jagged pieces of a puzzle. In the distance, farmlands, which had once been plowed in straight rows, bore verdant circles carved into the earth. Vultures glided on thermal pillows below us. I could hear nothing but the sound of the wind vibrating the cables and beams, and even the bulk of the tank, each at a different pitch, or frequency, a harmony of sounds rising and diminishing, continuously, like an improvised, ethereal symphony.

"Makes you see how small Newton really is." She pointed toward the horizon at tiny spires trailing strings of smoke, and bleak buildings barely visible through a dome of yellow, coagulated smog. "That's Knoxville."

I took my hands off the rail and held my arms straight out to the sides. "I wish I could fly."

"I know," she said. "Wad your fist." She held it in front of her face. "Close one eye and you can block Newton out completely."

And she was right. I no longer felt the chill or sensed the methodical clockwork of time.

"You remember Friday afternoon, when I was gone?" she said after a few minutes.

"Yeah."

"They gave me some tests. They want to skip me on to high school. I guess they're sick of my bullshit."

Although she sat next to me, for a moment I felt her drifting away. She was as close a friend as I'd ever had; I sensed a trusted clarity existing between us, but if I mentioned it, I was afraid the implied intimacy and its obligation might drive her away.

"That's great," I said as enthusiastically as I could. She locked her ankles and swung her feet, her wrists draped over the railing, her eyes fixed on the horizon. She didn't say anything. "So what are you going to do?"

"I don't know. I don't want to do anything, really. I get so sick of people wanting me to 'make something of myself,'" she said, framing the sarcasm with imaginary quotation marks using her fingers. "I guess I'd like to stay up here forever, if I can't escape." She doubled her fist again and closed one eye.

"But you're smart, probably one of the smartest people I've ever known. You could get through high school and get a scholarship, and then you could go anywhere, do what you want."

"What do you want to do?"

"I don't know, but that has nothing to do with you."

"Maybe it does," she said.

I thought for a moment.

"I know."

We said nothing for a long moment.

"So I get a scholarship and ace whatever college I choose, and then what?"

"What do you want to do?"

"Whatever it takes to be free. I hate this place as much as I hated Toledo. Seeing the same things, the same stupid people day after day." She swept her hand along the horizon. "There's more to life than this. Living like a fucking tree. Have you ever seen the ocean, Wes, the deserts, the Northern Lights?"

"No."

"And you never will. You'll grow up, do what's expected until one day you'll die a bitter old man, knowing there could have been more."

Straight out from us, hundreds of silhouetted birds swam in waves, changing directions smoothly and in unison, as if anticipating the others' intentions.

"Look!" I said and pointed. "It's like they're dancing."

"They cluster for protection," she said. "Flocks confuse predators like hawks. They can only concentrate on a single bird, so they have to wait for one to stray."

The tower began throwing its long, purple shadow across the town and its worn hills. Bruised thunderheads hovered in the eastern sky, sheet lightning flickering below the horizon. Behind us the sun had swollen and turned crimson.

Petey stood and dusted her seat.

"We better go. It will be dark soon."

"I wish we could stay," I said, still sitting, scanning the tiny world we would return to.

"Think about it, Wes. We could leave. We wouldn't be missed. Have you ever been to Florida?"

"No," I said as I stood, holding onto the rail, my legs cramping for a moment.

"It's always warm. They have oranges. The beaches are white as snow. My dad's brother runs a charter boat out of West Palm Beach. He and my mom don't get along. At the funeral he took me aside and said if I ever needed anything to let him know. We could be there in two days. He'd give us a job."

"But how?" I said.

"I'll take care of it. Don't worry. Nothing to be afraid of. Do you trust me?"

"Of course."

"Do you want to stay?"

"I want to go with you," I said, the fear of being left behind clouding all reason.

"Then it's done," she said. "Pack some things. We won't need much. Just show up at the corner tomorrow morning and leave everything to me."

We laced the fingers of our right hands between our faces. Her enthusiasm had become infectious. I could already feel the Florida sun warming my bare back.

But I couldn't sleep that night. I don't know what it was exactly, a confusion of fear and regret. I would be missed. Mother would be alone. I was all she had. But then again, we had seemed to share less and less the older I got; if I left, it would be just a few years before the inevitable. And if I didn't go, I would be letting Petey down, and myself. Imagining what it would be like not having her in my life forced me to realize just how important she had become, but I also knew she was possessed by a kind of divine irrationality. She was a spirit, tolerating the absurdity of our lives; I was mortal, addicted to convention, and would always be.

I woke the next morning groggy-eyed. The promises made on the tower the afternoon before seemed to have occurred in a dream. I felt nauseous. I asked mother to call in sick for me, but she felt my forehead and insisted I get ready. I could not look at myself in the bathroom mirror. I left early, taking the long way so that I wouldn't have to face Petey at the corner. I passed slumbering houses beginning to wake. My heart felt like a cup from which the bottom had been removed. The water tower, pink with the emerging sun that had yet to bathe the town, while picturesque, compounded my guilt. I had broken my word; I had no excuse. I sat in homeroom, dreading the moment she would enter, but she attended none of the classes. She wasn't in school Tuesday, either. I moved numbly from class to class. On Tuesday afternoon I went by her house, but no one answered the door. I pedaled down to Feathers, but they wouldn't let me in. Laughter and down-home music spilled out each time the door swung open. I asked several men entering if they would ask Petey's mom to come out. Most ignored me; one told me to go home, but then an older man with a cherry red nose and bloodshot eyes, walking as if he was unsure of his steps, tweaked my cheek and agreed.

She squinted as she emerged, her hair in disarray, holding the door open with a knee. Her pale cheeks sagged, as if something inside had slipped away. In the full light she looked older than I remembered, deep crevices etched into the corners of her mouth and eyes. She kneaded her hands on a towel.

"She ran away," she said, emotionlessly, as if giving me the time. She had lipstick on her teeth. Then a severe coughing episode ensued, something rattling as if she had a marble trapped in her throat. When it subsided, she cleared her throat noisily and spit something thick to the side. She let the door swing closed behind her.

That night as I lay in bed, unable to sleep, I felt desperately alone. I remembered something Petey had said: we were living our lives being told what to do, moving to the scream of bells, and waiting, but for what?

On Thursday I heard that the police had picked Petey up hitchhiking in Georgia. I heard nothing else about her Friday. I had waited at the corner, but eventually walked to school alone. I stayed inside Saturday and Sunday, except for church, hoping she would call or come by, but she didn't. I walked to school alone on Monday. She was in none of our usual classes. But that afternoon, I saw her leaving the high school building, which was separated from the middle school by a chain link fence and a narrow, grass easement. She cradled several books in her arms. She passed a group of tanned cheerleaders in halter-tops and short, pleated skirts practicing cheers, some spinning cartwheels agilely. Islands of students drifted across the parking lot, but she walked alone. My heart was veiled in guilt and sorrow, but I never talked to Petey again. I took the longer route to and from home. Most afternoons I would see her leaving the high school, always by herself. One Sunday I rode down Holston River Drive and stopped at Boyd's Pike. Across the river and nursing home parking lot, Petey's bike lay against the hedge beside the entrance. I returned home and watched television for a while, but then I turned it off. I had nothing to do. I stretched on the couch with a cushion behind my head. I had never noticed a squeak the ceiling fan made as it rotated with a slight wobble. It sounded like an insect chirping from some great distance. My mother read her Bible in the kitchen. I had begun to think of her as unfulfilled and damaged, although her faith would never permit her to admit it.

When classes ended for summer, I attended a church camp in North Carolina for three weeks of swimming, outdoor sports, and hiking. When I returned, I heard that the old house Petey and her mother had rented was sold, and they'd moved. Hoping it wasn't true, I rode over, but painters in white coveralls, and carpenters, their nailers popping like rifle fire, swarmed the house like bees. Men in yellow hardhats pored over blueprints spread across the hood of a pickup. What had been gritty and neglected had begun to assume its original elegance. I went by Feathers. Petey's mom had quit, so I knew they'd left town.

As days folded into weeks and then into seasons, memories of Petey occupied my thoughts less and less often; still, when I see a flock of silhouetted birds swimming in flawless harmony, I remember us standing on the catwalk circling the water tank that Sunday, plotting our escape, the thought of the unknown seeming, at least for an afternoon, clean and limitless. I always shade my eyes, mesmerized by their grace, and search the sky for something I might never see.

Jacob M. Appel

The Rod of Asclepius

A FIRST PULSE OF MEMORY: My father, broad-shouldered and dashing, sliding his arms into a long white coat that smells of bleach. It is springtime in St.-Arnac, a balmy Sunday afternoon snowing crabapple petals. We've parked in the physicians-only lot atop the roof of the hospital's garage, the same hospital where, the previous Thanksgiving, my pregnant mother died of a ruptured uterus. What my six-year-old self doesn't realize then, though it is clear to me now, is that this may be the first time my father has left our apartment in several months, that I am witnessing the man emerge from a winter-long twilight of raw anger. He drapes his stethoscope around his neck, retrieves his leather bag from the trunk of our Oldsmobile. "Are you ready to change the world, princess?" he asks. At that moment, I am suddenly persuaded that the world does indeed require changing, that the entire cosmos yearns for radical transformation. Vigorous nods earn me a kiss on the forehead.

My father leads me by hand across the broad granite plaza, colonized with lunching nurses and orderlies on smoke-break, where statues of North Carolina's war heroes guard the revolving doors. At the security desk, a red-faced officer with a bulbous nose and greasy comb-over greets my father with a genial, "Hi, doc," and then salutes me with a more formal, "Good afternoon, ma'am." I am still too young to distinguish personal from business relationships, friends from sociable strangers—it will be another several years before I realize, in an innocence-shattering blast, that our postman is *paid* to deliver the mail—so I swell with pride as the officer waves us past the visitors waiting to register, believing a personal honor is being bestowed upon my father, not realizing the privilege is afforded *all* white-coated medical gentry.

We ride the elevator to the top. The doors open directly onto the lobby of the VIP atrium, where angelfish and gouramis cross paths in a colossal aquarium, while a sad-eyed pianist plays cocktail-lounge standards on a baby-grand. Panoramic windows reveal the rolling, sun-drenched hills of the Piedmont and the wood-shingled rooftops of St.-Arnac's commercial district—an assortment of family-owned specialty shops, like my Aunt Hannah's millinery, which have since been swallowed by suburban Greensboro. Papa's grip is tight on my hand. He crosses the lounge and strides briskly down the adjacent corridor, practically sweeping me along the tiles behind him. We pass the nursing station where, beneath the cardiac monitors, a solitary aide reads a magazine. A whiff of disinfectant hangs in the stagnant air.

And then—without warning—Papa veers through an open door. Suddenly, we stand inside a patient's private room, the temporary home of an ancient, one-legged man dwarfed by his own wheelchair. The man's truncated knee is wrapped in gauze, suggesting a recent amputation. At his side, perched at the foot of the tidy bed, sits an equally wizened woman. To my surprise, my father apologizes for disturbing the couple and we retreat back into the corridor.

A moment later, we've entered another room. Here, a skeletal woman watches television from a stack of pillows. She cannot be much older than my father, but her eyes are sunken and her pale skin drapes off the bones of her face. On the end table, two photographs depict the same woman in the full bloom of health. In one picture, a handsome man clasps his arm around her waist; in the other, she cradles an infant. A basket of fruit and gourmet items—still wrapped—sits on the radiator. When the woman sees my father, she uses the remote control to lower the TV's volume.

"Have you seen Dr. Hagerman?" she asks.

Papa touches the woman's shoulder to offer reassurance. "I'm covering for Dr. Hagerman today," he informs her—in the same confident voice he uses to comfort me when I have a nightmare.

"He swore he'd be here before noon," says the woman.

"I'm sorry. Dr. Hagerman had an emergency. Something personal."

The emaciated woman seems partially assuaged. Papa opens his leather bag and methodically fills a syringe. "We need to give you some blood thinner," he explains. "Dr. Hagerman was concerned about your most recent laboratory values, especially the risk for spontaneous clotting…." As he speaks, my father rolls up the sleeve of the woman's gown; she winces and the injection is over. "That should do the trick," he says. "Dr. Hagerman will be here to see you in the morning…."

My father discards the syringe and removes his gloves. Even as he shuts the clasps on his bag, the woman drifts into slumber, a tranquil smile settled upon her lips. We are already halfway down the corridor when an alarm bell sounds from the woman's room; as we approach the nursing station at a rapid clip, a junior physician in aqua scrubs charges past us headed in the opposite direction.

We traverse the VIP atrium again, descend the elevator to the lobby. My father and the red-faced officer exchange another greeting. I feel anxious, but I cannot say why. Out on the granite plaza, a swarm of starlings blankets the austere statues of Confederate generals and colonels.

My father lifts me into his powerful arms.

"The reason we went to the top floor," he explains, "is because that's where the doctors' wives and mothers go when they get sick." Papa's eyes are level with mine, his nose so close I could touch it. "Don't be afraid to ask your father questions, Lauren," he adds. "I want this to be a learning experience"

Or maybe that is *not* a first pulse of memory. Quite possibly, that visit to the hospital occurs *after* Aunt Henrietta comes to live with us. I can vividly remember her boyfriend—one of my aunt's *many* boyfriends—transporting her suitcases from the trunk of his car into the guest bedroom. She'll be twenty-eight that summer, five years younger than my father, and stunningly gorgeous. I don't recall if Papa is also present that afternoon, but I do remember the two of them arguing bitterly, a few days later, while Aunt Henrietta drains bottles of whiskey into the hollyhocks. Only years in the future did I discover that my aunt's arrival hasn't been Papa's choice: It is part of the custody arrangement he has agreed to with Guilford County's Bureau of Child Welfare after I go truant from kindergarten.

If my aunt resents her premature summons to child-rearing, I never recall her showing it. Since I have no memories of my biological mother, a direct comparison remains impossible—but I cannot imagine anyone being more devoted to my welfare than is Aunt Henrietta. After school lets out for the summer, I accompany her to the millinery each morning, where she assigns me various "useful" tasks around the bustling shop. Some days, I sort ribbons or buckles. On other occasions, I unwrap exotic hats that arrive from the warehouse packed in newsprint. Once, I have an opportunity to pose in various bonnets for a professional photographer from the St. Arnac *Beacon* who is compiling a full-page spread on juvenile fashions. Yet I spend most of my time with the young African-American fitters who "mind the store" while my aunt enjoys half-day lunch breaks with her various suitors. One of these shop-girls, an olive-skinned teenager named Lila, takes a particular fancy to me, because, as she phrases it: "We're both orphans, so we have to look out for each other."

"I'm *not* an orphan," I insist. "My father is still alive."

Lila hugs me to her ample bosom. "Silly girl," she says. "Fathers don't count."

What I do know with certainty is that our visit to the hospital precedes my conversation with Aunt Henrietta about what I hope to become when I grow up. That talk occurs while we're on an excursion to pick our own peaches. My aunt is dating a dental student whose family owns vast orchards south of Asheboro, so I'm ensconced between the two of them on the front seat of the young man's Cadillac. The open windows bring a gentle breeze and with it the scent of drying alfalfa. My aunt's boyfriend, whose marriage proposal she will soon reject, has urged her to invite me along on this outing; he is doing his utmost to keep me entertained—to prove, I suppose, that he'd make a satisfactory partner with whom to raise children of his own.

He addresses me in a high-pitched, sing-song voice, as though I am an infant and not a rising first grader. "So, young lady, do you have any career plans yet?"

"I don't know," I answer.

Aunt Henrietta asks, "Do you know what a 'career' is?"

"Nope."

Her boyfriend tries again. "What do you want to be when you grow up?"

"I don't know."

I've folded my arms across my chest.

"Would you like to be a princess?" he asks. "Or how about a mermaid?"

Both sound like perfectly reasonable occupations to my six-year-old mind, but the young man's tone makes me feel contrary. "I want to be a doctor," I announce.

"Nothing wrong with that," says the dental student. He is grinning. "We could use more lady doctors."

Aunt Henrietta also appears amused. "That's the first I've heard of this," she says. "I'm curious, Lauren. *Why* do you want to be a doctor?"

I don't have a good answer. Even when I apply to medical school two decades later, my various justifications—to help people, to expand human knowledge, even to save lives—somehow never seem adequate. I suppose the real reason I become a physician is because I can't imagine doing anything else, but it takes another thirty years of reflection to reach that degree of insight. The explanation I serve my aunt is far more concrete: "Because Papa is a doctor."

The dental student flashes my aunt a puzzled look. I sense that I've said something wrong, but I'm honestly not sure what.

"Your papa isn't a doctor," says Aunt Henrietta—her voice kind but firm. "What on earth would ever give you that idea?"

I understand that I must not mention our visit to the hospital, that my father will want that to remain our secret. "I don't know," I say.

"Her father *was* an architect," my aunt informs her date. "*Before*."

The young man nods sympathetically. "Does she know about…?"

He lets his sentence trail away, as though the word *mother* were toxic.

"She *knows*," says Aunt Henrietta. "But I don't think she really *understands*."

I can't be certain whether my father visits the hospital again on his own, but the next time we visit together, it is already late summer and the corn along the county highway towers over his Oldsmobile. Instead of the community hospital in St. Arnac, we drive forty-five minutes to the freshly-minted women's clinic in Greensboro. My aunt is away for the weekend with her new boyfriend, a veterinarian, who will soon become my Uncle Conrad, and will later become my former Uncle Conrad, and will eventually move to Florida and open a theme park featuring exotic animals. Papa has finally mustered the wherewithal to warn me against discussing our hospital field trips with his sister, but when I tell him that I already know they are our secret, he grins. "Your mother would be so proud of you, princess," he says. Later, as we pull into a metered space opposite the clinic, he adds, "Never forget *why* we're here, Lauren. This is for your mother. So that those doctors who butchered her learn what it feels like."

And his voice is compelling, although even at the age of six, I'm already aware that his thinking itself is muddled, that my mother had never stepped foot inside the women's clinic in Greensboro.

The security guard on duty, a dour young woman, takes her job far more seriously than the jolly old-timers in St. Arnac. She asks my father for his ID card and, when he apologizes that he has left it in his car, she suggests with a firm civility that he retrieve it. "If you insist," he replies genially. But we do not return to the Oldsmobile: Rather, we circle the building until we arrive at the ambulance bay. "Pretend you're sleeping, princess," instructs Papa, scooping me up and carrying me into the emergency room as though I were an accident victim. A genuine trauma patient has arrived ahead of us, so the ER is a maelstrom of clattering equipment and frantic resuscitation efforts. An elderly woman pleads with God for her son's recovery, at top volume, while medics shear the clothing off a blood-drenched body. Nobody takes much notice of Papa when he strolls confidently through a graveyard of gurneys into the belly of the hospital. Soon enough, we've found ourselves another private room on an upper floor of the building.

This room appears far fancier that the one we visited in St. Arnac; oak-paneled walls and rosewood furniture lend it the ambience of a private library. Years later, when I reconstruct these events from newspaper articles, I learn that the room belongs not to a physician's relative, but to a physician herself: Dr. Jane Barnwell, the forty-two year-old head of pediatric nephrology, who has suffered minor complications following the birth of her first child and is being held overnight for observation. Fortunately for us, Dr. Barnwell sleeps soundly. Papa takes great care not to wake her. He loads his syringe in her private bathroom, instructs me to wait for him, then returns several seconds later and tucks the spent needle and rubber gloves into his leather bag.

"All done, princess," he says. "Good job."

He snaps shut the satchel and gives the room a final once-over. Dr. Barnwell doesn't look any different than she did ten minutes earlier, except her chest no longer heaves.

"What do you say we stop for ice cream on the way home?" asks Papa.

"Strawberry?"

"Whatever your heart desires," agrees my father.

We exit the hospital as we have entered, through the emergency room, again drawing virtually no attention. On the avenue, however, a squad car with flashing lights has drawn up behind the Oldsmobile. One of the officers remains seated in the vehicle, while the other stands on the sidewalk, comforting a distraught young woman in a burgundy smock. The woman has fiery red hair—

like my own mother's—and wide, child-bearing hips; if she wore less makeup, she'd be prettier.

I am still at an age when I find the presence of police officers to be reassuring, rather than threatening, yet that afternoon I suspect their arrival bodes trouble. My father, however, does not appear at all unnerved by their presence.

"Is something wrong, officer?" he asks.

The officer looks up. "Your car?"

"I'm afraid so," says Papa. "Did I park in the wrong place?"

"Yes, you did," says the cop. He's a gaunt bulrush of a man who looks as though a strong wind might topple him. "You parked right behind this woman's vehicle...."

I now notice—for the first time—that glass shards blanket the asphalt, remnants of the Oldsmobile's left headlight. A deep cleft forks the vehicle's front bumper, which buckles over the grill. The redheaded woman has apparently backed her car into ours.

"I'm *so* sorry, doctor," the woman apologizes to Papa, who still sports his white coat. "I honestly don't know what happened. I thought I was in drive, and I must have been in reverse, and I can't believe I could ever be so stupid...." She sounds as though she is seconds away from tears.

"Not a big deal," says Papa. He turns to the slender cop. "Officer, is there any way we can just forget this ever happened?"

These days, I practice medicine in Manhattan, and asking a question like that in this city can get a person arrested, but three decades ago, in Greensboro, the rules are more flexible. The slender officer steps over to the patrol car to confer with his partner. The second cop, an older man with a shock of white hair, climbs out of the vehicle.

"What are you going to do about the insurance?" he asks.

"Absolutely nothing," replies Papa. "It's not worth it. I'll just patch her up in my garage and she'll be as good as new. If I can operate on a human brain, I can operate on a busted bumper. Anyway, there's no reason this lady's insurance rates should skyrocket over a minor accident."

The veteran cop shrugs. "Suit yourself, doc," he says.

The older cop nods to the younger cop, and the pair depart into the urban web of Greensboro, leaving us alone with the grateful redhead. "I don't know how to thank you," she says. "I've never even been in an accident before. I'd offer to buy you lunch in the cafeteria sometime, but this is the last day of my rotation. I'm a nursing student—did I mention that?—and I go back to the hospital in Winston-Salem next week." She looks at Papa, who hasn't said a word, and blushes. “Oh, goodness. I’m talking too much, aren’t I?”

“Not at all. Why don’t *we* buy *you* lunch? Right now.”

The nursing student, whose name I later learn is Suzanne, glances at me with apprehension. “Won’t this girl’s mother worry if you’re not home on time?

“This girl’s mother,” replies Papa, matter-of-fact, “is dead.”

Suzanne’s expression flutters from shock to sympathy, but possibly sympathy tempered by relief. “I’m sorry,” she says.

“Not half as sorry as I am,” says Papa. “But now that we’ve broken the ice, how do you two beautiful ladies feel about barbecued chicken?”

Papa’s mood improves considerably after he starts dating Suzanne Shale. We drive out to Winston-Salem every Friday and spend the weekend at her cozy, cluttered apartment two blocks from Wake Forest’s medical center. At the time, I take for granted that Papa brings me along with him on these romantic getaways; in hindsight, I’ve come to recognize that Suzanne’s physical similarity to my late mother is not a coincidence—that my father, in some perverse way, hopes to reconstruct the family he has lost. For her part, Suzanne is twenty-four years old and thrilled to be dating a neurosurgeon—even one endowed with so much integrity that he refuses to help her with her pharmacology homework. That doesn’t stop her from begging for assistance, especially as she is barely passing her exams.

One evening, at a crowded steakhouse near the undergraduate campus, Papa nearly makes a fatal mistake while resisting her pleas. It is my seventh birthday dinner—my *second* seventh birthday dinner, because my father never brings Suzanne to St. Arnac—and he is working his way down the cocktail menu.

“What use will me helping you be when you’re alone with a sick patient?” Papa asks her. “Are you going to phone me from the hospital so I can convert cc’s into milliliters for you?”

Suzanne appears confused. “Cc’s are milliliters,” she says.

Papa smiles. “Just checking,” he replies. “So they *are* teaching you something in that nursing program after all.”

I am impressed—even at age seven—by my father’s talent for deception, his ability to meet every challenge and contingency. However, I am still too young to be thinking about long-term consequences. In hindsight, I find myself wondering whether he has given any mind to his end-game, to what will happen when Suzanne insists upon meeting his family or planning a wedding. Does he really think he can keep his ruse going forever? Does he care? Twenty-five years later, hoping to glean some insight, I write to Suzanne Shale—she is Suzanne Stanley now and teaches biology in Creve Coeur, Rhode Island—but my father's ex-girlfriend responds with a curt note asking me to leave her alone. I can't say I blame her.

Yet that autumn, for a brief interval, the three of us do feel like a family. We purchase a trio of pumpkins for Halloween, and while Papa and I carve jack-o-lanterns, Suzanne bakes pies from the pulp. We go hiking in the foothills north of the city to view the foliage at its most colorful. In early November, we enjoy a weekend road-trip to Virginia, where Suzanne introduces us to her mother. Thanks to Papa's seven-digit malpractice settlement with the insurance company, he has no need to return to his architecture firm. In his leisure, he drives me to school every morning.

Our hospital visits drift into memory, vestiges of a darkness that has lifted. So I am caught entirely off guard one weekend, around Thanksgiving, when Papa rouses me from my slumber in Suzanne's apartment for a "medical emergency."

"They need a consult on a bullet wound. A very tricky case," my father tells Suzanne. "We'll be back as soon as we can."

At first, I assume we are returning to St. Arnac. Instead, we drive five blocks to Baptist Hospital and park in the staff-only lot. My father adjusts his necktie with the help of the rearview mirror and then slides his arms into his white coat. He pins a Wake Forest ID card to his lapel—a forgery, I imagine, but it looks real enough.

"Can I ask a question?" I ask.

"What, princess?"

My stomach flutters. "How long are we going to keep visiting hospitals for?"

"Until we're done," he says.

All these years later, I'm still not sure what he means.

By now, of course, I know what to expect. So I am not at all surprised when we climb the stairs to the VIP floor and work our medical magic, as Papa calls it, upon a middle-aged woman with a nasty rash across her forearms and neck. Yet rather than making a quick getaway, my father ducks into a second room and injects an elderly man who is listening to a baseball game on his transistor radio. We "treat" two more patients before a "Code-1000" is called over the PA system. Thirty minutes later, we're eating French fries at a café and rehearsing our alibi for Suzanne.

"We've changed the world quite a lot for one day, Lauren," says Papa. "I couldn't have done it without you."

I fill my mouth with French fries and ketchup.

Papa asks, "Let's review, princess. Why are we doing this?"

"For Mama."

That is precisely what Papa wants to hear—what I have been coached to say— and he beams with approval. To strangers, he appears just another doting father accompanying his daughter out for a snack.

"Tell me one more thing, princess," he says. "What have you learned today?"

In the absence of guidance, I answer honestly. "I want to be a doctor."

My words are hardly out of my mouth when the sting of my father's palm sets my cheek aflame. I am too shocked to cry. The cashier at the café register flashes Papa a look of intense hostility; an elderly lady at a nearby table glances away. Nobody intervenes, of course: This is long before child abuse becomes a public concern. That does not make my face hurt any less.

"Doctors are the enemy. *Never* forget that," says Papa. "Is that clear?"

"Okay," I say. "I'm sorry."

"I didn't mean to hurt you, princess," he says—his tone gentle once more. "But I'm counting on you. *Mama* is counting on you. You won't disappoint us, will you?"

I promise that I won't let him down and he never raises a hand against me again. Of course, I never give him reason to do so. By the time we return to Suzanne's apartment that evening, my upper lip has swollen to twice its normal thickness—an injury we blame on a doorknob.

"She's still the most beautiful girl in the world," says Papa. "But in the future, she has to be more careful."

I am very careful from that day forward: So painstakingly careful that I take to eavesdropping on my father, amassing a secret stash of knowledge to avoid any more mistakes. After bedtime at Suzanne's apartment, I tiptoe into the foyer and press my tiny ear against the ventilation duct. From beyond the groaning of pipes comes the murmur of pillow talk. It's like having a radio broadcast directly from inside my father's head. That is how I learn that they are arguing, that Papa refuses to have the nursing student to St. Arnac for Christmas. "I can't handle it yet," he insists. "It reminds me of Ellen. I'm sorry." Never before, as far back as I can remember, has Papa called my mother by her given name; it takes me a moment to realize who he's talking about.

"Is that the *only* reason?" asks Suzanne.

"What's that supposed to mean?" demands my father. "Not wanting to be reminded of my slaughtered wife isn't a good enough reason?"

Suzanne responds in a soothing tone; I cannot make out her words. But her volume rises as she says, "All I want is the truth. I love you. You can trust me."

A long pause follows. I can hear footsteps, presumably Papa's, pacing the hardwood floor. "What are you driving at?" he finally asks.

"I want to be a part of whatever you're a part of, Phil," begs Suzanne. "I'm going to put my cards on the table: I know you're not a brain surgeon. None of the girls who've rotated through Greensboro Women's this fall has ever heard of you.... But I'm fine with whatever you are: an undercover journalist...or an FBI agent...even a Russian spy. After six months together, I have a right to know."

This is Papa's opportunity to save himself. Obviously, he doesn't need to reveal that he murders physicians' relatives as a hobby, a revelation that might test the limits of Suzanne's commitment. He merely must admit that he's a widowed architect with no medical training; I don't know how he'll explain away the white coat, but I'm confident that doing so is well within my father's capabilities. What will happen, I wonder, if he confesses and puts his hospital career behind us? Alas, I never find out.

Mattress springs creak at a distance, announcing that Papa has settled onto the bed beside Suzanne. He may have his hand on her knee or her bare thigh.

"You *do* have a right to know," says Papa. "But I can't tell you."

"Phil—"

"No, please hear me out," he continues. "You're right. I'm not a brain surgeon—or at least I'm not a brain surgeon at Greensboro Women's. I wish I could tell you what I *am* doing at the hospital, but can't. It's not that I don't trust you. Or love you. But telling you what I'm doing would put you in danger, and it would put my project in danger, and people's lives are at stake." I doubt so many falsehoods have been concealed with so much truth. "You'll have to trust *me*, Suzanne. Can you do that?"

"I don't know. That's a lot to swallow," she replies. "And Christmas?"

"Not this year," says Papa. "I have my reasons."

Suzanne responds with a gust of sobbing, then a high-pitched wail that breaks periodically against my father's protestations of devotion; I tiptoe back to my own bedroom and cry myself to sleep.

In the morning, a Sunday, Suzanne cooks up a pancake feast on the griddle. My father's girlfriend seems less chatty that unusual; otherwise, she appears as cheerful and affectionate as ever. When she walks us to the car after breakfast, she kisses Papa on the lips and reminds him to call her when we arrive home safely. Then she hugs me, her warmth a contrast to the atmospheric chill. It is raw, overcast day in mid-December—the sort of day when hugs always feel the most loving—and a light dusting of snow still blankets yards and hedges. It is the last day I ever see Suzanne Shale.

A final vestige of memory: My father, slumped and intoxicated, fumbling to unsnap the clasps on his satchel. Sixteen days have elapsed since our return from Winston-Salem, sixteen days since Suzanne Shale delivers her ultimatum. If she does not come to St. Arnac for Christmas, she'll find another partner. But we share a holiday supper only with Aunt Henrietta and my future uncle, who depart early the next morning for a week-long vacation on the Gulf Coast. It is now December 27th, approaching evening, but Papa has made no effort to turn on the lights.

My father sits at the kitchen table. He has grilled me a cheese sandwich, has poured me a tall glass of chocolate milk. I chew in silence, watching him unpack his medical supplies, bracing myself for another visit to the hospital, but Papa isn't planning any more excursions.

"I think it's time to teach you something, princess," he says. "Do you want to learn how to give an injection?"

"I don't know."

Papa finally manages to unsnap the claps on his bag. "What I'm going to do, princess," he says, "is fill this syringe with sodium chloride. Salt water. Totally harmless, but excellent practice. All I need you to do is give your father an injection…."

"I don't want to," I say.

"I'm not asking you, Lauren. I'm telling you."

My father insists that I pull my chair up alongside him. He is far too drunk to fill the syringe, too drunk even to hold the needle steady, so I am forced to draw the fluid out of the bottle on my own. My fingers ache from the multiple attempts. Nausea builds under my tongue. Papa clenches his free hand around my other wrist; even if I wish to flee, I cannot.

"All right, princess," he says. "Just like a doctor."

His breath, his body, the entire kitchen stinks of whiskey.

I insert the bevel and draw back the plunger. I know that the syringe contains more than sodium chloride—that even as the toxic contents fill my father's veins, he is sharing with me his final gift: the horror and thrill of saving lives.

Robyn Art

Frost, Beleagured Plains, Augeries of Dew, Whatever

Often it's attempting to be many
things at once not unlike the very body
itself: part time amateur violinist,
full time bullshit artist.
Sometimes two things
at odds, uxorial and kempt,
yet continually
misusing the turning lane.
A wind. A harkening. Sometimes exhaustion
clings to me like leaves to a wet porch.
I imagined once being a man
but couldn't hack the tearless,
light-truck-driving,
dozen-eggs-a-week eating.
When we play marching band
my daughter says *there is so much to be*
but so little time to be it.
Am I a drum?
I am not a drum.
Am I a maraca?
I am not a maraca.

Allister MacMartin

The News

I wonder for how long,
on the log in the shadow
of a trailer with busted windows

splattered by paint balls as the sun
goes down behind a hill covered in pine
and the grass grows tall except for where earlier in the summer,

and every week since then, the riding mower shaved out
a diamond and the rototiller turned over baselines
which were raked smooth, we can sit here

not saying a word even with the news
that she was probably pregnant
and it was probably his.

Roberta George

Reading Palms

The Palm Reader of Barneysville, Georgia,
cannot tell her: "You'll never leave, never stop
standing on a slanting porch,
watching children, your thin brown legs
hanging out of cut off, rolled up jeans,
showing your ass.

"In the late afternoons, you'll walk down to
your granny's, see the impossible
purple red earth of the driveways, the bronze
day lilies blowing in ditches, the
white D cup magnolias with
patent-leather green leaves.

"You'll spend Sundays at the Holiness Church,
or your mama and Jesus, and Fridays
at Shorty's for the height of a bar stool,
for the sweet music saying, 'Baby, I love you,'
repeating the cool blankness that comes
when a man touches the inside
of your thigh."

The Palm Reader of Barneysville, Georgia,
cannot tell her: "You'll work for white ladies five
days a week and watch their daughters, the ones
who hate cheese grits and greens,
go off to schools in Atlanta, driving black
Nissans, marrying doctors and lawyers,
hitting the Prozac and freeways
at seven each morning.

"In the evenings, you'll carry home leftovers and

old dresses to turn into quilts, the velvets and satins, a
Victorian crazy you found in a book. You'll
find an hour of daylight to work your back garden,

the purple eggplant, the fuzzy green okra, the yellow squash.
You'll see color and pattern in everything
and everywhere but in yourself."

Gregory Loselle

My Cat has an X-ray

> "Outside of a dog, a book is man's best friend;
> inside of a dog, it's too dark to read." —*Groucho Marx*

First the room with its pane
milk-white as a window shade
in summer evening sunlight,

then the animal all creaking knots
and pelted leverage in the crook
of my arm, paws fanned out pricking
mirrored constellations in my chest,
reared up, pushing itself into the dark
beyond my hand spread behind
the shims of its shoulder-blades.

And then the picture on the screen
in celluloid, more darkness added
to the dark, but light drawn into
wire-thin lines that map the landscape
of the night within: this chain
of ornamental links conforms
a spine, the tented shoulder-joints
and the pear-shaped hollow of her chest
divided by the diaphragm: the lungs
as thick and viscid as two clouds,
the heart, stilled here, a fretted knot
between; below, the coiled rope of the gut.

Consider by what mechanism we arrive
at the occulted volume of this space,
the patent of the undisclosed, how
radiation pierced the flesh to map
a live thing explicated on the screen,
and whining, sighing, stirring in my arms.

Gabriela Tiessen

Composed

—after Billy Collins

I set the book
down on the tray table.
I really should write more poems
I think as I contemplate
    the red and salmon flowers
    on my dress,
    my daughter sleeping on my lap.
At three she fits, scrunched,
in two airplane seats.
I search the passengers' heads,
    the clouds,
    the fasten seat belt sign
for some catching metaphor,
some transforming rhyme.

I scrounge quietly for a pen.
My bag, the black hole
of motherhood, has absorbed
    lip balm,
    an aqua top and shorts for Lily,
    a bag of mixed nuts (we are traveling to vacation)
    a small Etch-a-Sketch
but no pen.
I find crayons in my girl's backpack
and pick green
(blue would be more lyrical,
or purple)
But this little person

sighs, moves her head.
Any moment now she will
            sit up with hazy eyes,
            shiver into wakefulness,
            ask me to draw her name with this crayon
and then this ending
will have to do.

Mary Morris

Dinner with Hades

It's my birthday, yet he sends me an invitation. I get so tired of his knock, knock jokes. Knock, knock. Who's there? Hell. Hell who? Knock, knock. Who's there? Obsolete. Obsolete who? And he goes into this lather of hysterical laughter, prepares a cake with mercury and Roman candles. His house, a collection of figures from ancient Greece, Asia Minor, Major, carvings of rich woods, mother-of-pearl, carpets of extinct animals and rugs dyed with botanicals no longer in existence. From Mongolia, a red lacquer bed, made up with sheets of silver, fur, and blood. He has a rather proportionate body, calls me his favorite sleek filly, says he wishes to mount me, could he play the flute for a minute and pretend he is Pan? He serves everything foreign to my tongue. If I had known the delicate meat stuffed with heavy cream were the body parts of fallen angels, I would not have eaten them. He devours his food voraciously, the thin bones of those lofty creatures dropping from his glossy fingers. I glance out the French windows with black steel bars and note his hunting sleigh made of cast iron, his vehicle for carnage. Above a table of marble hovers a candelabra with ivory tapers. The wax drips slick. He peers at me with pharmaceutical eyes, blue and amber. Closes them. Opens only one eye, like the hinged lid of a pot. Boiling steam. White mist. How cunning he is as he rises, walks by the beveled mirror vacant of reflection. His frame, weathered but fine, like a man who has worked all his life in different worlds, grown tired; a few slight rolls in his middle and a melted wave of slack skin down the back, fallen chest. He removes his robe, a gold flame. Scent of cinders. Shows me the birthday cake, lit. My name is written in pomegranate seeds. He extends, becomes ample, disappears into the abstraction of my body. We are horizontal, then vertical, then vertical-horizontal. He creates a collage of body parts with infinite directions. It's like vertigo. He rocks me with his internal storm and I'm his boat. Suddenly, it's cold. I want my mother.

M. Callen

History of Romance

Dressed all up
in lightning, My hair teased
to the tenth degree, I was wanting
to be wanted,
A sweet talker
at twilight, Tried to memorize
my life, Rehearsed all the dances,
Knew the songs on the radio,
In a room
of pig straw huts, In an ever-
trembling tundra, I am not beyond
suggestion, Working
for the man's gut,
My lover
struck out & said *humble*, Produced
his stash of sorry's, His dealer's snake
around my neck,
& I was sleeping
when they stole me, Put
a stop between my teeth,
I was
the outrage of cocooning, The res-
ignation of an old man's lie,
Saw the moon
but wanted thunder, An electrician to fix
the vacancy sign.

Tamra Wilson

THE COZY CORNER

THE FIRST WEEK AFTER WE moved into our rattletrap hotel apartment in Illinois, Mama had already taken to avoiding crowds and sleeping late with a pillow over her head. She had left this town to marry Daddy twelve years ago and her coming home to stay wasn't going to be easy, especially with all the whispering about Daddy's new business.

This particular day, she teased and sprayed her hair into a presentable shape by the time the noon whistle sounded. The signal was the Wakefield Fire Department's way of reminding everyone that the day was half over and it was time for lunch. The crowd had thinned by the time we arrived at the Cozy Corner Café, which had to be a relief to Mama. If we showed up when the restaurant was full, more folks might see us and whisper among themselves. I could imagine them gossiping, *There's that Vannoy girl. Didn't she run off with that Putnam boy? What's she doing back here?*

Billy hated the restaurant because the grilled sandwiches tasted like fried onions, but the main problem was the layer of dead chewing gum under the tables. If we leaned under to count the dried wads, Mama would tell us to keep our faces and hands where she could see them.

We picked a booth a fair distance from the front door as the juke box belted Patsy Cline's "Crazy." Mama glanced down at her bosom. "Heavens to Betsy!"

She was no Marilyn Monroe chest-wise, but she was bosomy enough to gap a blouse. She fumbled with the buttons and told us to bow our heads to bless the meal though we hadn't even ordered yet. It was my turn.

"God is great, God is good. Let us thank Him for our food. God bless us all, especially Daddy. Amen."

"Amen," she repeated with clenched jaw. Daddy had left the minute we settled in to the apartment and from the looks of things he wasn't hurrying back any time soon.

"That's such a dumb prayer," Billy sneered.

"There aren't any *dumb* prayers," Mama corrected.

"Right, only dummies saying them. All she did was a sing-song."

Ever since Billy got himself saved two years before, he's gotten way too big for his britches.

"No fussing, you two. It's all I can do to keep this headache at bay." Mama fished a little tin box of aspirins from her purse and squeezed the corners. As she reared her head back to swallow two of the tablets, her eyes flew wide open. We turned to see what caught her attention. At the back of the restaurant sat Aunt Connie. Bobby pins formed a tic-tac-toe pattern across her scalp. She had dared to come downtown with her hair pinned up, something Mama wouldn't dream of doing in a million years. From visiting her last summer, I knew that Aunt Connie sometimes escaped the heat of the Speedy Press for a quick lunch and would be bringing a take-out back to Uncle Wayne.

"Why don't we tell her hey?" Billy said.

"Connie's on her lunch hour. It's not polite to bother people while they're eating. And don't point, young man. They'll think we're hicks," Mama warned.

The last thing she wanted us to look like was hicks, though it was hard not to. Growing up in a big place like Tampa hadn't helped us much. We hung around a lot of Cubans who didn't know good English. As Daddy said, you could take the hick out of Wakefield, but not the Wakefield out of the hick, referring to Mama's poor ways. They had married too young and uneven, he said, a big mistake. Daddy was upper crust; Mama was from the river bottom side of town. She had married him on the fly and followed him to a string of Air Force bases across the South: Barksdale, Lackland, Keesler, MacDill.

Mama handed each of us a menu, though we were sure to order the usual: three hamburgers with everything but cheese which cost extra, and two orders of fries to split three ways, root beer for me, coffee for Mama and for Billy, a Grapette that smelled like juice served during Communion.

"When you were growing up, did you get to come here and eat?" I asked.

"You know the answer to that. Your folks didn't use restaurants, did they Mama? I'll bet they've never been here before."

"As a matter of fact, I got my first job here at the Cozy Corner." Mama fingered the fringe of her hairdo.

I tried to imagine her in a pink uniform, taking orders from hungry customers, refilling glasses, scooping tips into her apron pocket. I figured she'd been a good waitress, being as how she paid so much attention to details and cleanliness.

"How did you learn to carry all those plates at one time?" I asked.

"Practice." She grinned, then lowered her voice. "Did you know Connie's real name is Contadina?"

"Like the tomato sauce?" Billy said.

"That's right. Mom craved tomato sauce before she had Connie," she said. "I didn't realize it was her actual name until she registered her for school. There it was on her report card: Contadina Louise Vannoy. The Louise part was for my grandmother."

"Why didn't your mama name her Louise?" I said.

Mama shrugged. "All I know is that she saw Contadina on the can and thought it sounded pretty."

I couldn't believe that anybody would name a baby after canned goods. I wondered why she was telling us this odd story. I knew that Grandma Gladys had more than a few problems: a sorry husband, too many children and a steady stream of washing and ironing. Three boys and four girls lived in their rabbit hutch of a house.

"What's craved mean?" Billy asked.

"Women want to eat certain foods before they have a baby. They want it real bad. They can't help it."

I figured it was something similar to my hard wishing for Daddy. He'd been gone only a few days and the loss of him already felt like a hole in my sock pinching my toe.

The waitress swiped the table with a damp cloth and scattered silverware at each place. "Just you three today, Hon?" as if she knew Daddy was missing.

Whenever we ate out he'd hurry us along, "Tell the girl what you want," he'd say, winking at the waitress. Then he'd order Billy "a man's plate" and me a "half a woman's plate," which made me feel grown up. And Mama would say, "Don't encourage them to waste food." But this particular day I didn't like people noticing that we were one person short. It made what felt part-ways empty seem positively gutted.

After we gave her our order, Billy asked, "Did you crave anything before you had us?"

"Why yes. Before you came along, I craved angel food. I took that as a sign that you'd be called to do the Lord's work." She gave him a vague smile. "If I couldn't get angel food cake, I'd settle for honey buns." She opened a pack of cigarettes and tapped the butt end on the table.

"Was I honey buns?" I said.

"Ha. You were devil's food." Billy blew the paper jacket off his straw. It fluttered to my plate.

"Show some manners, son." Mama lit her cigarette then shook out the match. "No Kelly, to answer your question. I'm afraid that you were corn on the cob. I couldn't find it in a Texas winter for love or money. Lord, those were some times."

I wadded the paper from his straw. I'd been born at Lackland Air Force Base at San Antonio, where Daddy was stationed. Daddy said Mama would croon along with country singers on the radio, something she kept doing until the past year or so. She refused to carry a tune. Here lately, she'd open the hymn book at church and not even bother to move her lips.

"You craved corn because she's corny." Billy laughed.

I wanted to pop him. I was no more of a cornball than he was, though Mama had craved those sweet kernels when I was in her stomach. She had to be making up that story about Billy and the angel food. He no more had wings than a rabbit. I wondered what awful thing she had craved for Baby Hank that would let him die so young, but I didn't dare ask for fear it would send her on one of her crying jags.

"Charlotte! What brings you to town?"

Mama leaned back to catch her breath as Aunt Connie hovered over our table. A straw purse was in one hand and a guest check and small paper bag in the other. Mama reached to give her a hug.

Mama sputtered. "What a surprise to see you!"

"Likewise," Connie said in a cloudy voice.

Mama didn't ask her to have a seat. Instead, Aunt Connie stood there awkwardly. "Billy you're the handsomest young man, and Kelly, you sure do favor your Daddy. How's he doing these days?"

Mama explained how Daddy had left the service and gone into business with his Cousin Ev, but she didn't say what they were doing: selling fallout shelters, which were like caskets—you didn't want to admit you owned one because people would think you were crazy.

"I just had lunch and picked up a sandwich for Wayne. He mentioned something about seeing a fellow who looked like Gale driving through town, but we didn't see your car at June's so I figured he must be mistaken. We had no idea that all of you were back up here."

"Gale's going to be away for a while," Mama said, quickly adding, "We're looking for property."

I couldn't understand why Mama was telling such a lie. She hadn't so much as skimmed a newspaper these two weeks, much less read the real estate ads.

"So you're moving back?"

Supposedly the town grapevine had somehow missed Aunt Connie.

"Say, how about you and the kids join us for dinner Sunday?" she said. "I've invited the folks. I'm sure they'd love to see you."

"I'm sure," Mama said bitterly.

"Oh please come, Charlotte. It's been years since we've all been together."

Mama paused. "Thanks, but we're still getting settled in. Maybe some other time."

"Of course, you must be busy and all. I'll give you a ring. You're staying at June's, right?"

"Not exactly." Mama bit her lip.

In summers past we'd stayed with Grandma June, Daddy's mother, because she had a big house and nobody around to fill it up.

"The Wake 'n Wink is awful nice. I hear they have one of those kidney-shaped pools."

Billy stopped dawdling with his food. "We're not staying there, either. We're at the Lincoln Hotel."

Connie looked surprised. "The Lincoln?"

"We're renting an apartment for the time being. It gives us little more room than at the motel." Mama blushed when she said this.

"Well then I'll have to give you a ring there." Connie's voice had a slippery streak, as if she was looking for a firmer grip.

"We ain't got no phone," Billy said.

I felt something move under the table. Billy leaned forward as if he were grabbing his shin and stared up at Mama.

"These kids are such savages," Mama hissed.

"Well, I guess I'll have to come see you then, won't I?" Connie said. "I've got to get back to work right now. Stop by when you can." She headed off to the cash register.

"Why'd you kick me?" Billy grumbled.

"We don't need to advertise about the phone, Billy. It's not technically true. There's one in the lobby we can use."

It was pure Mama. Always wanting to pretend things were fine when they were far from it.

The waitress brought our lunches and as usual, the French fries were a bone of contention. Mama divided them among the three of us by splitting the lion's share between us kids and saving a half dozen for herself.

"Hey look. It's John Glenn," Billy said, pointing to the door.

I swerved around, hoping to see the astronaut hero, as Billy pinched a French fry from my plate.

"Hey, that's not fair." I reached to snitch one of his fries to even the score. Mama grabbed my wrist. "Enough of that foolishness or we won't come here again."

Billy would welcome her threat. He didn't like the Cozy Corner in the first place, but eating there was our chance to get out of the apartment. Going here was better than nothing.

"Mama, do you think Aunt Connie and Uncle Wayne will come see us?" Billy asked.

She studied the guest check and pulled out her coin purse for the tip. "I hope not. We aren't set up for company."

I wasn't sure what she meant by "set up." Aunt Connie and Uncle Wayne were family and they weren't planning to stay all night. We could make do. They could sit on the fold-out sofa or the easy chair or on the flowered turquoise chair that Daddy had called a bad dream. We could serve them some Kool-Aid. And if Mama was embarrassed about the furniture, she could pull the blinds tighter.

I finished my sandwich, leaving the dill slices for last. "If we're looking for property, does that mean we're rich?"

"We don't want to be rich," Billy said.

"Why not? Grandma June's rich. She must be a millionaire," I said. June was Daddy's mother. As in: June was Daddy's mother, a ritzy relative who hadn't treated her money like a used snot rag. She still owned her first dollar, Daddy used to say.

"She doesn't have a million dollars," he said.

"If she isn't a millionaire then she's a thousandaire and we're hundredaires."

Billy scoffed. "There's no such thing. Besides, you aren't supposed to brag about money. It's hardest for a rich man to squeeze through the eye of a needle, isn't it, Mama?"

She snapped her purse shut. "Why Billy Graham Putnam, I believe you *are* going to be a preacher sure enough. But you're going to have your work cut out in this old world. There's only so much you can do with hard hearts." Her words wore a thick coat of warning.

Billy picked at the crust of his sandwich. "I know all about hearts from Sunday School. You have to have a good one to get into Heaven, don't you?"

"Well that's sort of true," Mama said

"Aunt Connie has a good one, right? And Uncle Wayne?"

Mama smiled. "Why, yes, I suppose so."

He was playing her to the hilt, bringing up churchy stuff. I wondered what he was aiming for—maybe some candy or a chance at the bubble gum machine by the front door.

"What about Daddy?" he asked.

Her chin quivered. I hoped she wasn't going to cry like back in Florida when someone had mentioned Baby Hank's name at the Howard Johnson's. As soon as we ordered, somebody sat down next to us with a fussy baby and Daddy looked at his watch and said it was so many years since "the time back in Tulsa." Then Mama burst into a bawling fit that wouldn't stop sobbing. I wanted to crawl under the table, she was boohooing so much. Our waitress came over and asked what was the matter. Daddy said that we were fine, which was the biggest lie in the state of Florida. Mama was making such a scene I wanted to pretend I didn't know my parents. Everyone was staring at Mama sobbing as if Hank had died that very second. It was more embarrassing than Billy teasing me about Guido, a boy in my class who smelled bad.

This time, Mama's eyes misted but they didn't spill over. She probably figured Daddy wasn't coming back. I could feel it. I studied the dill chip on its edge. It was cut thin enough to see through to the saw-tooth pattern on the rim, round and round in a perfect circle. My eyes felt stingy too.

There was nothing more dismal than a hot afternoon in a stuffy apartment, especially when you were nine years old and bored. By one o'clock we could hear people stirring upstairs and out in the hall as the old men had no doubt crawled out of bed after a late night at the Sit 'n Sip. The tavern was only a block away. For many of the old men, Mama said, it was home away from home. "They drink their trouble away, then come back to sleep it off."

I knew some didn't make it all the way home with the liquor they'd drunk. Billy had spotted puddles of throw-up on the sidewalk out front for two mornings in a row, which made me glad to stay inside.

Of course neither of us was allowed to do anything loud and boisterous or leave the premises. That particular day Mama huddled under her bed lamp reading a dog-eared copy of *Photoplay* and her Bible-in-a-Year devotional. Reading was something she did most any afternoon when she didn't want to watch *The Price is Right* or *Queen for a Day* with me and Billy, not that she ever wanted to watch women tell hard-luck stories for new household appliances. It was bad form, she said, though I couldn't imagine her turning down a free chest freezer or washer if given the chance. If it had been me on the show, I'd have picked bus tickets to Tampa so I could visit Elena, or go to Mayberry to visit the people on *The Andy Griffith Show.*

"There's no such place," Billy said. "They film TV shows in California, just like they film movies. I learned that in social studies."

"Then how come Andy Griffith talks like us?" I said. "He doesn't sound like other TV people."

Billy thought for a minute. "That's because he's from North Carolina, like in the show."

"That doesn't make sense. You said the show was in California."

Mama stepped in to explain that Mayberry was based on Andy Griffith's hometown in North Carolina. "He's from there, but the show is filmed in Hollywood."

"Why not the real place?" I asked.

Billy spoke up. "It's because they don't have the stages and cameras and stuff back in North Carolina."

"That's crazy," I said. "Why they would need to make up the place when they could use the real thing?"

Billy pointed at my sketching pad. "It's like those pictures you draw, Dummy. We already know what the real stuff looks like, but you keep drawing your goofy version of it."

"That's called artistic expression, Billy. That's not goofy," Mama said in her show-offy voice.

Artistic expression was a mouthful, but at least she saw my side of the matter. But I was still confused about which bus ticket I would buy to see Mayberry. Would the show people be in Hollywood or in North Carolina? And when I considered the matter, I figured Mama and Billy didn't know any more about it than I did.

Shows like *Andy Griffith* didn't run on Sunday. Instead, *Photoplay* was Mama's entertainment, her window on starlets, regular movie stars and old ones like Princess Grace who had taken off to Monaco. I had noticed this in *My Weekly Reader*. The country wasn't much bigger than a school district. Mama studied who was fixing to marry who, who was getting a divorce, what movies were coming out and which star preferred what kind of perfume and mouthwash and then tried to find whatever it was at the drug store, even though they didn't carry the fanciest brands.

The devotional leaned to her religious side which hadn't been exercised much since we'd left Florida three weeks ago. She'd started with Genesis in January and was moving at a fast clip until she bogged down midway at the Song of Solomon. I could tell because her book mark hadn't budged since our move into the Lincoln Hotel apartment.

That afternoon Billy said he was tired of messing with his stamp collection. He rooted around in his makeshift chest of drawers and dragged out his toy Army men. He hadn't paid them much mind since we'd arrived in Wakefield, but on that particular day he felt like war games. He set up a miniature battle scene on the linoleum, complete with molded plastic foxholes. Tiny stretchers and a scale-model Red Cross tent were set up to treat the wounded.

As Billy made artillery sounds and raced toy tanks across the floor, I drew heart pictures in my tablet, fat ones, skinny ones, broken ones. I remembered what Mama had said about hearts. If they were so hopelessly hard-boiled, why did people mess with church? There was nothing soft-hearted there, not the hard pews, not Brother Dirk's sermons or the gory hymns: "There is a Fountain Filled with Blood," "Are You Washed in the Blood of the Lamb?" or "Nothing but the Blood of Jesus." The lyrics made me break out in goose bumps. Who wanted to see a fountain of blood spurting like water out of a garden hose? It might thrill Billy and the Army men, but the songs didn't bother the church people one bit. If they were that bloodthirsty, maybe God wouldn't want them in Heaven. That was where Baby Hank lived, hanging around with the angels and heavenly hosts. I had seen his picture in Mama's billfold. His eyes were closed because the snapshot had been taken of him in his casket. I took out my pad to draw what I remembered from the picture: the satin baby-sized pillow, his round face, the rosebud touching his chin, the same pointed chin like Billy and Mama had. Whenever I got to Heaven, I'd finally get to meet him, only by then I'd probably be an old lady and he would still be a baby. It would be strange all right. I'd introduce myself: *Baby Hank, I'm your little sister Kelly. I was born after you died.* Or maybe *Hank, it's me, Kelly*. That would sound friendlier. I was already more than four times older than he was when he died, though somehow he was considered older. Cemetery arithmetic made no sense.

Billy had said that dead people stopped growing when they were buried. That was why babies didn't need to be dug up and put into larger caskets, so it wasn't necessary for us to check Baby Hank's grave out in Oklahoma. Once when I asked Mama about going out there to see where Hank was buried, she had said that Jesus, God and the angels would keep Hank company. It wasn't necessary for us to go. Angels flew around like Sky King. They could fly anywhere and fight any evil. And if you ever got to Heaven, your guardian angel would help interpret your words for you like Elena and Mrs. Estrada. I had seen this miracle happen for real. Back in second grade our teacher wanted Elena to understand the assignment. It was as if Mrs. Estrada had a magic decoder inside her brain that let her talk English and switch to Spanish in one breath. Elena smiled and said "*Si*," which meant she could see what the teacher meant.

Elena's English improved and she could write complete sentences by Christmas and give a complete book report by Easter. I asked if her Spanish words weren't getting crowded out by English ones and she laughed. "No *amiga,*" she pointed at her forehead. "I have two parts: one for the Spanish and one for the English. The English part grows bigger now."

When we left Tampa, I wondered if her head might explode or at least grow lop-sided, packing all those new English words in there. It had been more than three whole weeks since I'd seen Elena. Her head might have blown up already. Maybe that was why she hadn't written.

I leaned back from my drawing paper. I realized I'd made Hank's head lop-sided and his hair too wiry. The drawing was as ugly as the cigarette burn on the edge of the kitchen table. Once things were damaged, they couldn't ever be completely right again, just like with Daddy. Even if he came back this minute and pretended nothing had happened, all of us would know the real story about his girlfriend.

I added a big heart above Hank's head, but it looked bad. I wadded up the drawing.

Billy looked up. "What are you throwing away?"

"No. It's nothing."

"You lie. I'll bet it's a dirty picture."

Billy often came up with that excuse because he'd been caught drawing dirty pictures back in Tampa. He had traced some photographs in one of Daddy's naked-woman magazines. Mama was shocked that Billy had discovered Daddy's stuff and made him write "I will not draw dirty pictures" seven hundred times because seven was a special number from the Bible. Mama said sevens were all over the Book of Revelation, for example: seven seals, seven churches, seven trumpets, seven dooms. When Billy said it wasn't fair that Daddy had naughty magazines, Mama said, "Stop being a wise guy or I'll make your pants smoke for seven hours."

Billy yanked the balled paper from my grasp and smoothed the creases. "Hey, this looks like Guido."

"Give it back." I reached for the crinkled drawing.

"No way, Jose. I'm keeping this. I'm showing it to Guido, just see if I don't."

"Mama, Billy's got my drawing." I sounded whiny.

"Cry to Mama. You drew Guido's picture because you like him." He made kissing sounds. "Lookie here: a heart. I'm going to tell him next chance I get. Kelly's got a boyfriend. Kelly's got a boyfriend."

"Shut up! You aren't going to ever talk to him. He's way down in Florida."

"Ha. Then I'll mail it to him."

"No you won't. Give it back." I swung in his direction, barely missing his face. My foot scattered his Army men in all directions.

"Don't tear up my stuff," he yelled.

I slapped back at him.

"Ha! You can't hurt a flea." He tackled my waist and threw me sideways. Sofa cushions scattered as I kicked the air. He held his bed pillow across my face. I struggled against my own hot breath and the greasy scent of Butch wax on the pillowcase. I kicked harder, gasping for air. I broke out in a sweat. This is how it was to smother. Everything would turn dark and muffled and you'd run out of air. Stars would come out. Maybe I would get to meet Hank this very day. My arms and legs fell limp. Sounds drifted. Just as everything went black and hot, Billy raised the pillow.

"Hey Dummy, you dead yet?"

Marc Mewshaw

Happy Accidents

WHEN MAUREEN FIRST SUGGESTED a visit to his mother, Mike hadn't been too hot on the idea. He hadn't gone back home since he'd left the farmhouse on the shore of lake Okeechobee twenty years ago, not even for his dad's funeral, and that thought alone made him feel squirrelly. Plus which, now that things were starting to come together again after a long period of ugliness he felt he ought to stay in Destin, where the action was. Though he'd been reduced to working for his brother's construction outfit—Bill, the golden child—the dry-wall business was booming. Houses were being thrown up in places where there didn't seem to be much call for them, and with the money rolling in like it was he hoped to clear his debts inside six months, maybe even save up enough to move out of the trailer the ebb tide of his fortunes had beached them in.

Also, at least for the past few weeks, he'd demonstrated a high degree of rectitude in his personal conduct. On those occasions Maureen didn't know about when he'd knocked back a few cold ones with buddies from work, he'd limited himself to beer and the occasional shot of clear spirits only, not a drop of whiskey or tequila, and even with a buzz on he'd managed to restrain himself from calling up Felipe or Pedro or any of the usual suspects who, despite all the unpleasantness that had gone down between them, he was sure would be as pleased as punch to resume cordial dealings with him—so long as he paid up front this time.

But no, he'd fought down the urge whenever it cropped up and he saw this as a token of progress, part of the larger trend in his life. So why walk away from it now, even for a week or two, when things were going so well? Especially since it was idleness that usually got him in trouble. But Maureen kept saying, "For the kids' sake, for the kids." And when Mike gave in, it had as much to do with the kids as appeasing Maureen herself, who for some time now had been acting odd and secretive, chatting on the phone in a hushed voice late into the night, shrinking from Mike's touch and generally moping around like she was looking for any excuse to blow up at him.

So far, the drive from Destin down I-95—an artery permanently clogged these days by U-hauls with New York and New Jersey plates—had been like any other family outing. They could have been shooting down to the mall or Chuck E. Cheese's. It had started without fanfare and kept on in the same droning monotony and he could scarcely stand it anymore. Try as he might to remind himself that this was a vacation, the flatness of the terrain and the straightness of the road inspired a terrible certainty in him that what awaited on the far side of the horizon would be worse than what he'd just quit. It got to where he slipped into the notion he wasn't making progress at all, the road a belt feeding a loop past his car, the same stretch of scrub pines and gas stations and Spanish billboards cycling by again and again.

To remind himself on whose account he was going to all this trouble, Mike checked repeatedly on the kids in the rearview mirror. Leaning against the taut seat belt, errant whorls of hair curled over the nylon strap like golden talons, Sarah, Maureen's child from a previous marriage, slept with a doll clutched to her chest. Alton, the side-effect of Mike's own abortive marriage, you couldn't be sure if he was sleeping or what. Head lolling on his shoulders, arms and legs jumping around, drool on his chin, eyelids fluttering in the breeze stirred by a clip-on fan that served as his pacifier on road trips, he might have been dreaming. Or it could have been one of his fits: slow burns of twitching, a far cry from the thrashing grand mal deals you saw on TV but disturbing all the same.

"Think Alton's okay?" Mike asked.

"Yep," Maureen said without much interest.

Up ahead, a filthy red smear marred the road, beaten so deep into the asphalt it was anybody's guess what animal all that sun-blackened gore and fur once added up to. A mosaic of tread was printed over it and the hum of his tires briefly quieted as they recorded their own signature in the carnage.

"He's doing that thing with his head. The bobbles. Maybe he needs a Depakote. Or a valium."

"I'm sure he's fine," she said absently.

"You didn't even look."

"I know what you're trying to do, Mike, and I'm not falling for it again."

Mike tightened his hands on the wheel, knuckles paling. "Honest to God, Maureen, it's the boy I'm worried about."

"If you really cared about that boy we wouldn't be living in a double-wide, would we?"

Somewhere around mile marker 300, a jungle rankness blanketed the cart. "I have to go," Alton announced. But Mike was pretty sure the past tense was the appropriate one. He volunteered to handle it. As if there was any doubt who bathroom detail fell to.

They pulled in at the next rest stop, a long bunker-like complex in front of which a stars-and-stripes and a black POW-MIA flag, both about the size of a football field, hung slack from their poles. As Mike climbed out of the car, Maureen stayed him with a hand on the shoulder. For a second, he thought it was a gesture of tenderness.

"Just in and out, now," she said. "Don't tarry."

"Yup." He brushed her hand off.

"I mean it, Michael. No pit stops."

"Come on, gimme some credit. I've been good for a long time now."

"Define 'good'," she said.

"Pass me Alton's travel kit."

"*Michael.* I told you. You're not gonna make a rube of me today."

"You wanna be the one to wipe his ass, be my guest. But I ain't going anywhere without that kit."

She stared at him for a good long while, arms folded. "Fine." She removed the small red kit from her purse and handed it over. "Just FYI, I know how many are in there. I counted."

"Jesus, woman, you got any idea how paranoid you sound?" Stuffing the kit in his pocket, he slammed the door.

The boy sniffled as Mike gentled him up the stairs and through the smoked-glass doors of the Flying-J Travel Plaza.

In the bathroom, Mike stood him in the corner and swept the stalls for glory holes bored through the partitions, obscene graffiti advertising trysts or any other evidence of deviant activity. Satisfied, he beckoned to the boy and locked him into one of the cubicles, then fetched a wad of moist paper towels and passed it to him under the door.

"You okay in there by yourself, Alton?"

The boy just kept on sniffling.

"Hang tight for a sec. Your old man's gonna see if he can't scare you up a fresh pair of shorts somewhere."

Before leaving, he had a look at himself in the soap-spackled mirror and was appalled by the sorry sight he presented. Raddled, florid, eyes bloodshot, he looked older than his thirty-seven years. He opened Alton's emergency kit on the rim of the sink—a syringe primed with sodium valproate, surgical gloves, various prescriptions—and took out of the bottle of valium and tapped out a small pile of off-white tablets into his palm, counting. Then he pitched one into the back of his throat and dry swallowed and stood there brooding and regretting before deciding that one valium was just a tease, and so he nibbled gingerly at the edge of another pill, then decided to hell with it, and swallowed the whole thing with a splash of water that tasted like sweat wrung from athletic socks.

Out of the bathroom, he wove his way across the concourse, dodging long-haul drivers wearing the miles in their benumbed stares, and into the Super-Six convenience store. Charging past the newspaper racks, aisles of alligator-themed knick knacks, an insulin shock of zit food and a ginger-haired young girl who looked half-asleep at the cash register, he made a direct line to the medicine shelf in the rear of the store. He browsed the selection of pain-killers, sifting the gel-caps and candy-coated analgesics until he came across garden-variety aspirin. Slipping the blister pack out of a box, he forced one of the pills through the foil and examined it. These would do fine as decoys. Turning his back on the cashier, he popped out a dozen or so tablets and deposited the box back on the shelf. He fished out the valium bottle, poured several into his mouth and replaced them with aspirin as he chewed the tranquilizers to a chalky cud. Then, lips tingling with the mild buzz of petty theft, he made for the exit only to hesitate at the threshold, held up by a nagging feeling...like he was forgetting something... Something crucial...

Shaking it off, he cruised back across the complex and through the front door.

As he stepped out into the heat of afternoon, a damp foul breeze like the breath of some carrion-feeder washed over Mike's face. With the first effects of the valium whispering through his bloodstream, he lit a cigarette and looked out over a honey-mellowed world. There was a slow, syrupy aspect to the raking sunlight; the cars out in the parking lot seemed to float in it. Somewhere above him, ropes beat a gentle rhythm against the flagpoles like the bells of distant buoys in calm seas. Easing deeper into the languid atmospherics of late afternoon, he sat on the top step and soaked his lungs in a giant drag of nicotine. Things didn't seem half as grim as they had a few minutes ago.

Maureen had been right, he realized, to insist on this getaway. He hadn't had a week off for more than a year and you could see how the stress had built up behind his eyes and in his cheeks and aged him to where he was a dead-ringer for the old man. And Maureen herself was due a holiday. He owed her that much for all the shit he'd put her through—twitchy goons in the hire of the Latin Kings showing up on their doorstep at all hours of night to collect debts, repo men whisking the furniture away right out from under their asses… Plus which, he had her service in the childcare department to thank her for. Looking after Alton was no walk in the park. The world was an unforgiving place for such a defenseless child…you couldn't afford to lose sight of him for a second…

Not a second.

"Sheeeee-it!" Mike growled. Hauling himself to his feet by use of the handrail, he lumbered back into the rest stop as fast as his valium-ballasted legs could carry him.

In the bathroom, his calls for Alton echoed back to him unanswered through the odor of urinal cakes and the dribbling of leaky faucets. He flung open the stall door, but there was no trace of his boy except the soggy clump of paper towels Mike had passed him. He stood there staring at it, a pulpy mass press-molded into the shape of Alton's tiny fist, struggling not to indulge the superstition that this would turn out to be the last earthly relic of his son. Then, suddenly, he was convulsed with anger, incensed at Maureen for dragging him away from Destin, and doubly so for sending him to tend to the boy with a medical kit full of temptation. What was she thinking? How could she have been so goddamned stupid? Sometimes, he could swear, she set him up like this on purpose—just to prove a point. Fury licking up the back of his neck, he stalked out into the foyer.

After five minutes of jogging laps around the premises and calling out his son's name, five minutes of shouldering aside weary travelers who stubbornly refused to grasp the gravity of the situation, and scanning for the most vulturine face in the crowd and finally accepting it was futile since everybody here had the vice-wasted, unsavory air of a potential sexual predator or child murderer, he found himself careening towards the Cold Comfort Bar and Grill, thinking to calm his nerves with a highball, wondering too if it wasn't time to get on the PA or issue an Amber alert, when he collided with a gale-force squall of AC that stopped him dead. He gazed into the vent, at the fan blades spinning behind the grating, for he didn't know how long, absorbed in the blades' inexorable circles and striving to make out what this furious motion that always led back to the same place was trying to tell him, a message that he sensed might help him become a better man, a better parent, if only he was smart enough to read it. In the end he gave up and went outside, where he knew he'd find his son.

Mike discovered him, as expected, around back of the rest stop, staring into an exhaust fan as large and nearly as loud as a jet engine. The boy had a way of gravitating to the biggest one around. Not for the first time, Mike felt thankful for his son's peculiarities. In a world fraught with so much of the opposite, there was something to be said for the predictability of the unsound mind.

Sidling up to him, Mike cinched an arm around his scrawny waist and turned him face-to. The boy's dark lozenge eyes were blank and glazed.

"What do you see in that damn thing?"

The boy said nothing.

"Alton?"

"I see…stuff."

"Alright, well, that's…whatever it is. I'm just glad you're okay. Gave your old man a scare, you little shithead."

The boy seemed not to take any of this in. He was looking at Mike in a way that made him feel like something was sneaking up behind him. "Daddy? Where are you?"

"What do you mean, 'where am I?' I'm right in front of you."

"I can't see you."

"You can see that, can't you?" Mike asked, waving his hand in front of Alton's face.

"You're there, but you're not. Like a ghost."

Mike let out a nervous laugh. "What is this, the goddamned *Omen*?"

"Will you come visit? After you go away?"

Mike shuddered at Alton's spacey nonsense. He had a feeling, looking into Alton's delicate face, like he was observing something as weird and proof against understanding as a bug. It scared him to feel this way about his own flesh and blood. "Nobody's going anywhere," he said gruffly. "Only one that went anywhere was you. How many goddamned times have I told you not to wander off on your own?"

To Mike's annoyance, the boy grinned, seeing humor in something. Mike grabbed him by the shoulders and gave him a shake. "Why don't you knock it off, you goddamned spaz? You got any idea how much trouble you give me?"

The boy cringed and Mike realized he'd said this more angrily than he'd meant to, and also that he was grasping Alton harder than he'd thought. As soon as he loosened his grip the boy tore free of him and spun away, rubbing his upper arms and pouting, and backed himself up against the wall. The fear and hurt quivering in his boy's eyes cut Mike to the quick.

"Alton," he said, kneeling down to his level and holding out his hand. "Alton, I'm sorry. Look, I'm sorry. I didn't mean to…you gave me a scare, kid—that's all. You go traipsing around this part of Florida, you don't know what kind of trouble you'll wind up in. Out here, a gator's liable to eat your ass for dinner and save your nuts for dessert."

That seemed to crack Alton's petulance: despite his best efforts to restrain it, he let out a little giggle that righted his frown. Mike's dirty turns of phrase never failed to have this effect on the boy, and it gratified him to see there was still one person left in the world who found him amusing. Encouraged, he pounced on his son, but even as he tickled him and made farting noises on his belly with his lips, Mike wasn't able to fully give himself over to the moment. Once he'd worked the boy into a wriggling frenzy, he stripped off his shorts and soiled britches and handed over his own Bermudas, but Alton's words—"you're here, but you're not"—kept rattling around in his skull like a hand grenade in a cement mixer. Up above, thick dark clouds had begun to mass in the sky and the air tingled with the promise of rain.

The two of them marched around the side of the rest stop and across the parking lot, Mike free-swinging in his Hooters boxers, Alton droopy-drawered in his dad's shorts and still hiccupping with the aftereffects of laughter. Halfway back to the car, they passed an elderly couple who had stopped in their tracks to gawk, plainly bemused by the sight of a grown man in underwear walking hand in hand with a small boy. "Don't mind us, ma'am," Mike said, chuckling. "Just passin' through."

It wasn't until he saw Maureen that the joke went flat. She was leaning against the side of the car, her arms still crossed, as if she'd never uncrossed them. Her face was hard and closed, like some kind of invisible shutter had been lowered over it. As Mike and Alton approached, she opened the rear door and motioned for the boy to climb in, shutting it gently behind him. When she turned back to her boyfriend, her face was no longer ironed out, but creased along familiar fault lines.

"Mike," she said with controlled venom. "What the *fuck?"*

Her use of profanity shocked him unresponsive.

"I think the words you're looking for are, 'I'm sorry.'"

"I'm sorry?"

"Where have you *been*, Mike? You were gone for almost twenty minutes!"

"There was…complications."

"Complications? What were you doing back there, performing surgery?"

"No," he said, adding on an extra syllable so it came out as, "Noah."

"I'm listening," she said.

"We were just…out back there doing some father-son bonding-type stuff. Is what we were doing."

A little ripple of shock passed through her like she'd jumped into ice cold water, her eyes flashing and the sinew bunching at her jaws. Mike braced himself. He knew that look. Maureen held out her hand, palm up, and said, "Travel kit."

"Say what?"

"Give me the travel kit," she said, dead calm.

Shrugging, he dug the red kit from his pocket and laid it in her palm. Maureen took out the prescription bottle, poured out a few pills, glanced at them, then slid them back in and recapped the bottle. The brevity of her inspection gave Mike the idea the decoys had passed muster. But then she held out her hand again, palm up, same as before, and said, "Keys."

"The hell you want the keys for?"

"I may not be the sharpest thorn in the rose bush, Mike, but I know valiums don't have 'Bayer' scratched into 'em."

"Oh!" he said and chuckled stiffly. "Okay, yeah, I remember now. Now I remember. I think, a few months ago, back in the dark days there, I musta snaked a few pills to help me with a comedown and threw in a couple of aspirins and I never got around to replacing them. Sneaky, I know, but that was a while ago, Maureen. A lot's changed."

A yelp of laughter burst from her throat like something in her coming unstopped.

"Maureen, you gotta believe me, I'm done with that kind of shit."

"Oh, for Chrissake, *Michael.*" Her face tautened with rage, but then she re-crossed her arms, like she was holding it all in, tamping it down. "You know," she said, "we could sit here all day in this heat and play this game, and we could have the same conversation we had a thousand times in the past. I could tell you that I'm wise to your tricks, and that I've been smelling the booze on your breath when you come home from work for weeks now, and that I know where all this leads and it's just a matter of time before it goes from bad to Armageddon. I could lecture you on what a lowdown sonofabitch you are for stealing your own son's medication, and how fucking crazy and stupid to boot for putting us in danger driving under the influence. But it would be a waste of breath, because it's obvious you don't care. And, you know what? Neither do I. Not anymore I don't. Just can't afford to."

Mike felt his equilibrium give. He couldn't begin to imagine what kind of excuse was sharp enough to hack his way clear of this tangle of utterly valid accusations. She didn't even seem interested in hearing any. That was the unsettling part. Her tirades, he knew how to handle. But this resignation was new. "What's this…what's this all about?"

"You'll find out soon enough." She consulted her watch. "In about half an hour, I'd say."

"What happens then?"

"I called your brother ten minutes ago. All we have to do is sit tight until he shows."

"Bill?" His brother's name made his brain ache. "It's gonna take him a damned sight longer than half an hour to get down from Pensacola."

"He isn't coming from Pensacola."

Mike studied her through the swirling of his bewilderment.

"This trip," she said, "isn't a vacation. Never was. It's been in the works ever since I knew you were drinking again. I'm sorry if I misled you, but it was the only way this thing was ever going to work."

Mike moaned in exasperation. "What thing?"

"Bill and your mom've been waiting at her house with the interventionist. Everyone can see that you're going to end up like your dad if you don't straighten yourself out. Everyone 'cept you."

"So it's an ambush?" he said. "One of those sneak attacks where everybody guilt trips you into some drunk tank where they pump Jesus and sunshine up your ass?"

"It's only ninety days, Mike. Ninety days at most."

He reeled at the figure. "What about Alton?"

"He'll stay with his grandma."

"What's wrong with *you*? You got something better to do then looking after your own son?"

"Mike, Alton's not my son. He's yours." She paused, her eyes drifting to the asphalt. "Look, it's only fair that I level with you. It's not just your mom and brother I been talking to. I'm going up to Jacksonville. Believe me, I know it can't be easy hearing this, but Sarah needs a father figure in her life. And maybe her real dad's the one best cut out for the job."

Mike thought he might be sick. He looked up into the sky to clear his head, but superimposed over the quilting of cloud was the image of a turning fan blade that only made the wooziness worse.

"Here you are, a man that's been building homes all his life," Maureen continued, "and you don't have a proper one to live in. And what little I had going for me, even that your bad habits stole away. I'm afraid you'll rob so much from me I'll have nothing left to start over with." Her voice, which had risen to a doleful whine, became suddenly very businesslike and firm. "Bottom line, Don said he'd take me back, and that's the best offer I got going right now. Sorry, but that's just how it's gotta be."

"Don," Mike sighed. "Of course. *Don.* It would have to be him, wouldn't it?" He groped his body, patting himself down, and finding the car keys in his shirt pocket, fished them out. Then, in the same firm tone she'd put on, he said, "I'm going to need everybody to get out of the car now, please."

Maureen looked at him like he was crazy.

"Last chance, Maureen. I'm gonna drive away in that goddamned car whether the kids are in it or not."

Whatever Maureen saw in his eyes was enough to tell her he meant business. Blanched, shaken, she corralled the children and walked them across the parking lot as Mike set about emptying the Subaru of their possessions—Sarah's doll and child safety seat, Alton's fan, a pile of comic books, a makeup kit Maureen had left in the glove compartment, her pack of gum in the console, a long strand of her brown hair. He piled it up into a cairn outside the car then jettisoned their suitcases and duffel bags.

Panting from the exertion, he looked over to see Maureen and the kids staring at him from a picnic table sheltered by shabby palmetto thatch—staring at him as if he were some grotesque sideshow curiosity caged behind bars they didn't fully trust to keep him in. He gave them one last look then turned away. Punchy as he was, his mind ran cool and clean on the fuel of a single overriding conviction: he'd sooner kill himself than wait around for his brother to show up and drag him off to the drunk tank.

He slumped in behind the steering wheel, jammed the key into the ignition and stroked the engine to life. He checked his wing mirrors, adjusted the angle of the rearview, slapped the car in gear, then twisted around to look out through the back window and released the hand brake. As he toed the gas, he watched in befuddlement as every car in the lot reversed away from him in perfect unison. When he understood what was happening, there was still plenty of time to hit the brakes, still plenty of time to stop what had been set in motion, but a strange hopeful impulse took hold of him and he stomped on the gas. The car revved and, bucking over the curb, pitched down a slope and Mike turned just in time to see the front of the hood slosh into brown water and the molded curve of the steering wheel rearing up to meet him like a set of black knuckles.

When he came to, his nose was numb, a wet crackle accompanying his exhales, and an unpleasant salty warmth dribbled over his lips and chin. With only the dimmest sense of how this state of affairs had befallen him, he watched the car's hood sink to its windshield in the roiling water of a drainage ditch. He probed the pulpy mass of his face with his fingertips and a ringing pain shot through his teeth.

Once he'd recovered his wits, he shouldered the door open against the weight of the water, and a brown scum sluiced in, swamping his legs. He stepped out and lumbered along the ditch, one lurch at a time, his stride occasionally churning a flash of spiny appendages like a soupspoon dragged through some nightmarish stew, until, just shy of the bank, he hit a pocket of mud and sank to the ankles, then to his knees. Yellow bubbles of swamp gas burbled around him.

His father had drowned in water no deeper than this. Knee-deep water, they'd said. At the age of fifty-three, he'd managed to pass out fully-clothed in the bathtub, a half-empty bottle of whiskey floating above him like a buoy. A fittingly stupid end for a boozy fool who'd beaten and berated the kids he claimed to love. Peering down at his shaky reflection, his mangled nose raining blood, Mike understood that his own life, such as it was, seemed destined to end in the same ignominy.

From the brow of the drainage ditch, Maureen called. "Mike? Mike? You crashed. You crashed the car."

Silhouetted against the glowing white cloud cover, she presented a figuration of such strange, vibrant clarity, such unspeakable sadness and beauty, that it appeared to be a message of mystical origin. "Certainly seems that way."

She descended the slope, grabbed hold of his wrists, and tugged until the muck released its grip with an obscene sound. Together, they clambered up to the top of the bank where Mike flopped on his back.

"You crashed the car," Maureen said again.

"In case I missed it," Mike managed to wheeze through blood bubbles.

While she went to the kids, Mike remained on his back watching the clouds skim by, bathing in the soundtrack of his childhood, the same soughing and whirring and croaking that had lulled him to sleep as he grew up, often drowning out the shouts and sobs from distant rooms. It purled over him, a euphony as broad as the sheet flow that every rainy season cleansed the marsh, sweeping away all traces of the past, reshaping the channels and gouging new sloughs, washing out the dead and feeding them to the living, wiping the slate clean for another year. Drifting under the white river of cloud overhead, he had a pretty nice feeling going, notwithstanding the ache in his face, the groggy load of valium and the knowledge that he'd suffered some heavy losses on this day. As fine points of mist began drifting over him, he realized he hadn't felt something like this for a long time. Months or maybe longer. Maybe not since he left this part of Florida all those many years ago.

Benjamin Rybeck

Perfect, Starting Now

1.

LAST WEEK, THE NEWS BEGAN to spread that Steve Scanlon's mother had died, making him the second person in the school, after Randy, to have lost a parent. It's sort of an odd coincidence too. The Scanlons have been close to Randy's mother since the passing of her husband. Or, at least, Steve Scanlon's *father* and Randy's mother have been close. They know each other from work. For the last week, Steve Scanlon hasn't been at school. His lacrosse team sits alone, looking confused about whom to throw straw wrappers at, which nerds to call fags, and which girls to stare at without their captain present to guide them.

Today, on this afternoon before the comet comes—Madden's Comet, passing close to the earth for the first time in twelve years—Scanlon, out of nowhere, rises from the parking lot as Randy unlocks his car and climbs inside. Scanlon wedges open the door with rugged arms. Randy can feel the boy's breath on the tip of his nose. Scanlon doesn't look weak or anything. He looks thick as ever, heavy-necked, like his body is one big muscle. But small patches of hair splotch his face. He's not dressed, like usual, in school colors; instead, he's in a pair of cut-off jeans and a white V-neck. "Move over," Scanlon says.

Randy looks at the stick shift in between the two front seats. "I can't move over."

"Move the fuck over," Scanlon says.

Scanlon's hand grips the door, almost like if the fingers curl away from the metal he will drop into some abyss. Randy climbs awkwardly over the stick shift, the rubber of it catching the bottom of his pants, and plops into the passenger seat. Scanlon gets in and closes the door.

Like always, Randy is parked in the farthest possible spot from the school entrance, and nobody else is parked around him. Randy watches the other students get into their cars across the parking lot, a flood of them stepping over discarded autumn leaves, stepping into shiny vehicles. Randy cannot spot Scanlon's BMW anywhere, but he wonders what the lacrosse captain's friends might think if they saw him sitting in the used Geo Prism at the back of the parking lot—easily the cheapest car on the property—let alone in such a car with someone like Randy.

Scanlon turns the keys in the ignition and the motor whirrs to life. "My dad," Scanlon says, "thinks we should talk."

Randy feels like his body, his mind, has slowed. "We can talk if you want," he says.

"I put my dad's head in the oven. Said I'd turn it on if he mentioned your family again."

A car goes by with its bass turned all the way up, and rap music shakes the pavement around Randy's car, startling him. When Randy looks into the window of this car, he cannot see anyone driving it; he just sees a faceless black mass behind the wheel.

Randy understands: Scanlon has broken down. He's weak and he may never be able to get beyond this pain in the way that Randy did as a young boy, when Randy's own father died. But Randy doesn't dare tell him this. Scanlon's hands have tightened around the steering wheel.

"Well, tell you what, Muteboy." It surprises Randy that Scanlon still remembers this nickname from so many years ago. But Randy wouldn't act *mute* if more people were deserving of his attention. "Tell you how you can help me," Scanlon says. "You're going to tell me where you live now, and we're going to go there, cause I know your slut mom doesn't come home until five. So we're going to go there together this afternoon."

"I don't understand..."

Scanlon, like a snake uncoiling, removes a hand from the steering wheel and powers it upward, into the roof of the car. Randy jumps. He's scared of emotionally weak people who happen to be physically strong. There's no telling what Scanlon can do. He's lost control.

"You think I don't know," Scanlon says, "where my dad was the night my mom died? You think I don't know why she left the house that night? Why she went *looking* for him? What she was looking *for*?" Scanlon's voice sounds husky in the way a cigarette-smoker's does, although Randy is certain Scanlon has never smoked a cigarette in his life. "Tell me where you and your whore mom live and we're going there together."

"How did it happen?" Randy says. "How did she die?"

"Badly," Scanlon says, like he's answering a question about the weather. "Now tell me where you live."

The old man's heart gave out when Randy was six. That was that. He went to sleep one night and didn't wake up. Randy never cried. School counselors and seldom-seen relatives asked if he was okay, if he needed anything. They told the boy his father went to Heaven and was in a good place. But Randy didn't need anyone to tell him this. It was the strangest thing, really, how peaceful he felt. Randy's mother sent him to a few psychiatrists, but all of them came back to her and said, "The boy seems fine." Randy touched his mom's hand one morning when she started to cry. "We need to stick together now," she told him. "I'm going to help you through this because I love you." Randy let his mother say this. He went to the psychiatrists. Even at six, seven, eight, he knew his mother needed this—to feel like she could help her son. Randy knew he had more strength than his mother.

Now, Randy watches Scanlon hunch over a box of Randy's mother's things, papers and jewelry and so on, sorting through them like an animal devouring a carcass. Scanlon reaches the bottom of the box and pushes it away from him; it topples over, but nothing remains to be spilled out. "Where's the rest of your mom's shit? Come on, come on," Scanlon says. Randy thinks this might be a taunt, or an imperative, but he doesn't know how to respond. Scanlon stands and wipes dirt from his shorts. He puts his hands on his hips and looks around the room. He takes his tongue between his teeth. "Come on, come on," he says again, a little louder this time.

Scanlon has been here for an hour already. The comet will come in three hours, and Randy needs Scanlon out of the house by then. He will not share the comet with anyone.

Randy was worried as he let Scanlon inside; he felt a pang of shame as he looked at his mom's ashtray, overflowing with cigarette butts—as he opened the door to the slim living room with no television, with a cigarette-burned couch—as he led Scanlon through the kitchen that has no microwave and a clunker of a fridge—as he led Scanlon into the bedroom, which made Randy nervous that Scanlon was going to ask to see Randy's bedroom too, and wonder why the place is so small and how two people can possibly live there comfortably. But Randy realized pretty quickly that Scanlon wasn't interested in anything other than Randy's mother. He stormed into the house like an obsessed man, said, "Where does your mom keep her shit," and didn't ask a single question like, "Why is this place so small," or, "Where do *you* sleep?"

Scanlon continues to look for whatever he's looking for. He looks in the closet, pushing hanging clothes out of the way. He looks under the bed, but just finds a laundry hamper. He looks in the pockets of jackets and pants. His pace quickens. He flails around the room. He stomps. He pants. He keeps saying, "Come on, come on." His face is red. Randy has never seen anybody act like this before; he keeps at least six feet away from Scanlon at all times.

But after going through the pockets of jackets and pants, Scanlon freezes. He lowers his head and stands there kind of slumped, like he's fallen asleep. And he doesn't mutter anything. And he doesn't move for a minute. His breathing quiets.

"Scanlon?" Randy says this without commitment, although he takes a few steps toward the boy. "If you tell me what you're looking for, I can try to help you find it."

"I don't want your help." Scanlon keeps his eyes on the carpet.

"Why are you here?" Randy says.

But Scanlon doesn't answer. Instead, he looks up, and turns toward Randy, but looks just beyond him. Randy turns around and sees what Scanlon's looking at. A photograph on the bureau in the room. Randy's mother and father, the one photograph of the man they still display, the two of them at some water park as twenty-somethings, Randy's father looking mock-strong, flexing his arms comically, his mother in a bikini top, eating an ice cream cone.

"I asked my dad about it last night," Scanlon says. "Your mom and him would lie next to each other. Never touching. He said they never touched except for a handshake, but that they talked. Do you understand it?"

Randy doesn't, but he nods. "I think so," he says.

"My mom and dad never talked," Scanlon says. "I don't know what they did together, but they never talked. Maybe he was all talked out from being with your mom so often. And what I want to know is if they wrote letters to each other. I want to know what they said to each other when they laid there and didn't touch."

"When they *lay* there," Randy says.

Scanlon's eyes narrow. "What?"

"Never mind," Randy says. "Please don't cry."

"I'm not going to cry, you little shit."

"You need to leave now," Randy says. "Can you please leave?"

"Can I leave?" He takes a couple steps toward Randy, his face growing redder. "Can I *lay*, can I *lie*, can I *leave*, you little shit?"

Randy backs up and pushes himself against the bureau. He hears the photograph clatter against the wood and fall to the carpet.

Then Randy hears something else. He hears a car outside. Hears the engine turn off. He moves away from the bureau and pulls aside the window's blind and sees his mother step out of the car in the parking space below the apartment, a cigarette in her mouth, her hair shining in the sunlight as she un-bunches the bottom of her dress.

"That's her, right?" Scanlon lifts up the bottom of his shirt and wipes sweat off his face. Randy sees his hairy stomach, flat and muscular. "I'm going to wait. I'm going to talk to her."

"No." Randy looks at the mess. "We need to clean this up."

"I'm not cleaning up shit," Scanlon says. "She's been with my dad today, you know. I'm staying right here and I'm *waiting* to talk to her."

Randy knows he can't stop this. Whatever's about to happen he cannot do anything about. He hears his mother at the door, unlocking it, and he hears the door open, and his mother calls his name, and Randy cannot speak. He stares at Scanlon, whose face is still sleek from sweat. Randy's mother is going to come into the bedroom, she's going to see the box of her stuff emptied on the floor, and what will Scanlon do then? Will Scanlon attack her? Will he put her head in an oven, just as *claimed* he put his own father's head in an oven?

His mother comes to the doorway. She looks into the bedroom, looks down at the box of stuff, spilled on the floor, and then back up at Scanlon. She doesn't look at Randy. She looks at the other boy instead. And Randy watches him too. They both watch him, like they're waiting to see what he'll do. When he will snap. When he will lunge. When he will attack.

"Oh God," Randy's mother says. She takes a breath, and when she exhales, she shakes her head and says, "You poor thing."

All at once, Scanlon seems to collapse, like the scaffolding in him breaks and takes him down with it, deep inside himself, to the very bottom. The rest of it happens smoothly. Randy's mother holds out her arms, and, almost like she's magnetized, Scanlon goes toward her, and she wraps him up, folds him into herself, and they embrace. Scanlon's so much bigger than the woman, but he looks like a baby in her arms, his head on her shoulder. Randy's mother says, "Shh," whispers this to him over and over again, although he's not making any noise.

Randy feels like a stranger—like he doesn't belong in this house. After his father died, his mother tried to hug him more often, and he let her, sometimes, but he always tried to pull away. But Scanlon and Randy's mother hold each other tightly, like letting go of the other one would mean to fall, and to keep falling, and to fall forever without ever hitting the bottom of anything. Randy would be lying if he claimed to understand what's happening here.

2.

Whenever Scanlon looks at Randy's mom, he resembles a child. This is what Randy starts to think, anyway, watching them at the table in the kitchen. Randy's mom invited Scanlon to stay to eat, and Scanlon didn't hesitate longer than to shuffle his feet on the carpet before saying, "Sure." Now, Scanlon observes polite behavior, and seems almost terrified to offend. Whenever he needs more Parmesan cheese, he clears his throat and then says, "Could you please pass the Parmesan please?" He always says please twice. What has changed in this lunatic?

Randy's mother doesn't say much. She twirls spaghetti around her fork and sets it down on the edge of her plate without taking a bite. She rotates the wedding band on her finger, but never looks at it. Scanlon never takes his eyes off Randy's mother. He scrutinizes her. Randy watches the two of them and feels cold. Somebody should turn up the heat in this house.

After the spaghetti's gone, Randy's mother stands. Scanlon says, "Can I help you clean?"

Randy stands too, and starts clearing plates off the table.

"No," his mother says, holding up her hand, palm flattened at him. "Randy, relax. Steve and I will do this."

Randy doesn't say anything. He lowers himself back onto his chair and watches the two of them clean. Scanlon picks up the plates and stacks them neatly, like this is something he's done before. Once all the dishes are piled, Scanlon and Randy's mother move into the kitchen, leaving Randy alone at the foldout table in the living room.

Randy looks at the clock. 6pm. An hour until the comet comes. He needs to gather some blankets and maybe make a cup of hot tea to bring with him when he climbs onto the roof. When he looks into the kitchen, he can't see his mother, but he *can* see Scanlon, leaning against one of the counters, head down, and he can *hear* his mother's muffled voice, but he cannot hear what she says. Scanlon nods from time to time, almost like he's being admonished for something. But he nods and looks brave. A phrase comes into Randy's head. He looks like a little adult.

A little adult. This is what people told Randy after his father died. At the funeral, he shook hands with all the people who came to pay their respects, and they all smiled graciously and said, "What a little adult you are." They took his mother aside (she told him later) and said, "What a little adult you have for a son. He'll be running the house in no time." A little adult. This gratified Randy, to know it was working, the peace he'd made since the death.

After a few minutes, Scanlon and Randy's mother emerge from the kitchen. They stand together in the doorway, like they're coming to deliver some sort of bad news. And Randy looks at them. Nobody says anything for a second. And then his mother says, "I need to go."

"Where are you going?" Randy asks.

"Errands," she says. "But let me talk to you for a minute in the kitchen."

Scanlon keeps his head down, as though trying to avoid eye contact. The whole thing seems so inexplicable to Randy: Scanlon's transformation from a wild boy into a polite young adult, and the conversation in the kitchen... Randy feels suspicious of all of it. "Why?" he says.

"Because," his mom says, and leaves it at that.

"Listen," she whispers a moment later in the kitchen. "Steve is going through a hard time, okay? You understand? Just like you did too. You should spend some time with him tonight."

"No," Randy says without thinking.

His mother tightens her face into a frown. "Yes," she says. "You can help him."

"He wanted to hurt you," Randy says. Maybe if he can convince his mom that Scanlon is a threat, she won't make him do this.

"We talked about it," his mother says. She makes her hand into a spider on Randy's shoulder. "I think you two can understand each other. It would be good for you both."

"I don't need it," Randy says.

"Okay," his mother whispers.

Randy doesn't want to do this. God, he doesn't want to do this. But he cannot bring himself to say no. So he looks away from his mom and nods his head gently, as though a suspect finally confirming something shameful about which the police have been drilling him for days.

"Good," she says, and that's that.

He looks at her again. Her eyes are wide and she looks almost like she's about to cry. But of course, she doesn't cry. Instead, she smiles. Not a big smile—just small electricity at the corners of her mouth.

Without another word, Randy's mother stands and leaves the kitchen. Randy doesn't move for a minute, but instead he listens. He hopes to hear his mother say something to Scanlon, but she doesn't say anything. She gathers up some things and heads out the front door.

Scanlon isn't in the dining room. Randy listens for a second, and hears rustling from the bedroom. When he goes inside, he sees Scanlon cleaning up. Scanlon snaps the cover of the box back on and stands. He bites the inside of his mouth and rotates his head, looking around the room as though hunting for something else to do.

"What are you doing tonight?" Randy asks. Of course, he can still back out of it. He can still tell Scanlon that he needs to be left alone. He can tell Scanlon to leave his house and Randy will still have plenty of time to get to the roof to watch for the comet. But Randy remembers that look in his mother's eyes—like his mother was at her husband's funeral all over again, like his mother was searching for some way to turn on a light to cut through the darkness around her. So Randy says, "You know, that comet passes tonight. I don't know if you heard about it, but I was going to go on the roof and watch."

Scanlon locks his eyes on the bureau across the room.

"I watched it years ago with my dad," Randy says. "Maybe you'd like to see it."

Scanlon heads to the bureau. He picks up the framed photograph of Randy's mother and father, and he studies the image, holding the frame gently in his hands like he's afraid of snapping it. How many times has Randy looked at this photograph in passing, glancing at it while getting his clothes out of this bureau? Randy has never tried to count this, because it's too many times to count—an infinite number of times, perhaps. But Scanlon stares at it, biting the inside of his mouth and squinting. Whatever Scanlon searches for in the faces of Randy's parents is something Randy has never taken the time to see.

After a minute, Scanlon sets the photograph down on the bureau. He looks around the room. "Everything is okay with you, isn't it."

Because Scanlon doesn't inflect this like a question, Randy doesn't answer. "Would you like to come watch the comet with me?" he says.

Scanlon hangs his head for a moment. Randy wonders if cleaning up is something his mother told Scanlon to do, or something Scanlon did on his own.

3.

The night has grown cold, and the blankets, Randy realizes, are more for warmth than comfort. Randy holds one of them out for Scanlon, but Scanlon doesn't look at Randy; instead, he looks into the sky. "Hey," Randy says, and wiggles the blanket. Scanlon doesn't respond. Randy wraps the blanket around his own shoulders and the fleece itches his bare arms.

Randy hasn't been up here since the night with his father, when the old man had to stand on a chair and hoist his son onto the roof. Tonight, Randy had to do it himself, stumbling a bit, almost falling off the chair as he scrambled to the top. Scanlon made it to the top with minimal effort. It seemed to Randy the athlete simply willed his legs off the ground, rocketed his whole body upwards with no energy expended, and landed perfectly on the steel ridges of the roof.

Randy presses his palm against the steel and it freezes his skin. He throws his second blanket down, sits on it, and stares at Scanlon, who does not take a seat; instead, he keeps his eyes on the stars. It's a thankfully clear night, and out in the suburbs no light pollution exists. Once he realizes Scanlon wants to stand, Randy spreads out on the blanket. The steam drifts off the tea like a fire crackles in the mug. Randy tries not to let it burn his tongue. The comet will come any minute now. Randy waits. He watches, and he waits.

Randy can barely remember what the comet looked like twelve years ago; he can only remember his father watching it, his eyes lighting up as he caught a glimpse of something from far off, an object from another part of existence that made itself visible for just a few seconds, reminding him of such unimaginable space beyond what we can conceive. This is what Randy's father told him, anyway. He told him about the vastness of everything, and how you really can only notice it, and begin to understand it, when something from the other corner of the universe brushes so close that you feel you can reach out and hold it. So much light shines everywhere in the universe, Randy knows. He knows that wherever his father has gone, his father has gone somewhere out there, and he is warm, and he is safe.

Any second now. Randy breaks his eyes away from the darkness to see if there's anybody else visible out here, on other roofs in this complex—other people ready to see what the universe casts out at them. But nobody else watches. What's wrong with people? How is the entire world not on one collective roof right now, waiting? Randy understands what the rest of the world doesn't. He feels bad for the others. So much he knows at such a young age. Will the others ever catch up with him? Most days he doubts it. Everybody else is stuck behind him somewhere: Scanlon, his mother, and everybody else, trying to understand what Randy already knows.

Randy looks back to the sky, and he mutters, "*Scanlon*," but Scanlon answer. In this moment, Randy sees it, the streak of light crawling across the sky, and he climbs to his feet, and the blanket falls from his shoulders, and he doesn't care about the cold. He sees it, the streak of light, and he doesn't care about the cold because this light warms him, makes his body hot inside, and he feels the light on his face, as though the whole sky brightens, as though everything around him brightens, as though he's watching the sun cross the sky. The sight overwhelms him, this golden rope unspooling against the darkness, and he reaches his hand toward the light. Randy feels softness against his palm. He feels the softness of his father's hand, his father's fingers, intertwined with Randy's own, as they watch together, breathe together. "God," Randy says. The light leaves the sky. He falls backwards, onto the blanket, and curls himself up, wrapping his arms around his chest.

Scanlon's voice startles him when he asks, "It's over?"

"It's over," Randy says.

He looks at Scanlon again, but Scanlon doesn't move, except to take his hand down from his forehead. He stands straight. "That's… it?"

Randy doesn't understand. *That's it?*

"My mother isn't in the sky," Scanlon says. "My mother's in the ground."

Of course. What did Randy expect—that Scanlon would understand? Of course Scanlon didn't understand. "I feel sorry for you," Randy says.

Scanlon looks away from the sky. Randy cannot see his eyes, which scares him a bit. "You feel *sorry* for me?" Scanlon says.

"Maybe one day you'll see it," Randy says.

"I'll see what? What *you* can see?"

Randy starts to lift himself up from the blanket. But before he can climb to his feet, Scanlon comes at him and kicks the cup of tea. The hot water spills across the roof and creates a bath of hissing steam. The mug spins away from them, out into the darkness, and Randy hears it shatter against the pavement somewhere below. Scanlon puts his hand around Randy's throat and holds him down. Scanlon's eyes are chunks of obsidian. He bares his teeth. His fingernails dig into Randy's skin. "What do you understand?" Scanlon says. "You're alone. You have nobody. Your father's dead and my mother's dead. What the fuck do *you* understand?"

"Let go of me," Randy chokes. His body doesn't feel numbed by fear, but feels, instead, heightened—like Randy feels everything, but like the fear makes him feel it all on a delay.

"Why are you up on this roof?" Scanlon says. "Why do you come up here to see your father if you spend all your time pretending that you're okay—that there's nothing the matter with you? I can feel something. And you're dead inside. You're fucking dead inside."

"That's not true," Randy mutters.

"Let me tell you something," Scanlon says, getting closer to Randy now—so close that Randy can feel the heat of his breath. Scanlon turns Randy's head to the side and leans down, pushes his lips against Randy's ear. "You were six when your father died. What do you remember about him? He died in his fucking sleep. I got a call in the middle of the night. My father wasn't around because he was with your mom. I had to go out. I had to see her in the car. She was unrecognizable. Her *head*… I could have plucked it with my fingertips. So tell me again what you understand that I *don't.*"

"I hate you," Randy says. He spits this out. His teeth are clenched. He doesn't know where this comes from, but he says it again with more force—with as much force as he can muster. "I hate you," Randy says. He's never felt this afraid before. He's never before had his brain shut down, but his brain has shut down, and his body has become pure sensation—nothing but an ocean of nerve-endings.

Scanlon laughs. "Good," he says, and releases Randy's throat. The rush of air that comes back to Randy's lungs almost knocks him out. "I hate you too. And I hate your mother. You tell her she's wrong about me, about what she said to me in the kitchen. Tell her that just cause she fucks my dad and thinks she understands him doesn't mean she understands me." Scanlon wipes his mouth with the back of his hand. "I'm going home now," he says, "and if your mom is there with my dad, I'm going to hold her down and fuck her in front of him. And you need to get some help. You're more fucked up than I am."

Scanlon raises his foot in the air and stomps the steel an inch away from Randy's ear. The racket rattles a moment in Randy's head. He covers his face with his hands like it's a bad dream he's trying to make go away. "Good," Scanlon says, quietly now, almost like he's expended all remaining energy. Randy hears Scanlon's footsteps get quieter.

When Randy finally uncovers his face, Scanlon is long gone. Randy lifts himself off the blanket and looks around. He cannot hear anything. He cannot see anything, except for the stars overhead. Across the way, a neighbor turns out a light.

In the darkness, which feels complete and suffocating, Randy starts to laugh, although nothing about any of this is really *funny*. It's just that Randy can't believe what's happened. He cannot believe how scared Scanlon made him, as though Scanlon is actually strong enough to harm Randy, to do any of the stuff he promises to do. Scanlon's out of control, but he's fragile. Randy is almost angry with himself for feeling so weak. For feeling so scared. He stops laughing and makes a decision. Never again will he let such weakness and fear into his life. He needs to be stronger than that. He can be stronger than that.

Because, see, for a moment, as he stood up to watch the comet, as he whispered Scanlon's name, he thought, stupid Randy, he thought that maybe this could help him too—that maybe Scanlon seeing something beautiful would validate what Randy saw, what Randy *feels*. Randy thought, for just a moment, that this might be a good thing, and that the two of them could share this, and that maybe they'd feel a little less alone. But Randy *wants* to be alone.

In all of this, Randy sees how fragile Scanlon is, and he hates him for it. He hates him for trying to ruin the experience of the comet. Next time, Randy will not watch it with anyone. He will wait another twelve years, and he will be completely alone by then, and he will not need anyone to watch it, and maybe even his mother will be dead, and she will not be able to tell him what to do. Randy hopes for this, and it gives him some small comfort, but right now, the sight has been ruined. And Goddamn it, he hates Scanlon for this.

Across the way, the woman turns her light back on, as though she's realized something she forgot to do before sinking herself into the evening's darkness.

Randy is already in bed when he hears his mother unlock the front door and come inside. She doesn't turn on any lights. She slips into the bedroom and, without changing into her usual pajamas, lies down next to him. He can smell her—her soap, her perfume, her cigarettes—and he tries to smell something else, some other scent mingling with it, still attached to her skin from where she's been tonight. But he cannot. Since they started sharing the same room after moving into the smaller apartment, Randy has gotten to know the way his mother smells. Some days he can smell her all afternoon on his fingertips. She puts her hand in his hair and massages his scalp, pushing her body against his. "Are you awake?" she whispers.

"Did you see Steve?" Randy asks.

"No," she says. "His father is out looking for him right now."

"This is not a new family," Randy says.

"Why would you say that?"

"I don't want Mr. Scanlon to be my dad. I don't want Scanlon to be my brother."

"You poor thing," she says, and kisses Randy on the back of his head. He can barely feel her lips through his hair.

"You're with Mr. Scanlon," Randy says, "but that doesn't mean I have to be with Steve."

"I'm not *with* him," Randy's mother says. "We understand each other. We always have. And I think you can talk to Steve. I think you and Steve can understand each other too."

But how can Randy understand him? Randy can think of no way that he and Scanlon can cross the river between them. Randy cannot understand Scanlon's weakness, his anger. Randy cannot understand grief that manifests itself in that way. He feels strong. He feels perfect.

Randy says, "I hate him."

"Shh," Randy's mother says.

"I want him to die."

"No you don't."

"I want *you* to die."

"Sweetie," Randy's mother says, but already her voice softens. She's close to sleep, he knows. "You're still hurting," she says. "But you'll understand one day."

"I understand more than you," Randy says.

"You'll understand," his mother says, "that we need other people around us. We need to feel close to one another. We can't go it alone."

"*I* can go it alone," Randy says. "I don't need anybody. I don't want anybody."

"You poor sweet boy," she says. "Every day I miss him too. Now go to sleep."

"I don't want to go to sleep."

"I miss him too," she says. "Now go to sleep."

Go to sleep? He doesn't need to sleep. He hears his mother already snoring, already locked in unconsciousness, but Randy will not sleep, doesn't need to sleep. He is stronger than they are. His hatred for them—for the Scanlons, for his mother—has hardened like a crust on his skin. He can stay up all night. He can stay up forever.

He begins to count. "One…two…three…"

He can count forever, because the numbers will never end. He can count forever.

"…four…five…six…"

It will never end. The numbers crawl before him, one after another, lit up, unspooling in a line across the sky as he closes his eyes, as he sees them, the unbroken stream of them, the stream that will never end, that he will count forever.

"…seven…eight…nine…"

Before he climbs beyond single digits, Randy falls asleep.

Justin Burnell

I Think I Know What You Mean

ON A NORMAL THURSDAY, I GOT HOME from work to find a box stuck between my front door and screen door the way the post office does, as if that hides the package instead of making it more obvious. The return address said CA and above that, "Delia." I took the box in and set it on my glass coffee table. I got a beer from the kitchen. I like to have a beer or two after work each day. I don't think it's trouble. Every once in a great while someone sticks their nose in and says maybe it is. I guess I spend a decent amount of time alone. Back in my living room—some might call it a TV room or a sitting room, but I like the idea that of all rooms in the house it is the one I live in—I popped open the beer and stared at the box. I'd met her in Denver where I worked a just-out-of-college internship in logistics. We got along so well,

I applied for jobs in the area, but when the internship ended none of those organizations had buzzed my phone. I moved to my current employer where I plan direct routes of transportation, which I enjoy.

I thought she might have found something I'd left behind when I moved. Maybe she had just completed her move to California and in unpacking she found something of mine. At that sad thought, I hesitated further. I'd rather her keep whatever it was. I'd obviously long forgotten about it, and I'd be happier if something hung around her new place reminding her of me. A little reminder fit us more than a note or a lingering voicemail. Delia and I could not talk for hours, or, rather she could not talk for hours. I tend to get nervous in prolonged silence and blurt out some half-thought without any context as if in mid-conversation. She'd smile with a symmetrical part between her lips and tell me I talked too much. I remembered her voice as I stared into the box. I saw all the time I'd lost and got up to leave. Feldman and I had a standing agreement to meet at The 13th Step on Thursdays.

"Yeah, the box. I assume you opened the box." Feldman asked.

"I open the box and, well, it's a hand."

"What? Like off a model or a prop?"

"No. A human hand. A severed human hand." Feldman stopped twisting his pint glass on the table.

"A real, once-on-a-body hand?"

"Yes, like that."

"What the fuck?" Feldman finished his beer in a long drink. "You think she went psycho, and it's, like, a hand from her victim. She sent it to you because you're her ex?"

"I'm not terribly sure. I didn't think of that."

"What? I mean, she might be sending out body parts to all her ex's. Maybe she's killing her ex's and sending the still living ones the parts, like, as a warning."

"I seriously doubt that. Delia was always pretty even keeled."

"I need to think about this. Do you need another? Never mind, you need another. Vodka today?"

I nodded. I drink beer at home. At bar's I order vodka tonics or cape cods or ginger and whiskies. Feldman went to the bar to order drinks. We sat at a table instead of the bar, as I must request each time he and I meet up. I think he likes the idea of two buddies sitting shoulder to shoulder, drinking a couple beers, facing forward, and talking without directly looking at each other. Along with the lack of facial cues, sitting at the bar invites people into your conversation or at least makes it much easier for people to listen. And they do listen—especially in a conversation where someone like Feldman gets so instantly excited—until the temptation to join what should clearly be a private conversation is too great, and they tell you exactly what you should do, or some personal story impossible for anyone but themselves to delineate the connection to the previously private conversation. Feldman put the drink in front of me. "Man, so what are you going to do?"

"What do you mean?"

"Like are you going to get in touch with her, or, like, give it to the cops?" Feldman pushed his hair back as if trying to solve a complex equation he'd eventually give up on. I just wanted a rational conversation, to get some advice from a friend about what to do or what it meant. I admit a lack of focus on the actual item sent. Delia and I tried to stay in touch, but the phone calls got awkward. An hour of silence on the phone is different than an hour of silence face to face. I don't mean to make her sound like a bore. She chose her words carefully. I didn't think it'd be useful to call her.

"I know this isn't a normal situation. I think you're not understanding me. I recognize that. But Delia has never been exactly normal. On our one-month anniversary, she brought me a bird's nest filled with unhatched eggs. Meaning, she killed or I guess she prevented those baby birds from being born. Do you know how that works with eggs? Is it the same as a fetus?" I tore away the excess napkin that stuck out from under my drink by feel.

Feldman leaned back in his chair and made a theatrical motion of looking away from me. "No, I'm not sure when life begins in the egg. So you are going to . . .?"

"Well, she didn't write a letter or anything. Now that you mention it though, do you think I should send her something back? She might think I missed the point if I just write her. I think I've told you a little about her. Delia was the not very talkative girl."

"Yeah, 'not very talkative.' You mean the girl that liked to sit in silence, who told you, of all people, that you talk too much. I mean, with all due respect, she sounds not all there. Before, I thought she sounded boring, but now, I understand she's insane."

"Okay, there wasn't any respect in that comment. Delia wasn't boring, anything but. She had a different way of interacting. I guess I'm not saying this very well. I will admit, her way of thinking seems off, outside of the box. Anyway, should I send her something?"

In lieu of verbal communication, Delia and I went for walks or "little adventures" as she called them. We gave each other gifts. She'd make small things—a print of a leaf, a chain of daisies—or give me things she found.

"What are you going to do, send her a foot? An elbow joint?" He tilted his beer until the liquid reached the rim. I glanced around to be sure we weren't attracting attention.

"Okay, firstly, an elbow joint? That's not even a self-contained thing. It's part of the arm. So, no to that. Secondly, I don't know where to get stuff like that. I was thinking a stuffed bird. Maybe a cat's head. I'm not sure how comfortable I am with cutting a cat's head off though or looking for a dead cat."

"Okay, firstly, what the fuck is wrong with you? You're like sitting here telling me this isn't way, way fucked up. Now you're asking me if you should, I don't know, maybe cut the head off a fucking cat." The beer in his glass sloshed side to side in a swirl.

"Feldman, friend, there are all types of weird things that go on. You told me the story about that guy in London who found someone who would eat his leg. You said it was some sort of fetish. Not to mention all the body modifications people make. It could be from a cadaver. Maybe she bought it online."

"Online? Like, there's a service that will send body parts to your ex-lovers? I haven't heard of that, could you please give me the web address? I'm sure I know someone who could use an ear. You, Gabe, friend, are missing the point."

"Please, don't mock me." I spun my glass with the tips of my fingers. "I don't know how exactly to say it. You're sitting across from me, telling me Delia is insane, a horrible person, someone who murders. This is or was an important and good friend." I felt around my glass. It now sat on a fitted circle of napkin.

"A severed human hand, sent to you unceremoniously in a cardboard box. Gabe, I don't think it's a far stretch to question her mental state. That's crazy."

"You're presuming without context or any outside knowledge of this person aside from this and the few things I've told you about our relationship. I don't think it's bad or wrong of me not to instantly assume the worst about someone I knew very personally. Am I expressing all this?"

I could tell from his face I wasn't using the correct words to convey my meaning. I started to think this must be fun for Feldman, getting to talk at me like this, and talk about what a boring yet simultaneously crazy and murderous sadist Delia must be. His hands running through his hair, all his gestures were all melodramatic signs of frustration, whereas, he probably felt rather proud of how right he assumed himself. His eyes shone with each exaggerated point. He laughed with a small sneer. He'd decided his position correct, and I must be enlightened. If he were right and Delia killed me in the coming months, I'm not sure he could help thinking 'I told you so.' He might sit at this bar with another person and through sadness and even tears say, 'Right there, at that table, I told him.'

"Fine," Feldman said. "I guess I'm the one who should calm down.

Because, I guess this is, like, a perfectly normal thing to do."

"Thanks. So about the bird. I remember she had this old wrought-iron birdcage. The type with a chain to hold it up. If she still has that, a bright, stuffed bird would look nice in it." Without the extra napkin, condensation ringed my drink.

"You understand I was being sarcastic, right? Like, this is not normal. I'm starting to wonder which of you is crazy. We have the girl who probably has a larger cage where she keeps people to harvest body parts from, and a guy thinking how best to reciprocate the gift of a severed hand. A human fucking hand."

"Listen, I don't want to be mean here, but I think you're being a little sensational about this. I'm not saying this is normal. Did I say that before? I think I said that before. It's shocking. It's outside of expectable gifts, but haven't you dated a few odd ones in the past?"

"Who? Mina? The girl who slashed my tires when she caught me cheating? Honestly, don't you think that's, like, a little more cliché? I was pissed and thought it was childish. I think this is more like if she, I don't know, sent me pictures of her fucking animals or something."

Mina is exactly the odd I was referring to. Feldman's former girlfriend/partner/lover, who asked him why he needed to spend time with his friends if he had her, and what was there he couldn't talk about with her? When he could get away, his chief complaint was she talked or wanted to talk so much. It's this kind of thought that lead to his drab jokes about Delia sounding like the perfect woman. Re: her quietude. Delia and I did have conversations. I imagine Feldman has this idea she and I sat in a room staring into each other's eyes not making a sound. In a popular film, an attractive and odd character herself said you know you've found someone special when you can shut the fuck up and comfortably enjoy the silence. I repeated that quote to Delia. She laughed. I didn't make her laugh very often. She said people too often don't listen. If she were here, she'd nudge me under the table to say, "See what I mean?" She thought that people think of words as precise little tools, which, if perfectly linked, acted like a scalpel lined with diamonds, each sharp word ready to carve out meaning, but really those well thought out verbalizations were ham-fisted and about as precise as a bulldozer. She said all of this to me while we watched the snow fall over the parking lot of my apartment complex, her face very certain and serious. Then she looked over and said, bull in a china shop. We both laughed like it was the wittiest thing we'd heard. When I remember it, I'm not sure exactly what she meant. Maybe she meant bulldozer in a china shop.

Feldman stared at me. His hand clutched his beer, his back off the chair.

"That's different." I told him. "Animals can't consent to sex with people.

So technically it's abuse. Either way, both actions are irrational. In fact, don't you think slashing someone's tires is more aggressive, more threatening?"

"What about where the hand came from? Are you trying to convince me that someone said sure, please, cut my hand off?"

I suggested maybe we should play darts or something. I'm not very skilled at bar games, but the conversation wasn't headed anywhere.

"How do you think a normal person would react? Not you, a rational human being. How would someone normal react at getting a fucking hand in the mail from some girl they dated for five months, what, six years ago?"

"I hope they wouldn't react like you. Pushing their hair back and waving their arms in the air. Spouting worst-case scenarios. So, could we please drop the subject?" The condensation expanded. Each time I set my hand down it came back wet, and I had to discretely wipe it on my pants.

"Seriously? I can't drop this. What am I supposed to do, talk about work? Tell you about getting new tires? Ask you about routing lines and shipments? You brought this up. This is way better than our typical stuff."

Feldman stopped listening to anything I had to say. He was too preoccupied with how right he was. I thought of leaving without a word to see if he'd even notice, which of course he would, so I sat across from him, but the need for my participation in the conversation had ended. I waited for a moment then told him it was getting late, and I had a lot to do the next day. We both knew this was probably a lie, a manufactured, meaningless something to excuse myself from his company. I don't like these social grace lies, but I was tired of talking to him and wanted to leave but not further any annoyance at the other, which from the spiral of our conversation I assume he understood as well as I.

When I got back to the house, I popped a new beer and sat down on the couch, bending at the knees then letting my back sink into the cushion, so I could feel the bend of each joint in the controlled way I sit anytime I'm annoyed. What Feldman didn't have the patience to pause and realize was even if one of his absurd—to me anyway—scenarios proved true, I'd rather help Delia than turn her over to the authorities or shun her. I should have sat straight, looked him in his eyes, and said, Look now, this is my friend. What if you, on one of your not-so-sober trips home, nodded off or lost control of your car in some way and wrecked your car, or caused injury or death in some fashion? Wouldn't you want me to honor our friendship? Oh and he'd say something about this hand situation being different and not an accident. To which I'd say, No, no. We're talking about assumptions here. The assumption some people would make about you in the case I just proposed would be you were a person who had so little regard for human life, your own and others, you couldn't even be bothered to take a cab or ask a friend—me—for a ride. And although I'd agree, through your own foolishness, you caused harm or death by an extremely avoidable accident, I'd still say it was an accident, and you are a person who has the utmost respect for human life. Re: this conversation. Or maybe a simple, stop being such a dick about someone who, while I haven't spoken to in years, I obviously care about. I think that would have sufficed, but even simple phrases always eluded me when I'm presented with the time to use them. In French it's called *l'esprit de l'escalier*. The feeling of knowing the perfect phrase to shut someone up, but putting together that sequence of thoughts long after they're due. Although, any snarky retort from me would have been steamrolled by him and deliver the inverse-action of shutting me up. I'd leave annoyed. Come home, pop a beer, and sit down in a careful motion, focusing on each joint bend and the feel of my back absorbed into the cushion of my sofa. Which, more or less, is exactly what happened.

The box sat on my coffee table with the hand inside. I'd been so flustered by the opening and the finding, I'd completely lost sight that I should put the hand in the refrigerator, if not the freezer. When I'd opened the package it was not noticeably cool. I assumed the USPS did not climate control the shipment. The questions raised by asking for an air-conditioned freight might have been too invasive for Delia. The USPS may have codes and restrictions on sending body parts, given the possibility of health risks. Not to mention the overall creepiness of the contents and, compounding the creepiness, her lack of viable reason to send a hand to a residential address.

I opened the box flaps one at a time, carefully as if a small animal lived inside and would escape at the first chance. Instead, the hand was poised on its fingertips, slightly arched, the palm's center hovering. The hand had been removed in two diagonal cuts, one from the top, and the other from bottom. This left exposed meat and bone and made the hand look small and incomplete. Visually, the wrist is part of the hand and cutting at the wrist hurt the aesthetic. Where the skin broke, it curled in and wrinkled. It had grayed even more since I first opened it. I should have put it in the refrigerator. Despite this, the hand was free of dirt or blood flakes. Even the exposed meat looked wiped clean but had darkened to the color of old steak. With the hand removed, there was no way to tell what the box had carried. I'm not sure what enabled me to hold the hand and review it in such a detached way. I didn't cup it or intertwine my fingers with it; I held it as a delicate thing. Somewhere in my mind, something retreated from the thing as a human hand. The knife strokes so precise they removed all trace of gore or instance of horror. Neither of the cuts had the jagged signs of hesitation all the crime scene investigation cop shows talk about. Although, all my forensic knowledge comes from those shows and must be taken with a TV-sized grain of salt. I guess because it was so well removed from the body and the action of removal, I held it as if I were in a lab or what I imagine med school is like when students practice on cadavers.

A light scar marred the back, behind the knuckle and a thick callous bubbled under the pointer finger. The thing wasn't as large as my hand, but I didn't lay it flat and splay the fingers to measure it. It felt frail. The skin like putty, it weighed in my hand. I touched the back and softened my grip. I feared the bones might break and the stiff crack would clack through the skin. That gave me a chill, realizing again what I held had bones, and those bones once attached it to an arm and that arm to a human body. I put it down on the table and sat back to finish off my beer. I didn't turn the television on, as I usually do.

When I left Denver, Delia was the last person to see me off. My car packed, the backseat filled with my possessions, the rearview mirror useless. The two of us stood on the driver's side. She put her hands on my hips and kissed me. An abbreviated, small good-bye kiss. If I remember it correctly, we didn't say good-bye. I'm not sure we said anything. I assume we must have, but retrospect is fallible. In my memory of it, we don't say anything. I got in the car, and she walked away. She didn't turn back once. I completely recall her not turning to look back. That part might sound cruel, but it fit with us. I watched her walk away, as if I weren't the one leaving.

I'd stocked up on vacation days. I like my job more than most people in my department, but decided I'd use one of those vacation days. Some basic household duties were past due. It'd been some time since I took a walk just to be in the sun. The thought of spending the next day planning road routes and connecting product to supplier felt unfulfilling.

I leaned forward on the edge of my sofa and picked up the hand again. I looked over to the door and to the TV, as if someone might interrupt, before I raised the hand up to my face. It smelled sour and musky, like old, sick meat. My stomach turned with the scent, but I brought the hand closer until I let the fingertips drag across my nose and cheek.

I'm not some sad hump, pining after the last love he ever felt, in fact, Delia and I never used the word. Until now I don't think I've ever used that word in conjunction with her name. I've had relationships with women since I left Denver, a few, I would say a respectable amount. A couple were serious. I took them out to meet Feldman and a few other friends. They put their arms around the small of my back at social events. What I mean is, I'm not a person who ever worried about ending up alone. I don't think I've ever thought about it either way.

I dated one for a year. I said, "I love you." It wasn't the first time, but it was the most recent. She said it to me one night, and I paused unsure how to respond. I said it back and smiled because it didn't feel completely unnatural From then on it became our idiom for good-bye, like "aloha" means "hello," "good-bye," and "I love you." But the Hawaiian word means more than that. It means a general kindness for others, goodness. "I love you," meant that for us or at least for me. We said it at the end of phone conversations or when we left each other's apartments. I liked saying it to her because I meant "good-bye with a great level of care and affection." I tried to explain to her one night that it was nice we had a phrase that meant so many things and fit different situations. I guess I didn't do a very good job of saying what I meant. We got into a fight about it that night and a few more over the next week. She said she didn't think I understood what love was, and the word meant one very real, very specific thing, and if I didn't understand that I was a fucked up guy. I tried to tell her I thought it was much bigger and better than one thing, but I realized we were talking about different things.

Feldman laughed at me when I told him the story. He said I needed a friend. I shouldn't be alone at a time like that. He took me out, pushed drinks on me, and said, "Okay, tell me everything. Anything you want." He said I was an idiot. But there would be others. I like Feldman, but I still get annoyed when he calls me an idiot or insults my intelligence, so I asked him how exactly he defined "I love you." I said, "What do you mean when you say it?"

He said, "Okay, I think you need a good dose of honest simplicity sometimes. Really, it's just something you say to make a woman feel special. Sure it means something, but really it's just the next level of 'I like you,' which you only say to make someone feel good. I mean, I don't tell you I like you because it should be pretty obvious. I guess I'm agreeing with you."

I told him I didn't think he was getting my point, but I did agree with what he said about the unstated emotion of our friendship.

I felt something more than 'the next stage of like' for the person, but the best definition I could come up with, even when said to a person I would tell others I loved, meant little more than "I really like spending time with you. There are few others I'd rather be with," which doesn't sound much different. Delia and I never even thought to say it.

I couldn't think of the right gift to send back to her. I could buy her a stuffed bird and a cage in case she had lost hers or used it in some other way. Given Feldman's thoughts on the hand, I thought it might be better if I killed a bird myself and put it in the cage. That felt closer to our conversations, more personal, but the thought of killing something revolted me. I couldn't decide, so

I gave up for the night. I put the hand back in the box and into the refrigerator. Falling asleep, I thought of lying in the snow with Delia outside my apartment complex in Denver, with no urge to speak or need to fill the air with sound.

Even on Saturdays, I wake up early without an alarm. I make coffee using a plastic tablespoon measure, adding one for each cup of water. When I opened the refrigerator to retrieve the cream, I had to reach past the box. I lost my appetite and skipped breakfast. Normally, I'd cook a nice meal to start the morning, something like eggs with spinach and toast. I couldn't think of the last morning I hadn't woken with a raging hunger. I sipped my coffee and got out my running shoes. I go running on the weekends, especially if I've gone out to the bar. It helps clear my head, and I thought today I could go for an extra long run. Maybe a thought would pop into my head, and I'd have my answer for how to respond to Delia. Although, it was during a run I got the idea for my relationship ending articulation on love.

There was a knock on my door while I washed my breakfast dishes. I thought it was Feldman coming to prod me. Delia stood framed by the early sun. She looked tired, circles fringed under her eyes. Not dark, ugly circles, faint ones that hinted at worry or fear. Her arms hung at her sides. She stared at me, and I stared at the place her hand should be. The abbreviated limb ended in a stitched nub, instead of the hand, which was cooling in my refrigerator. She said a shallow hello, and I remembered to look at her face.

"You're here," I said.

"Yeah, I took a plane the day after I overnighted the package." She stepped inside the doorway. The sun crested behind her. It was dark in my house, and the dust-fattened light fused around her, through her brown hair that absorbed the sun. It was a moment you remember as it happens.

"Your hand."

She looked down at her wrist. "I didn't know any words for it."

I told her I was never actually sure how to say anything.

She nodded. Her eyes flicked down and shone wet. I decided she was happy.

"What?"

"You're grinning."

I hadn't noticed, but I couldn't stop. "You know you could have just come. You didn't have to, you know."

She smirked. "I've always been a little dramatic. Better to show than tell, and all."

"How did you?"

"A girl at a piercing shop did it. I didn't think I could do it, and her way was cleaner, professional. Some people are into strange stuff." She laughed and glanced down. "Happens all the time, right?"

She stepped forward and put her arms around me. Her face pressed against the cheek I'd put her unattached hand on. I felt where her hand should be on my back. She made a sound. I kissed her. I felt her warmth against me. One hand across my back, its fingers curled around my side. And the missing hand left an absence of pressure, like the relief of putting together something you've been trying to say.

Paul Brown

TWO RUSSIANS AND AN AMERICAN WALK INTO AN IRISH PUB

I CAN TELL YOU EXACTLY what Katya's thinking. She's thinking that life is a snowball's tumble down a precipitous mountainside that accumulates more unwieldy complications than you can stick a carrot into. I'm thinking of all the complications that arise from the habit of carrot sticking period, but Katya would not find my mental quip amusing. She stands in the snow with a rust-brown scarf coiled about her neck like a snake, a Dunhill cigarette between her fingers and at her lips. She wears a double-breasted, black wool coat, a plaid skirt that matches her scarf, black stockings and flats. Her curly auburn hair is ruffled. She looks out over the frozen pond in the distance, avoids eye contact, and takes quick, deep drags off her smoke. Married to other people, Katya and I are/were having an affair. Her husband, Dmitri, has found out about it. Katya called me at work to set up an emergency meeting. We've been on a couple of picnics here at the pond. It's lunchtime. It's biting cold out, so no one is around but the two of us and one old lady on the other side of the pond wrapped in a winter coat and feeding bread crumbs to a few scraggly looking ducks.

I want to give Katya my undivided attention. After all, this is a serious situation. But I work as an accountant, and accounting work can be quite dull, so I sometimes sneak a joint to make the mundane labor a bit more stimulating. No one drug tests accountants, and admittedly, I'm the only accountant I know that indulges. So, despite the urgency of the situation, I feel a little abstracted. I notice, for example, that the altocumulus clouds slashing across the blue sky over the pond resemble fish scales. I think about the Chinese invasion of Tibet. I think about affairs and why people have them. I come up with a pat assessment.

If you've never had an extramarital affair, then kudos. No, really, I mean that sincerely. However, you may be at least familiar with the urge to step outside. For men and women both, it's partly the thrill of a new lover, a forbidden lover, a lover who's still on his or her best, sexiest behavior, not the lover that sits on the can for an hour in the morning and forgets to shave and maws on a bowl of greasy potato chips while watching the same stupid television shows that you personally despise every Thursday night. The new lover always smells his or her best. The new lover grooms before every meeting. The new lover seldom complains about work or the kids unless they somehow interfere with your plans to meet up later. Substantial affairs are not drunken one night stands on some out of town trip. They allow you, sometimes compel you, to escape what can feel like a slow death.

Consider that we may experience a brief rush of freedom when we're teenagers and for maybe a decade thereafter while we take the reins and point our lives haphazardly into one or more directions. Pretty soon we realize, however, that we're no longer riding a glimmering white stallion and lashing it forward with the vigor of our hormonal and professional ambition and the curiosity of our minds and bodies; instead, one day we find ourselves sitting in a cart behind a haggard plow horse and nursing a bad case of hemorrhoids as old soap-bones pulls us along a road of ruts and potholes. In other words, less abstracted, less interesting words, life, for what it's worth, begins to take charge of us. Suddenly we're obliged. The script of who we are and what we do is written for us by circumstance. I'm not trying to justify my behavior. I'm just a little flummoxed, and I'm trying to tell you why I leapt off the wagon for a picnic with Katya who now detests me like you might detest inhaling spoiled cabbage. She thinks rightly that I may have cost her the deeper love, the firmer foundation, the steadier, plodding existence of the wagon that she's come to rely on, come to prioritize in the grander scheme. You risk it all when you step out. Everyone knows that. There are potentially severe consequences. I sympathize with Katya's plight to the point of nausea but remain selfishly grateful that Dmitri knows next to nothing about me and certainly does not know my wife.

"He wants to meet you."

"Excuse me?"

"Don't be a prick, Tom. He wants to meet you."

"No way in hell."

Katya is an incredibly sexy Russian. She has an accent. She's strong, aggressive, quick to pout, exotic, exciting. Her legs are curvaceous, her breasts pert, her stomach flat. She laughs loudly, also with an accent. She bites down a little too hard on your nipple before apologizing with a lick. Occasionally sweet as clove honey, she can be as obdurate as the gelid winter.

The trees around the pond are black and bare. The snow around the pond is fresh and white and undisturbed. Katya's pale cheeks have roses.

"Did he hit you?"

"It's the cold."

"It's not okay for him to hit you."

"Oh, shut up, Tom. Just shut up. It's not okay what I've done. What you've done. He wants to meet you."

"Why?"

"How the hell should I know? He just said that he needed to see you face to face."

"No way. I'm sorry that he found out, Katya, but a man does not meet with another man when that man knows that he's been sleeping with his wife."

"He won't shoot you."

"He'll just stab me to death?"

"He doesn't want to hurt you. He's very upset, Tom. He wants to know why."

"So, tell him why. Why did you sleep with me?"

"Because I was stupid."

"Thanks."

"You were stupid, too."

"Thanks."

"Are you stoned? You bastard, are you stoned?"

"I did it before you called."

"You son of bitch."

"I did it before…"

"It's all so easy when it's not your marriage. You don't care. It's not your world falling apart."

And it isn't. I'm thinking that I could still walk away. I could still get out of this. What did you expect me to think? I'm a first rate bastard, but I'm a first rate bastard with a wife and two kids that love me. I'd rather have my boys grow up without knowing just how much of a first rate bastard their father really is, and I'd rather that my wife still love me. I still love her, but perhaps only another bastard like myself would understand that.

"I'm sorry, Katya. I really am."

"I will tell your wife."

Katya never did beat around the bush. During our secret rendezvous, this aspect of her personality was something I appreciated. Always sex first. If there was time, and we were inclined, then sex later too. But always we would get right down to it. Then maybe after, we'd lie in bed and talk or visit the zoo or go for ice cream. Aside from sex—naughty, lustful, forbidden, passionate sex—we both needed a little romance. We went on dates. We saw a couple of movies together, across town, of course, where we couldn't possibly meet anyone either of us knew, someplace out of the way, a little run-down, with the soda-sticky floors and the stale popcorn and the auditorium-type metal chairs with the torn beige fabric that reminds you of the fabric that used to stretch across the front of your old man's stereo speakers.

"You wouldn't do that, Katya."

"Yes, I would."

"We promised we…"

"To hell with promises. I have to try and save my marriage, Tom. If I have to destroy yours to do it, I will."

"That's cold-blooded."

"You have to help me."

"If I could, I would. But I really don't see how sitting down with your husband over a cup of Joe at the local Starbucks is going to help matters."

"He wants resolution."

"Resolution my ass, Katya. He wants to beat the shit out of me. I can't blame him either, Katya. It's a lose-lose."

"Then let him."

"Excuse me?"

"Let him punch you in the face."

"I've got to get back to the office."

I turn to leave.

"Would you rather I tell your wife everything? Do you want your kids to know, too?"

"You fucking bitch."

"Yeah, so I'm bitch. What about you? You're no better than me."

How quickly people turn. We used to cuddle with and coo at one another. When we were "out of town on business" we used to lie in bed all day together in a four star hotel. She used to run her nails up and down my back for fifteen minutes at a stretch while I lay across the king sized mattress and drooled. I made her breakfast at a cabin we'd rent by the lake. We'd go on lovers' strolls together, take a rowboat out to Pelican Island, make love there on the strand. Well, you can be lustful, affectionate. You can play. But you can't pretend to be moral, to be good. There's no faith between the faithless. She'll destroy my life if she wants.

"Can't you figure out another way," I suggest. "Tell him I won't do it. What can he do? Tell him I'm scared. Tell him I'm a cheat and a coward and I disgust you. Tell him I'm not worth the effort."

Katya lights another Dunhill and takes another deep drag. She breaths smoke like a dragon. It's sexy the way she handles her cigarette. It's an extension of her personality. It's like a conductor's baton that communicates her emotions to an invisible orchestra—angry trombones, despairing violins, determined trumpets.

"You bastard..."

"Let me tell you a joke, Katya. Two Russians and an American walk into a bar."

"I'm American you asshole."

"Fine. Two naturalized but ethnically Russian immigrants and an American walk into an Irish pub. One naturalized Russian shoots the American dead while the other naturalized Russian watches in horror because she knows that not only is her former lover now dead on the floor, but her marriage is doubly destroyed because her husband will now spend his remaining years in prison. Ha ha."

Katya is both stubborn and impulsive, so it surprises me a little when she decides to consider my statement. Her right elbow is level with her breast, almost as if she were raising her hand to ask a question, but her palm is turned toward her. The sides of her pointer finger and middle finger pinch against the cigarette's filter. When she exhales, she blows the smoke out to the side as if she doesn't want it clouding her vision. Her other hand is on her cocked hip. She stares out over the pond in the distance to her right, but of course it's the type of stare that searches for nothing in particular in the scenery. There is no interaction with or curiosity about the stage props forming the background. It's just a place to point the eyes while the mind sorts through its dilemmas. I actually want to hug Katya. I want to reach out and pull her to me, to warm her, to comfort her. But it's obvious that cannot happen. We will never again hold each other close. We will never kiss. We may never talk again. It's sad really. It's like the day you leave summer camp for home, and the girl you met there goes home too to someplace far away. You'll exchange a letter or two and that will be the extent of it. I suppose these days you'd friend each other on Facebook and drag out a childhood summer crush until even the memory is tarnished beyond recognition, and it would all turn unbearably saccharine and yucky. Thankfully, though, when I was a kid, you lost track of people. People moved on. It was healthier that way. That's beside the point really, especially because I don't feel like a preteen at summer camp during the late seventies. I feel stoned, but beyond that, I feel depressed.

"Maybe he does want to punch you in the face, Tom. Maybe he does want to punch you. I don't know. But is that so bad? You walk away with a bruise on your cheek. I have to try and fix a ruined marriage. Would you rather try to explain to your wife why you cheated on her, would you rather spend years trying to regain her trust, would you rather look your guilt in the eye every morning and every night, or would you rather get punched in the face?"

I'd rather get punched in the face. There's no clean break here. And I think that maybe the best affairs really do occur out of town with a stranger one night in a hotel. I even think that perhaps affairs are not the way to go at all. You laugh. You've known this all along. You feel, rightly so, as though I'm getting no less than I deserve. In fact, I deserve worse. I know I do. We bring these things on ourselves when we hop out of a moving wagon. And to be fair, it's not like my wife is boring or frigid. It's the modern world that I blame. Over half my life is spent working. A third is spent sleeping. Much of the rest of it is spent caring for the kids, mowing the lawn, doing the dishes, driving to some store or other or watching television, maybe going out to eat occasionally. My affair is not my wife's fault. It's a weakness born of the battle we rage against routine. It's the joint that spikes another dull Friday night spent watching the same Disney movies for the umpteenth time in a row. And now we have to pay for it, and the price is too high. It's emotionally too high. I know exactly how miserably ruined Katya feels, how terrible, how dirty and self-loathing she feels. And I want to take full responsibility for being an asshole. But I'm a coward. People who have long term affairs are tinged by cowardice. Sneaks usually are. I go from missing Katya before she's gone to wishing I'd never met her.

"Give me one of those," I say.

She hands me a Dunhill and lights it. I haven't smoked in fifteen years. I cough a little, but it quickly passes. Like riding a bike. We share this moment together, Katya and I. We stare out at the snow and the blue sky with the clouds and the frozen pond and the black etchings of trees. And perhaps we are closer now than we've ever been. Prisoners to our collective guilt, our pain, our dread. We find each other physically repulsive. All the glamour and intrigue has disappeared, and we're now skeletal, bare, covered by the dirty tincture of our trespass. To think that we ever wanted to touch the other person at all, well, it leaves a bad taste in the mouth. Or maybe that's just the cigarette you're smoking, but you keep smoking it because self-destruction mollifies. The nicotine and the view is all the two of you have left to share, the only salve for the bloody pulp you've made of yourselves. You think, God this sucks. And God says, I told you so. And there's a strong urge to weep openly on your knees. And Katya steals a sideways glance at you. She's waiting. Commiseration is over. She's plotting now. Thinking about damage control. Thinking about how she wants to prove her loyalty to her husband, how she needs to bring her lover to him to be judged and punished, how she must make amends, how she can maybe make you the scapegoat. You see, Katya and I have selfishness in common. We reveled in our baser natures, and now we must turn on each other. It's inevitable. There was attraction. There was play. And now we must be willing to cut each other to pieces if necessary. We must fuck each other one last time. I meet her glare and feel her hatred. I briefly want to sleep with her again because she hates me. It's a rather twisted desire. It passes. She's a block of ice.

The 'ol lunch break is creeping past the hour. Duty calls. We will have to call duty and take a sick day.

I don't know if I decide to go to the ironically suggested O'Leary's pub across town because I think a punch in the face might bring some relief to my growing guilt, or if I'm worried that Katya will follow through on her threat to tell my wife, or if I feel that I owe her something, or if I am just a little too stoned to think clearly. It's probably an amalgamation of these that drives me to put myself at the mercy of a man I've made a cuckold. By the time we get to the bar, however, my marijuana buzz has mostly gone away. I order a glass of whisky immediately. The husband is en route. I inform work that I have to pick up a sick kid from school. Before Dmitri arrives, I manage to drink two Knob Creeks on the rocks and a Newcastle. I decide to switch to beer because I don't want to be too drunk. I don't want to swing back, for example. Katya has all but convinced me that if I take the hit, she and I can get out of this and move on with our real lives. I feel reassured by the fact that we are at least meeting in a public place and not in some back alley or on some deserted country lane. It still feels very clandestine, though, very spy vs. spy. The fact that Katya and Dmitri are both Russian creates the sensation that I am an undercover operative in the Cold War about to get my ass handed to me by the Kremlin. When Dmitri arrives, I am a little relieved. He's a small, balding man that stands at about 5'9". His muscles do not bulge. He has no discernible military tattoos or the like. He wears khakis and a tie. He's clearly coming from an office job himself. Between his mundane appearance and the drinks, I almost feel at ease except for the fact that Katya looks absolutely terrified.

"So, you are the man that has been fucking my wife?"

"I'm sorry."

"Sorry for what? She's a beautiful woman. She knows how to give it to you good, eehh."

I don't respond.

Dmitri turns to the bar across the room an orders a vodka, neat. He takes a seat.

"Katya tells me that you too are married."

"Yes."

"Does your wife not know how to give it to you good, huh? Tell me, does she not suck your wee wee?"

"Umm."

"Does she not like it like doggy style?"

"No, my wife is fine. It's…"

"If your wife is fine, Tom, then why do you fuck mine?"

"I don't know. It just happened. It was a terrible mistake. Katya and I both feel…"

"Don't you do that! Don't tell me how you and Katya feel."

The bartender drops off the vodka. Dmitri pauses to drink it and orders another.

"You fucking *cobaka*. You stupid dog. You do not know Katya. You cannot possibly know what is Katya, how she thinks, what she feels. Katya is ungrateful whore, and she needs to be reminded where she came from. But you know nothing about that."

"Katya's not a whore."

"Oh *REALLY*! Are you going to defend her honor, you pig? You going to tell her husband what is his cheating wife? You too are whore. You are piece of shit."

"Look, I'm sorry about all this. Believe me, I am…"

"Oh, he's sorry. That fixes it, ya? You're sorry about your little dog penis in my wife, ya?"

"I'm sorry. I don't know what else to say."

"It's okay. Enough talk."

Here it comes. Instinctively, I clinch my jaw. He's belittled Katya, berated me, and now the grand finale. I don't like feeling this way, and I don't like watching Katya, fearless and bold Katya, cowed and silent and stooped in her chair like a mouse in its hole, but despite his cruelty, Dmitri is justified. We have wronged him unconscionably. I know that I would feel much the same if it were my wife and another man. I experience an added shame, an oppressive wave of shame, because I can never be like Dmitri. I am irrevocably stained by my own guilt and can never again don the cuirass of righteous wrath. At best, I can take my punishment like a man.

"I want fifty thousand dollars."

"Excuse me?"

"For what? For fucking my wife? Fifty thousand dollars."

"I don't have fifty thousand dollars."

"My wife's a whore but she's expensive, no? Fifty thousand dollars, and we forget this. Clean slate."

"Hey, I'm sorry about having an affair and all, but I can't just give you…"

"Fifty thousand dollars or Katya here tells your wife everything. How much is your marriage worth?"

Son of a bitch. I stand before you abashed, ashamed. I stand before you a first rate bastard that deserves to be punished. You loyal wives and husbands, you dearly beloved and faithful, I realize you don't like me much. But fifty thousand dollars? That's a big chunk of cash. That could cover college tuition for the kids (almost). I could pay off the house with that (almost).

"Katya, you can't let him…"

"Shut up! Shut up. You never talk to my wife again, do you understand? Never speak to her again or I'll cut off your fucking testicles."

The bartender who drops off another vodka for Dmitri has clearly been listening to our conversation and looks at me like, *"Oooo, you're in deep shit, buddy. Mad Russian gonna mess you up bad, bro."* The bartender's probably mid to late twenties. He's clearly enjoying this. Can't wait to tell his pals what happened today at work. I want to smash his face in but impotently order another whisky instead. When you've been busted for cheating on your wife, when the woman's husband with whom you cheated is in the process of blackmailing you for fifty thousand dollars and has just threatened to remove your testicles, beer doesn't really seem sufficient. The bartender returns quickly and hands over the drink with a smile.

I take a big gulp. "My wife already knows about the affair. I told her about it months ago. She wasn't happy about it, but we've been having some problems. You know, we talked about it for a long time. It's a different century. We decided to try an open marriage. I haven't told Katya about it. I've kept things the way they were. It's just easier emotionally if my wife and I keep our affairs separate from our marriage. It's really..."

"That is bullshit," Katya snaps. "You've never told your wife nothing."

I just want to smack her across the face.

"Maybe the liar is telling the truth. Let's find out. Call his house."

Katya begins scrolling down her number list. I wonder what pseudonym she has my home phone under. I don't even recall when I gave it to her. I wonder why Dmitri isn't more enraged by this open display.

Katya hits the send button and holds her cell to her ear.

"Wait! Hang up the phone."

Kayta looks at Dmitri who gives her a slight nod. She hangs up. This is a lesson in marital psychology. The cheat is now fascistically loyal to the cheated. We're a table of mercenaries.

The honorable play here would be to confess my sins. But Heather, my wife, would not understand. She would not try and patch things up. She would take the kids and leave me. That's just the way it is. I crossed a line that I cannot uncross. I skittered over the Rubicon. She'll hand me divorce papers before the week is out after she makes sure to carve her initials into the sides of my classic Mustang convertible with a kitchen knife, set fire to my record collection, and throw the contents of the china cabinet at my face. My boys, being good boys, will side with their mother. I would henceforth be Dad, the bastard. I have to pay the man.

I finish the whisky.

"I have a classic car in the garage that I can sell for maybe eighteen thousand. I have about five thousand left in mutual funds and a few thousand in savings. I can maybe come up with thirty thousand if you give me time to sell the car."

Dmitri cracks a grin. "I want fifty thousand, Tom, or your wife finds out."

"I can't give you fifty thousand without her finding out anyway. Look, I'm going to have a hard enough time coming up with a reason for this as it is. I'd have to take her money too and sell the house and do God knows what else to get you the money you're asking for. Thirty thousand cleans me out to zero. After that, I can't, you understand? I can't."

Dmitri glares at me for a long minute. His eyes bore into my skull. Unless he knows Russian samba or something—and for the record, I wouldn't be surprised if he did—I could take Dmitri in a fight. If we were two boys in the schoolyard, he'd be outmatched. I have him by three or four inches and a good thirty pounds of muscle. Still, even though he's not the hulking mass of steroids that I feared he might be, he's got blue ice and razor blades behind his corneas. You get the sense that he's accustomed to suffering, that he's come close to starving to death in a gulag or that he's surmounted great rocky peaks in the Urals. You could take him once, but he'd keep coming at you. You'd be thinking, break his nose; he'd be thinking, slit your throat. There's a weakness to being too civilized, and you imagine that maybe you're too civilized to stay up nights wondering if and when a man was going to break into your home and shoot you dead. Dmitri holds up a finger and summons the bartender over.

"Another vodka for me, and another whisky for this man."

The bartender leaves and returns.

"Thirty thousand then. I guess I can accept thirty thousand, Tom. I will give you two weeks to sell your automobile and then we meet here again, eh? You bring the money in cash, we part ways, and you never see my wife or me again. Agreed?"

"Yes."

"Good. If you do not bring the money to me in two weeks, then you know what will happen."

"Yes."

"Good. We drink to it."

He downs his vodka, and I follow with my whisky.

"Good." He sets down his empty glass and stands up. "Katya."

They leave, and without having worked out the details, I know that Katya will call me in two weeks and that I better have the money.

I am close to drunk after all the drinks which is at once alarming and a relief. In an hour, I really won't be fit to drive. So, I settle up the tab which includes all the vodka drank by Dmitri and head home. It's terrible because Heather is just arriving at the house after picking the kids up from school, and I'm greeted by all three of them. I feign enthusiasm, hug the boys, and tell Heather a lie about a luncheon with some colleagues that turned into an afternoon off.

"Jesus, Tom. How much did you drink?"

"Well, it was one of the guy's birthdays, and another's kid just got a job and is moving out finally. You know how it is."

"Whose birthday is it? It's not Bob's or Kenny's."

"Shit, you know. It was a new guy. I mean, not a new guy. New to the group. It was a fella from the mail room. Bret or Burke or something."

"Well, okay."

"I'm just going to watch some TV. Hey, guess what?"

She fiddles with the front door lock. The boys are chattering loudly about something school related. The front door swings open. The kids run in. Heather seems annoyed.

"What?"

"I'm going to sell the old Mustang."

"You must be really drunk, Tom. You shouldn't have driven home."

"No, it's okay. I had a window."

"Why don't you turn on the television. I'll bring you some coffee."

And so it goes. Except, I tell her not to bother with the coffee and continue drinking beer. Heather's put out, but she keeps the boys busy. I watch some Charles Bronson movie and part of a game show and a couple innings of a Yankees game and part of an infomercial about a get rich quick scam selling crap online. But, of course, I don't pay much attention to any of it. Heather goes to bed around ten, and I stay up worrying about what I've done and what I have yet to do.

Being blackmailed galls like nothing else. Somebody has you by the balls and will start to squeeze and twist if you don't pay up. I didn't see this one coming. I mean, I don't know if I were in Dmitri's position exactly what I'd do, but profiting financially from my wife's infidelity seems, not that I'm one to talk here, but, I don't know, immoral? It's not exactly a conventional divorce settlement. I've gone and diddled on the dark side. What would normally be foul ball is suddenly fair game. I figure that I'll either have to pay him, find something to counter-blackmail him with, or murder him and Katya and dump their bodies in a lake. I could use the sleeping bags in the garage and fill them with rocks so their two bloated carcasses wouldn't float up to the surface. I'll keep them in the trunk and then motorboat out at night to the middle real quiet and dump them over the side. It'll take a few days to get the gun. After, I'll file off the serial number, run a needle file down the barrel and across the firing pin, disassemble the thing, and fling the different pieces in different directions across the water. Except, perhaps I'm not really a killer at heart. Furthermore, my conscience firmly believes I deserve to be punished. Finally, I'm not a religious man, but there's a lingering doubt regarding murderers and hell. Blackmail? I've got nothing on him. Plus, it'd have to be really big, considering. Nope. I'm a squirming worm on a hook.

On top of it all, now that it's over, I can't even stand to look my wife in the eye. When I run the scenario in my head of just how much it would hurt her, just how much she would despise me for being so awful to her, I start to tremble in the chair. I cry quietly. It's hard for me to believe just how much I love her. It's hard for me to believe just how awful I've been to her. I can't even explain it to myself, can't even really fathom my own behavior. WWI veterans were the first to coin the phrase and the very idea of being beside one's self. They claimed that lying in the trenches with the shells falling all around them and then leaping up for a deadly charge across No Man's Land divided the identity. There was an overwhelming sensation that they were two people, the one doing, and the one watching. Based on letters from the front and biographies and numerous documented accounts from V.A. hospitals, this feeling was quite common. The point is, I guess I just feel like there's the me that finally grasps what I've done and that other me that I want to shoot repeatedly with a carbine. When it was happening, it was like a fantasy. Now that it's real…

When I was in high school, my 11th grade English class read Tennyson's *Idylls of the King*, and I remember wondering why on earth Guinevere risked everything on a tourney knight when she was already married to the king and living in a castle. I was very flustered by this. She flees to a nunnery and whatnot and realizes at the end after Arthur forgives her that Arthur was always, had always been, the better man. She loved him then and wanted to be his wife in heaven. Well, I can relate to her now. It's like Cinderella, not the fairytale but the band: *"You don't know what you got till it's gone."* Or in my case, nearly gone.

You think of the woman who has stood by you through the long years, the one who has cared for you with her heart and soul, who has genuinely desired your happiness and has gotten your back time and time again. As the night wears on, you feel like such a worthless idiot, such a low down, no good, filthy little, petty little criminal. You flagrantly, foolishly risked the real thing for a side piece, and you kind of want to disembowel yourself with a short sword. But she doesn't know, and despite a near crippling urge to tell her everything, you realize that she can't know, that you are just going to have to try to live with yourself. So, you get drunk and stoned more often than usual, you buck up and bear guilt's anvil, you sell a classic automobile that you cherish at less than half of what's it worth, you say you're considering a risky investment, you liquidate the mutual funds, and you call the cell phone of a woman whose husband holds your balls in his angry, calloused hands and tell her that you've got the money.

O'Leary's. Midnight.

"So, Katya tells me you've got the money."

Dmitri and I sit alone at a corner table. Long shadows stretch across the floor. There's the smell of stale lager in the air.

"I do."

"Where is the cash?"

"I've got it here. It's a money order. Just as good."

"I said I want cash."

"But it's a money order."

"Fine. Like you say, just as good."

"So, it's settled then? We're square?"

"Sure. It's settled."

"Good. Um, one more thing."

"What?"

"I'm sorry, Dmitri. I'm truly sorry."

"Ha. Well, not all is bad. Katya and I have come to understanding. We may fix what is broken now."

"Good. I'm happy to hear that."

"Just remember one thing, Tom. Empathy is more stronger than sympathy."

"Right."

"Oh, and if you change your mind and come for the money, I will kill you and your family."

"Hey, there's no need for that."

"For your sake, I hope not. Good evening, Mr. Tom."

When Dmitri leaves, I stay and have one more beer. The deal's done, and I feel relieved. Shit, I even manage to laugh a little. I mean of all the bizarre situations to get yourself into. Dmitri is a real person, flesh and blood, skin and bone. Katya is a real person, soft lips and cold fingers. Yet, now that it's over, it all seems to have taken place in Minsk during the Reagan era. Right down to the threats and the seedy bar and the underhanded deals. Maybe I've had my taste of the fantasy, and it didn't turn out quite as expected. Maybe in addition to Guinevere, I can relate to Marx too. But I will go back to bean counting for wealthy capitalists and babysitting the hellions and be happy about it. I will focus on the joys of fatherhood. I will learn to once again be sexually invigorated by my wife. I will do penance by being a better husband.

The living room light shines through the window when I pull into the drive. I figure Heather is still up and worrying about me being out so late. I figure because I'm sober, she won't be particularly upset. I have an explanation prepared about the risky but potentially lucrative investment I'd told her about, that I'd been meeting with a guy in finance.

When I open the front door, Heather is waiting for me in the foyer. She is red-faced and angry, and she has been crying. The kids are up. They're on the couch in the living room and have also been crying. She sends them back to their beds.

"A woman named Katya called, Tom."

"Heather…"

"She said the two of you have been having an affair for the past eight months. She gave me dates and times and everything, Tom. It all adds up. You son of a bitch."

"Oh God, please forgive me, Heather."

"Forgive yourself, you bastard."

All the tears. All the pleading. All the begging for second chances and explaining how you learned your lesson and all the bargaining and the groveling, and you're left just where you knew you'd be. One random night, maybe—after much suffering. But eight months? No. You must go to hell and stay there. Heather takes the kids and the house, and I go to live in a cheap motel. I don't see the boys for a long time. I don't know what to say to them. I almost lose my job because of the drinking. I start smoking cigarettes again: Merits. One night when I am really drunk, I call Katya's cell phone. The number is no longer in service. I wonder if it hasn't all been a scam, if Katya and Dmitri, or whatever their real names are, haven't set me up to con me out of my money. But logic does not dictate this scenario. If that were their game, they would have kept taxing me for their silence as long as they could. No, Dmitri loves his wife and wanted his revenge. Well, he got it. My life is over, and I'm really fucking sad about it, and I know I deserve it, and I hate myself, and I have to try and live with myself. And my boys, Jason and Lee, will never feel the same about their daddy ever again. I keep a journal now because I'm the only one from my former existence, including my mother who loves Heather like the daughter she never had, that will still talk to me. I wouldn't talk to me either. Strangely, I begin patronizing the very same Irish pub where the deal went down. I guess it's like the criminal revisiting the scene of the crime. Whatever it is, I sit slumped in a chair at that same corner table every evening when I get off work. I begin reading Tolstoy. I recently started paying a therapist to make me a better person. I don't even believe in therapy.

Twenty Questions

Lewis Robinson

1) How has Maine informed your writing life? And how does place affect your work in general?

When I think about how Maine has informed my writing life I think about my teenage years in Yarmouth, my fearless friends, our interest in ritual (poker, athletics, cannabis), driving off road through the woods in our parents' cars, my fear of girls, the allure of bonfires and sandpits, always feeling like I was living on the periphery of the real action.

2) How did you come to be a writer?

I read a lot as a young kid. In high school I started scribbling stories—little episodes without much shape. In college I had two teachers (Jay Parini and David Bain) who encouraged me to stick with it. What a huge boon to get permission from them to keep my head down and practice. After college it helped that my parents didn't mind that I spent years driving a moving truck.

3) What are your biggest roadblocks as a writer?

During a given week: staying up late, getting up early with my kids, feeling brain dead and soulless and sitting down in front of pages I've recently written and not liking them. I'm glad that I've been writing long enough, now, to know that those periods of discouragement are usually followed by something better.

4) Who are your writing heroes?

I like knowing that John Cheever would put on a coat and tie in the morning, ride the elevator to the basement of his apartment building (the businessmen would get out on the ground floor) and with his whiskey and cigarettes spin those amazing stories. Nicholson Baker is another hero. I love his books, his idiosyncratic and humane voice. Also: Elizabeth Bishop, Arda Collins, Aaron McCollough.

5) What are you working on now, and how did you get there?

I'm working on a novel told from four alternating points of view, set primarily in Portland, featuring the smuggling of mountain lions, adultery, regret, redemption, gambling, and public indecency.

6) How do you work—please let us know something of your writing life and discipline.

I write between breakfast and lunch. I've been writing for the last two years in a windowless room in the basement of a library. A hot thermos of coffee and a good desk lamp make up for the lack of sunlight.

7) How do your characters speak to you? Or not? Is it a process of engagement with yourself or with extraneous voices?

My characters don't speak to me. My preferred situation is to string together many consecutive days of uninterrupted work, so that the world I'm creating starts to feel tangible. In other words, I try to enter the world of my characters. I don't want them popping up into mine! That would be scary, in my opinion.

8) How much do politics and/or personal/cultural identity weigh for you in terms of your writing?

More and more. I used to be stubborn about not wanting to consider my writing—or any good writing—political. But I know better now. It's all highly political, but the obviousness of the angles will vary.

Do you aim to create a greater message in the body of your work? And, do you think your separate works create their own overall narrative arc?

I don't aim to create a greater message, no. As a reader, if I get a whiff of "Message," I'm usually annoyed. I like lower-case messages: i.e., here are situations and details that are of interest because they are sad and/or funny. As for an "overall narrative arc," how badass would that be? In my case, though, it seems unlikely.

9) How much impact does your childhood, or personal life, have on your writing? Generally speaking, does your work live in the present, past or future? Most often

I draw upon images and emotional scenarios from the past.

10) Writers are often encouraged to "kill their darlings," as the saying goes. Does this come easily? Do you enjoy it?

The darlings I kill deserve their fate, so I don't sweat it too much. I've set aside hundreds of pages that will never see the light of day, thank god.

11) Are you jealous of other writers/how do you feel when you read a bad review/ why do you think what you do matters/who do you think you are?

Unfortunately/pissed/why not/gentleman farmer.

12) How does humor play in, in terms of your writing? What would your alter-ego writer's name be? Or: tell a joke!

How did the hipster burn his tongue? He took a bite of pizza WAY before it was cool.

13) If you could snap your fingers and everything would suddenly be absolutely perfect (buy the ticket and take the ride here…just imagine this is possible) what would be perfection for you?

I'd like to have an island in Casco Bay at my disposal, where my family and I could host weekly pig roasts with all of our friends, and somehow pull this off without killing a pig every week. In the winter I'd play for the Celtics.

14) Which metaphor do you most often use to talk about writing craft (as in food-making, music, etc.) and why? And, how important is metaphor in your work? Symbolism?

Architecture and wizardry. Metaphor: yes. Symbolism: no.

15) It's commonly said that writing is re-writing. How do you edit? How many readers of your own work do you have— and If you feel like telling us, who are they?

I edit while I'm writing the first draft but I also edit—much more—when I'm done. Key readers for me are Curtis Sittenfeld, Aaron McCollough, Alix Ohlin, Theo Emery (a high-school friend who is a journalist), and my wife CC.

16) E. M. Forster famously said, "How do I know what I think until I see what I say?" When you aren't able to write for some reason, what happens to you? And, are there other art forms in which you work?

When I don't write I usually feel great for a day or two and then I start to be a royal asshole.

17) Do you enjoy writing or is it simply something you must do? Is there some other occupation you'd rather have besides being a writer?

All in all, I love writing. It's grueling sometimes, but come on, seriously—drinking coffee and dreaming up stories? I'll take it! Other occupations that would be a good fit for me: bassist for Radiohead, shooting guard for the Celtics, or Vice-President of the United States.

18) Do you have anyone you'd like to thank in particular for a writing success? And is there anything you'd like to say to your readers?

When I was living in Brooklyn in my twenties, I wrote stories that I never sent out and drove an art-moving truck for money. My mom kept harping about how I should go to grad school. I ignored her for a while but finally, I listened to her. Obviously, getting an MFA is not for everyone, but for me, it was huge. It gave me two years to see what it was like to spend the day writing and reading, and group of peers to obsess with. I would also like to thank Jane Lindholm, Vermont Public Radio host, the only person who ever introduced me at a reading by praising my basketball skills. She was quite specific and effusive, and for that, I will always be in her debt.

19) What advice you have to give to fellow writers?

A while ago I read an interview with Richard Ford, who avowed the value of putting one's nose to the grindstone, but he also said it was okay to take the occasional break to watch SportsCenter. (I'm paraphrasing.) I continue to cherish that advice, and hereby pass it on.

20) What question have you always wanted to be asked in an interview?

I'll go with a question that was asked of me earlier in this interview: "who do you think you are?"

Patrick Quinlan

Twenty Questions

1) How has Maine informed your writing life? And how does place affect your work in general?

I moved to Portland, Maine for the first time nearly a decade ago. I came up from New York City with my young wife, now ex-wife. She was black. I was white. I was young, but I felt old. I'd written a couple of novel manuscripts before then, but hadn't gotten a publishing deal. I had basically given up on writing. I had an awesome literary agent, who is my agent to this day.

One day my agent called me. He said: "What are you doing?"

I said: "I don't know. Living in Maine. Working. Doing whatever."

He said: "Do you have any ideas?"

I said: "Yeah. Maybe I have one."

"Then write it. I think you're a great writer. What's the harm?"

So I wrote a story about an old white guy from New York, way past his prime, living in Portland, Maine. He's dating a young, energetic black woman. Turns out the guy is an explosives expert, who used to work for the mob. He killed a Mafia don and stole $2.5 million dollars. He changed his identity and is actually hiding out in Maine. The mob finds out where he is, and sends up a team of thugs to collect him.

It seems to me that I wrote that book in less than three months during the spring and summer of 2004. I was really wired at that time. Generally speaking, summers in Maine are fantastic in every way, and many times I have felt very alive during Maine summers. But they're also very brief. So I was writing that book, and was on my bike every day, and was ocean swimming a lot off of Willard Beach in South Portland and Fort Williams in Cape Elizabeth. Just raring to rip because the summer is here and gone, and there's no time to lose before it gets cold and dark again.

The book was called SMOKED. Two weeks after I sent it to my agent, we had a deal in the United States. A few weeks later, we had a worldwide deal. And the deals just kept coming. Translations. Film options. Deals for more books. It was a heady time. And I think part of what people liked about the book was the Maine setting, somewhat unusual for a thriller. And I think what drove the writing was just the sense of someone being a newbie in a new place, and the energy and "get it all in now" fire of a Maine summer.

Usually I tell people that place has nothing to do with my writing. That if I just stare at a blank wall long enough, the images start to come. Maybe now I'll have to rethink that.

2) How did you come to be a writer?

I was a freshman in college, and I had a Composition 101 class with a sexy woman professor from England. She was probably 35. Her husband was away a lot, for whatever reason. And I had no idea what I was going to do. I didn't expect to live very long, actually. I was in college on a scholarship, and I figured I would just drop out sooner or later. Who cares? Most of the kids there were from another planet. Or I was. They were all going to be something good and wonderful. Their mommies and daddies said so. I was going to be a skid row bum.

But I was a good looking kid. It was the only thing I had going for me. I had hair halfway down my back, and I used to work physical, grunt-labor jobs, so I was in good shape. And everybody, man, woman and beast, used to try to get a piece of me. They said I was like Jim Morrison, or the guy from INXS. This isn't me telling stories. It's just how it was. It's been 20+ years, and I'm ugly now, so there you go.

And this Comp 101 professor wanted to take me home. She kept inviting me to her house, saying things like, "Well, my husband is away in Europe this week."

And maybe to soften me up, or groom me, or whatever, she would say things like, "I think you're a wonderful writer. That 50-word essay you wrote about the clock ticking, and time lapsing away? It was brilliant. Let's have dinner and drinks at my house and we'll talk about writing."

I was a kid. I didn't know shit about writing. Except this nice woman said I was good at it. For some reason, I took that to heart.

3) What are your biggest roadblocks as a writer?

I am, in all ways, the biggest roadblock to achieving my desires, regardless of the field of endeavor.

4) Who are your writing heroes?

These: Ernest Hemingway (The Old Man & The Sea), F. Scott Fitzgerald (The Great Gatsby), Norman Mailer (Tough Guys Don't Dance and An American Dream), Alice Walker (The Color Purple and some of her poems), Carolyn Chute (The Beans of Egypt, Maine and Snowman), Graham Greene (Our Man in Havana and The Quiet American), Elmore Leonard (too many good ones to mention), James Ellroy (L.A. Confidential and American Tabloid), Charles Bukowski (too many), Stephen King (too many), Dean Koontz (too many).

Non-fiction, I have really liked self-help authors like Martin Seligman (Learned Optimism), Deepak Chopra (7 Spiritual Laws of Success) and Stephen Covey, who just died (7 Habits of Highly Effective People). Some people hate self-help books, or look down on it. Not me. I've read a couple hundred self-help books. Listen, you're born, you get kicked out of the nest, and nobody explains any of this shit to you. You're like one of these newborn seagulls running frantically around the streets of Portland, can't fly, getting run over by cars. How great is it that you can get a library card for free, and here are people telling you, in books, how it all works? Pretty great.

Among non-writers, I once had pretty serious man-crushes going, on Muhammad Ali ("I ain't got no quarrel with them Viet Cong. No Viet Cong ever called me nigger.") and John Brown (raid on Harpers Ferry, instigator of the Civil War).

5) What are you working on now, and how did you get there?

I am finishing up a novel called Demons Among Us. It is the story of Jessie James, an 11-year-old girl who is psychic. She comes to believe that another little girl is trapped behind a cinderblock wall in the basement of an abandoned hospital near where she lives. One day she goes there and discovers a large man looking at the very same wall. Now, one of the ways Jessie is psychic is if she touches you, she can know nearly everything about you. When she touches this man, she finds out he is a serial killer of children. Worse, he isn't a man at all—he's a demon from an alternate reality, and the cinderblock wall is a doorway between worlds. The way he passes from one world to the next is by spilling the blood of an innocent.

I ended up working on the book like this: In 2008, my wife and I split up. At the time, I was contractually obligated to finish a book, a novel called The Hit. Which I did. I thought it came out pretty good. After that, I was toast. It was 2009. My marriage was over, and I had written five books in less than five years. I had some money left, so I did nothing for about a year. I sat on the couch, drank beer, and watched professional sports on TV. I gained about 30 pounds.

Suddenly it was 2010.

I decided I wasn't going to write novels anymore. I probably wasn't going to write anything anymore, but if I did, it would only be short stories about my childhood. So I started writing this short story about how when I was a kid, there was this abandoned mental hospital near my house. They had closed many of the mental hospitals in the 1970s, and years later this one was just sitting there, mostly empty, but with a lot of stuff, like beds and equipment and furniture, still inside. The place was broken open, and my friends and I used to go in there and wander around. Over time, I became a girl named Jessie James, and that story became Demons Among Us.

Oh, and then I started exercising four or five times a week, and I lost all the weight I gained.

6) How do you work—please let us know something of your writing life and discipline.

Generally speaking, I often go for months without writing. When I am writing, I work from about 11pm or midnight until dawn, and sometimes well past dawn, like 9 or 10am. It's very hard for me to get started, but once I get into a groove, I write pretty much every night. The hours fly by, and I barely notice. Like, I sit down at the computer and then four hours have passed. So I get up, take a leak, and make a cup of tea. Then I sit down again. When I look up, it's day time and people are out making noise, driving cars, going to work. So I go to bed. I draw the shades, put earplugs in, and pull a hat over my eyes. Otherwise it can be hard to sleep.

A lot of times, I only sleep for a few hours. Then I get up and do daytime-type stuff, often in a sort of fugue state. At night, I get some energy going and start to write again.

I write on a computer with no internet access. In the old days of wireless cards, I used to take the wireless card out of my computer and put it downstairs or in another room. Nowadays, I have one computer with internet access, and one that I've disabled its networking capacity. I use the disabled computer for writing. It's more or less a fancy typewriter at this point. I can't write on a computer with internet access. Too many opportunities for distraction and time wasting.

My agent recently suggested that I use voice recognition software to speed up my writing process and gain more direct access to my subconscious. I have toyed around with this, without success. But check in with me a year from now, and I may tell you that I just dictated an entire book to my computer.

7) How do your characters speak to you? Or not? Is it a process of engagement with yourself or with extraneous voices?

I basically stare at a blank wall. After a while, a story starts to unfold and it's like I'm watching it happen. Then I start writing it down. Typing it. I'm watching and typing, but eventually I don't realize I'm typing anymore. So it seems to me like I'm just watching, but at the end I have all this material I've written.

Of course, what I've written is pretty bad, so I have to edit. But even the re-writes are often like I'm just watching the story, and fixing the wording as it goes by.

I am one of the main characters in every novel I've written so far. In that sense, I suspect I may be trying to tell myself something. Maybe: "Don't worry, kid. You're okay. Everything is gonna be okay."

8) How much do politics and/or personal/cultural identity weigh for you in terms of your writing? Do you aim to create a greater message in the body of your work? And, do you think your separate works create their own overall narrative arc?

I was very involved in Green politics for a long time. I identify myself as working class, and I identify strongly with working class people. If Bruce Springsteen singing "Youngstown" or "This Land is Your Land," comes on the radio, I might have to pull the car over for a good cry.

I believe that this comes through in my writing.

That said, when I first started publishing books, and my books thus far are basically pulp-fiction style thrillers, some people who knew me would say, "This is it? This is what YOU wrote?"

I believe that people read thrillers primarily to be entertained. As such, I aim to provide as much entertainment value as I possibly can for my readers. My books also tend to be morality tales in which people who do bad things eventually reap the consequences of their actions.

The most overtly political book I've written is called The Hit. It's set against the backdrop of financial and societal collapse. In the ensuing confusion, a very rich man has hired some bad actors to carry out a bio-terror attack against the impoverished inhabitants of a Caribbean island. I'd say that premise accurately sums up my perspective of how things work in the real world.

9) How much impact does your childhood, or personal life, have on your writing? Generally speaking, does your work live in the present, past or future?

My father was a serious alcoholic, and not a cheerful one. When I was a child, everyday life was like welcome to the terror dome. So I got accustomed to high adrenaline situations. As life went on, I did many, many, many crazy things. The kids that were crazier than me are dead now. So when I started writing, I naturally gravitated toward pedal-to-the-metal, action-oriented, suspense thrillers.

I've traveled quite a bit, and nearly all of the settings in my novels are places I've been. I witnessed or participated in a fair amount of violence as a young person, and much of the violence in my books is at least partially based on that. Many of the characters are partially based on people I've met or known. At least some of the events in my books are exaggerated or idealized versions of events I participated in.

The paranoid, they're-coming-to-get-you feeling in my novels is how I feel most of the time.

Come to think of it, I don't really have much of an imagination.

10) Writers are often encouraged to "kill their darlings," as the saying goes. Does this come easily? Do you enjoy it?

I've heard it as "Kill your babies," but no matter.

I sold my first short story when I was 21. I started writing regularly for pay when I was 23. Copywriting, magazine writing, grant writing. You learn pretty quickly that the editors or clients are going to kill your babies, and that it can improve the writing a lot. In that sense, I don't mind it. I write a lot of dumb things that on second look, really need to go.

11) Are you jealous of other writers/how do you feel when you read a bad review/ why do you think what you do matters/who do you think you are?

Most of the writers I've known are pretty seriously impaired, often in numerous ways. It's hard to be jealous of them. Usually I feel a certain empathy toward their plight, which is they are trapped inside a burning inferno, or conversely, are alone on the dark side of a cold, far distant planet. When things go their way, I tend to feel good about it, especially considering how unforgiving the publishing industry is.

I used to get pissed off at bad reviews. Now I enjoy them. I'd rather get a really bad review, especially if it's funny, than a middling review.

I don't think that what I do, or what you do, or what anybody does, matters all that much. Generally speaking, the human race are a howling pack of somewhat clever monkeys, myself included. It would be a mistake to get very excited about our wondrous achievements.

I think it's important to be gentle and kind to others as much as circumstances will allow, but beyond that...

12) How does humor play in, in terms of your writing? What would your alter-ego writer's name be? Or: tell us a joke!

I can never remember the whole joke, but I often do remember the punch line. With that in mind, here are a few:

"Yeah, and deep, too."

"Nun."

"My son's a doctah."

"Thirteen. One to hold the light bulb, and twelve to turn the house."

"You forgot the coffee!"

13) If you could snap your fingers and everything would suddenly be absolutely perfect (buy the ticket and take the ride here…just imagine this is possible) what would be perfection for you?

Kelly Slater and I are surfing at Pipeline on the North Shore of Oahu, and we're getting tubed like crazy. When we come in, Kelly's like, "Dude, that was some gnarly set, but you were really killing it out there." So he buys me a beer at this beachfront bar, and suddenly we're catapulted back in time to July, 1976, in London, England. We're in the crowd at a Ramones show with the Sex Pistols and the Clash, and I'm like, "I'm from New York. I know these guys." So I bring everybody back stage with me, and then it's just me, Kelly Slater, the Ramones, the Sex Pistols, and the Clash hanging out, but we're in Los Angeles, and we're all rolling down the street in this huge gold Plymouth Satellite low-rider convertible from the early 1970s. Except now, in addition to me, and Kelly, and the various punk bands, Dr. Dre is driving and Snoop Dogg is chilling in the shotgun seat, and there's no traffic anywhere, and we've got all these chicks in bikinis in the car with us, not to mention Joan Jett and the Runaways (it's a big car), and the song on the radio is "Let Me Ride."

14) Which metaphor do you most often use to talk about writing craft (as in food-making, music, etc.) and why? And, how important is metaphor in your work? Symbolism?

I can only remember using one metaphor in relation to writing. Sometimes I've talked about the difference between writing for pleasure and writing for money, and compared it to the difference between gardening and farming.

I wrote a book called "The Takedown," or as an e-book, "The Falling Man." In that book, my secret point was that the main character, Dick Miller, who is trying to get rid of the dead body of his ex-girlfriend, has actually died and gone to hell, but doesn't know it. In the book, hell is New York City. That's the only time I've made extensive use of symbolism or metaphor, and it's very subtle. In fact, so subtle that no one got it.

15) It's commonly said that writing is re-writing. How do you edit? How many readers of your own work do you have— and If you feel like telling us, who are they?

Once I have an entire novel draft in hand, I start over at page 1 and go through the whole thing, cutting out huge chunks of it, and rewriting huge chunks of it. I cut and paste entire sections and put them somewhere else. I add entire sections and new characters. Once that's done, I start over at page 1 and go through the whole thing again. Once I finish doing that, I start over at page 1 and go through the whole thing. Each time I do it, it goes faster and I make less changes.

Eventually, I start giving it to people. My friend Brian Dunleavy is a writer and editor in New York and has read and edited early drafts of every novel I've written. He generally gets it first. But various other people, maybe as many as a dozen over the years, have also read my novel drafts. Sooner or later, but usually later, I show it to my agent. I want to give him something that I think is very close to done. Often he's got some ideas for me, and I incorporate those. It's a long process.

16) E. M. Forster famously said, "How do I know what I think until I see what I say?" When you aren't able to write for some reason, what happens to you? And, are there other art forms in which you work?

I go long periods of time without writing, and so far nothing has happened to me.

I play the guitar a little, and from time to time, I've written songs. In fact, at one point, I did an experiment, which was for several months I tried to sell some songs I wrote and recorded. That was hard, but I did get some personal feedback, generally negative, from a couple of producers. In one case, I was pitching one of my songs, and I'd had a very talented singer perform it for the recording. And a producer wrote me a letter, saying, "I really like this singer, but you have to get her some better material."

17) Do you enjoy writing or is it simply something you must do? Is there some other occupation you'd rather have besides being a writer?

I have enjoyed writing immensely. Not always, but certainly at times. I feel privileged and grateful that I have had some moderate success at it.

I have worked on numerous political campaigns, and have enjoyed that kind of work. I think I will get back to it at some point.

I sometimes feel like I would like to invent something, but I have no idea what. I have less than zero mechanical or engineering ability.

I have done quite a bit of public speaking, and have enjoyed that.

I have organized events, and enjoyed that kind of work. In fact, I wouldn't mind being some kind of festival organizer or promoter, if only once.

I would like to start a website where creative people can get together, and smash ideas off one another, and come up with weird and wonderful solutions to the world's problems. I might even call it CleverMonkeys.com. If you have any thoughts, let me know.

18) Do you have anyone you'd like to thank in particular for a writing success? And is there anything you'd like to say to your readers?

There is no doubt in my mind that none of this would have taken place without the help and guidance and persistence of my literary agent. However, he doesn't like people throwing his name around, so I will refrain from mentioning it here. I love you all very much.

19) What advice you have to give to fellow writers?

Get out of that chair! Hit the weights at least three times a week. Don't injure yourself, nothing too heavy, just light weights. Start your workouts with squats to get the blood pumping and the fat burning, then move on to the smaller muscle groups. Also, cardio two or three times a week. Not too much. Most of the benefits come in the first 20 minutes. Fruits and vegetables, five to ten servings a day. A little red wine. Garlic. Dark chocolate. Green tea. Watch a couple of funny YouTube videos every day. Now you're all set.

20) What question have you always wanted to be asked in an interview?

I have never once thought about this. I can't even seem to make something up.

Elizabeth Miles

Twenty Questions

1) How has Maine informed your writing life? And how does place affect your work in general?

I moved to Maine about six and a half years ago; I have been more creative here than anywhere else I've lived. I co-founded a theater company. I fell in love with a Mainer. I've walked in so many woods and swam in lakes and trudged through snow and all of that shows up in my books. I feel comfortable here, and my horizons expanded as a result.

2) How did you come to be a writer?

My parents were both New York City educators and encouraged my early love for reading and writing. I am an only child, and books were my best friends. Writing was and is an natural extension of my affinity for reading.

3) What are your biggest roadblocks as a writer?

Self-confidence and time-management. I think my lack of the former leads to my issues with the latter. It takes me a while to get going sometimes.

4) Who are your writing heroes?

There are so many. I gobble up everything Anne Carson does. I think Rebecca Solnit is brilliant and thoughtful. One of my journalism peers, Chris Faraone—he has such incredible energy and seems to be one of the most productive writers of all time. Colin Woodard is a fantastic reporter and writer. Stephen King, of course, is an inspiration. And there are many young adult authors I admire, including Lauren Oliver (who was instrumental in my fiction-writing career), Leila Sales (one of the funniest YA writers around), and Moira Young (whose *Dustlands Trilogy* is *awesome*).

5) What are you working on now, and how did you get there?

I am promoting *Eternity*, the third (and final) book of the Fury series, which came out in September, 2013. I'm also working on a new young adult fiction idea—a standalone, contemporary novel. I'm about eight chapters in and really enjoying it so far. And I am working at my day job. This might be a good time to segue into the whole "pen name" thing. I don't want things to get too complicated here! But yes, Elizabeth Miles is a pen name, which I adopted for a variety of reasons, mostly because I also write full-time for a newspaper. I didn't want those two worlds to get mixed up.

How did I get here...Well, there I was, happily working in the world of journalism, when my close childhood friend (and successful YA author) Lauren Oliver decided to launch a boutique literary development agency called Paper Lantern Lit. She wondered whether or not I wanted to submit a writing sample. I did so—mostly on a whim—and here I am now! PLL works with unpublished writers, guiding them from the "raw talent" phase through plotting, outlining, drafting, and ultimately selling a novel. The Fury series sold to Simon Pulse as a trilogy in June 2010, less than six months after we started working on the book.

6) How do you work—please let us know something of your writing life and discipline.

Well, I spend most weekdays standing up at my desk in downtown Portland. Writing news articles and the like. Reading blogs and other newspapers and interviewing people and doing research. Then I *try* to work on the books approximately three to four additional nights/weekend days per week. It all amounts to about twelve fiction-writing hours, or two chapters, per week, with more of a push when I'm close to deadline. I also have a standing desk at home. I cannot listen to music with lyrics when I'm writing. I am a journalist by training, and therefore very deadline driven.

7) How do your characters speak to you? Or not? Is it a process of engagement with yourself or with extraneous voices?

My characters do not speak to me. I can envision them clearly, I can hear their voices, but they're never speaking TO me. I wonder sometimes if that will ever happen—or if the fact that they don't reflects poorly on me as a crafter of worlds... Never mind. I'm just going to leave it at that.

8) How much do politics and/or personal/cultural identity weigh for you in terms of your writing?

Very much so at my day job, obviously, where I've worked to hone a writing voice that is informed, personal (and personable), and authoritative. In terms of the books, I hope that the issues and themes of the series are relevant to today's teenagers. I believe that they are. Questions of bullying, revenge, forgiveness, and love—they're all things I want to address because I care about them, and because I've pondered them myself.

9) Do you aim to create a greater message in the body of your work? And, do you think your separate works create their own overall narrative arc?

I don't think I want to convey any specific messages. I hope that my readers are entertained, and that what I write makes them think. That's all.

(Of course when it comes to the series there is an overall narrative arc, but I hope that's evident!)

10) How much impact does your childhood, or personal life, have on your writing? Generally speaking, does your work live in the present, past or future?

A lot. I write for teens and young adults, and I mine my own experiences extensively to make sure I'm staying honest and real. I've always been very emotional and sensitive and that comes out a lot in my characterizations, especially the females, but the males too. I am a person who is in love with love, and has had very intense romantic relationships and that certainly has informed my characters' interactions. I would say that my work lives in the present and the past—I'm more interested in processing what has happened and what is happening than in speculating about what might happen.

11) Writers are often encouraged to "kill their darlings," as the saying goes. Does this come easily? Do you enjoy it?

Because of my background in journalism, I am very used to the editing process—I go through it week after week! I enjoy the collaborative nature of the revision phase, where editor and writer put their heads together to make the story better. There have only been one or two passages that I was truly bummed to cut...and those (at least the ideas behind them) will probably show up somewhere else someday.

12) Are you jealous of other writers/how do you feel when you read a bad review/ why do you think what you do matters/who do you think you are?

Oh god, this question...Yes. Yes to all of it! I am jealous of other writers. I feel terrible when I read a bad review (Have you ever been on Goodreads? That place is toxic for authors.). Who DO I think I am???

13) How does humor play in, in terms of your writing? What would your alter-ego writer's name be? Or: tell us a joke!

My alter-ego already has a name! You're talking to her! And let me tell you: having two names is very weird sometimes. Are you confused now?

14) If you could snap your fingers and everything would suddenly be absolutely perfect (buy the ticket and take the ride here…just imagine this is possible) what would be perfection for you?

Other than world peace and income equality and healthcare for all and gender equity? My idea of perfection is quiet, surrounded by nature, reading a book, fire in the fireplace, my love nearby, the smell of something cooking in the kitchen.

15) Which metaphor do you most often use to talk about writing craft (as in food-making, music, etc.) and why? And, how important is metaphor in your work? Symbolism?

My husband is a carpenter; he makes beautiful furniture and cabinetry and the like. In some ways my work is very similar to his. We absorb stylistic influences and then work with others to shape ideas, to make a framework into which we can pour our creativity. We take great pride in the craft of it—in clean lines, clean prose, the ability to imbue something for public consumption with our personal sensibilities.

Metaphor is extremely important in my fiction writing. There are lots of emotions and experiences that are difficult for teenagers (and adults, let's be honest) to fully articulate, and metaphor often allows my characters to more deeply explore a scary, uncomfortable feeling. Also, Fury is a very frightening read, and there are only so many ways to describe fear—I had to come up with creative ways to do so, and that often involved metaphor.

16) It's commonly said that writing is re-writing. How do you edit? How many readers of your own work do you have— and If you feel like telling us, who are they?

I edit in chunks. I'll write a few chapters, edit them, and then move forward to the next bunch. Then once I have a complete manuscript I'll go back through it a couple of times, doing more editing. Like I said, I truly enjoy this part of the process. There are two fantastic women (young adult author Lauren Oliver and Stonecoast MFA grad Lexa Hillyer, who co-founded Paper Lantern Lit) who read all of my material before its passed on to my editor at Simon Pulse. Their input is invaluable; I really trust them both.

17) E. M. Forster famously said, "How do I know what I think until I see what I say?" When you aren't able to write for some reason, what happens to you? And, are there other art forms in which you work?

I love that quotation. I definitely process a lot of my thoughts through writing, whether it be by email, in my non-fiction work, in fiction, or even sometimes by text message. I also love theater. I think there's a great overlap between theater and fiction writing. Many of the characters in the Fury series were developed at least in part by asking myself the same questions I'd ask if I was cast in that role on stage.

18) Do you enjoy writing or is it simply something you must do? Is there some other occupation you'd rather have besides being a writer?

I cannot imagine making a living by doing something other than writing. I guess that means it is something I simply must do? It is the only thing that I know I am good at, other than, like, loving cats. I know I am good at that too. I would also love to be a Broadway musical theater star, but that ship has clearly sailed.

19) Do you have anyone you'd like to thank in particular for a writing success? And is there anything you'd like to say to your readers?

I would like to thank Lauren and Lexa, who I mentioned earlier. I'd like to thank my new husband Keagan, for being incredibly loving and patient with me (even when I'm acting bananas, because, well, writers do sometimes). I'd like to thank my fantastic friends who have been so supportive through the publication process. I'd like to thank my cats, Ender and Bean, who cannot read or understand anything I say to them. I'd like to thank the broad and enthusiastic community of YA book bloggers who offer huge support and encouragement to me and many of my author friends. And of course I'd like to thank my readers for being engaged, thoughtful, and honest.

20) What advice do you have to give to fellow writers?

It's difficult to come up with answers that haven't been said a million times (read a lot, write a lot, etc.). I suppose one thing that really helps me, and that I think might help others, is taking care of myself physically. I know there's a romantic notion of the author hunched in a garret, smoking cigarettes and drinking whiskey. At least I used to romanticize that image. But I tossed that out a while ago. It just doesn't work for me. I'm a better thinker and a more productive writer when I'm well-rested, well-exercised, breathing well, and in touch with my body. When I'm taking the right steps to manage my various psychological impediments. This isn't to say that I don't inhale Ben & Jerry's when I'm on deadline (I do) or that I run five miles every day (I don't). But I just know that I have to be a whole person in order to do the kind of work I'm proud of.

21) What question have you always wanted to be asked in an interview?

What is your favorite type of pie? The answer is strawberry-rhubarb.

BIOGRAPHIES

JACOB M. APPEL, MD, JD, is a physician and bioethicist based in New York City. He is a graduate of the MFA program in creative writing at NYU and currently teaches at the Gotham Writers' Workshop. His most recent publication is a collection of short stories entitled *Scouting for the Reaper*.

LESLIE ANDERSON is a writer and communications strategist in Arlington, Virginia, where she lives with her husband, girl-children, Brittany spaniels, a hermit crab, and 80,000 honeybees. She was most recently a finalist in the *Washington Post* @Work Advice Contest. Anderson received an MFA in creative writing from Columbia University and has previously taught writing in Barnard's Pre-College Program and Central Texas College. She is currently and interminably working on a novel.

ROBYN ART grew up in Lincoln, Massachusetts. Her first book, *The Stunt Double in Winter*, was a finalist for the Sawtooth Poetry Prize and the Kore First Book Award. Recent work appears in *Yew*, *The Burnside Review*, *Word For/Word and The Denver Quarterly*. Her text-visual collaboration with artist Robin Barcus Slonina, *Dear American Lovechild, Yours, The Beautiful Undead* is forthcoming soon. She lives with her husband and daughters in Matawan, NJ.

QUENTON BAKER is from Seattle, Washington. He writes.

RICK BASS has published more than 20 books of essays and novels, and has worked passionately for environmental causes all over the world. His honors and awards include a PEN/Nelson Algren Award Special Citation for fiction, a National Endowment for the Arts fellowship, and the James Jones Literary Society First Novel Fellowship for *Where the Sea Used to Be*. He was a finalist for the Story Prize in 2006 for his short story collection *The Lives of Rocks*. He was a finalist of the National Book Critics Circle Award for his autobiography, *Why I Came West*. Bass lives in the remote Yaak Valley of Montana, where he works to protect his adopted home from roads and logging. He serves on the board of both the Yaak Valley Forest Council and Round River Conservation Studies. His papers are held at the Southwest Collection/Special Collections Library at Texas Tech University and Texas State University–San Marcos.

VINCENT M. BASSO is a doctoral student in the English Language and Literature program at the University of New Mexico. He received his MFA from the

University of Southern Maine, and his BA in Creative Writing and MA in Education from the College of Santa Fe. His interests include American literature and critical theory, oral history, poetry and poetics, and comics. His poetry has appeared in *Black Renaissance/Renaissance Noire, Future Earth Magazine*, and *Nth Position.*

BRIAN BEARD was born and raised in Houston, Texas. After graduating from the University of Texas at Austin, he served as a Peace Corps Volunteer in Benin, West Africa from 1999-2001. He has worked as a bar musician in Paris, a construction worker in rural Georgia, a middle school English teacher with New York City public schools, and, since 2009, a high school French teacher in Maine, where he lives with his wife and their two sons. His writing appears in *Poetry East, Red Rock Review*, *Hoot Translation Review* and *Quiddity*, and is forthcoming in *The Prose-Poem Project.*

JEANNE MARIE BEAUMONT is the author of *Burning of the Three Fires*, a finalist for the Writers' League of Texas Book Award *Curious Conduct* and *Placebo Effects*, selected by William Matthews as a National Poetry Series winner. She is co-editor of the anthology *The Poets' Grimm: 20th Century Poems from Grimm Fairy Tales.* Her poems have been published in numerous anthologies and magazines including *Court Green*, *Harvard Review*, *The Manhattan Review*, *The Nation*, *New Letters*, *Poetry Daily*, *Good Poems for Hard Times*, *The Year's Best Fantasy & Horror 2007*, *When She Named Fire: Contemporary Poetry by American Women*, and *World Literature Today.* She teaches at the Stonecoast MFA program and at the Unterberg Poetry Center of the 92nd Street Y in New York, where she lives.

ERIN BELIEU is the author of four poetry collections, all from Copper Canyon Press, including *Slant Six*, forthcoming in September 2014. Poems from the new collection have appeared in places such as *The New Yorker*, *Slate*, *Ploughshares*, *The Awl* and *The Rumpus.*

JOHN BLAIR'S short story collection, *American Standard*, was the 2002 winner of the Drue Heinz Literature prize and was published by the University of Pittsburgh Press. He has also published two books of poetry, *The Occasions of Paradise* and *The Green Girls*, along with two novels. His poems and stories have appeared in *Poetry*, *The New York Quarterly*, *The Sewanee Review*, *The Antioch Review*, *New Letters* and elsewhere.

MADELEINE BLAIS is a Pulitzer-prize winning journalist and the author of three works of narrative nonfiction, *The Heart is an Instrument*, *In These Girls Hope is a Muscle*, (finalist for the National Book Critics Circle award) and *Uphill Walkers*, a memoir. She is a professor of journalism at the University of Massachusetts in Amherst and has also recently taught in the Goucher College low-residency MFA program in creative nonfiction and has been a writer in resident in the Creative Writing Program at Florida International University.

BRUCE BOND is the author of eight published books of poetry, most recently *The Visible, Peal* and *Blind Rain*, which was a finalist of The Poet's Prize, in 2008. His tetralogy of new books, entitled *Choir of the Wells* was released this year. Presently he is a Regents Professor of English at the University of North Texas and serves as Poetry Editor for *American Literary Review*.

CONOR BROUGHAN lives in Indiana with his wife. He teaches creative writing and composition at Purdue University, where he served as the fiction editor at *Sycamore Review*. He has co-translated that appeared in *The Coffin Factory* and is currently working on a novel.

PAUL TOLLIVER BROWN has an MFA from Eastern Washington University and a Ph.D. from the University of South Carolina where he is currently an English instructor.

TAYLOR BROWN'S short fiction has appeared in *CutBank*, *Plots with Guns, Thuglit, Pindeldyboz*, *storySouth*, *Porchlight*, *The Dead Mule*, and *The Liars' League*. His fiction has been anthologized in *The Press 53 Open Awards* and *Press 53 Spotlight* anthologies. His story, *Rider*, received the 2009 Montana Prize in Fiction. He lives in Wilmington, North Carolina.

JUSTIN BURNELL moved to New Orleans ten years ago. He received his MFA from The University of New Orleans. His writes fiction and non-fiction for *NOLAFugees* publications.

CHRISTOPHER BURSK is the author of ten books, including *The Infatuations and Infidelities of Pronoun*, *Cell Count* and *The Improbable Swervings of Atoms*. He is a recipient of NEA, Guggenheim, and Pew Fellowships. Most importantly, he is the grandfather of six.

M. CALLEN is a multidisciplinary artist and poet from Pittsburgh, PA. She is the recipient of fellowships from the Atlantic Center for the Arts, the Bucknell Seminar for Younger Poets, and the Vermont Studio Center. Her work has appeared in *Fence*, *Gigantic*, and other publications.

Writer, editor, journalist, essayist, and lecturer, EDIE CLARK has written extensively about New England in award-winning feature stories for more than thirty years. She has been a Fellow at The MacDowell Colony, Hedgebrook Writer's Colony, and Visiting Writer at Northern Michigan University. She teaches writing and journalism at graduate and undergraduate level and is a frequent lecturer. Her essay, *Mary's Farm*, is a regular feature in *Yankee* magazine and is beloved by many. She also writes a regular feature for *Yankee* on home cooks. Her books include *Monadnock Tales*, *The View from Mary's Farm*, *Saturday Beans and Sunday Suppers: Kitchen Stories from Mary's Farm*, *The Place He Made*, *States of Grace: Encounters with Real Yankees*, and *Night Sky*, an audiobook. Her new book, *What There Was Not To Tell: A Story of Love and War*, has just been published.

KEVIN CONNER is a poet and screenwriter living near the Susquehanna River in Wilkes Barre, Pennsylvania. He currently manages advertising campaigns at the local newspaper while pursuing other creative projects on page and on screen. His short film, *Pitchfork*, is in post-production and scheduled for release soon. He recently completed a chapbook entitled *Love Letters to No One.* Kevin graduated from Wilkes University in 2012 with an MFA in Creative Writing.

CHRIS CONNOLLY was born in Dublin, Ireland in 1983. His work has appeared in the *Global Shorts* short story anthology and *Boston Literary Magazine*, among others. In 2012 he was the winner of the Canon Sheehan Perpetual Literary Award. He was also shortlisted for the RTE Francis McManus Short Story Award, the Fish International Short Story competition and the Fish International Flash Fiction Award. Chris is currently completing a short story collection and working on a novel.

TRACY DEBRINCAT is the author of the prizing-winning books, *Hollywood Buckaroo* a novel, and *Moon Is Cotton & She Laugh All Night,* a story collection. Another short story collection, *Troglodyte*, was recently awarded the 2012 Elixir Prize is forthcoming in 2014. Her short stories and poems have appeared in journals from *Another Chicago Magazine to Zyzzyva.* San Francisco is her hometown, but she loves living in Los Angeles, where she is a freelance creative advertising consultant.

MEGHAN DUNN was born and raised in upstate New York and currently lives in Brooklyn, where she teaches high school English. She holds an MFA in creative writing from Emerson College and a BA in English from Boston College. She has been the recipient of a St. Botolph's Club Foundation Emerging Artist Grant and a fellowship from the Writers' Room of Boston. Her work has appeared in *Narrative, Ploughshares*, and *Post Road*, among others.

STEPHEN DUNN has written over a dozen books of poetry and several books of prose. His honors and awards include The Pulitzer Prize, The National Poetry

Series Prize, the James Wright Prize, an Academy Award for Literature and fellowships from the National Endowment for the Arts and the New Jersey State Council on the Arts. Distinguished Professor of Creative Writing at Richard Stockton College, Dunn lives in Maryland with his wife, the writer Barbara Hurd.

Currently studying for an MA in Creative Writing at Kingston University, London, TOMEK DZIDO is a disciple of the down and out and dirty. With an interest in survival and how each and all attempt to somehow cope and see life through, Tomek is attempting to record the unique and universal to portray small segments of what it is to exist today, and how and why and if it can be done. He is currently working on a collection of short stories to be titled *Soapsuds Island*, set in his home town of Acton, West London.

BD FEIL has credits in *Mississippi Review*, *Slice Magazine*, and *Cleveland Review*, and was nominated for a Pushcart in 2012. He lives in Michigan with quite the brood.

DORIS FERLEGER is the author of three volumes of poetry, *Big Silences in a Year of Rain, As the Moon Has Breath* and *When You Become Snow.* She is the winner of the New Letters Poetry Prize and the *A* Room of Her Own (AROHO) Creative Non Fiction Prize, among others. Her work has been published in numerous journals, including *Cimarron Review*, *L.A. Review*, and *South Carolina Review.* She holds an MFA from Vermont College of Fine Arts and a Ph.D. in psychology from Temple University. She also maintains a psychotherapy practice in Montgomery County, PA.

ROBERTA GEORGE was born in Bisbee, Arizona, and lived in California, Arizona, and Texas, where she went to Catholic girls' schools. She spent most summers with her German grandmother on a 200-acre farm in the South, which left her with an overwhelming desire to pick blackberries every spring—and to make wine. She teaches yoga and a writers' workshop called "The Snake Handlers" at the Turner Center for the Arts. She founded *Snake Nation Press* in 1989. She has seven children, all grown and gone, and lives with a third-generation Lebanese husband, two dogs and a cat in Valdosta, Georgia.

SARAH GERKENSMEYER'S short story collection, *What You Are Now Enjoying*, was selected by Stewart O'Nan as the 2012 Autumn House Press Fiction Contest winner and was published this year. A selection of her short-short fiction garnered a finalist spot in the 2011 Italo Calvino Prize for Fabulist Fiction. Sarah's stories have appeared in several journals, including *The Massachusetts Review*, *Hayden's Ferry Review*, *Sonora Review*, *North Dakota Quarterly*,

The Nebraska Review, Redivider and *Cream City Review.* Sarah was named the 2012-13 Pen Parentis Fellow. She received her MFA from Cornell University and is now a visiting assistant professor of creative writing at SUNY Fredonia.

VAN NEWELL received his BA from the University of Montevallo, his MFA from Columbia University, and a Certificate from the Act One Writing Program. In 2003, he was awarded a fellowship from the US Department of Education America Reads program. His screenplays have been nominated as finalists of the Warner Brothers Writers Workshop, the David Angel Humanitas Prize, and the Sidewalk Film Festival Sidewrite Prize. His short story, *The Man's Angels*, received a fiction award from the Alabama Writers Conclave. His writing has been published in *Postscript*, *Aura*, *First Draft*, *Birmingham Arts*, online at Writersforum.org and Ala-lit.com. He is currently working on a novel and teaches at the University of Alabama.

LEWIS ROBINSON is the author of the novel *Water Dogs*, a *New York Times* Editors' Choice selection, and *Officer Friendly and Other Stories*, winner of the PEN/Oakland-Josephine Miles Award and a Whiting Award. His short fiction and essays have appeared in *Tin House*, *The Missouri Review, Sports Illustrated, The New York Times Book Review* and on NPR's program *Selected Shorts*. Robinson lives in Portland.

KRISTEN MALIA HAY received a BA in English and Psychology from the University of Washington in 2004. In 2009 she enrolled in a Literary Writing Certificate Program at UW. There she was lucky enough to meet her writing group. She credits them for providing inspiration, support, and much laughter during what can often be a challenging process. Kristen recently moved from Seattle to San Francisco, and when she's not working she can often be found on her yoga mat, hiking, or maybe just taking a nap.

RICHARD HOFFMAN is author of *Half the House*: *a Memoir*, and the poetry collections, *Emblem*, *Without Paradise*, and *Gold Star Road*, which won the 2006 Barrow Street Press Poetry Prize and the 2008 Sheila Motton Award from the New England Poetry Club. He is a fiction writer as well; his book, *Interference & Other Stories* was published in 2009. A new memoir, *Love & Fury*, is forthcoming. He is Senior Writer in Residence at Emerson College.

JOAN LEE HUNTER leads writing workshops at her retreat, Fifth House Lodge, in western Maine. The enclosed story, *The Dog*, is part of a collection of stories she is working on about all manner of characters living in the hidden folds of that rolling terrain.

BARBARA HURD is the author of three books of creative nonfiction and two books of poetry. The recipient of an NEA Fellowship for Creative Nonfiction, winner of the Sierra Club's National Nature Writing Award, three Pushcart Prizes, and four Maryland State Arts Council Awards, she teaches in the Stonecoast MFA program at the University of Southern Maine.

JOHN JOHNSON'S poems have appeared (or will soon appear) in *BOXCAR Poetry Review*, *Chaparral*, *The Comstock Review*, *DMQ Review*, *OVS Magazine*, *Triggerfish Critical Review* and *Verse Wisconsin*. One of his poems was a broadside winner in the Sebastopol Center for the Arts Bibliophoria contest.

WAYNE LEE is a Canadian/American who lives in Santa Fe, New Mexico, where he works as an educator and journalist. Lee's poems have appeared in *Tupelo Press*, *Slipstream*, *The Floating Bridge Anthology*, *Conversations Across Borders* and other journals and anthologies. He is winner of the 2012 Mark Fischer Poetry Prize and has been nominated for a Pushcart Prize and a Best of the Net award. His collections include *Doggerel & Caterwauls: Poems Inspired by Cats and Dogs* and *Twenty Poems from the Blue House*.

KATE LEVIN is a native New Yorker who has read her poetry, short stories, and excerpts from her unpublished novel, *Punk Prophet*, at venues throughout the city, including the 2013 Annual New York City Poetry Festival. Her article, *It Happened to Me: I worked at Marvel Comics*, was published by XoJane.com, and her short story, *Riding Redbirds*, was published in the Fall/Winter 2013 issue of *Newtown Literary*. Levin is a member of the Buffalo Poets and works as a graphic designer. She graduated with a BFA in creative writing at the University of Maine at Farmington.

WULF LOSEE lives in Northern California with two cats in imperial disguises who loll through long afternoons among the stacks of books and his friends come and go from his house and after a glass of wine or a meal he'll write as memories surface on the tip of his pen until he can resist sleep no longer and sometimes on a night of a blank moon his dreaming mind sets off on its own to find his muse in her house of twilight out at edge of things where the stars fade away but she's always always somewhere else.

GREGORY LOSELLE has won four Hopwood Awards at The University of Michigan, where he earned an MFA. He has also won The Academy of American Poets Prize, the William van Wert Fiction Award from Hidden River Arts, and The Ruby Lloyd Apsey Award for Playwriting. He also won the Lorian Hemingway Short Story Competition, The Robert Frost Award and the Rita Dove Prize for poetry. His has published three chapbooks *Phantom Limb*, and *The Whole of Him Collected*. His short fiction was featured in the and *The Saturday Evening Post*, and his poetry has appeared in *The Ledge*, *Oberon*, *The Comstock Review*, *Rattle*, *River Styx*, *The Spoon River Poetry Review* and *The Pinch* among others. He teaches Language Arts and Art History in Grosse Ile, Michigan, drilling his students in the distinctions between can and may, good and well.

JENN CHAN LYMAN is a fiction and non-fiction writer based in Shanghai. Her articles have been featured in *Tatler Magazine* (Hong Kong and Asia), (Hong Kong), and in the Los Angeles-based digital magazine. She has also written about music and jazz for AllAboutJazz.com and *That's Shanghai* magazine. Jenn has a Bachelor's degree in Comparative Literature from Stanford University and a Masters in Fine Arts in Creative Writing from City University of Hong Kong. She re-wires her brain from finance to writing on a daily basis, resulting in the occasional fractured psyche.

ALLISTER MACMARTIN was born and raised in Northfield, Vermont. His poems have appeared online at "What Light: This Week's Poem" on mnartists.org and elimae.com. In 2009 he received a BA in English with an emphasis in creative writing from Macalester College, where he was awarded the Bennett Cerf Endowed Prize for work as an English major. He has been a summer intern at MQR and an editorial assistant for *Canarium Books*. Allister is currently a Zell Postgraduate Fellow residing in Ann Arbor, having recently received an MFA in poetry from the University of Michigan.

ED MADDEN is an associate professor of English at the University of South Carolina. He is the author of two books of poetry: *Signals*, which was selected by Afaa Weaver for the 2007 SC Poetry Book Prize, and *Prodigal: Variations*. His work also appears in *Collective Brightness* and Notre Dame's *The Book of Irish American Poetry*.

EAMON MAHONEY is a Rhode Island native. He has taught creative writing at AS220 Youth and the R.I. Youth Detention Center. Currently, he is a low-residency student at Goddard College, studying education and prison practices and policy. He lives in the west of Ireland.

KRISTINA MCDONALD received her MFA from Eastern Washington University and currently works at Rice University. Her poetry has been published or is forthcoming in *Narrative*, *Sugar House Review* and *Shelf Life*.

MARC MEWSHAW has a BA from Princeton and an MFA in creative writing from NYU. His work has been nominated to be part of *Best New American Voices* and has been published in a number of literary journals. The enclosed piece, *Happy Accidents*, is an excerpt the novel Marc is presently working on, which is set in south Florida. He is a recent transplant to Portland, Maine.

ELIZABETH MILES is the author of *The Fury Series* for young adults. A graduate of Boston University, she has taught creative writing workshops for The Telling Room and works as a full-time journalist in Portland. She is also a co-founder of the theater company, "Lorem Ipsum." She recently moved with her husband and two cats to a brick farmhouse in Gray.

JENNY MOLBERG, a Texas native, earned her BA at Louisiana State University and her MFA at American University. In Washington, D.C., she worked as the assistant editor at *Poet Lore* and was a Lannan Fellow at the Folger Shakespeare Library. She is currently a teaching fellow and a second-year PhD student at the University of North Texas, where she works as the assistant poetry editor at *American Literary Review*. Her work has recently appeared in *Copper Nickel*, *Louisville Review*, *Smartish Pace* and *Mississippi Review*, among others. She lives in Denton, Texas.

MARY MORRIS lives in Santa Fe, NM. She is the winner of the Rita Dove Award and the New Mexico Discovery Award. Her work has been published in *Quarterly West*, *Southern Humanities Review*, and *Poet Lore*. She has written book reviews for the *Montserrat Review* and the *Patterson Literary Review*.

LESLIE MUNNELLY lives on Nantucket Island, a small community off the MA coast. Married and the mother of two adult children, she's an avid reader, writer, and runner. This summer has marked her breakthrough in the writing world with three short stories pending publication. Currently, she's working with an editor on the revision of her first novel, a thriller set in the western mountains of Maine.

SHARON OLDS is the 2013 recipient of The Pulitzer Prize in Poetry and the T.S. Eliot Prize for her book, *Stag's Leap*. She has won numerous awards, including the National Book Critics Circle Award and the first San Francisco Poetry Center Award in 1980. She is the author of several poetry collections and has contributed poems to many anthologies. She currently teaches creative writing at New York University.

CINDY ST. ONGE is the author of three collections of poetry. *Curse of the Firstborn*, *Traffic Along the Ghost Roads* and *Vigil*. Her chapbook, *The Gospel of Self-Annihilation* will be released in December, 2013. Her poetry has appeared in *New Millennium Writings* and has been presented live for the Broken Word and Stonehenge reading series in her hometown of Portland, Oregon.

JOSE PADUA'S poetry and fiction has appeared in *Bomb*, *Beloit Poetry Journal,*

Exquisite Corpse, *Another Chicago Magazine*, *Unbearables*, *Crimes of the Beats*, *Up is Up, But So Is Down: New York's Downtown Literary Scene, 1974-1992*, in many other journals and anthologies and online at Salon.com. He was a featured reader at the 2012 "Split This Rock" poetry festival. He lives in Virginia with his wife, the poet Heather Davis, and their son and daughter.

LESLIE JILL PATTERSON teaches in the creative writing program at Texas Tech University, where she also serves as editor of *Iron Horse Literary Review*. Her prose has appeared most recently in *Texas Monthly*, *Creative Nonfiction*, *Colorado Review*, Baltimore Review, and Meatpaper. She also serves as the case storyteller for the Texas Regional Public Defender's Office for Capital Cases, helping to represent indigent defendants facing execution.

SARA PATTON holds a Bachelor of Science in Botany from the University of Washington. She's climbed mountains, hiked canyons, swam in oceans and raised two children who she loves beyond measure. Currently she lives in North Routt, Colorado. On a good day, she rides a horse named Blue.

MARGE PIERCY'S 18th poetry book, *The Hunger Moon: New & Selected Poems 1980-2010* was recently re-released in paperback. *The Crooked Inheritance*, *Colors Passing Through Us*, *What Are Big Girls Made Of* and *The Art of Blessing The Day* are all available in paperback now as well, plus the earlier selected poetry collection. Piercy has published 17 novels, most recently *Sex Wars. Dance the Eagle to Sleep*, *Vida* and *Braided Lives* have both been re-released with new introductions by Piercy. Her memoir is entitled *Sleeping With Cats*. Her work has been translated into 19 languages and she's given readings, workshops or lectures at well over 450 venues nationally and abroad. Every June she gives a juried intensive poetry workshop in Wellfleet, limited to twelve workshop participants of the hundred or so who apply.

JUDITH PODELL is a fiction writer, book critic and lapsed lawyer. *Blues for Beginners*, a collection of Podell's short fiction, was published this year. *The Muse*, an excerpt from her novel-in-progress, was published in the inaugural issue of *The New Guard*. A recipient of fellowships and grants from the Virginia Center for the Creative Arts, Ragdale Foundation, the MacDowell Colony and the District of Columbia Commission for the Arts and the Humanities, her work has appeared in numerous publications. She has also performed stand-up comedy in bars. One bar, really, but it was in Ireland. She received her MFA from Stonecoast and lives in Washington, DC.

PATRICK QUINLAN was the youngest child in a big, noisy, New York Irish-American family. Other kids in the neighborhood wanted to become cops, or firemen, or crime kingpins. He wanted to become Jimi Hendrix. He is the author of six novels— *Smoked, The Takedown*, *The Hit, The Drop-Off*, *The Girl Inside the Wall* and *The Demon.* He is also the co-author, with legendary actor Rutger Hauer, of Rutger's memoir, *All Those Moments*, *a Los Angeles Times* bestseller. One of his favorite things is travel. He is happiest when surrounded by people he can't understand and who can't understand him, reducing him to frantic hand gestures. He likes to get things cookin'.

LESLIE RODD is a retired public librarian who spent over three decades promoting books and reading to blind people, prison inmates, and adult literacy students in San Francisco and Oakland, California. Her novel, *Good Mother Lizard*, was a quarterfinalist for the 2009 Amazon.com Breakthrough Novel Award, and an excerpt from an early draft won a Hackney Award for Short Fiction and was published in *Cyanosis*. *The First Blind Man on the Moon* is her current novel-in-progress. She has been published in such magazines as *Transfer Magazine*, *Bosque* and *The Sun*, among others.

BENJAMIN RYBECK fiction has received "notable story" and "special mention" distinctions from *The Best American Nonrequired Reading* and *The Pushcart Prize Anthology*, respectively, and his book reviews regularly appear in *Electric Literature* and *Three Guys One Book.* He recently finished a novel titled *The Sadness*, a literary thriller about cinephiles, movie stars, orphans, and missing people.

GREGG SCHROEDER is a fiction writer based in Hong Kong. The California native has lived half his life abroad and more than 20 years in Asia. A journalism graduate of Cal Poly, San Luis Obispo, CA, he is a freelance textbook editor. He recently earned an MFA in fiction from City University of Hong Kong. Gregg is currently working on a novel set in the Chinese territory. *Apartment 6D* is his first piece of published fiction.

LONES SEIBER is a retired aerospace engineer living in Morristown, Tennessee. He has been writing fiction for six years. His stories have appeared in *GSU Review*, *The Pinch*, *Lynx Eye*, *Wordstock Ten, Roanoke Review*, *Tall Grass Writers Anthology*, *Pearl*, *Indiana Review* and *Inkwell.* His nonfiction has appeared in *American Heritage.* He won the 2005 GSU Review Fiction Contest, the 2007 Pinch Fiction Contest, the 2008 Leslie Garrett Award for fiction, the 2011 Indiana Review Fiction Contest, and the 2011 Warren Adler Prize for Fiction. His short story, *Icarus*, was selected for inclusion in The Best Mystery Stories of 2012.

An international journey is the best description of GABRIELA TIESSEN'S life so far:

she was born in Bolivia and grew up in Mexico before her family moved to the Midwest when she was 12. After graduating from Hope College in 1998, she joined a team in Europe to do research on minority languages. After three years of working together, she and one of her colleagues decided to make the arrangement permanent, going on to make their first home in Central Asia. She currently is wife, mother and linguist living in southeastern Europe.

Erica Vega does her poeting in Illinois where she also teaches high school English. She is working on a novel.

Mark Wagstaff lives in London. Since 1999, he has had stories published across a range of journals and online, including *Stone Highway Review*, *Scissors & Spackle* and *Inkwell.* Mark has published four novels and a novella. His most recent novel, *In Sparta*, a story of radicalism, conformity and terror, is available in print and on E-book. Mark's first collection of short stories appeared in 2002 and his second collection will be published in 2012. He is also working on an E-book project with *Folded Word.*

Matt Welch grew up in Pittsford, NY and attended Babson College and Maine College of Art (MECA). He taught art at Aucocisco in Cape Elizabeth for seven years and was owner and founder of Flat Iron Gallery, which he ran until 2012. His family has always been his strongest source of inspiration and the reason why he was exposed to the universe of art. He began painting seriously at MECA around 2000. He enjoys changing the scale of objects and animals as well as employing a sense of light in his work. He is also attracted to subjects revealing a sense of humor or attitude. Matt lives in the heart of Portland with the loves of his life: his wife, Andrea, and his children, Henry and Fiona.

A native of Central Illinois, Tamra Wilson has spent most of her life in North Carolina. She is the author of *Dining with Robert Redford & Others Stories,* parts of which previously appeared in *Epiphany*, *North Carolina Literary Review*, *Gihon River Review*, *The MacGuffin* and elsewhere. She won the 2009 Jesse Stuart Prize for Young Adult Fiction and is a Road Scholar for the North Carolina Humanities Council. The Cozy Corner is an excerpt of her MFA thesis at the University of Southern Maine's Stonecoast program.

Ian Withrow is the author of several short stories. He currently resides in western Montana, where he worships good music and great books. He sleeps with every limb tucked safely beneath the covers.

CHARLES WYATT is the author of two collections of short fiction, a novella, and two poetry chapbooks. He holds degrees from the Curtis Institute of Music, The Philadelphia Musical Academy, and Warren Wilson College. He presently teaches for UCLA Extension and in the Low Residency MFA Program of the University of Nebraska. Before devoting himself exclusively to writing and teaching, he was principal flutist of the Nashville Symphony for 25 years.

Thank you to all who make The New Guard a continued success. Our team is made up of wonderful writers, readers, artists, enthusiasts, friends and family. Many have contributed to The New Guard since its inception in 2009, from contest readers to advertisers to journalists to designers to copyeditors. The list is long. Thank you so much for your good work and your good cheer, one and all. We are very lucky to have worked with such talented, passionate people over the years. We haven't forgotten you!

Many new people have come aboard and given generously of their time and energy. Thank you, Richard Hoffman, for cheerfully rolling up your sleeves and working side-by-side with us on our contest. Thank you to our featured poet, Marge Piercy, with your distinction of being nominated for a Nobel Prize in Literature in 2013. Thank you to our Love Letter section contributors: Stephen Dunn, Barbara Hurd, Erin Belieu, Madeleine Blais, Judith Podell, Van Newell, Edie Clark, Ian Withrow, Kate Levin and Leslie Z. Anderson and Sharon Olds, who won the 2013 Pulitzer Prize for her book of poetry, "Stag's Leap." Thank you to our judges, Rick Bass and Jeanne Marie Beaumont. Thank you to Maine artist Matt Welch—we're honored. Thank you to our submitting writers, whose work came in from all over the world. Thank you to our winners, finalists and semi-finalists. It is an honor to publish your work.

Thank you to our inspired web artists, James Provenzano, Sergei Chaparin and Eleanor Leonne Bennett. Thanks to David Lydon for your years of excellent web service. Thank you to Lisa Greenleaf, for putting together a massive manuscript like a pro. Thank you, Scott Vaughan, for being such a terrific help. Thank you to The Kirby Family Foundation, in cooperation with Portland Creative Corporation, for your incredible gift. Thank you for your kind support: Maggie Cushman, Magdalen Braden, Judith Podell and Christina Ricciardelli.

Thank you to the good people of Longfellow Books, who have graciously hosted our reading series. Thank you in particular to Julia Gersen, who arranged the series and oversaw events. Thank you to Longfellow Books owners Chris Bowe and Stuart Gersen. Thank you to all of our series readers: Charles Simic, Tess Gerritsen, Melissa Roberts, Bill Roorbach, Jaed Coffin, Sarah Braunstein and Jefferson Navicky.

Thank you to our new friends via The Writer's Hotel, *The New Guard's* editorial arm, where we teach adult writers online and in a face-to-face Master Class environment. We are grateful to the folks of Literary Manhattan, especially to Michael del Castillo and Aaron Siewert, for all your help and to the folks at all three of our upcoming summer "campus" hotels, especially Hilaire Curry of The

Bryant Park, Kelly Fitzgerald of The Algonquin and Ivana Bolf of The Library Hotel. We are also grateful to have worked with all of our TWH writers—you know who you are!

Thank you for believing in us. We are only as good as the sum of our parts. Thank you all.